ECONOMICS and EMPIRE
in the ROMAN WORLD

CENTER AND LIBRARY FOR THE BIBLE AND SOCIAL JUSTICE SERIES

Matthew J. M. Coomber, series editor
The Center and Library for the Bible and Social Justice Series produces scholarship for the academy, churches and seminaries, and activist communities so as to fulfill The Center's mission to connect biblically informed activists and justice-oriented scholars.

Laurel Dykstra and Ched Myers, editors
Liberating Biblical Study Scholarship, Art, and Action in Honor of the Center and Library for the Bible and Social Justice

Norman K. Gottwald
Social Justice and the Hebrew Bible
3 volumes

Elaine Enns and Ched Myers
Healing Haunted Histories
A Settler Discipleship of Decolonization

Richard A. Horsley
Jesus and the Politics of Roman Palestine

Matthew J. M. Coomber
Re-Reading the Prophets through Corporate Globalization
A Cultural Evolutionary Approach to Economic Injustice in the Hebrew Bible

ECONOMICS and EMPIRE in the ROMAN WORLD

Guide to the Bible and Economics, Volume 2

Edited by
Matthew J. M. Coomber

CASCADE Books • Eugene, Oregon

ECONOMICS AND EMPIRE IN THE ROMAN WORLD
Guide to the Bible and Economics, Volume 2
Center and Library for the Bible and Social Justice Series

Copyright © 2025 Wipf and Stock Publishers. All rights reserved. Except for brief quotations in critical publications or reviews, no part of this book may be reproduced in any manner without prior written permission from the publisher. Write: Permissions, Wipf and Stock Publishers, 199 W. 8th Ave., Suite 3, Eugene, OR 97401.

Cascade Books
An Imprint of Wipf and Stock Publishers
199 W. 8th Ave., Suite 3
Eugene, OR 97401

www.wipfandstock.com

PAPERBACK ISBN: 978-1-6667-1243-8
HARDCOVER ISBN: 978-1-6667-1244-5
EBOOK ISBN: 978-1-6667-1245-2

Cataloguing-in-Publication data:

Names: Coomber, Matthew J. M., editor.

Title: Economics and empire in the Roman world : guide to the Bible and economics volume 2 / edited by Matthew J. M. Coomber.

Description: Eugene, OR: Cascade Books, 2024. | Center and Library for the Bible and Social Justice Series.| Includes bibliographical references and indexes.

Identifiers: ISBN 978-1-6667-1243-8 (print). | ISBN 978-1-6667-1244-5 (print). | ISBN 978-1-6667-1245-2 (epub).

Subjects: LSCH: Bible. NT—Criticism, interpretation, etc. | Economics in the Bible. | Sociology and the Bible.

Classification: BS2545.S55 E23 2024 (print). | BS2545.S55 (epub).

Unless otherwise noted, Scripture quotations are from the New Revised Standard Version Bible, copyright © 1989 National Council of the Churches of Christ in the United States of America. Used by permission. All rights reserved worldwide.

Scripture quotations marked (RSV) are taken from the Revised Standard Version Bible, copyright © 1946, 1952, and 1971 the Division of Christian Education of the National Council of Churches of Christ in the United States of America. Used by permission. All rights reserved.

In loving memory of my mother, a dear friend and ever-faithful champion,
Eleanor Ruth Coomber
1942–2023

Contents

Contributors | ix
Acknowledgments | xi
Abbreviations | xiv

1. Biblical Economics as an Essential Tool
   for Biblical Studies | 1
   MATTHEW J. M. COOMBER

2. Economic Relationships Found in the Worlds of the Bible | 12
   ROLAND BOER AND CHRISTINA PETTERSON

3. The Political Economic Project of Jesus
   vs. the Roman Imperial Order | 44
   RICHARD A. HORSLEY

4. Imaginings of Jesus and the Economic Questions of His Day | 101
   JAMES CROSSLEY

5. Women and Economics in the Roman World | 118
   CAROLYN OSIEK

6. Urban Economy and Economics Relationships
   in the Roman Empire and Pauline Assemblies | 141
   WARREN CARTER

7. An Alternative Society of Local Communities
   among Peoples Subject to the Roman Empire | 187
   RICHARD A. HORSLEY

8. Apocalypse in Response to Roman Economic Ideology | 230
   KELLY J. MURPHY

Ancient Document Index | 273
Author Index | 287

Contributors

Roland Boer is a professor in the School of Philosophy at Renmin University of China, Beijing, where he teaches Marxist philosophy. His research areas include Marxism and religion, the history and theory of socialist governance, and the relations between Marxism and the best of traditional culture. Among his many publications, are *The Sacred Economy of Ancient Israel* (2015), *Postcolonialism and the Hebrew Bible* (2013), and *Marxist Criticism of the Bible* (2003). His most recent monograph is *Socialism in Power: On the History and Theory of Socialist Governance* (2023).

Warren Carter is the LaDonna Kramer Meinders Professor of New Testament at Phillips Theological Seminary in Tulsa, Oklahoma. Previously he was professor of New Testament at Brite Divinity School and at Saint Paul School of Theology. His publications include *Jesus and the Empire of God* (Cascade, 2021); *Gospel of Mark* (2019); *Seven Events That Shaped the New Testament World* (2013); *What Does Revelation Reveal?* (2011); *The Roman Empire & the New Testament: An Essential Guide* (2006); *Matthew and Empire* (2001); and *Matthew and the Margins* (2000). Forthcoming is a commentary on Matthew's Gospel.

Matthew J. M. Coomber is professor of biblical studies and theology at St. Ambrose University in Davenport, Iowa, and serves as an Episcopal priest. His publications in include *Re-Reading the Prophets through Corporate Globalization* (2010; paperback ed., Cascade, 2022) and *The Common Good: A Biblical Ethos against Poverty* (forthcoming). He is the editor of *Bible and Justice: Ancient Texts, Modern Challenges* (2011) and *Economics and Empire in the Ancient Near East* (Cascade, 2023), and is coeditor (with Gale A. Yee and Hugh R. Page Jr.) of *The Old Testament and Apocrypha* (Fortress Commentary on the Bible) and (with Ludwig Beethoven J. Noya) of *Class and Intersectionality in the Hebrew Bible: Engaged Biblical Studies in the Academy and on the Streets* (Cascade, forthcoming). Coomber also serves as the series editor of the Center and Library for the Bible and Social Justice Series.

James Crossley is research professor of Bible, politics, and culture at MF Oslo and academic director of the Centre for the Critical Study of Apocalyptic and Millenarian Movements, UK. He has published widely on Christian origins and religion in English political discourse. Among his latest publications is *Spectres of John Ball: The Peasants' Revolt in English Political Discourse, 1381–2020* (2020). He is also coeditor (with Chris Keith) of *The Next Quest for the Historical Jesus* (2024). His latest project is a biography of the English Communist A. L. Morton and a history of the English radical tradition, including interpretations of the Bible.

Richard A. Horsley, Distinguished Professor of Liberal Arts Emeritus at University of Massachusetts Boston, is author of many books, including *Empowering the People; Jesus and the Politics of Roman Palestine* (2014; rev. paperback ed., Cascade, 2021); *Jesus and Empire* (2002); *Galilee: History, Politics, People* (1995); and *Covenant Economics* (2009).

Kelly J. Murphy is a professor in the Department of Philosophy, Anthropology, and Religion at Central Michigan University. She is the author of *Rewriting Masculinity: Gideon, Men, and Might* (2019) and coeditor of *Apocalypses in Context: Apocalyptic Currents through History* (2016) and of *Biblical Themes in Science Fiction* (2023).

Carolyn Osiek is Charles Fischer Catholic Professor of New Testament Emerita at Brite Divinity School of Texas Christian University. She was also for twenty-six years professor of New Testament at Catholic Theological Union, Chicago. She holds a doctorate in New Testament and Christian Origins from Harvard University and is a past president of the Catholic Biblical Association and the Society of Biblical Literature. She is the author of many books and articles on topics of family and social life in early Christianity, including *A Woman's Place: House Churches in Earliest Christianity*, coauthored with Margaret Y. MacDonald (2006).

Christina Petterson is an adjunct lecturer at Ilisimatusarfik, University of Greenland. Petterson's primary research considers Christianity through the lenses of theology, history, and cultural theory. Her publications include *From Tomb to Text: The Body of Jesus in the Book of John* (2018); *Apostles of Revolution? Marxism and Biblical Studies* (2020); *Acts of Empire: The Acts of the Apostles and Imperial Ideology* (2020); *The Moravian Brethren in a Time of Transition* (2021); and *Early Capitalism in Colonial Missions: Moravian Household Economies in the Global Eighteenth Century* (2024).

Acknowledgments

In a project of this breadth it is difficult to know where to begin thanking all of those who made it possible, so I will start at the beginning. The series to which this volume is connected was born out of an idea that Neil Elliot had during his years at Fortress Press: to create a repository of what is known about biblical economics and how this subfield of biblical studies is relevant to both the academy and also to the nonacademic world. Elliot invited me to edit the series, and we brought together a fantastic group of scholars, as is evident in the tables of contents. Due to a change in company structure at Fortress Press, however, the project was let go. Elliot assisted me in finding a new home for the series and its contributors' works, which were already under way. I cannot thank him enough for his dedication to this series and assistance in finding it safe harbor. K. C. Hanson and Cascade Books was that harbor, and I am immensely grateful to Hanson for his assistance in helping me to shape this series into what it has become. Hanson's years of experience in the publishing world, alongside his academic expertise in biblical studies, were invaluable in helping to move the project forward.

Next, I wish to thank the late Norman Gottwald. Shortly after completing my doctoral studies, Gottwald read my book, *Re-Reading the Prophets through Corporate Globalization*, and invited me to join the Center and Library for the Bible and Social Justice's board of directors, on which I served from 2010 through 2023. I jumped at the chance to be involved with an organization that connects sound biblical scholarship with activist communities that endeavor to create a just world. Gottwald's guidance and encouragement were highly formative in both my development as an early scholar and also in how I approached my editorial work in this series. My colleagues at the Center and Library for the Bible and Social Justice have been incredibly supportive in the development of this series, for which I am very deeply thankful.

I wish to offer special thanks to Richard Horsley, whose guidance, encouragement, expertise, and support during some unexpected surprises that came along the way were essential to the creation of this book. I also wish to express my gratitude to Elisabeth Schüssler Fiorenza who, like Horsley, has played a large role in the development of this volume, and the series as a whole.

I would like to express my thanks and respect to those who continue to shape my scholarship and lead me in new directions of study. Their influences have played no small part in the creation of this series. I do not believe I would have been approached to edit this series had it not been for the experience and guidance that I gained through coediting *The Old Testament and Apocrypha* (Fortress Commentary on the Bible) with Gale Yee and Hugh Page Jr. Both Yee and Page were outstanding colleagues with whom to work, and continue to be. I am also profoundly thankful to the contributors to the CLBSJ Guide to Bible and Economics. Their works, both in these volumes and also in their other publications, have helped to shape my scholarship, priestly vocation, and advocacy work for a just world. It is an honor and privilege to collaborate with such great minds and good people.

In addition to the works of this volume's contributors, my understanding of ancient southwest Asian and Roman micro- and macroeconomics has been greatly impacted by the research of Roger Nam, Samuel Adams, Candida Moss, Kelly Murphy, Ronald Simkins, Davis Hankins, Brendan Breed, and Kenneth Hirth. The postcolonial scholarship of Jione Havea, Monica Melanchthon, Steed Davidson, and Raj Nadella have shaped my understanding of biblical interpretation and how imperialism has shaped its trajectories. Their work has not only given me insight into modern receptions of the Bible, but has helped me to explore new questions pertaining to the experiences of colonized peoples in the ancient world. Examining biblical economics through the gender-focused works of Elisabeth Schüssler Fiorenza, Gale Yee, Margaret Aymer, Davina Lopez, Mitzi Smith, Jessica Keady, Cynthia-Shaffer Elliot, Katie Edwards, Carolyn Osiek, Lynn Huber, and Christy Cobb continues to shape my understanding of the ancient world, for which I am grateful. Activist-centered scholars such as Gerald West, Diana Swanncutt, Crystal Hall, Noelle Damico, Ched Myers, T. Christopher Hoklotubbe, Micah Kiel, and so many others have helped to open my eyes to the possibilities that exist for both asking new questions of the Bible's ancient contexts and also seeing various points of relevance that biblical texts hold for today. I would also like to extend my gratitude to Richard Horsley, a mentor and friend who has been an invaluable consultant in the development of this series. I also wish to thank my colleagues in the Theology Department at St. Ambrose University. Profs. Mara Adams, Robert "Bud" Grant, Ella Johnson, Michelle Petersen, and Lisa Powell make my life more intellectually rich and are incredibly supportive.

I would also like to thank a scholar who will remain anonymous. She had agreed to write one of the chapters for this volume but, upon having her academic position taken away, needed to withdraw from the academy and—subsequently—this project. In a time of departmental downsizing, institutional closures, and increased reliance on "part-time" academic labor, much important work in the humanities will, tragically, remain unwritten. All sorts of ideas and areas of knowledge waiting to be discovered will continue to lie dormant. This scholar's work is exceptional and her loss is far from her own. Her impact on both on New Testament studies and the students who studied under her were great. Her efforts, and those of many other scholars who have endured what she has, deserve our gratitude.

Last, in a project such as this there are so many folks to thank that I fear it is inevitable that I have left out key individuals and groups. I offer them my sincere apologies and extend my gratitude.

Abbreviations

Modern Journals, Series, and Societies

ABS	Archaeology and Biblical Studies
BibInt	*Biblical Interpretation*
BibInt	Biblical Interpretation Series
BibSem	The Biblical Seminar
BJS	Brown Judaic Studies
BPC	Biblical Performance Criticism
BTB	*Biblical Theology Bulletin*
BSR	*Bulletin for the Study of Religion*
BZAW	Beihefte zur Zeitschrift für die alttestamentliche Wissenschaft
CBQ	*Catholic Biblical Quarterly*
CPJ	*Corpus Papyrorum Judaicarum*. Edited by Victor A. Tcherikover. 3 vols. Cambridge: Harvard University Press, 1957–64
CurBR	*Currents in Biblical Research*
ECL	Early Christianity and Its Literature
FC	Fathers of the Church
HdO	Handbuch der Orientalistik
HeyJ	*Heythrop Journal*
HTR	*Harvard Theological Review*
HTS	Harvard Theological Studies
HUT	Hermeneutische Untersuchungen zur Theologie
HvTSt	*Hervormde teologiese studies*

IDB	*The Interpreter's Dictionary of the Bible*. Edited by George A. Buttrick. 4 vols. New York: Abingdon, 1962
ICC	International Critical Commentary
IEJ	*Israel Exploration Journal*
Int	*Interpretation*
ITC	International Theological Commentary
JAC	*Jahrbuch für Antike und Christentum*
JBL	*Journal of Biblical Literature*
JBS	Jerusalem Biblical Studies
JESHO	*Journal of the Economic and Social History of the Orient*
JJS	*Journal of Jewish Studies*
JRA	*Journal of Roman Archaeology*
JRH	*Journal of Religious History*
JRS	*Journal of Roman Studies*
JSJ	*Journal for the Study of Judaism in the Persian, Hellenistic, and Roman Periods*
JSJSS	Journal for the Study of Judaism Supplement Series
JSNT	*Journal for the Study of the New Testament*
JSOT	*Journal for the Study of the Old Testament*
LAI	Library of Ancient Israel
LEC	Library of Early Christianity
LHBOTS	The Library of Hebrew Bible/Old Testament Studies
LNTS	The Library of New Testament Studies
Neot	*Neotestimentica*
NovT	*Novum Testamentum*
NovTSup	Supplements to Novum Testamentum
NRSV	New Revised Standard Version
NTS	*New Testament Studies*
OTL	Old Testament Library
PEQ	*Palestine Exploration Quarterly*
RBS	Resources for Biblical Study
RSV	Revised Standard Version
SBL	Society of Biblical Literature

SCM	Student Christian Movement
SemeiaSt	Semeia Studies
SNTW	Studies of the New Testament and Its World
SPCK	Society for Promoting Christian Knowledge
STDJ	Studies on the Texts of the Desert of Judah
SWBA	Social World of Biblical Antiquity
SymS	Symposium Series
TSAJ	Texte und Studien zum antiken Judentum
TynBul	*Tyndale Bulletin*
WBC	Word Bible Commentary
WJK	Westminster John Knox
WUNT	Wissenshaftliche Untersuchungen zum Neuen Testament
ZNW	*Zeitschrift für die neutestamentliche Wissenschaft und die Kunde der älteren Kirche*

Ancient Authors and Texts

1 Clem.	1 Clement	
1 En.	1 Enoch	
Athenaeus	*Deipnosophistai*	
CIL	Corpus Inscriptionum Latinarum	
Dio.	Dio Cassius	
EA	El-Amarna	
Eusebius of Caesarea		
	Hist. eccl.	*Historia ecclesiastica*
Gos. Thom.	Gospel of Thomas	
Hermas, Shepherd		
	Herm. Mand.	Mandate(s)
	Herm. Sim.	Similtude(s)
	Herm. Vis.	Vision(s)
Ignatius of Antioch		
	Ign. *Pol.*	*Letter to Polycarp*
	Ign. *Smyrn.*	*Letter to the Smyrnaeans*

Josephus

	Ant.	*Antiquities of the Jews*
	J.W.	*Jewish War*
	Life	*The Life*

Justin Martyr

	1 Apol.	*First Apology*

Pliny the Younger

	Ep.	*Epistulae* (Letters)

Philo of Alexandria

	Spec.	*De specialibus legibus*

P.Oxy — Oxyrhynchus papyri
Ps.-Aristotle — Pseudo-Aristotle
4QFlor — Florilegium (from Qumran)

1. Biblical Economics as an Essential Tool for Biblical Studies[1]

MATTHEW J. M. COOMBER

Biblical economics is a quickly developing subfield within the discipline of biblical studies, and for good reason. Neither the Bible as a whole nor its individual books can be fully understood without an awareness of their economic underpinnings. As is the case with any culture, ancient or modern, religious beliefs and practices cannot be divorced from the economic environments in which they were developed and formalized.

It is for this reason that the first two volumes of the Center and Library for the Bible and Social Justice Series's Guide to the Bible and Economics were created: to offer readers what is currently understood about the economic contexts of ancient southwest Asia and the Roman world. The purposes of this volume and its predecessor are by no means to present a final word on the subject, but are intended to facilitate further research on the economic environments that shaped and were also challenged by the communities who developed texts that would eventually become biblical.

The chapters within *Economics and Empire in the Roman World* illuminate the economic realities that underpin the books of the Christian New Testament. Before delving into the volume's main body of work, this chapter explains the importance of the field of biblical economics and addresses some of the challenges faced by those who pursue its approach.

1. This introductory chapter is a revised and updated version of the introduction to the first volume of this series, *Economics and Empire in the Ancient Near East*, "The Importance of Biblical Economics to the Field of Biblical Studies."

Importance of the Study of Biblical Economics to Biblical Studies—and Beyond

The Bible is most often read without consideration for either its economic underpinnings or their implications. More often than not, the Bible is thought of in regard to its devotional value, with many readers' first encounters taking place in houses of worship, religious educational programs, or another sort of religious setting. Others gain their first exposure to the Bible through the evangelism of its devotees, either via direct contact with an evangelist or the more indirect approach of Gideons International, which, among its other activities, makes Bibles available in hotel rooms. At other times, the Bible may be introduced through the promotion of a specific verse. During televised sporting events in the United States, for example, it is not uncommon to see "John 3:16" held aloft on poster board or written under an athlete's eyes. But while the Bible is unquestionably religious, it is also undeniably economic. The economic nature of biblical texts is a very important factor for academics who study them and the social realities of the ancient world and also for scholars of other fields of study that engage the cultures and geographic settings that surrounded the Bible's development.

Economics and economic concerns do not run parallel to the field of biblical studies: they run straight through it. Recognizing and understanding the influence of the Bible's economic underpinnings affords two primary benefits. First, a recognition of the Bible's economic backdrop reveals previously undetected levels of meaning in even the most familiar of texts. For scholars, the detection of these underpinnings cultivates a greater awareness of recurring economic themes and values—many of which were adopted from yet earlier societies—that are revisited in various parts of the Hebrew Bible and New Testament. Such awareness can also facilitate a recognition of previously unseen connections between texts as disparate as the legal writings of the Holiness Code, Hebrew prophetic oracles, Jesus' parables, Paul's letters, and John of Patmos's Revelation. Conversely, cultivating this knowledge can also help scholars to better recognize and dispel eisegetical interpretations. Understanding the economic systems of ancient southwest Asia and the Roman Empire, which functioned much differently than our own, better equips readers to recognize when modern paradigms—such as capitalist or socialist ideologies—are imposed upon biblical ideas. Additionally, for scholars and non-scholarly readers alike, paying attention to the Bible's recurring economic themes can help bring into view those texts that either confronted or reflected ancient forms of economic exploitation and manipulation that are also present today: e.g., political corruption, predatory resource extraction, and the worship of political figures.

A second benefit to be gained from recognizing the Bible's economic underpinnings is the potential to uncover clues pertaining to the economic realities that colonized peoples were made to face in ancient southwest Asia and in the Roman world. Beyond offering value to the field of biblical studies, insights that can be gleaned from the Bible are of great importance to scholars of economic anthropology, ancient history, or other humanities and social-scientific disciplines that have an interest in the lives and times of those who inhabited what is now commonly referred to as the "biblical world." Extracting such insights from biblical texts, however, is complicated and fraught with potential for missteps, many of which the contributors of volumes 1 and 2 of this series address. Before outlining these challenges, the intertwining nature of economic development and religious formation should be addressed.

Centrality of Economics in Religious Activity

Concerns over the allocation and distribution of resources have preoccupied almost every aspect of human life since kinship groups started banding together into larger communities. From the development of the earliest hunting and foraging societies to the modern ambitions of billionaires seeking to colonize Mars, communities have developed and augmented strategies to procure, secure, and distribute goods. In addition to forming societies to collectively engage in the cultivation and storage of foodstuffs, broaden genetic diversity, and form security alliances, economic activity has shaped the creation, development, and evolution of religious beliefs, ethics, and practices.

In the ancient world, little divided environmental phenomena from the spiritual realm. Rates of rainfall and the flow of rivers, the spread of crop-killing diseases and pests, and other natural events were often connected to either the will or neglect of divine actors. It was for this reason that communities believed the pursuit of divine favor to be essential. Ensuring fruitful harvests and avoiding the catastrophic consequences of successive crop failures were believed to depend upon the successful navigation of religious rituals and observances. Thus these religious practices were designed to guide planting and harvest seasons, regulate relationships between neighbors, and determine the management of arable lands.[2] Numerous texts within the Bible represent these same concerns, from seeking rain through divine intervention (1 Kgs 18, Ps 68, Zech 10:1) to parables that addressed how personal finances and community

---

2. Hirth, *Organization of Ancient Economies*, 117–23; Rappaport, "Sacred in Human Evolution," 37–39.

resources should be managed in relation to one's neighbors (Matt 25:14–30, Luke 16:19–31).

Connections between economics and engagement with the divine realm, however, went beyond simply seeking deities' favor and avoiding their rage; religious rituals and beliefs were used to facilitate economic administrators' ambitions. As economic systems evolved, religious beliefs shifted to meet and support new societal goals. Bernard Knapp notes that as a result of the strong connections that develop between agrarian strategy and divine engagement, "ritual activities serve as the interface between religion and techno-economic or socio-political activities."[3]

As spiritual-economic traditions solidify over time, the ritualization of producing, storing, and allocating goods erodes any divisions that might have once existed between religious ethics and economic activity. The economic system becomes imprinted onto the deity or deities to which the rituals are connected.[4] Consequently, the characteristics of divine actors become indistinguishable from the community or society's economic systems and goals. This process happens so completely that shifts in economic goals are rarely mitigated to any large extent by religious doctrine or tradition. The reverse, rather, is more often the case. Doctrine and tradition—as well as the deities to which they are connected—undergo a transformation that facilitates the desired economic changes of local and regional administrators, and/or their imperial overlords. This appears to have been the case in the late eighth century BCE, when the Southern Kingdom of Judah was absorbed into an expanding Assyrian Empire, and the region experienced numerous religious reforms, particularly in relation to the temple cult in Jerusalem.[5] In the New Testament, members of the early Jesus movement struggle to determine how the teachings of Jesus should shape individual and community conduct within their Roman imperial contexts: a struggle complicated by some members' belief that Jesus' return and the dawn of a new world was imminent.

Marriages between economic systems and religion, and the pull that economics forces exert on religious belief and practice, are not limited to the ancient world. An increase in trade between Europe and Asia during the fifteenth century CE overturned numerous long-held religious taboos, such as

---

3. Knapp, "Copper Production," 157.
4. Coomber, "Caught in the Crossfire," 419–21.
5. Coomber, *Re-Reading the Prophets*, 97–134. For example, King Hezekiah's decision to remove worship sites from Judah's countryside and centralize worship, and its flow of temple revenue, in the capital city of Jerusalem (2 Kgs 18:22, 2 Chr 32:12).

making various Chinese spices—which had once been strictly reserved for ceremonial use—available for general consumption on European tables.[6] So too in the twentieth century CE, Libyan dictator Mu'ammar Qadhdafi reinterpreted Muslim doctrine and altered the Islamic calendar in his country in an effort to reshape his nation's economic strategy. For example, in order to liberalize Libya's economy to more effectively engage with international capitalism, Qadhdafi privatized the nation's sacred land endowments, known as the *waqif*, which had been religiously managed for centuries in order to offer subsistence farming for impoverished agrarian workers.[7] Such examples of economics influencing religious practice and their connected belief systems and institutions go on into the present day, including the rise and spread of prosperity theology and Christian nationalism among sectors of the ruling elite in the United States.

Considering the links that bind religious development and economic practice, it should be no surprise that economic desires, activities, and changes underpin the writings found within the Bible. Recognizing biblical authors' reactions to economic needs, events, and ethics—whether as supporting economic realities or as forms of resistance—can offer insights into the effects that economic and theological developments create. In the context of Hebrew biblical texts, the authors' communities witnessed massive changes in the first millennium BCE, including advancements in the processing and manipulation of iron, the introduction of monetary economics, a centralization of oil and wine production, the advent of speculative taxation, and the introduction of sustained imperial control over the Southern Levant.[8] Authors connected to the early Jesus movement in the first centuries of the first millennium CE had to contend with the reassertion of economic norms expressed in the Hebrew texts, alongside of new teachings that ran counter to Roman-imperial social and economic agendas. While an awareness of how such socioeconomic changes affect religious systems serves to highlight economic realities that were imprinted onto biblical texts, this awareness can also shed light on biblical interpretations that developed as a result of economic shifts in those societies that later adopted biblical texts as sacred.

Much is to be gained by studying the economic environments that shaped

---

6. Bayly, "'Archaic' and 'Modern' Globalization," 52–53.

7. Anderson, *State and Social Transformation*, 266.

8. Coote and Whitelam, *Emergence of Early Israel*, 72–80. The Southern Levant refers to the geographical region of ancient Canaan, which encompasses modern-day Israel, Jordan, and Palestine.

biblical texts, but ancient economic systems can be exceedingly difficult to decipher. The following section addresses some of the challenges that scholars of biblical economics face, challenges that have been met by the contributors of this volume.

Challenges to Creating an Overview of Biblical Economics

When one considers the economic realities of the Bible, the information provided in the Bible's texts is far from clear. The contents of the Hebrew Bible, for example, represent perspectives that are largely, if not entirely, limited to those of male urban elites. They are driven by religious and other cultural biases, and present their audiences only with what the authors wanted to reveal. Furthermore, the books of the Hebrew Bible, as with New Testament texts, underwent several levels of revision before being set in those forms from which our modern translations are derived. This led to some texts being set quite clumsily and haphazardly, as can be found in the book of Micah. In short, there is no *original text* in either the Hebrew Bible or New Testament with which to work.[9]

To uncritically receive biblical accounts of their economic authors environments would result in images that are either incomplete or wholly inaccurate: take, for example, the false claims of King Solomon's unmatched wealth and imperial influence (2 Chr 9:13–29), for which there is evidence to the contrary. But when read together with contemporaneous literature, histories, archaeological evidence, and the heuristic aid of social-scientific theories, the Hebrew Bible can serve as an indispensable partner in uncovering those economic realities and challenges that shaped biblical communities. While our understanding of the economics among biblical communities is incomplete, clues within the Bible—whether presented overtly or hidden within context—can serve as useful tools for developing a clearer picture. The contributors to *Economics and Empire in the Roman World* have incorporated such tools in order to offer the clearest picture that we currently have of those economic environments, their goals, and the challenges that shaped the composition of biblical texts. Outlined here are a few of the more overt challenges to engaging in this process.

---

9. Philip Davies offered a helpful treatment of the urban-dominant perspectives of the Hebrew Bible ("Urban Religion").

Scarcity and Nature of the Literary Evidence

A common challenge faced by those who study the economic practices that surrounded biblical communities is a lack of literary evidence dating back to when the texts were originally composed or, in the case of literature first developed orally, put into writing. In regards to the Hebrew Bible, any original texts have been lost to time. Whereas the Assyrians and Babylonians left legal texts and accounting records preserved in baked clay—some dating as far back as the third millennium BCE[10]—such was not the case among the Hebrew Bible's authors' communities; research must be conducted without either access to original texts or knowledge of how those texts may have read. Aside from the fact that much of the Hebrew legal corpus appears to have originated and been transmitted as oral tradition, any law codes, contracts, or supply lists that had been committed to writing were recorded on animal skins, which decayed. The continued survival of these texts depended upon the time, energy, and resources of generations of scribes who continued to remake copies as the previous versions of these texts aged and became unusable. Aside from the Dead Sea Scrolls, not discovered until the twentieth century CE, the oldest existing examples are centuries younger than their originals, edited and redacted to fit the evolving circumstances and ideologies of the communities into which they were received. While we have more fragments and less orality surrounding texts of the early Jesus movement, found in the New Testament, there are also no "original texts" to which scholars can turn. As with the texts of the Hebrew Bible, the New Testament texts we have today are products of generations of editing and redacting.

In addition to the literary limitations that scholars of biblical economics face, certain kinds of documents that would help researchers to better understand rural economic practices of ancient Hebrew communities are entirely absent. As an example from the Hebrew Bible, key documents pertaining to how usufruct[11] was managed in ancient southwest Asia are entirely absent. While some Hebrew legal, prophetic, wisdom, and narrative texts address usufruct (e.g., Lev 25, 1 Kgs 18, Prov 22:28, Isa 6:8), legal documents pertaining to land conveyance and deeds of land ownership are entirely absent from the biblical record. In addition to working without either land conveyance documents or landholding deeds, Baruch Levine notes that there are no official correspondence or royal edicts from either the Northern Kingdom of Israel or

10. The Code of Ur-Nammu dates to between 2100 and 2050 BCE.

11. *Usufruct* is the legal right of an individual or kin group to access the productive capabilities of farmable land.

the Southern Kingdom of Judah.[12] In order to contend with this lack of literary evidence, scholars of biblical economics have found various means through which to glean information, including comparative studies with neighboring cultures and various social-scientific methods.

Contextual, Cultural, and Paradigmatic Differences in the Authors' Times

Another set of challenges faced by those who research the economic realities of the Bible is the sociocultural gulfs existing between biblical texts and their modern audiences. While this is challenging enough in itself—considering differences in economic goals, strategies, and religious norms between ancient and modern cultures—scholars of biblical economics must also consider the disparities that existed between the different ancient communities that gave rise to the texts of the Bible.

Many ancient authors of the Bible were separated from each other by culture, time, geography, and theology, and their works represent and reflect theological assertions, questions, and assumptions of communities that had worked apart and, therefore, came to differing conclusions. These divergent societal and religious contexts led to what would later become intra-biblical disparities pertaining to economic rules and ethical paradigms. For example, in the Covenant Code it is commanded that a male slave should be freed without debt in the seventh year of bondage (Exod 21:2), but no command for manumission is afforded to female slaves (Exod 21:7). In the Deuteronomic Code, however, both men and women are to be freed in the seventh year (Deut 15:12; see also Jer 34:9). Gleaning economic information from the Bible is further complicated by the fact that their writings emerged and were copied before notions of intellectual property had developed. Thus, as mentioned in the previous section, biblical texts were frequently subjected to revisions that either augmented or added material to texts so as to represent later writers' theological and ethical viewpoints. While theological differences existed between various biblical authors, far greater are the socioreligious and paradigmatic dissimilarities between the ancient authors and their modern audiences. For many modern adherents—taught that the Bible is a univocal "book"—acknowledging such differences is difficult to either see, understand, or accept and, therefore, are frequently overlooked, explained away, or ignored.

---

12. Levine, "Farewell," 224.

Projecting Modern Economic Paradigms onto the Ancient Past

A key impediment to understanding the economic landscapes of either ancient West Asia or the Roman Empire, as addressed in Boer and Petterson in chapter 2 of this volume, is the temptation to impose modern paradigms onto the ancient past, whether consciously or unconsciously.

When a person is presented with a situation or object that they do not understand, the mind looks for potential connections to what it *can* understand in order to make sense of it. This may be why so many foods with nondescript flavors appear to taste like chicken when tried for the first time. While ancient and modern humans' primary hopes and anxieties are quite similar, the paradigmatic worlds they inhabit—be they cultural, religious, scientific, or economic—are foreign to each other. It is only natural, therefore, for modern readers of the Bible to approach those texts with what tools they have at hand: for example, labeling a particular economic strategy as *proto-capitalist* or *proto-socialist*. While this process may be understandable, forcing modern systems and ideas onto the ancient past can impede our attempts to develop clearer understandings of ancient economic contexts as they were.

In the context of the field of medieval studies, Norman Cantor addressed the issue of imposing modern realities onto earlier cultures. He found that people had a high propensity to project their worldviews onto the medieval world, which led them to reinvent the past in their own image: an issue that has also been addressed by current medievalist Courtney Luckhardt in relation to white supremacist impositions of modern biases onto medieval Europe.[13] As this phenomenon appears in the study of medieval Europe, examples are frequently found in artworks that portray biblical characters, such as Gerard van Honthorst's seventeenth-century painting *King David Playing the Harp*. In this painting, Van Honthorst presented David as a primarily European-style king, save a few Orientalist adornments. In much the same way, readers of the Bible are prone to think of and express biblical economic concepts and goals in terms of the capitalist, socialist, or other economic systems to which they are accustomed. Such anachronisms may readily make sense to author and audience alike, but do not represent these texts' ancient contexts. While it is difficult to avoid the projection of modern paradigms onto earlier contexts—to escape doing so entirely is scarcely possible—attentiveness to this hazard can help scholars avoid its worst effects as they work to understand realties outside their own worldviews.

---

13. Cantor, *Inventing the Middle Ages*, 156–58; Luckhardt, "Confronting Race."

While the challenges outlined above may impede our understandings of the economic realities that surrounded the Bible's authors and their communities, all hope is not lost. As readers will find in the following chapters, scholars of biblical economics, culture, and religion are able to employ numerous models, tools, and strategies to help decipher the macro- and microeconomic realities that surround the composition of biblical texts. Through working with clues derived from the Bible; archaeological evidence; the literary resources of neighboring civilizations; and social-scientific models that can be tested against the evidence we have, the field of biblical economics is offering new insights into the economic realities in and around ancient southwest Asia and the Roman world. Additionally, studies in biblical economics are shedding light on long-hidden meanings behind numerous biblical texts.

Lack of Consensus within the Field of Biblical Economics

As in any academic field of study, scholars will interpret data in different ways, which leads to divergent conclusions. Such disagreements are not unwelcome, as the divergent viewpoints that emerge from such differences can be incredibly fruitful to both sharpening and also furthering discussion and discovery. Debate is the whetstone of the mind, and when collegially and successfully engaged, its friction helps to grind the false away so as to lead us closer to truth. Within this volume, readers will occasionally find opposing points of view in areas where our contributors' research overlaps. This was to be expected and it is welcomed by the editor. *Economics and Empire in the Roman World* was by no means intended to be the final word or represent a consensus on the subject. The goal here is to present an overview of what is currently understood about the economic landscapes out of which the New Testament developed and to facilitate further exploration into their study. To present a univocal collection of essays would be a great disservice to that end. Readers can be assured, however, that any discrepancies between our contributors' interpretations of evidence do not stem from a lack of academic rigor from one author or the other. Rather, areas of difference should be recognized as guideposts for the sort of reflection and exploration that this volume intends to promote, highlighting areas for further investigation.

On behalf of the contributors, the editor wishes to express our hope that *Economics and Empire in the Roman World* will offer valuable insights into how the New Testament's economic environments, both real and imagined, shaped the communities and individual lives of those living under the Roman Empire, while also highlighting what the area of biblical economics has to offer to the field of biblical studies, and beyond.

Bibliography

Alfaro, Juan. *Justice and Loyalty: A Commentary on the Book of Micah*. ITC. Grand Rapids: Eerdmans, 1989.

Anderson, Lisa. *The State and Social Transformation in Tunisia and Libya: 1830–1980*. Princeton: Princeton University Press, 1986.

Bayly, C. A. "'Archaic' and 'Modern' Globalization in the Eurasian and African Arena: c. 1750–1850." In *Globalization in World History*, edited by A. G. Hopkins, 47–73. London: Pimlico, 2002.

Boer, Roland. *The Sacred Economy of Ancient Israel*. LAI. Louisville: Westminster John Knox, 2015.

Cantor, Norman F. *Inventing the Middle Ages: The Lives, Works, and Ideas of the Great Medievalists of the Twentieth Century*. Cambridge: Lutterworth, 1992.

Coomber, Matthew J. M. "Caught in the Crossfire? Economic Injustice and Prophetic Motivation in Eighth-Century Judah." *BibInt* 19 (2011) 396–432.

———. *Re-Reading the Prophets through Corporate Globalization: A Cultural-Evolutionary Approach to Understanding Economic Injustice in the Hebrew Bible*. Center and Library for the Bible and Social Justice Series. Eugene, OR: Cascade Books, 2022.

Coote, Robert B., and Keith W. Whitelam. *The Emergence of Early Israel: In Historical Perspective*. SWBA 5. Sheffield: Almond, 1987.

Davies, Philip R. "Urban Religion and Rural Religion." In *Religious Diversity in Ancient Israel and Judah*, edited by Francesca Stravrakopoulou and John Barton, 104–17. New York: T. & T. Clark, 2010.

Ekholm-Friedman, Kajsa. "On the Evolution of Global Systems, Part I: the Mesopotamian Heartland." In *World System History: The Social Science of Long-Term Change*, edited by Robert A. Denemark et al., 152–84. London: Routledge, 2000.

Hirth, Kenneth. *The Organization of Ancient Economies: A Global Perspective*. Cambridge: Cambridge University Press, 2020.

Knapp, Bernard A. "Copper Production and Eastern Mediterranean Trade: The Rise of Complex Society in Cyprus." In *State and Society: The Emergence and Development of Social Hierarchy and Political Centralization*, edited by J. Gledhill et al., 149–72. One World Archaeology. London: Unwin Hyman, 1988.

Levine, Baruch A. "Farewell to the Ancient Near East: Evaluating Biblical References of Ownership of Land in Comparative Perspective." In *Privatization in the Ancient Near East and Classical World*, edited by Michael Hudson and Baruch A. Levine, 223–52. Peabody Museum Bulletin 5. Cambridge, MA: Peabody Museum of Archaeology and Ethnology, 1996.

Luckhardt, Courtney. "Confronting Race and Medieval Fantasies: Teaching the Middle Ages in the Modern South." *Perspectives on History*, Sept. 22, 2021. https://www.historians.org/publications-and-directories/perspectives-on-history/october-2021/confronting-race-and-medieval-fantasies-teaching-the-middle-ages-in-the-modern-south?fbclid=IwAR2N1N33gi2LTolZoyyrCH2cuQ87ZrkuXTkumRNtbvKdZ2bWmozuEOsLTdY.

Rappaport, Roy A. "The Sacred in Human Evolution." *Annual Review of Ecology and Systematics* 2 (1971) 23–44.

2. Economic Relationships Found in the Worlds of the Bible[1]

ROLAND BOER AND CHRISTINA PETTERSON

This study focuses on specific biblical texts that concern economic relationships in ancient Near East and the Greco-Roman world. It will soon become clear that we need to avoid the assumption that "economics" concerns solely trade and commerce. Instead, the primary economic activity for more than 90 percent of the populations of the ancient Near East and the Greco-Roman world was agriculture, which included both crop growing and animal husbandry.

We have selected three topics from the Hebrew Bible and two from the New Testament. The first concerns the narrative tension between Joseph and Moses, a literary manifestation of an economic tension between subsistence-survival agriculture and estate systems. This is followed by an analysis of exchange in texts concerning Solomon and Tyre, and then comes a discussion of specific practices associated with transactions over land—often but erroneously regarded as "private property." The New Testament examples concern Gospel parables of rapacious landlords and demonized peasants and tenants, and the much-debated question of slavery in Paul's few writings.

Throughout, we assume three layers of economic activity derived from *régulation* economic theory: (1) the building blocks of institutional forms, which coalesce at different times into (2) regimes. These regimes provide

---

1. This chapter, designed to cover economic relationships reflected in both the Hebrew Bible/Old Testament and also in the New Testament, appears in the first two volumes of the Guide to the Bible and Economics. It was first published in *Economics and Empire in the Ancient Near East*, the first volume, in 2023.

relative stability over a period of time, but they are inherently unstable, eventually giving way to another regime. Finally, the aggregate of regimes forms (3) a mode of production. In what follows, from the Hebrew Bible we analyze texts concerning three regimes, each of them dominated by one institutional form: a subsistence regime (dominated by subsistence survival), a palatine regime (dominated by estates), and a regime of plunder (dominated by patterns of tribute and exchange). From the New Testament we analyze two texts concerned with the colonial and slave regimes (with the *polis-chōra* relationship in the Greek and Roman colonies dominating in the first text, and slavery dominating in the second). Although we are unable to go into detail here,[2] this time line provides a sense of how the regimes related to one another.[3]

Economic Timeline

Uruk	Akkad(e)	Ur III	Old Assyria & Babylon	Neo-Assyria, Neo-Babylonia, Persia *(Israel)
Palatine regime				Regime of plunder
←——————[*SR]—————→ [*SR]—————→[*SR]←—————————→				
vs. Subsistence regime				vs. Subsistence regime
4000 BCE	**3000**	**2000**		**1000** **0**
				*(Israel: SR vs. brief palatine)

* SR: prolonged dominance of subsistence regime

Further, we operate with two methodological positions. First, a regime's relative stability is enabled by a mode of *régulation*,[4] which we understand as a set of behavioral patterns and institutions that enable and challenge the ideological reproduction of a given regime. This takes place in three domains: (1) constraint (laws and rules) and compromises, (2) patterns of behavior and assumptions, and (3) the methods by which these are socially reinforced and undermined. A mode of *régulation* need not be religious, but in the context of the Bible, the primary nature of such a mode was deeply and inescapably religious. Further, during periods of relative stability, a mode of *régulation* provides the necessary social and ideological glue to enhance such stability. Yet, during times of turbulent change, modes of *régulation* become plural, exploring ways to challenge the problematic status quo, attempting to find ways through to a new consensus. Additionally, as part of a mode of *régulation*, texts relate to

---

2. See further Boer, *Sacred Economy*; Boer and Petterson, *Time of Troubles*. The examples used in this text are drawn from these works, as well as from Boer, "Economic Politics."

3. Boer, *Sacred Economy*, 194.

4. Boyer and Saillard, "Summary of *Régulation* Theory," 41; Jessop and Ling Sum, *Beyond the Regulation Approach*, 42; Lipietz, "Accumulation, Crises."

their contexts in mediated and unexpected ways, attempting to resolve socioeconomic tensions in the production of their stories, poetry, myths, and song. Neither windows onto reality nor expressions of the ideologies of the various groups that purportedly produced them, texts have indirect and contradictory connections with the socioeconomic context to which they respond.

Joseph and Moses

The first exhibit concerns the struggle between Joseph and Moses (Gen 41 to Exod 15). "Joseph?" you may ask. Is not the fight to the death between Pharaoh and Moses? The text attempts to exchange the protagonists, suggesting that the new pharaoh did not know Joseph and thus began to oppress the Israelites (Exod 1:8). Instead of charging the text with subtly redirecting the reader's gaze, we prefer to see this as one of the many mediations of the basic conflict in the text.[5] To draw out this conflict, we focus on four features: the opposition between estate and subsistence regimes itself; the insertion of geographic or spatial distance between the opposed regimes, now in terms of Egypt and Canaan; the pattern of traversing that distance; and the depth of rupture required to break the stranglehold of the estates.

First, Joseph clearly establishes a hyperestate system—a central feature of the palatine regime—once he achieves recognition and then power in Egypt.[6] Genesis 41 tells the fabulous story in which Joseph is first called from prison to interpret the pharaoh's double-dream. Indeed, the fat cows of the dream (Gen 41:1–8) already signal the tone of the narrative. Over-fattened cows were a distinct marker of relative affluence and power, and one can well imagine the idle rich dreaming about them. By contrast, the small number of bovines in rural villages were normally used not for consumption but for traction, since they consume vast amounts of water and fodder.[7] Having successfully interpreted the dream, Joseph is promptly appointed as the overseer of not one estate among many, but of a hyperestate that is the land of Egypt itself (Gen

---

5. As observed earlier, we tend to analyze the tensions within a text as indirect and mediated representations of socioeconomic tensions. That said, it is sometimes possible to identify a dominant ideological position, which then reveals its internal tensions in unexpected ways. Thus, the account of paradise in Gen 2–3, or its reframed version in the Song of Songs, assumes the normality of estates and the palatine system. The same could be said of the account of Joseph and Moses, except that the text attempts to valorize both by shifting the blame to the unnamed pharaoh.

6. On estates as an institutional form, as well as subsistence-survival and their perpetual economic tensions, see Boer, "Production and Allocation."

7. Brewer, "Hunting, Animal Husbandry," 434–38. For the *fatted calf* as a symbol of power and excess, see 1 Sam 28:24; 1 Kgs 1:9, 19, 25; 15:17; Jer 46:21; Amos 5:22.

41:33–45).[8] Joseph does what any estate manager would do if given free rein: he gathers up all the grain so that the people have nothing left for themselves and have to come to him for sustenance (Gen 41:46–49, 53–57). Yet produce is only half of the story, for the key lies with labor; and the best estate labor is indentured labor. So, later in the story (Gen 47:13–26), Joseph manipulates the situation so that people are forced to sell their bodies into slavery.

The text says less concerning the opposition to the estate system (Gen 46:8–27), although the clan of Jacob may be seen as the textual presence of the village community—central to the subsistence regime. The clan of "keepers of livestock" numbers seventy persons. Although this is an ideal number (marking fullness), that does not equate with the genealogical list (Gen 46:8–27); it also marks—if we include women and children—the normal range of a village-commune. Clan and village-commune were usually coterminous, as suggested by Judg 6:24; 8:32; 2 Sam 14:7; Jer 3:14.[9] Their apparent semi-nomadism was very much part of village existence, as was the tendency for nomadic groups to settle periodically. Both pastoral nomadism and sedentary agriculture were variations, with many overlaps, on the resilient patterns of subsistence survival.

The tale has already provided one instance of exacerbation (Joseph's mega-estate), but another follows. Instead of the tension between estates and subsistence agriculture taking place within close proximity, this tension is stretched out, as it were, with each end pushed as far apart as possible—among other peoples and in other places (Canaan versus Egypt). The distance is emphasized by two features: the physical amount of text that concerns this spatial separation (Gen 41–50) and the constant but onerous travel between the two places. Narrative distance emphasizes the economic gulf between estates and village communities.

Distance traveled leads to the third point: co-option of labor for the estates. Ostensibly, the story concerns clan squabbles and a grand reconciliation, but it also enables the securing of labor. This co-option begins with hostage taking (Gen 42:18–25) and then includes the "surety" of other family members (43:8–10), the fear that all the brothers will become slaves (43:18), and whatever trick it takes—the golden cup—to secure their labor (44:10–13, 18–34). From the perspective of the village community, someone indentured for estate labor seemed to be "no more" (Gen 42:6). Yet, this is only the beginning, for eventually Joseph manages to indenture his whole family into the estate system (already foreshadowed in Gen 44:16–17 and given divine approval in 45:4–14,

---

8. Skinner, *Commentary on Genesis*, 501–2.

9. Jankowska, "Communal Self-Government"; Schloen, *House of the Father*, 155–65; Liverani, *Israel's History*, 21–22.

46:1–4).[10] Upon arrival in Egypt, they become indentured laborers, keepers of the landlord's livestock (Gen 47:1–6). Joseph—and not the new pharaoh—has indentured the labor of his own clan. The text hints that Joseph and the oppressive pharaoh become one, for the name of the territory where Jacob's clan is settled is Rameses (47:11), the same name connected with slave labor and storage facilities in Exod 1:11.[11]

While the various metaphorical items of the story—golden cups, foreign places, hostages, and then enslavement—indicate the convoluted strategies used to co-opt labor for the estates, they also indicate the constituent resistance of village communities to co-option. Despotic power and its system of estates are not at the center of the narrative; rather, that power must constantly adapt to find new ways to commandeer the labor so desperately needed for the estates. This brings us to the final point of the narrative: the depth of the rupture required to break the hold of the estate system. Exodus 1–15 may be read as a massive story of breaking with the estates and their indentured labor. The story attempts to shift the blame not only onto a cruel pharaoh (see above) but also onto the increasingly oppressive labor conditions (Exod 1:8–22, 2:23–25, 5:10–21). Would Joseph's labor conditions have been any different? Yet, the key is the amount of effort required to break away from the estate system. In this legendary tale, the effort takes the form not of sporadic violence (Exod 2:11–15) but of the drawn-out account of the divinely ordained plagues (Exod 5:1—12:36). It becomes even tougher since God hardens Pharaoh's heart time and again. Then we have not only violence against the firstborn of the Egyptians, but also the drowning of Pharaoh's horses and charioteers in the sea (Exod 13:17—15:21). This violence marks not merely the rupture between the powerful and the powerless but also the sheer eagerness with which people would seek the destruction of despots and their centers and symbols of power.

The twenty-five chapters that cover the transition between Genesis and Exodus may then be seen as a tale in which the struggle between estates and village communities—and thus between palatine and subsistence regimes—leaves its traces on one of the most significant accounts in the Hebrew Bible. These traces have been mediated and metaphorized in terms of clan struggles, exotic places, foreign despots, and miraculous escapes. But let us close this section with another signal of the depth of the tension we have been tracing. When Jacob

---

10. Some are seduced by the divine approval of Joseph while others note the negative tone, albeit for other reasons (Kim, "Reading the Joseph Story"; Stone, "Joseph in the Likeness").

11. Brodie, *Genesis as Dialogue*, 397.

hears that Joseph is alive and powerful in Egypt, the text reads, "He was stunned; he could not believe them" (Gen 45:26). We suggest that Jacob expresses surprise, not that Joseph is alive, but that the traitor is managing a mega-estate.

Solomon and Tyre

The previous section concerned literary mediations of the tensions between subsistence and palatine regimes (dominated by subsistence-survival and estate-institutional forms)—the main regimes of some three millennia of economic history, from the rise of Uruk in the fourth millennium to the early first millennium BCE. The texts in the present section deal with exchange, which is often described as "commercial" exchange. Under the Persians in particular, such exchange became relatively widespread, as the Persians deployed markets and coinage to deal with logistical (usually military) problems over a somewhat vast empire. Indeed, the Persians had refined a regime already established by the Neo-Assyrians, which we have termed a regime of plunder, in which tribute exchange was dominant. But why connect exchange with plunder? The first step involves making a distinction between polite internal plunder (commonly known as taxation) and brute external plunder. Both are forms of extracting goods and wealth from others. The second step concerns the rise of markets, which were developed for the double purpose of taxation and military logistics. With the invention of coinage and its adoption by rulers (especially the Persians in this part of the world),[12] it became apparent that the strange new items with abstract value attached to them could be deployed for military provisioning. Instead of using as many people to provision an army as those in the army itself, rulers hit on the idea of paying soldiers in coin and simultaneously demanding taxes in coin. How could agricultural laborers acquire coins? By selling produce and goods to the soldiers in question.[13] Thus, the first widespread markets were determined by state concerns of logistics and tax, with profit clearly a secondary phenomenon.

Given this context, it is surprising that representations of exchange, let alone entrepreneurial merchants, are quite rare in the Hebrew Bible. Two are notable: Solomon and Tyre, in 1 Kgs 10 and Ezek 27–28. In 1 Kgs 10:22, Solomon appears as the quintessential merchant king, who brings prosperity by engaging in trade: "For the king had a fleet of ships of Tarshish at sea with

---

12. Coinage was invented at roughly the same time in Lydia, India, and China, with different technologies and no apparent contact.

13. Even in this situation, however, old practices of customary price rather than the vagaries of supply and demand dominated.

the fleet of Hiram. Once every three years the fleet of ships of Tarshish used to come bringing gold, silver, ivory, apes, and peacocks." Two items are worth noting. First, these ships "used to come" (*bw'*) every three years. No exporting and importing take place here, for the ships bring items to Solomon and his court. Their function is to acquire items, but what items? Valuable metals (gold and silver), expensive ornamental material (ivory), and exotic animals (apes and peacocks, or perhaps rare fowl).[14] No mention is made of bulk goods, such as grains, meats, dairy products, or vegetables. Instead, acquisition and preciosities are the key elements of an ideal image, projecting a picture of how an Israelite Empire might have appeared. It is clearly drawn from the realities of actual empires, whether Neo-Assyrian, Neo-Babylonian, or Persian, each of them providing an ideal to which the "little kingdoms" might aspire.[15]

The crucial distinction is between exchange in bulk and in preciosities: trade in bulk has small profit margins and requires cheap transport and complex logistics; by contrast, the exchange of a small amount of nonessential preciosities with high value (tangible and intangible) takes place when these items are difficult to acquire due to high risks, prohibitively expensive transport, and limited logistics. While bulk trade is for the whole population, preciosities are for those who can afford it—the small ruling class. It follows that in precapitalist societies, bulk exchange is marginal, decentered, and local, while exchange in preciosities may take place over greater distances, for it requires minimal and sporadic interaction.[16] The only form of bulk acquisition was for feeding palace and estate, a command economy that operated by means of estates and taxation. Occasionally, in a preciosity-poor region, some bulk goods might be sent to a neighboring little kingdom for the sake of acquiring preciosities.

To return to the text, within the wider context of 1 Kgs 10:22 the focus remains consistent: a concern with acquiring preciosities. In one year, the gold that "came" to Solomon was a mythical 666 talents, which were made into shields, cups, and other vessels. They were used to overlay an ivory throne. So much gold was available that silver was counted as nothing. Not short on hyperbole, our anonymous author (or authors) says this about Solomon's throne: "Nothing like it was ever made in any kingdom" (1 Kgs 10:20). The queen of

---

14. For comparable and much longer lists, see EA 14, 22, 25; Moran, *Amarna Letters*, 27–37, 51–61, 72–84. See also Nam, *Portrayals*, 70–73.

15. Many were the minor potentates who attempted to emulate the Assyrians and the Great (Persian) King (Briant, *From Cyrus to Alexander*, 172, 201–2; Long, *1 Kings*, 75–76).

16. On the distinction between preciosities and bulk, see Wallerstein, *Capitalist Agriculture*; Chase-Dunn and Hall, *Rise and Demise*, 52–54, 204, 248.

Sheba, too, arrives, riding camels laden with spices, gold, and precious stones.[17] As she unloads these exotic items, she is overwhelmed by Solomon's wealth and wisdom, which surpass any report she has heard. To add to the influx, an appended couple of verses (1 Kgs 10:11–12) include Hiram of Tyre, who brings from Ophir yet more precious stones and the rare almug wood, which is used for temple and palace building, and for lyres and harps for the singers.

The important feature of these stories is what may be called the idea of exchange, the purpose of which is to acquire goods. All of these preciosities travel in one direction: to Solomon (see also 1 Kgs 4:20—5:6 [Eng. trans. 4:20–26]). Even within the "commercial" Persian Empire, the emphasis was thoroughly centripetal, in which tribute and trade merge into one.[18] There is little sense of exporting goods, let alone two-way exchange; a favorable balance of trade; or the weighing of risks, outlays, losses, returns, and investment. Nor is there any presence of the brisk trade in bulk agricultural goods. This applies just as much to the "men of the road and the to-and-fro of the busybodies" (*'anšê haṭṭārîm ûmisḥar hārōkĕlîm*) of 1 Kgs 10:15. Even in the Greek world and its phase of colonization, the prime function of trade was the acquisition of goods one did not have, to be paid for by whatever means were available— mines, plunder, or the necessary evil of merchants.[19] Wallerstein's observation may well read as commentary on this text concerning Solomon: the acquisition of preciosities "depended on the political indulgence and economic possibilities of the truly wealthy."[20]

Let us consider another text, 1 Kgs 10:28–29:

> Solomon's import of horses was from Egypt and Kue, and the king's traders received them from Kue at a price. A chariot could be imported from Egypt for six hundred shekels of silver, and a horse for one hundred fifty; so through the king's traders they were exported to all the kings of the Hittites and the kings of Aram.

This translation comes from the NRSV, which has conveniently turned

---

17. Finkelstein and Mazar imagine the queen of Sheba as Solomon's "trading partner," "undoubtedly" reflecting the presence of the "lucrative Arabian trade" (*Quest for Historical Israel*, 215).

18. Briant, *From Cyrus to Alexander*, 201.

19. Ste. Croix, *Athenian Democratic Origins*, 349–70. Evidence from ports such as the Piraeus or those of Egypt indicates that ships paid a flat tax for entering and leaving a port. If one was concerned to ensure a balance of trade in favor of exports, one would hardly tax ships *leaving* port (Briant, *From Cyrus to Alexander*, 385).

20. Wallerstein, *Capitalist Agriculture*, 20.

the text into the image of a fully-fledged and profit-driven market economy.²¹ It is instructive to consider the text without a neoclassical economic frame. A better translation is:

> And horses went out [*yṣ'*] for Solomon which were from Egypt and Kue [or linen; *miqwēh*]; the king's busybodies [*sḥr*] acquired [*lqḥ*] them from Kue at a price. And a chariot came up [*'lh*] and went out [*yṣ'*] from Egypt for six hundred shekels of silver, and a horse for one hundred and fifty; so for all the kings of the Hittites and the kings of Aram they brought them out [*yṣ'*] by their hand.

The terms used indicate a rather different impression. What the NRSV translates as "export" is simply "go out" (*yṣ'*), and the subject is either horse or chariot and not an entrepreneurial Solomon; "import" is actually "acquire" or "get" (*lqḥ*). As for *soḥar* (*sḥr*) and *rôkēl* (*rkl*), their semantic fields indicate that "busybody" or even "hustler" captures the sense best, or perhaps "groveling busybody."²² In this light, a different picture emerges: instead of a commercial enterprise for profit, it is a rather lucrative task given to despised and busybody merchants, who acquire horses for Solomon, as well as for the kings of the Hittites and of Aram. In this legendary tale, they needed horses and chariots, and someone was prepared to get them. That these busybodies would have been rewarded handsomely goes without saying.

To sum up, the texts concerning Solomon's exchange or "trade" have the consistent themes of acquisition rather than trade for profit; the overwhelming concern has to do with preciosities and with the denigration of merchants. And we have suggested that a better term for such "merchants" is "middlemen," or indeed "grovelers"—outsiders responsible for acquiring preciosities for the political indulgence of a small ruling class.

A third text remains, which is often used to depict commercial exchange in the ancient world:

> Tarshish scurried [*sḥr*] about with you due to your massive piles of riches; silver, iron, tin, and lead they gave [*ntn*] for your forsaken wares [*'zb*]. Javan, Tubal, and Meshech trafficked [*rkl*] with you; they gave human beings and vessels of bronze for your barren cargo [*'rb*].²³ Beth-togarmah

---

21. Some follow suit, such as by speaking of a *global economy* (Bright, *History of Israel*, 216–17). Our analysis draws on Petterson, "King Solomon."

22. See the full discussion of these two terms in Boer, "Production and Allocation."

23. The semantic field of *'rb* includes "exchange," "become dark," and "arid, barren, or sterile." It is also the name for Arabia. In its substantive form, "barren cargo" expresses these associations.

gave for your forsaken wares horses, war horses, and mules. The Rhodians swarmed [*rkl*] about you; many coastlands became your own busybodies [*sḥr*]; they brought you in payment ivory tusks and ebony. Aram scurried [*sḥr*] about with you because of your many shady dealings [*'śh*]; they gave for your forsaken wares turquoise, purple, embroidered work, fine linen, coral, and rubies. Judah and the land of Israel swarmed [*rkl*] over you; they gave for your barren cargo wheat from Minnith, millet, honey, oil, and balm. Damascus scurried [*sḥr*] about with you due to your many shady dealings—because of your piles of riches of every kind—wine of Helbon, and white wool. Vedan and Javan from Uzal gave for your forsaken wares wrought iron; cassia and sweet cane were for your barren cargo. Dedan swarmed [*rkl*] about you for saddlecloths for riding. Arabia and all the princes of Kedar were your favored busybodies [*sḥr*] in lambs, rams, and goats; in these they scurried [*sḥr*] about with you. The busybodies [*rkl*] of Sheba and Raamah swarmed [*rkl*] over you; they gave for your forsaken wares the best of all kinds of spices, and all precious stones, and gold. Haran, Canneh, Eden, the busybodies [*rkl*] of Sheba, Asshur, and Chilmad swarmed [*rkl*] over you. These swarmed [*rkl*] over you for choice garments, for clothes of blue and embroidered work, and for carpets of colored material, bound with cords and made secure; in these they swarmed [*rkl*] about you. The ships of Tarshish sailed for you with your barren cargo. (Ezek 27:12–25 author's trans.)

The initial impression is the predominance of preciosities, but a closer look reveals the wheat, millet, and honey supplied by Judah and Israel, and the lambs, rams, and goats from Arabia and the princes of Kedar. Thus, Tyre acquires goods from the two main areas of agriculture—basic crops and products from sheep and goats. Before we conclude that enterprising and profit-minded farmers have finally made an appearance,[24] note that the text does not mention farmers or peasants. Instead, given the nature of exchange between the "little kingdoms" of the ancient world, these transactions took place between the courts. For preciosity-poor minor potentates, the payment of grains and animals—acquired through taxation—was a necessary evil in the pursuit of preciosities. On this matter it is worth noting that despite all his supposed wealth, Solomon gives Hiram of Tyre both wheat and twenty towns in Galilee (1 Kgs 5:11; 9:11–13).[25] But when Hiram comes to view the towns, he finds them entirely useless.[26]

24. Odell, *Ezekiel*, 349–50.
25. Nam, *Portrayals of Economic Exchange*, 126.
26. Seibert argues that the material functions as a subtle critique, especially in light of

More significant is the emphasis of the Isaiah passage and its genre. In terms of emphasis, items flow into Tyre in centripetal fashion;[27] the lists are swamped by preciosities; the city's status is exceptional or anomalous—note especially the trafficking in human beings. It is a little kingdom that embodies the status of the middleman or busybody noted earlier. In terms of genre, not only is it a literary word picture, full of the obligatory literary license,[28] but it is above all a prophetic condemnation of Tyre.[29] The town is thoroughly denigrated for precisely what is does: accumulate wealth through the dirty business of exchange. This text is part of the wider image of the glittering ship of Tyre, decked out in all the finery acquired from here and there. That ship is about to come to grief: "By your great wisdom in trade / you have increased your wealth, / and your heart has become proud in your wealth" (Ezek 28:5).

This disdain of middlemen or busybodies appears throughout the prophetic literature, where they become a byword for all that is unsavory, taking all that is best and hoarding it (Isa 23:2–3, 8, 17; Ezek 17:3–4; 38:13; Hos 12:8–9 [ET 7–8]; Nah 3:16; Zeph 1:11; Zech 14:21; see also Neh 13:20). The mark of the busybody, the balances, is also condemned (Hos 12:8; Zeph 1:11; see also Lev 19:36; Deut 25:13; Amos 8:5–6; Mic 6:11; Prov 16:11; 20:10, 23).[30] Above all, these texts critique the activity of these merchants, who also happened to be tax collectors, usurers, and landlords for, like Tyre, they "prostitute" themselves "with all the kingdoms of the world on the face of the earth" (Isa 23:17).

The Question of Property in Land

The third item has to do with a fascinating group of materials concerning the transferal of what many have called "private" or "inviolable" property, inevitably of land. These include Abraham's acquisition of the field of Machpelah in Gen 23; Jacob and the issue of land for an altar in Gen 33:19–20; stipulations regarding inheritance, redemption, and jubilees in Lev 25 and 27; Boaz's acquisition from Naomi of both land and woman in Ruth 4; David and the threshing floor of Araunah in 2 Sam 24:18–25 (see 1 Chr 21:1—22:1); Ahab and Naboth's vineyard in 1 Kgs 21; Jeremiah and the field of his cousin Hanamel in

Deut 17:14–20 (*Subversive Scribes*, 174–80).

27. Launderville, *Spirit and Reason*, 162–63, 170–71.

28. Many are seduced by the word *image* as describing a commercial trade network (Liverani, *Israel's History*, 170; Launderville, *Spirit and Reason*, 162–63; Diakonoff, "Naval Power").

29. Launderville, *Spirit and Reason*, 150; Renz, *Rhetorical Function*, 95–96.

30. Law 94 in Hammurabi's Code also condemns false weights in lending or receiving money.

Jer 32:6–15; and various texts in the Psalms and Prophets that concern inheritance. The underlying issue of how land is represented is pertinent to all of the regimes that appear in the economic context of the Hebrew Bible: subsistence, palatine, and plunder. But how should we understand the question of land and its transfer? Our assumption in dealing with these texts is expressed best by Steinkeller: the category of private property in interpreting the relation to land in ancient economies is "useless, confusing and harmful."[31] This is not least because the legal-cum-economic category of private property was first invented by the Romans—in response to slavery—in the late second century BCE.[32] Before this time one cannot legitimately speak of private property without a serious anachronism. Of course, this raises the question as to how we interpret the texts we have mentioned.

Let us begin with some terminological clarification. Three main terms that have been assumed to refer to some form of private property are 'ăḥuzzâ, naḥălâ, and ḥelqat haśśādeh.[33] To begin with, 'ăḥuzzâ comes from the same root as the word for "tenure": 'ḥz means "to hold" or "seize." It is clearly not "property," as the lexica would have us believe. Thus, Abraham seeks to acquire some land, as a burial "tenure" ('ăḥuzzat qeber) (Gen 23:4, 9, 20),[34] from the "Hittite" clan of Ephron so that his own clan may have a place to bury their dead. There is no suggestion that the Hittites cease to be the overlords, even though the burial tenure passes on to Abraham's sons. Similarly, Hamor's granting of 'ăḥuzzâ to Jacob's sons in Gen 34:10 permits them tenure in and thereby usufruct—the legal right to use the products of—the land.

Often paralleled with 'ăḥuzzâ is naḥălâ. The standard meaning given is inviolable and inalienable property.[35] Yet the focus of the root nḥl concerns not the

31. Steinkeller, "Land-Tenure," 296. See also Steinkeller, "Private Economic Activity," 93; Brinkman, "Land Tenure," 6–7:74; Godelier, Mental and Material, 86; Deist, Material Culture of Bible, 143–44; Guillaume, Land, Credit and Crisis, 10–12. Of the many who continue to assert the existence of private property in land we cite a representative sample: Bright, History of Israel, 81; De Geus, "Agrarian Communities"; Dever, What Did Biblical Writers, 239; Matthews, "Physical Space, Imagined Space"; Houston, "Was There Social Crisis," 134; Levine, "Farewell"; Pastor, Land and Economy, 1; Thompson, Historicity of Patriarchal Narratives, 211, 295–96.

32. For a full presentation of this historical point, see Boer and Petterson, Time of Troubles.

33. The discussion of these terms is indebted, with some modification, to Guillaume, Land, Credit and Crisis, 18–21.

34. Here the lexica are a little confusing, suggesting both "possession" and "property" (Clines, Dictionary of Classical Hebrew, 1:187). Koehler et al. err even more with "landed property" (Hebrew and Aramaic Lexicon, 32).

35. Koehler et al., Hebrew and Aramaic Lexicon, 687; Clines, Dictionary of Classical

object itself but the process of transition or passing over. Thus, it means to "take possession" (*qal* verb form), "allocate" (*piel* verb form), and "give" (*hiphil* verb form), all with the association of inheritance. That is, it designates the acquisition (*qal* verb form) of something that is allocated or given (*piel* and *hiphil* verb forms). All of this means that *ăḥuzzâ* and *naḥălâ* are not synonymous: the former designates tenure, while the latter means the way such tenure is acquired.

The third term is *ḥelqat haśśādeh* (allocated field), more often functioning as a metaphor (Gen 33:19–20; Ruth 4:3; 2 Sam 14:30–31; 2 Kgs 9:21, 25; Jer 12:10; Amos 4:7; cf. the verb *ḥlq* [apportion] in Jer 37:12). This is a share of land usage between members of village communities and not, as it is so often rendered, a field or plot of land. Why not? In contrast to a field or even a farm, which is surveyed, measured, and demarcated from neighbors, a land share is a moveable strip or strips of land that are constantly reallocated on the basis of usufruct and labor.[36] Or rather, it is a reallocation of usufruct and labor rather than land; for this reason, it is better to speak of an allotment of land usage. In this light, it is possible to understand the various references to "boundary" or "landmark" (Deut 19:14, 27:17; Prov 22:28, 23:10, Job 24:2, Hos 5:10),[37] to "the lot [*gôral*] of their [*naḥălâ*]" (Josh 14:2 author's trans.; see also 18:2–10),[38] as well as to the "measuring rope" (*ḥebel*), the semantic field of which actually includes an "allotted portion" of land (Deut 3:4, 13–14; 32:9; Amos 7:17; Mic 2:5; Zeph 2:6–7; Zech 2:5 [2:1 Eng. trans.]; Pss 16:6; 78:55; 105:11). These are the means for measuring and demarcating strips of reallocated land usage in relation to one another.

Hebrew, 5:659. In his rather loose studies, Borowski, too, sees *ăḥuzzâ* and *naḥălâ* as synonyms and defines them as inherited private property within the context of the clan (*Agriculture in Iron Age*, 22; *Daily Life*, 26). Deist has a curious twist, noting all the terms mentioned here, even recognizing the process of allotment, but then assuming that they become inalienable property (*Material Culture of Bible*, 143–44).

36. A consistent thread of some awareness of this approach to agriculture may be found among biblical commentators, albeit with more or less specificity. Alt, *Kleine Schriften*, 3:348–72; Henrey, "Land Tenure"; Kohler, "Gemeinderschaft und Familiengut"; Karl Elliger, "Allotment," *IDB* 1:85–86; Chaney, "Ancient Palestinian Peasant Movements," 64–65; Kaufman, "Reconstruction," 280; Lemche, *Early Israel*, 196–98; Bendor, *Social Structure*, 141–60.

37. Among others, Wright and Matthews mistakenly assume that they refer to markers of personal property in land (Wright, *God's People*, 70; Matthews, "Physical Space, Imagined Space," 15).

38. The hypothesis that this was a once-and-for-all allotment of land (narratively speaking) that was subsequently inalienable misses the function of the terminology. Sweeney, *I and II Kings*, 249; Deist, *Material Culture of Bible*, 145. By contrast, Kitz explores the implications of the allocation by lot ("Undivided Inheritance").

What are the implications for the texts we mentioned earlier? Rather than reflections of real life, these engage in processes of metaphorization, in response to social and economic conditions and in ways that are unexpected and indirect. Frameworks, too, are crucial for understanding the function of these texts. To begin with genre, the four texts mentioned earlier (Gen 23; 33:19–20; Lev 25 and 27; Ruth 4) are part of a complex political myth running from Genesis to Joshua at least. This means the texts cannot be read as direct reflections of everyday life, for they form part of the metaphorical structure of myth. Overlapping with this mythic genre is the cultic focus of three of the texts, Gen 33:19–29, 2 Sam 24:18–25, and 1 Chr 21:18–22. The transfer of some land is here clearly not a matter of private property, but the designation of some collective, tribal land by a patriarch or a king for an altar.

Further, these texts metaphorize collective relations to land and inheritance, especially the means and relative ease with which land changes possession. In each case the collective dominates: explicitly in terms of named clan members, implicitly in terms of the paterfamilias (Abraham and Jacob). Or the collective is marked by the sign of YHWH. Jacob's altar, the acquisition of Araunah's/Ornan's threshing floor, and the instructions regarding what should be done with items dedicated to YHWH (Lev 27), may all be read as collective ownership at a higher degree. This assumption is summed up in Lev 25:23: "The land is not to be sold [*timmākēr*] in perpetuity, for the land is for me [*lî ha'areṣ*]; for you are strangers and sojourners with me" (AT).[39] This is the metaphor par excellence for collective relations with the land, precisely within the context of the founding political myth. Given that YHWH is the "God of Israel," anything that is YHWH's is thereby the people's as a whole—a necessarily imaginary community. At this level is YHWH the land's overlord; everyone else is merely a tenant on the land, and that tenancy is conditional.[40] Within this fictive framework, usufruct of the land is contingent upon observing the commandments. If the people do so, they will enjoy the vines and olive trees planted by others (Deut 6:11, Josh 24:13); if not, others will make the most of the houses and vineyards they have constructed (Amos 5:11, Zeph 1:13).

Genre and metaphorizing of collective relations and usufruct—these overlapping features frame the texts we mentioned earlier. In this context, the texts evince the following features: utopian and dystopian images; processes of transfer, or rather the contingent relation between land and human beings; the collective

---

39. In Babylonian terminology, *makkûr* designates the claim that the gods "own" the land (Van der Spek, "Land Ownership," 190–92).

40. Guillaume, *Land, Credit and Crisis*, 10, 17–18.

nature of such contingency; and the prime concern with usufruct. On the first point, the Psalms and prophetic literature present both dire and ideal images of allocatory life (characteristic of subsistence regimes). On the positive side, Ps 16:6 indicates that a blessed and bountiful time is when the measuring rope (*ḥebel*) falls favorably, providing a good *naḥălâ*, while Ps 105:11 speaks of the land of Canaan as a whole being subject to the measuring rope of a *naḥălâ*. Similarly, but in a more warlike setting, in Ps 78:55 enemies may be scattered so that the land may be measured out "by a rope for a portion" (*běḥebel naḥălâ*).[41] But the warlike setting may become more negative, for Yhwh may inflict punishment so there is an absence of casting the measuring rope by lot (Mic 2:5). Or indeed, as Amos 7:17 (see also Zech 2:5 [ET 2:1]) suggests, that someone else will come and turn women into prostitutes, kill sons and daughters, and apportion the land by means of a measuring rope (*běḥebel těḥulāq*). This process of metaphorization is not, simplistically, a reflection of real practices of daily life but rather a construction of a mythical image of ideal existence in an allocatory framework, which may become unstuck due to the disfavor of Yhwh. The precise function of this negative image is to reinforce the idealization of an allocatory form of economic life, with the bucolic village-commune as its basis.

As for contingent processes of transfer, the contortions of Num 27 and the various "laws" of redemption (*g'l*) in Lev 25:25–55 concern the means by which items are passed around within the clan. In other words, an individual's relation with any piece of land is highly contingent. So also Jeremiah's parable[42] of the "redemption" (*haggĕ'ullâ*) (Jer 32:7, 8) of the piece of land of his relative Hanamel features an internal shift within a clan. The land itself is a side issue, for the parable obsesses over the process. However, the utopian nature of the text reveals itself with the delightful absurdity of Jer 32:15: "For thus says Yhwh of hosts, the God of Israel: houses and fields and vineyards shall again be acquired [*yiqqānû*] in this land." Rather than a "free market" of buying and selling private property, people freely reallocate according to kinship lines.

The folktale in Ruth 4 tells of a comparable shifting sideways—for Boaz is a "kinsman" (Ruth 3:2). Here a characteristic feature of folktale and myth appears once again, exploring the edges and transgressions of acceptable norms, in part to assert the importance of those customary norms. This text also mentions two of the terms we mentioned earlier. The matter at hand concerns the

---

41. Enemy prisoners themselves may be forced to lie down and then be measured off with a rope, designating those to be killed and those to be spared (2 Sam 8:2).

42. Holladay enthuses that it is "the most detailed description of the transfer of property to be found in the OT" (*Jeremiah* 2, 214). By contrast, Carroll's focus on its fictional and prophetic role is a telling counter (*Jeremiah*, 2:618–23).

naḥălâ of Elimelech (Ruth 4:5, 10). Given the emphasis of this term on a flexible, even alternative, process rather than object transferred, the whole text of Ruth 4:1–12 is a quaint tale of that process of transfer: a meeting at the gate, ritual words, a sandal passed over, some trickery in acquiring three shares rather than one. Further, the land in question is *ḥelqat haśśādeh*, a share of land that would be regularly reallocated in the village-commune (Ruth 4:3).[43] That the focus of the land share is usufruct becomes clear when Ruth is acquired (*qnh*) and thereby the children that follow. Produce counts, whether of the land, animals, or indeed women.

The issues of usufruct and the boundaries of acceptable transfer of *naḥălâ* come to the fore in the story of Naboth's vineyard. Ahab seeks to extend his estate with a piece of land in order to grow some vegetables (1 Kgs 21:3).[44] As with Ruth 4, the term *naḥălâ* appears: Naboth abruptly replies to Ahab's approach, "Yhwh forbid that I should give you the inheritance of my fathers [*naḥălat 'ăbōtay*]" (1 Kgs 21:3; see also v. 4). And as with Ruth, the issue is the process of transfer rather than any notion of inalienable property.[45] A gruesome tale follows, without Ruth's quaint air. On the surface, it may appear that Jezebel's scheming seeks to overturn the inalienable nature of inheritance, only to be condemned by Elijah. However, a careful consideration of the text reveals that Naboth has refused the king's prerogative to take over tenure, even with a generous alternative; that Jezebel acts in terms of the king's power to do so; and that Elijah condemns Ahab not for violating Naboth's *naḥălâ*, but for his death (1 Kgs 21:19). In other words, the story deals clearly with usufruct and the transfer of tenure, whether this takes place by fair means or foul.[46]

Thus, these texts must be seen in terms of myth (whether utopian or dystopian), collective engagements, usufruct, and a concern with the process of transfer rather than the object itself. Instead of buying and selling of private property in land, we find a metaphorization of the edges and transgressions of inheritance transferal, of the intricacies of kinship, of what an ideal or baleful world might look like.

---

43. In this light one may understand Jer 37:12, where Jeremiah leaves Jerusalem to "apportion" (*ḥlq*) land in Benjamin (Guillaume, *Land, Credit and Crisis*, 45–46).

44. That it is a field share is indicated by 2 Kgs 9:21, for it is the specific allotment of Naboth where Jehu meets Joram. The story has been read as "proof" of private property in land in ancient Israel (Silver, *Prophets and Markets*, 74).

45. Contra Sweeney, *I and II Kings*, 249; Cronauer, *Stories about Naboth*, 127–28.

46. Contra Walsh, *1 Kings*, 319; DeVries, *1 Kings*, 257.

Parables in Landlord Eyes

With the fourth collection of texts, we move to the New Testament, dealing with nothing less than the parables. We are interested in particular in the troublesome parables in which God appears—sanctioned by the words of Jesus—as an exploiting landlord. The economic context is a colonial regime, characteristic of the lands conquered in the eastern Mediterranean by the Greeks under Alexander and then by the Romans. The pertinent feature of this regime was the colonial modulation of the *polis-chōra* relation, in which the *polis* became the colonial presence and the *chōra* the colonized territory that had to supply local and more distant *poleis* (Roman included). The small ruling class—including landlords—tended to be based in the *poleis*, although they also had a good number of exploited laborers and peasants.

In relation to the parables, the question arises: Are they told from a ruling-class, landlord, and *polis* perspective, or are they told from the viewpoint of "peasant life"?[47] Many would side with the latter, but the problem is that instead of the "families of peasants, fishermen, or day workers" we find instead a "significant number of individuals who belong to the elite families: rulers or aristocrats, who lived in big mansions, had servants to perform different tasks and owned large amounts of land."[48] Many are the explanations given for such a disjunction. Guijarro suggests that stories of peasant families would not have appealed to Jesus' listeners. And Moxnes opines that even though the parables are located in elite households, their perspective is from "below," with "neither the implied author nor the audience sharing the social location of the characters in the story."[49]

This tenet is difficult to hold. Let us take the parable of the wicked tenants in Mark 12:1–12 (also Matt 21:33–46, Luke 20:9–19). This parable produces myriad problems for interpreters who want to use the parables for a social justice agenda. The difficulty is ultimately a theological one, as Schottroff indicates:

> The matter-of-fact interpretation of the vineyard owner as God, which rules in the interpretative tradition with only a few exceptions, must be fundamentally called into question if we take the social-historical analysis of the text seriously. The owner of the vineyard acts like an opponent of God; he does the opposite of what the God of the Torah and the Lord's

---

47. Dodd, *Parables of the Kingdom*, 21.
48. Guijarro, "Family in First-Century Galilee," 48.
49. Moxnes, *Putting Jesus*, 43–44.

Prayer desires and does.[50]

The problem is the allegorical interpretation, which equates God with the owner of the vineyard, the violence perpetrated, and also the ensuing dismissal of the Jewish people as the heirs of the vineyard. Schottroff attempts to counter this allegory by means of her nondualist parable theory, attempting to emphasize the lives of ordinary people instead of treating them as signifiers for a theological meaning.[51] Thus Schottroff suggests that the tenants reflect "the economic hopelessness of the increasingly poor agrarian population and their hatred for their new master"—so much so that "in this parable we hear how indebtedness turns those burdened with it into violent people filled with hatred."[52] A problem remains: the perspective of the parable, which is clearly that of the slave-owning landlord rather than the tenants. The landlord is presented as the one who performed all the labor in establishing the vineyard and was claiming only that to which he was entitled. The tenants attempt to appropriate this through violence and murder.[53]

It is instructive to consider Schottroff's analyses of individual parables to see which ones she finds unacceptable (she has an excellent eye for the socioeconomic inequalities, and therefore refuses to see God as complicit in these structures). Any parable that depicts God as a slave owner, landowner, or king is regarded by Schottroff not as an analogy, but as an antithetical parable, which intends to present the listeners with the difference between God's kingdom and the current situation. Examples include the parable of the unforgiving servant (Matt 18:23–36), the laborers in the vineyard (Matt 20:1–16), the wedding banquet (Matt 22:1–13), and the slave parables in Luke (12:35–38, 17:3–10, 19:11–27).[54]

Schottroff follows Herzog in seeing the parables as expressions of class conflict. Thus, they must both read against the grain of the parable to detach God from the rich slave owner. While Herzog detaches the parables from their later Gospel interpretations,[55] Schottroff keeps them in their respective lit-

---

50. Schottroff, *Parables of Jesus*, 17.
51. Schottroff, *Parables of Jesus*, 2. See the methodological sections in pt. 2, 81–113.
52. Schottroff, *Parables of Jesus*, 17.
53. Mark's version is the harshest, which Matthew and Luke both attempt to ameliorate. The later versions are favored by scholars attempting an interpretation that presents God in a more flattering way. For example, see Bailey, *Jesus*, 410–26.
54. The parable of the weeds among the wheat, with God as a slave owner, is passed by with only a brief mention of its eschatological significance. Schottroff, *Parables of Jesus*, 207.
55. Herzog, *Parables as Subversive Speech*.

erary contexts, which means that she needs other arguments to support her antithetical readings. The main interpretive tactic she uses is her translation of *homoioun* and *homoios* as "compare" rather than "equate," because "compare" includes the possibility of seeing difference in the comparison rather than similitude. Schottroff and Herzog thus want to isolate God from the ongoing class conflict of which the texts are a product—or at least in Herzog's case to enlist Jesus (and thereby God) in a version of guerilla warfare against the ruling class. Our point is that class conflict is already represented from a certain class's viewpoint: that of the ruling class or the landlords, a perspective from which peasant resistance is depicted as self-serving rebellion.[56] We can reconstruct, flesh out, and read from below all we like, but the text simply does not recognize the viewpoint from below as valid.

Thus, the information on the conditions of production and the socio-economic history of the land, which provide a reading from below, comes not from the New Testament material, but rather from historical studies of Roman Palestine and Egypt, which suggests that the New Testament texts represent more the *polis*-based perspective of the ruling class rather than the common people. As in archaeological excavations, the lower classes are present in the texts only as traces. Given this feigned rural dress of the parables, we suggest that rather than coming from the mouth of Jesus, they originate in the *polis*.

Slavery

The final topic concerns slavery, which constituted a significant regime alongside the colonial regime. Obviously, slavery dominated this regime, but we are interested here in the "slave relation," which operated at social, intellectual, psychic, and textual levels.[57] As slavery became integral to economic activity, it influenced the modes of human social interaction. Such interaction became mediated through slaves, but the key is that mediation itself became a wider norm within human consciousness and thereby the literature, linguistic forms, and even religions produced at the time. Such was the saturation that slaves need no longer be actually present, for mediation itself became central to the way people thought and behaved. In this section, we focus on the first, and arguably most important, Christian ideologue, Paul, after which we examine the slave relation in the Gospels.

It would be self-deception if one failed to see that Jesus of Nazareth; the

---

56. As an instructive parallel, see the example of Ernst Bloch's reading of the sons of Korah (Num 16) in Boer, *Political Myth*, 20–21.

57. Martin, *Slavery as Salvation*.

apostles; and the church, in both its formative period and its later development, accepted the dominant system of labor of the time, including the slave structure, without hesitation or any expressed reluctance.[58] Further, the overwhelming tendency of biblical studies is to focus on household slavery, which is unsurprising given that this is also the major focus of the New Testament. The problem is that such a focus misses the prevalence of rural slavery on the estates and in agricultural production. Instead, the slaves in the parables either belong to a wealthy household or work for an absentee landlord.

With this in mind, let us turn to Paul, whose letters are full of slave metaphors. Above all, there is the Letter to Philemon concerning the slave Onesimus. In order to understand this letter, we draw on the work of Ulrike Roth, which shows how this letter may function as a productive starting point for early Christian attitudes toward slavery.[59] Roth's argument is that Onesimus was a contribution as human chattel to the *koinōnia*, and that Paul was a co-owner of Onesimus. She argues this point through attention to the letter's communication strategies, through analysis of the term *koinonia* and its practices of pooled ownership of various resources, through attention to Paul's display of mastery, and through an analysis of the parallel universe of Pauline Christianity, which brings the contradiction between Christian brotherhood and the economic system of slavery to the fore. Roth concludes:

> Whilst slavery, like citizenship, was irrelevant in the new world order, it was the order of the "old" world, which acknowledged slavery, that allowed Paul a double coup: in his dealings with Philemon and Onesimus, Paul embraces the order of both this world and the next, creating parallel universes that, with regard to slavery, could only have been understood by non-Christians (and probably by some fellow Christians) as an expression of a complete and unreserved acceptance of the slave system.[60]

We would like to address a number of significant points resulting from Roth's article. The first concerns Paul as a slaveholder. Based on a dual reading of *koinōnia* as both a practical association of pooling resources for a specific goal, as well as Paul's spin into a community of believers (*koinōia tēs pisteōs*), Roth argues that Paul is consciously mingling the two layers in order to assert his authority and undergird his demand for Onesimus. Based on the contractual arrangements inherent in *koinōnia*, to which Paul refers several times, he is

---

58. Westermann, *Slave Systems*, 150.
59. Roth, "Paul and Slavery."
60. Roth, "Paul, Philemon, and Onesimus," 128.

challenging Philemon to honor the agreements in this arrangement. The precise issue is Onesimus, who if he was a contribution by Philemon to the *koinōnia*, would make Paul the de jure part owner of Onesimus. This situation accords with the agreement entailed in the nature of the *koinōnia*, where material contributions become common property. Slaves, as chattel, would have been part of this contractual arrangement. Roth notes that a similar arrangement could be argued for the relation between Paul and Epaphroditus in Philippi.[61] She argues that there are two particular points in the letter that reinforce the master-slave relation between Paul and Onesimus. The first is Paul's readiness to take on possible debts, which shows him thinking as a slave master and acknowledging his legal responsibilities to Philemon.[62] The second is the presentation of Onesimus as Paul's agent—the physical extension of Paul, who is to be received by Philemon both in the flesh and in the Lord, thereby reinforcing Onesimus's status as a "thing," a sentient tool or the hands of Paul's mind, but also "of the old world."[63] This brings us to the second item of interest to take from Roth's article, namely, the idea of slave as a thing, used as a slave, within the church.

Scholarship on slavery and Christianity has come a long way since William Westermann's naïve assertion that the early Christians regarded slaves as human personalities instead of *things* as in Roman law.[64] In particular, the work of Glancy and Harrill has broken much new ground.[65] Another provocative example is Marchal's analysis of Onesimus as a sexual vessel. Yet, another step remains, which many scholars have been reluctant to acknowledge: the use of slave labor within congregations. These scholars attempt to insert a buffer against such a possibility in various ways: seeing Paul's perspective as *aligning comfortably with that of the slave owners*,[66] seeing Paul's possible interaction with slaves when accepting the hospitality of slaveholders,[67] using qualifiers

---

61. Roth, "Paul, Philemon, and Onesimus," 120–21 and n70.

62. Roth, "Paul, Philemon, and Onesimus," 123–24.

63. Roth, "Paul, Philemon, and Onesimus," 122.

64. Westermann, *Slave Systems*. See the helpful but already dated survey by Byron, "Paul and the Background." But see Osiek and Balch, *Families*. Here they state that "the human dignity of slaves was recognized by their acceptance into the community, without calling into question the mention of slavery itself" (188).

65. Glancy, *Slavery in Early Christianity*; Glancy, *Slavery as Moral Problem*; Harrill, *Manumission of Slaves*; Harrill, *Slaves in New Testament*.

66. Marchal, "Usefulness of an Onesimus."

67. Glancy, *Slavery in Early Christianity*, 45. See also Barclay, "Paul, Philemon." Barclay states that the slave context that would have been most familiar to Paul was "that of slaves living in the urban homes of their masters" (165), followed by a number of examples from Paul's letters and their references, for instance, to Chloe's people in 1 Cor 1:11.

when mentioning Paul and slave ownership ("as though"),[68] perhaps even regarding Onesimus as a runaway slave—since this avoids the notion put forward by Knox, Winter, and Roth, that Onesimus was sent by Philemon to assist Paul, which would make Paul someone who directly benefited from slave labor. It seems that most follow, whether explicitly or implicitly, Byron's assessment of the status quo: "As appalling as the notion of slavery is in any society, the fact remains that, in the context of the New Testament, slavery did take on some positive aspects. This is not to suggest, of course, that Paul was a supporter of slavery. But he and other New Testament authors were able to find something that was of 'redeeming' value for their theology."[69]

Following Roth, we follow the grain of the text: slaves were used in the service of Christianity. We mean not only that Paul would have benefited from someone's slave in someone's house, but that the various congregations made use of slave labor, as was the case with Onesimus and Epaphroditus. For example, the reference to Chloe's house in 1 Cor 1:11 suggests for Barclay "probably... the presence of slaves in the homes of some of his converts,"[70] and Osiek and Balch, following Theissen, acknowledge the possible presence of "slaves or dependent workers" in Chloe's home.[71] Both Glancy and Nasrallah go a little further and suggest that the message to Paul was conveyed by Chloe's slaves,[72] but without coming to the obvious conclusion that early Christianity exploited slaves as a matter of course—as did the rest of society.

In her conclusion, Roth follows and expands upon Barclay's point that the hospitality offered in the first house churches is unimaginable without slaves.[73] Roth points out that missionary activity could not have been carried out without the work of slaves (see also Acts 8:1–5, where Paul works with Aquila and Priscilla until Silas and Timothy arrive in Corinth).[74] While most commentators assume that Timothy and Silas bring funds, which enables Paul to concentrate on preaching,[75] the text says nothing about bringing anything.

---

68. For "as though he himself was the owner of Onesimus," see Arzt-Grabner, *Philemon*, 246. For scare quotes ("elsewhere, the epistle maintains the claim that Onesimus 'belongs' to the apostle"), see Frilingos, "For My Child," 101.

69. Byron, "Paul and the Background," 136.

70. Barclay, "Paul, Philemon," 165.

71. Osiek and Balch, *Families*, 99; referring to Theissen, *Social Setting*, 93.

72. Glancy, *Slavery in Early Christianity*, 49; Nasrallah, "You Were Bought," 64n45.

73. Barclay, "Paul, Philemon," 129–30.

74. Barclay, "Paul, Philemon," 130.

75. Bruce speaks of Timothy and Silas bringing "supplies" (*Acts of the Apostles*, 344). See also Marshall, *Acts of the Apostles*, 293–94, 452; Witherington, *Acts of the Apostles*, 448–49.

This opens up the possibility that Timothy and Silas work to support Paul, enabling him to preach full-time. This is emphasized by the order, or command (*entolē*),[76] issued by Paul to Silas and Timothy to join him as soon as possible (Acts 17:15).

Another place where Paul's use of slaves appears is in his letters, where he (and his disputed alter ego) steps in, indicating that he himself is now writing:[77]

> I, Paul, write this greeting with my own hand. (1 Cor 16:21)

> I, Paul, write this greeting with my own hand. This is the mark in every letter of mine; it is the way I write. (2 Thess 3:17)

> See what large letters I make when I am writing in my own hand! (Gal 6:11)

> So if you consider me your partner, welcome him as you would welcome me. If he has wronged you in any way, or owes you anything, charge that to my account. I, Paul, am writing this with my own hand: I will repay it. I say nothing about your owing me even your own self. (Phlm 1:17–19)

> I, Paul, write this greeting with my own hand. Remember my chains. Grace be with you. (Col 4:18)

We also have the example in Rom 16:22, where Tertius (a typical slave name, suggesting the possibility of a Primus and Secundus also under Paul's *potestas*), inscribes himself: "I Tertius, the writer of this letter, greet you in the Lord."[78]

Elsewhere, Roth pursues the topic of "Christian slavery," situating "Paul's use of slave labor in the wider context of the exploitation of slaves in the Roman Empire."[79] In terms of the economics of missionary success, "slave exploitation was a systematic [and, we would add, systemic] feature behind Christianity's early success."[80] Beginning with Meggitt's contention that full labor and ministry were incompatible within Paul's modus operandi,[81] and taking into account

---

76. Translations and commentaries usually translate *entolē* as "instructions," which softens the force of the word and assumes that they are *coworkers*, not subservient to Paul.

77. Petterson, *Acts of Empire*, 2–3.

78. For indications of Tertius as a slave name, see Solin, *Stadtrömischen Sklavennamen*, 152–53.

79. Roth, "Paul and Slavery," 156.

80. Roth, "Paul and Slavery," 170.

81. Meggitt, *Paul, Poverty, and Survival*, 76. However, it must be said that Meggitt's overall thesis, on the poverty of Paul and his communities, falls under what Roth astutely calls the "pauperising approach" to early Christians' social standing, which functions to minimize the possibility of implication in slavery and exploitation (which she also notes is not a given)

the efforts at staying connected with various communities, Roth concludes that the "demand for slaves to undertake some of the leg-work—in a literal sense—emerges as very real," of which Onesimus and Epaphroditus are suitable examples.[82] The travels and epistles (from *epistellō*, of course) that made the Pauline mission such a success were unthinkable without slave labor. Here we find offers of accommodation, financial and in-kind travel subventions, and courier services as examples of slave-based services that slave owners may offer Paul. We add the possibility of Paul's own co-owned slaves assisting him on travels, as the above example from Acts shows.[83]

All of this brings us to the contradiction between slave ownership in the early congregations and the ideology of equality espoused by Paul in his epistles (as noted by many).[84] If it is clear that the early Christian communities exploited slave labor in their missionary activity, then the issue becomes slightly more acute, needing an effort at a solution. Here we draw on the theory of an imaginary resolution of a real contradiction, first proposed by Lévi-Strauss and then elaborated by Fredric Jameson in an Althusserian framework.[85] In short, an irresolvable social and indeed economic contradiction often generates an attempt at resolution at an ideological level. Obviously, such a resolution cannot deal with the real social contradiction, so it reveals, through its very tensions and problems, the irresolvable nature of the problem.

In this light, we propose that Paul's use of metaphorical slavery is a desperate and brilliant attempt at working to resolve the actual contradiction at an ideological level. It consists quite simply in making everyone slaves, figuratively speaking, while maintaining, supporting, and benefiting from the fundamental inequality of this economic structure in daily life: as Roth says, Paul has his cake and eats it too.[86] The contradiction is not expressed in these terms, but relies rather on a difference between this world and the next, flesh and spirit, death and resurrection, and so on, which revolves around the fundamental problem

---

(Roth, "Paul and Slavery," 164).

82. Roth, "Paul and Slavery," 171.

83. More research needs to be done. A line of questioning, which we cannot pursue here, would be the passive verbs in the texts, since they may conceal the metaphorization of slave labor (e.g., Mark 12:1, Acts 8:28, 1 Cor 1:11).

84. Barclay mentions "the central tension in the present status of Onesimus as both slave and brother to Philemon" ("Paul, Philemon," 183).

85. Lévi-Strauss, *Tristes Tropiques*; Jameson, *Political Unconscious*; Althusser, *Lenin and Philosophy*.

86. Roth, "Paul, Philemon, and Onesimus," 124.

of the early Christians caught between this world and the next.[87] This means that the metaphor does not simply arise from everyday life[88] but emerges as an ideological effort to deal with an actual and pressing problem. It also indicates the inability to resolve this problem in practice.[89]

This metaphor of slavery took on a life of its own, wresting itself free from the problems that gave rise to it. One place in which the metaphor comes out quite clearly is in the parables of Jesus that deal with slaves and God as the slaveholder. As we mentioned earlier, Schottroff takes particular exception to the parables that present God as a slaveholder and argues that these must be seen as antithetical parables, pointing to the difference between the slaveholder and God. Crucial to her argument is the dubious move of translating *homoioun* and *homoios* as "compare" rather than "equate," since this translation loosens the connection between God and the slaveholder in these parables. Schottroff also insists heavily on non-allegorical interpretations of the various parables, because she wants to use the exploitative and violent content of the parables to signify the actual socioeconomic context and to separate a given parable from the kingdom of God.

However, many of the parables do contain the "keys" to their own interpretation, either through an extensive one-by-one exposition of the various elements, such as in the parable of the sower (Mark 4:2–20, Matt 13:1–23, Luke 8:4–15) or as in the weeds in the field (Matt 13:36–43) or as in the formula *homoiuon/homoios estin* (Matt 7:24–27, Luke 6:46–49). We wonder whether the existence of the allegorical key to the parables displays the contradictions of class struggle, in that the agricultural imagery is used to explain something else. However, the allegorical reading (broadly defined) was in Dodd's analysis set out in terminology much closer to that of Paul than that of Jesus.[90] This he understood to mean that Mark 4:11–12 ("And he said to them, 'To you has been given the secret of the kingdom of God, but for those outside, everything comes in parables; in order that 'they may indeed look, but not perceive, and may indeed listen, but not understand; so that they may not turn again and be forgiven'") indicates that this is a piece of apostolic teaching. Both Dodd's and Schottroff's rejections of the allegorical method are founded in their refusals to acknowledge anti-Judaism in Jesus' teaching; both see this facilitated

87. Boer, *In Vale of Tears*, 179–98.

88. As Glancy seems to suggest in her characterization of slavery as "fertile ground for generating metaphorical language" ("Slavery," 457).

89. Contra Turner, "Christian Life as Slavery."

90. Dodd, *Parables of the Kingdom*, 14.

and encouraged by the allegorical method and its inside-outside structure.[91] However understandable such an ideological position may be, it also seems to close down some interpretative options that we are keen to pursue—not so much in relation to the question of insiders and outsiders, but rather in relation to what the abstraction itself indicates.

This allegorical key, which is also present in Matthew and Luke, undergirds the dual nature of the material in question and, along with *homoiuon/ homoios estin*, encourages an allegorical reading. In this light, we suggest that the use of parables in the Gospels is an expression of the abstraction identified in Paul's writings, specifically in his attempt to overcome the contradiction between the use of slaves within the church and the equality of its members.

To go further, Christian metaphors of slavery include both negative and positive connotations: "The Christian can be termed both a slave of Christ and a freed person of Christ."[92] Crucial in this designation is not the positive or the negative valence, but the characterization of the Christian as a slave, one way or another.[93] This is not only the case in Paul and later uses thereof, but also in Jesus' parables, such as in Luke 16:13, which concerns a slave not being able to serve two masters. Here God and wealth are personified as masters, which means that the listener is interpellated as a slave. Further, in the various parables where God is characterized as slaveholder, the slaves are either obedient or disobedient, and are rewarded or punished accordingly—all of which provides the listener with a choice between being an obedient or a disobedient *slave*. Finally, Paul's instruction to become slaves to one another through love (Gal 5:13) echoes Jesus' pronouncement in Mark that whoever wants to be first shall become everyone's slave, following Jesus' own example.[94] We would see this the other way around: Mark's saying is an attempt to resolve an unresolved tension in Paul's letters.

Let us now add the question of private property, which the Romans first developed as a legal-economic category in response to the pervasive reality of slavery. Here we face a contradiction: Jesus at times argues against property, while in no way criticizing the institution of slavery, which he uses as a way to get theological points across. The problem is that there is a very close

---

91. Their motivations have different foundations. Over against Schottroff's liberative reading, Dodd's concern is more historically motivated, in his keenness to keep the original Jesus apart from the primitive church. Dodd, *Parables of the Kingdom*, 14–15.

92. Glancy, "Slavery," 457–58.

93. See also Meeks, *Moral World*, 157, 169.

94. Glancy, "Slavery," 459.

connection between property and slavery, so it would be possible to see the criticism of property as a criticism also of slavery. At the same time, we want to take our argument in a different direction and point out that the question of property in the Gospels is not without its problems. On the one hand, we note the various sayings about camels and eyes of needles (Matt 19:23–24, Mark 10:23–25, Luke 18:24–25), as well as the parable of the rich fool (Luke 12:13–21). Yet, we also have the parables in which God is apparently cast as a king or slaveholder, to the point of being in charge of substantial property, as we find in the parable of the faithful or the unfaithful slave (Matt 24:45–51, Luke 12:41–48), or in the parable of the talents (Matt 25:14–30). A particularly interesting example is the chapter in Luke containing three parables that illustrate repentance. Two of them concern property as metaphors for sinners, namely, the lost sheep (Luke 15:1–7) and the lost coin (15:8–10). Both parables equate the repentance of a sinner with the finding of something lost. The third is the parable of the prodigal son (15:11–32), whose father owns a large slave-run property. In all three cases, God is the property owner who rejoices in the return of what is lost.

On the basis of these examples, we propose that the Gospels propagate the slave ethos, or, in our terminology, the slave relation to the listener—continuing the metaphorical tradition springing from Paul's attempt to overcome the profound tension between slave exploitation and equality. In doing so, the Gospels are not really advocating an alternative society in regard to slavery, but remain within the parameters of the status quo. The odd rich person—who sells off property, gives it to the poor, and joins Jesus—does not change the dynamics of slaves and slave owners. Instead, he contributes to the endurance of the slave relation.

Luke 17:7–10 best sums up the slave relation, namely, the extension of the slave ethos to everyone, in submission to God:

> Who among you would say to your slave who has just come in from plowing or tending sheep in the field, "Come here at once and take your place at the table"? Would you not rather say to him, "Prepare supper for me, put on your apron and serve me while I eat and drink; later you may eat and drink"? Do you thank the slave for doing what was commanded? So you also, when you have done all that you were ordered to do, say, "We are worthless slaves; we have done only what we ought to have done!"

We have traced this ideological form back to the contradiction between ideology and practice in Paul's thinking, out of which the metaphorization of slavery arose as an imaginary effort at resolution. Slavery continued well after

Constantine, and Christianity's contribution to slavery seems to be more one of undergirding the system with an ideology that actually strengthened it, in the sense that the servile attitude was imbued as something desirable. This is what we designate the slave relation.

Conclusion

In this survey of key biblical texts concerning economic relations in the Bible, we have ranged over the struggles between estates and subsistence survival (Joseph and Moses), the despised presence of tribute exchange (Solomon and Tyre), the complex question of private property, the troublesome nature of parables that present the perspective of the ruling class, and the many levels of the slave relation, from Paul to the Gospels. In light of our economic framework, we have sought to challenge conventional interpretations and read the texts in slightly different ways, all the way from Joseph as a landlord to the persistence of slavery as an unchallenged feature, not only in Paul's usage of slaves, but also in their assumed role in the Gospels. Throughout, it became clear that the Bible—as an exhibit of a mode of *régulation*—offers not so much a reflection of actual economic relations, but rather a complex mediation, or indeed metaphorization, of economic realities—in unexpected ways.

Bibliography

Alt, Albrecht. *Kleine Schriften zur Geschichte des Volkes Israel*. 3 vols. Edited by Martin Noth. Munich: Beck, 1959.

Althusser, Louis. *Lenin and Philosophy, and Other Essays*. Translated by Ben Brewster. Modern Reader. New York: Monthly Review, 1971.

Arzt-Grabner, Peter. *Philemon*. Papyrologische Kommentare zum Neuen Testament. Göttingen: Vandenhoeck & Ruprecht, 2003.

Bailey, Kenneth E. *Jesus through Middle Eastern Eyes: Cultural Studies in the Gospels*. Downers Grove, IL: IVP Academic, 2008.

Barclay, John M. G. "Paul, Philemon and the Dilemma of Christian Slave-Ownership." *NTS* 37 (2009) 161–86.

Bendor, Shunya. *The Social Structure of Ancient Israel: The Institution of the Family (Beit 'Ab) from the Settlement to the End of the Monarchy*. JBS 7. Jerusalem: Simor, 1996.

Boer, Roland. "The Economic Politics of Biblical Narrative." In *The Oxford Handbook of Biblical Narrative*, edited by Danna Nolan Fewell, 529–39. Oxford Handbooks. New York: Oxford University Press, 2016.

———. *In the Vale of Tears*. Vol. 5 of *On Marxism and Theology*. Historical Materialism Book Series 52. Leiden: Brill, 2013.

———. *Political Myth: On the Use and Abuse of Biblical Themes*. New Slant. Durham: Duke University Press, 2009.

———. "Production and Allocation in Ancient Southwest Asian Economics." In *Economics and Empire in the Ancient Near East*, edited by Matthew J. M. Coomber, 44–74. Vol. 1 of *Guide to the Bible and Economics*. Eugene, OR: Cascade Books, 2023.

———. *The Sacred Economy of Ancient Israel*. LAI. Louisville: Westminster John Knox, 2015.

Boer, Roland, and Christina Petterson. *Time of Troubles: A New Economic Framework for Early Christianity*. Minneapolis: Fortress, 2017.

Borowski, Oded. *Agriculture in Iron Age Israel*. Winona Lake, IN: Eisenbrauns, 1987.

———. *Daily Life in Biblical Times*. ABS 5. Leiden: Brill, 2003.

Boyer, Robert, and Yves Saillard. "A Summary of *Régulation* Theory." In *Régulation Theory: The State of the Art*, edited by Robert Boyer and Yves Saillard, 36–44. London: Routledge, 2002.

Brewer, Douglas. "Hunting, Animal Husbandry and Diet in Ancient Egypt." In *A History of the Animal World in the Ancient Near East*, edited by Billie Jean Collins, 427–56. HdO 64, sect. 1: The Near and Middle East. Leiden: Brill, 2002.

Briant, Pierre. *From Cyrus to Alexander: A History of the Persian Empire*. Translated by Peter T. Daniels. Winona Lake, IN: Eisenbrauns, 2002.

Bright, John. *A History of Israel*. 3rd ed. Philadelphia: Westminster, 1980.

Brinkman, Carl. "Land Tenure." In *Encyclopedia of the Social Sciences*, edited by Edwin R. A. Seligman, 6–7:73–76. New York: Macmillan, 1933.

Brodie, Thomas L. *Genesis as Dialogue: A Literary, Historical & Theological Commentary*. Oxford: Oxford University Press, 2001.

Bruce, F. F. *The Acts of the Apostles: The Greek Text with Introduction and Commentary*. 2nd ed. London: Tyndale, 1952.

Byron, John. "Paul and the Background of Slavery: The *Status Quaestionis* in New Testament Scholarship." *CurBR* 3 (2004) 116–39.

Carroll, Robert P. *Jeremiah*. 2 vols. OTL. Repr., Sheffield: Sheffield Phoenix, 2006.

Chaney, Marvin L. "Ancient Palestinian Peasant Movements and the Formation of Premonarchic Israel." In *Palestine In Transition: The Emergence of Ancient Israel*, edited by David Noel Freedman and David Frank Graf, 39–90. SWBA 2. Sheffield: Almond, 1983.

Chase-Dunn, Christopher, and Thomas D. Hall. *Rise and Demise: Comparing World-Systems*. New Perspectives in Sociology. Boulder, CO: Westview, 1997.

Clines, David J. A., ed. *The Dictionary of Classical Hebrew*. 9 vols. Sheffield: Sheffield Academic, 1993–2012.

Cronauer, Patrick T. *The Stories about Naboth the Jezreelite: A Source, Composition and Redaction Investigation of 1 Kings 21 and Passages in 2 Kings 9*. LHBOTS 424. New York: T. & T. Clark, 2005.

De Geus, Cornelis H. J. "Agrarian Communities in Biblical Times: 12th to 10th Centuries BCE." *Antiquity* 41 (1983) 207–37.

Deist, Ferdinand E. *The Material Culture of the Bible: An Introduction*. BibSem 70. Sheffield: Sheffield Academic, 2000.

Dever, William G. *What Did the Biblical Writers Know and When Did They Know It? What Archaeology Can Tell Us about the Reality of Ancient Israel*. Grand Rapids: Eerdmans, 2001.

DeVries, Simon J. *1 Kings*. WBC 12. Waco: Word, 1985.

Diakonoff, Igor M. "The Naval Power and Trade of Tyre." *IEJ* 42 (1992) 168–93.

Dodd, C. H. *The Parables of the Kingdom*. Rev. ed. London: Collins, 1961.

Finkelstein, Israel, and Amihai Mazar. *The Quest for the Historical Israel: Debating Archaeology and the History of Early Israel*. Edited by Brian B. Schmidt. ABS 17. Atlanta: SBL, 2007.

Frilingos, Chris. "'For My Child, Onesimus': Paul and Domestic Power in Philemon." *JBL* 119 (2000) 91–104.

Glancy, Jennifer A. "Slavery and the Rise of Christianity." In *The Ancient Mediterranean World*, edited by Keith Bradley and Paul Cartledge, 456–81. Vol. 1 of *The Cambridge World History of Slavery*. Cambridge: Cambridge University Press, 2011.

———. *Slavery as Moral Problem: In the Early Church and Today*. Facets. Minneapolis: Fortress, 2011.

———. *Slavery in Early Christianity*. 2002. Repr., Minneapolis: Fortress, 2006.

Godelier, Maurice. *The Mental and the Material: Thought, Economy and Society*. Translated by Martin Thom. London: Verso, 1986.

Guijarro, Santiago. "The Family in First-Century Galilee." In *Constructing Early Christian Families: Family as Social Reality and Metaphor*, edited by Halvor Moxnes, 42–65. London: Routledge, 1997.

Guillaume, Philippe. *Land, Credit and Crisis: Agrarian Finance in the Hebrew Bible*. Bible World. Sheffield: Equinox, 2012.

Harrill, J. Albert. *The Manumission of Slaves in Early Christianity*. HUT 32. Tübingen: Mohr Siebeck, 1995.

———. *Slaves in the New Testament: Literary, Social and Moral Dimensions*. Minneapolis: Fortress, 2006.

Henrey, K. H. "Land Tenure in the Old Testament." *PEQ* 86 (1954) 5–15.

Herzog, William R., II. *Parables as Subversive Speech: Jesus as Pedagogue of the Oppressed*. Louisville: Westminster John Knox, 1994.

Holladay, William L. *Jeremiah 2: A Commentary on the Book of the Prophet Jeremiah, Chapters 26–52*. Hermeneia. Minneapolis: Fortress, 1989.

Houston, Walter. "Was There a Social Crisis in the Eighth Century?" In *In Search of Pre-Exilic Israel*, edited by John Day, 130–49. JSOTSup 406. London: T. & T. Clark, 2004.

Jameson, Fredric. *The Political Unconscious: Narrative as a Socially Symbolic Act*. Ithaca, NY: Cornell University Press, 1981.

Jankowska, Ninel B. "Communal Self-Government and the King of the State of Arrapha." *JESHO* 12 (1969) 233–82.

Jessop, Bob, and Ngai-Ling Sum. *Beyond the Regulation Approach: Putting Capitalist Economies in Their Place*. Cheltenham, UK: Elgar, 2006.

Kaufman, Stephen A. "A Reconstruction of the Social Welfare System of Ancient Israel." In *In the Shelter of Elyon: Essays on Ancient Palestinian Life and Literature in Honour of G. W. Ahlstrom*, edited by W. Boyd Barrick and John R. Spencer, 277–86. JSOTSup 31. Sheffield: JSOT, 1984.

Kim, Hyun Chul Paul. "Reading the Joseph Story (Genesis 37–50) as a Diaspora Narrative." *CBQ* 75 (2010) 219–38.

Kitz, Anne M. "Undivided Inheritance and Lot Casting in the Book of Joshua." *JBL* 119 (2000) 601–18.

Koehler, Ludwig, et al. *The Hebrew and Aramaic Lexicon of the Old Testament*. 2 vols. Translated and edited under supervision of M. E. J. Richardson. Study ed. Leiden: Brill, 2001.

Kohler, Josef. "Gemeinderschaft und Familiengut im israelitischen Recht." *Zeitschrift für Vergleichende Rechtswissenschaft* 17 (1959) 217–22.

Launderville, Dale F. *Spirit and Reason: The Embodied Character of Ezekiel's Symbolic Thinking*. Waco: Baylor University Press, 2007.

Lemche, Niels Peter. *Early Israel: Anthropological and Historical Studies on the Israelite Society before the Monarchy*. Translated by Frederick H. Cryer. VTSup 37. Leiden: Brill, 1985.

Lévi-Strauss, Claude. *Tristes Tropiques*. Translated by John Weightman and Doreen Weightman. Picador Classics. London: Pan, 1989.

Levine, Baruch A. "Farewell to the Ancient Near East: Evaluating Biblical References to Ownership of Land." In *Privatization in the Ancient Near East and Classical World* edited by Michael Hudson and Baruch A. Levine, 223–46. Peabody Museum Bulletin 5. Cambridge, MA: Peabody Museum of Archaeology and Ethnology, 1996.

Lipietz, Alain. "Accumulation, Crises, and Ways Out: Some Methodological Reflections on the Concept of 'Regulation.'" *International Journal of Political Economy* 18 (1988) 10–43.

Liverani, Mario. *Israel's History and the History of Israel*. Translated by Chiara Peri and Philip Davies. Bible World. London: Equinox, 2005.

Long, Burke O. *1 Kings, with an Introduction to Historical Literature*. FOTL 9. Grand Rapids: Eerdmans, 1984.

Marchal, Joseph A. "The Usefulness of an Onesimus: The Sexual Use of Slaves in Paul's Letter to Philemon." *JBL* 130 (2011) 749–70.

Marshall, I. Howard. *Acts of the Apostles: An Introduction and Commentary*. TNTC. Grand Rapids: Eerdmans, 1982.

Martin, Dale. *Slavery as Salvation: The Metaphor of Slavery in Pauline Christianity*. New Haven: Yale University Press, 1990.

Matthews, Victor H. "Physical Space, Imagined Space, and 'Lived Space' in Ancient Israel." *BTB* 33 (2003) 12–20.

Meeks, Wayne A. *The Moral World of the First Christians*. LEC 6. Philadelphia: Westminster, 1986.

Meggitt, Justin J. *Paul, Poverty, and Survival*. SNTW. Edinburgh: T&T Clark, 1998.

Moran, William L., ed. and trans. *The Amarna Letters*. Baltimore: Johns Hopkins University Press, 1992.

Moxnes, Halvor. *Putting Jesus in His Place: A Radical Vision of Household and Kingdom*. Louisville: Westminster John Knox, 2003.

Nam, Roger. *Portrayals of Economic Exchange in the Book of Kings*. BibInt 112. Leiden: Brill, 2012.

Nasrallah, Laura Salah. "'You Were Bought with a Price': Freedpersons and Things in 1 Corinthians." In *Corinth in Contrast: Studies in Inequality*, edited by Stephen J. Friesen et al., 54–73. NovTSup 155. Leiden: Brill, 2014.

Odell, Margaret S. *Ezekiel*. Smith & Helwys Bible Commentary. Macon, GA: Smith & Helwys, 2005.

Osiek, Carolyn, and David L. Balch. *Families in the New Testament World: Households and House Churches*. Family, Religion, and Culture. Louisville: Westminster John Knox, 1997.

Pastor, Jack. *Land and Economy in Ancient Palestine*. London: Routledge, 1997.

Pervo, Richard. *Acts: A Commentary*. Hermeneia. Minneapolis: Fortress, 2009.

Petterson, Christina. *Acts of Empire: The Acts of the Apostles and Imperial Ideology*. Critical Theology and Biblical Studies. Eugene, OR: Cascade Books, 2012.

———. "King Solomon and the Global Economy." Paper presented at SBL annual meeting, San Francisco, Nov. 19–22, 2011.

Renz, Thomas. *The Rhetorical Function of the Book of Ezekiel*. VTSup 76. Leiden: Brill, 1999.

Roth, Ulrike. "Paul and Slavery: Economic Perspectives." In *Paul and Economics: A Handbook*, edited by Thomas R. Blanton IV and Raymond Pickett, 155–82. Minneapolis: Fortress, 2017.

———. "Paul, Philemon, and Onesimus." *ZNW* 105 (2014) 102–30.

Schloen, J. David. *The House of the Father as Fact and Symbol: Patrimonialism in Ugarit and the Ancient Near East*. Studies in the Archaeology and History of the Levant 2. Winona Lake, IN: Eisenbrauns, 2001.

Schottroff, Luise. *The Parables of Jesus*. Translated by Linda Maloney. Minneapolis: Fortress, 2006.

Seibert, Eric A. *Subversive Scribes and the Solomonic Narrative: A Rereading of 1 Kings 1–11*. LHBOTS 436. London: T&T Clark, 2006.

Silver, Morris. *Prophets and Markets: The Political Economy of Ancient Israel*. Social Dimensions of Economics. Boston: Kluwer-Nijhoff, 1983.

Skinner, John. *A Critical and Exegetical Commentary on Genesis*. ICC. Edinburgh: T&T Clark, 1910.

Solin, Heikki. *Die stadtrömischen Sklavennamen. Ein Namenbuch. Barbarische Namen, Indices*. Forschungen zur antiken Sklaverei 2. Stuttgart: Steiner, 1996.

Ste. Croix, G. E. M. de. *Athenian Democratic Origins, and Other Essays*. Edited by David Harvey et al. Oxford: Oxford University Press, 2004.

Steinkeller, Piotr. "Land-Tenure Conditions in Third-Millennium Babylonia: The Problem of Regional Variation." In *Urbanization and Land Ownership in the Ancient Near East*, edited by Michael Hudson and Baruch A. Levine, 289–329. Peabody Museum Bulletin 7. Cambridge, MA: Peabody Museum of Archaeology and Ethnology, 1999.

———. "Towards a Definition of Private Economic Activity in Third Millennium Babylonia." In *Commerce and Monetary Systems in the Ancient World: Means of Transmission and Cultural Interaction*, edited by Robert Rollinger and Christoph Ulf, 91–111. Melammu Symposium 5. Wiesbaden: Steiner, 2004.

Stone, Timothy. "Joseph in the Likeness of Adam: Narrative Echoes of the Fall." In *Genesis and Christian Theology*, edited by Nathan MacDonald et al., 63–73. Grand Rapids: Eerdmans, 2012.

Sweeney, Marvin A. *I and II Kings: A Commentary*. OTL. Louisville: Westminster John Knox, 2007.

Theissen, Gerd. *The Social Setting of Pauline Christianity: Essays on Corinth*. Edited and translated by John Howard Schütz. Edinburgh: T&T Clark, 1982.

Thompson, Thomas L. *The Historicity of the Patriarchal Narratives: The Quest for the Historical Abraham*. BZAW 133. Repr., Harrisburg, PA: Trinity International, 2002.

Turner, Geoffrey. "The Christian Life as Slavery: Paul's Subversive Metaphor." *HeyJ* 54 (2013) 1–12.

Van der Spek, Robartus J. "Land Ownership in Babylonian Cuneiform Documents." In *Legal Documents of the Hellenistic World*, edited by Markham J. Geller and Hedwig Maehler, 173–245. London: Warburg Institute Press, 1995.

Wallerstein, Immanuel. *Capitalist Agriculture and the Origins of the European World-Economy in the Sixteenth Century, with a New Prologue*. Vol. 1 of *The Modern World-System*. Studies in Social Discontinuity. Berkeley: University of California Press, 2015. First published 1974.

Walsh, Jerome T. *1 Kings*. Berit Olam. Collegeville, MN: Liturgical, 1996.

Westermann, William. *The Slave Systems of Greek and Roman Antiquity*. Memoirs of the American Philosophical Society 40. Philadelphia: American Philosophical Society, 1955.

Witherington, Ben, III. *The Acts of the Apostles: A Socio-Rhetorical Commentary*. Grand Rapids: Eerdmans, 1998.

Wright, Christopher J. H. *God's People in God's Land: Family, Land, and Property in the Old Testament*. Grand Rapids: Eerdmans, 1990.

3. The Political Economic Project of Jesus vs. the Roman Imperial Order

RICHARD A. HORSLEY

Introduction

We have long understood the Lord's Prayer as a plea for the kingdom of God, the subject of its opening petition. The next two petitions of the prayer then immediately indicate what the kingdom is about more concretely: sufficient food, and cancellation of debts. Although it is usually unrecognized, the focus of the prayer for the kingdom of God is on economic subsistence. The people who pronounced this prayer, moreover, were affirming that, in connection with pleading that their own debts be cancelled, they were cancelling one another's debts. They were collectively *taking action* to deal with their debt, thus strengthening their communities, through mutual aid, against the political-economic pressures that had brought them into hunger and debt. Whatever the communities were doing, however, was evoking repressive action by the rulers. So they also petitioned God to deliver them from "the testing/trial" of being dragged into court (cf. Mark 8:34–38, 13:9; Luke 11:2–4, 12:2–12).

The Gospel stories portray the interactive mission of Jesus as engaged in collective *political-economic action*. Jesus was not teaching about attitudes toward wealth and poverty or attitudes towards other individuals. He was rather delivering commands about concrete social-economic relations and interaction. The command to "love your enemies" was more fully and concretely "love your enemies, do good, and lend"! He was addressing not individuals but whole communities, on the one hand, and pronouncing God's judgment against the people's rulers, on the other.

Standard interpretation of Jesus and the Gospels has blocked discernment of the political-economic conflict portrayed in the Gospel stories. It has also blocked recognition of how Jesus was generating a movement in the course of his mission in Galilee and beyond. The separation of religion from concrete political-economic life in modern Christianity and modern Western culture generally has been projected onto the Gospel texts. This has, for example, reduced Jesus' obstruction of operations in the temple to a mere religious "cleansing" and has domesticated Jesus' declaration "render to Caesar... and to God" into an illustration of the modern separation of church and state. Closely related is the projection of modern Western individualism onto the Gospels and Jesus and the focus on his individual sayings. Jesus is reduced to an individual "talking head" uttering pithy aphorisms to individuals, while unengaged in the fundamental social-economic forms of village life and the deepening political-economic conflict in Roman Palestine.

Two constructions of Jesus that became particularly prominent over a century ago and emerged again to prominence at the end of the twentieth century both exemplify the reduction of Jesus to an individual figure. One of these constructions presented Jesus as a wisdom teacher of an individualistic discipleship of piety and ethics in withdrawal from the world of political-economic affairs.[1] The other construction presented Jesus as an apocalyptic prophet of the end of the world in cosmic catastrophe.[2] Both of these lines of individualistic interpretation of Jesus are based primarily on individual sayings of Jesus (purposely) isolated from their literary context, thus ignoring our primary guide to the historical political-economic context (the Gospel stories and speeches). Even at the end of the twentieth century, moreover, we can discern underneath both of these diametrically opposed constructions a focus on Jesus as the unique individual revealer whose teaching led to the origin of the new religion of Christianity from the old religion of Judaism. According to this Christian theological scheme, Jesus attracted only individual disciples. Only after Easter did "the church" begin and expand rapidly, especially among "the gentiles," in the mission of Paul.

1. Harnack, *What Is Christianity* (1901); Crossan, *Historical Jesus* (1991). This book by the leading voice of the Jesus Seminar, which became highly influential partly because aggressively marketed by the publisher, recently merged into the Murdoch publishing empire, which continued to market competing theological constructions of Jesus.

2. Schweitzer, *Quest of Historical Jesus* (1906). Schweitzer's construction of Jewish apocalypticism, restated by Bultmann in his *Theology of the New Testament* (1951), had become standard as a controlling concept in New Testament studies. Schweitzer's apocalyptic Jesus was revived by Allison, *Jesus of Nazareth* (1996); and Ehrman, *Jesus: Apocalyptic Prophet* (1999).

The Gospel Stories of Jesus' Mission and Movement(s)

The Gospels, however, tell a different story. Since the 1980s, their interpreters have been discovering that the Gospels are not mere collections of sayings and "miracle stories" but are sustained narratives, with speeches, that are full of social and political conflict—a development largely ignored by interpreters of Jesus. While much literary criticism of the Gospels simply applied recent criticism of modern fiction, some interpreters attempted to understand the Gospels as sustained stories in their historical context.[3]

The Gospels, which purport to be historical stories of concrete events, portray a movement developing in response to Jesus' proclamation and healing as Jesus interacts primarily with villagers but also with the scribal-Pharisaic representatives of the Jerusalem temple-state and then with the high priestly rulers appointed by the Romans. It is remarkable, moreover, the extent to which the Gospel stories and speeches "fit" the historical context of Roman Palestine in which they are set: the fundamental political-economic conflict between the people of Israelite heritage and their Roman-appointed rulers had become increasingly unstable so as to evoke the rise of movements of renewal and resistance led by popular prophets. The Gospel stories fit into the historical context known from other sources, such as the accounts of the Judean historian Josephus: Roman imperial conquest and reconquests, installation of client rulers, intensified extraction of the people's resources, and increasing popular resistance. The Gospels are stories of a prophet-led renewal of the people combined with prophetic pronouncements of God's condemnation of the rulers for their extraction of resources that the people needed for their own livelihood.[4]

A brief summary of the Markan story and of the additions that the Matthean and Lukan Gospels made to the basic story can provide a sketch of the broader political-economic-religious conflict involved: Jesus was generating a renewal of the people in their village communities in opposition to and by the rulers and ruling institutions.

In the Markan story, after being divinely commissioned and tested in the wilderness (like Elijah), Jesus begins his mission in the villages of Galilee, proclaiming the direct rule of God and manifesting its presence in many exorcisms and healings. Narratives of sea crossings and feedings in the wilderness frame some of the exorcisms and healings, suggesting that Jesus is a prophet like Moses and Elijah, who later appear with him in a vision on a mountain. The

---

3. See, e.g., the investigations by Myers, *Binding the Strong Man*; Horsley, *Hearing the Whole Story*; Horsley, *Jesus and the Politics*; Horsley and Thatcher, *John, Jesus, and Renewal*.

4. See esp. Horsley, *Jesus and the Powers*; Horsley, *Jesus and the Politics*.

people respond with trust (*pistis*), reinforced by the rapid spread of his fame, generating crowds in and from many villages, a growing movement that he extends into the villages of nearby areas subject to other Roman-client rulers in cities such as Tyre and Caesarea Philippi. Giving the movement more explicit social-political form, he appoints the Twelve as representatives of the people of Israel undergoing renewal in his proclamation and healing, and commissions them to extend these works of renewal in village communities (the principal social-economic form in most agrarian societies). Woven into the sequence of episodes, the scribes and Pharisees come down from Jerusalem to confront his apparent challenges to the prerogatives of the temple-state. Jesus responds with prophetic condemnation of them, for example, for violating the basic commandment of God by manipulating the people to devote (*qorban*) to the temple resources needed by their families. As he completes his mission of healing and teaching in Galilee and beyond, he delivers a (Mosaic) covenant renewal in a series of dialogues focused on family, community membership, economic relations in the community, and leadership of the movement.

Jesus then goes up to Jerusalem and the temple where he engages in a sustained confrontation with the high priests: a prophetic demonstration in the temple, a prophetic parable that announces God's condemnation of the high priests (for economic exploitation), and an announcement that the temple (the central political-economic-religious institution) will be destroyed. Finally, the high priests have him arrested and hand him over to the Roman governor, who orders him crucified as "the king of the Judeans," that is, a (presumed) leader of insurrection. In the abrupt "open ending" of the Markan story (Mark 16:1–8), the women at the empty tomb are told to tell the disciples to meet him back in Galilee—where, presumably, they will continue the movement that he had generated. The Markan story thus presents the (hi)story of Jesus' renewal of the people (of Israel) in opposition to and by the high priestly rulers, who were the face of the Roman imperial order in Palestine.

The Matthean and Lukan Gospels tell the same basic story of Jesus' mission in the villages of Galilee and beyond and his confrontation with and then execution by the rulers, with two major additions. First, these Gospels begin with legends of Jesus' birth under Caesar's decree subjecting the people to pay tribute (Luke 2) or the Roman-client King Herod's massacre of children to prevent the deliverance from imperial domination that Jesus is born to lead— that leads to his family's recapitulation of the story of Israel's exodus from repressive rulers (Matt 2)—and genealogies that present Jesus' mission as the fulfilment of the history of Israel. Second, the Matthean and Lukan Gospel stories include speeches by Jesus on key issues of the movement of renewal he is generating. These include a long covenant renewal speech (commonly called the Sermon on the Mount/Plain); a commission of his disciples to extend his mission of healing and proclaiming the direct rule of God in village communities; and a series of woes indicting the scribes and Pharisees for exploiting the people.

The narratives and speeches in the Gospels thus portray Jesus' mission and movement as a renewal of the people of Israel in their village communities, in opposition to and by the rulers at the head of the Roman imperial (dis)order in Palestine. The Gospels are not just stories, but purport to be (political-economic-religious) histories (however embellished) of Jesus' mission and movement based in village communities, his prophetic pronouncement of God's judgment against the rulers, and his martyrdom that energized the further expansion of the movement. The Gospel (hi)stories also reflect the expansion of the movement that Jesus and his disciples generated in the village communities in Galilee to other areas in Syria-Palestine. The movements continued to evoke persecution by the rulers, but without the serious disruption that would have led the rulers to suppress them militarily. The Gospel stories and speeches continued to tell of the origins of the Jesus movements and of the ongoing collective identity and common life of the communities of those movements.

Exploring Economics in "Biblical" Texts and Their Contexts

Since the term *economics* is used in many different ways, it is important to clarify in what sense it may be used intelligibly in connection with the texts that were later included in the Hebrew Bible and New Testament and the historical situations they addressed. Biblical scholars have tended to project the "market economy" that developed in early modern Europe onto the texts they were interpreting.[5] As interest in economic issues has increased in biblical studies—surely partly as a result of disillusionment with neoliberalism and the 2008 crash of global finance capital—scholars in the related fields of ancient southwest Asian studies and of the Roman Empire, as well as biblical scholars, are casting about in search of economic theories appropriate to their subject matter.[6] The field of biblical studies now has the widely knowledgeable and deeply

---

5. The New Testament scholars who gave explicit attention to economics tended to be influenced by the works of Rostovtseff, *Social and Economic History*. On the development of the ideology of capitalism and "the market," see now the highly instructive critical survey by Boer and Petterson, *Idols of Nations*.

6. For example, the articles in Morris and Manning, *Ancient Economy*. Neoclassical economics, however, is alive and well in studies of "the Roman market economy," e.g., in Temin, *Roman Market Economy*; Mayer, *Ancient Middle Classes*.

critical theoretical work of Roland Boer, *The Sacred Economy*, that offers a solid and appropriate theoretical basis for study of the wider ancient southwest Asian context of the Judean temple-state and its villages.[7] This investigation of the historical political-economic context of Jesus' mission and movement(s) as portrayed in the Gospels and its historical background is broadly informed by Boer's work. The focus here, however, is on what is attested and portrayed in Judean and Gospel texts and pertinent archaeological studies.

What we find in texts that were later included in the Hebrew Bible and in the Gospels—and which were yet later included in the New Testament—is primarily people who were living in villages and producing crops to feed themselves as well as the kings, officers, and priests who extracted a percentage of those crops as taxes and tithes. The economy portrayed in these texts was basically agricultural. The basis of the economy were the many self-sufficient and semi-independent village communities comprised of multiple households linked by kinship who struggled to obtain a subsistence living from often unforgiving conditions. Those who wielded authority and/or power induced or coerced the productive villagers to yield a portion of their produce to support a more comfortable life for the ruling elite and their retainers and servants in cities. "Economics" was thus not something in itself, independent of other aspects of life, but was embedded in social-political-religious life. It thus is more intelligible and appropriate to think in terms of the political-economic-religious structure and its dynamics rather than of economics or "the economy" as if it were a separate sphere of life. It is necessary, moreover, to consider the cultural tradition in which people were embedded that guided their social-economic interaction and collective sense of identity and what was expected and acceptable.[8]

---

7. Boer, *Sacred Economy*. In the text and notes Boer includes telling criticism of other theories and how they fit in the history of "economics" and economic theory. See also Boer, "Production and Allocation." I find Boer's analysis and theory of the political economy of ancient southwest Asia more appropriate to and helpful in understanding Jesus and the Gospels in the context of Roman Palestine than the subsequent (Boer and Pettersen) *Time of Troubles* that informs my analysis of the Pauline letters in the context of the Roman Empire in this volume. *Time of Troubles* is most important for delivering a broad analysis of political-economic structures in the Roman imperial world and the historical movement toward the emergence of the colonate (tenant farmers or sharecroppers) that dominated in late antiquity as Christianity became the established religion.

8. In the last few decades some biblical scholars have been borrowing (the mainly structural-functional) Western social science of the mid-twentieth century. Such social science tended to understand social-political structures as stable and to downplay political-economic conflict and historical change. Its focus on social status and stratification tends to hide fundamental conflict between the dominant and the subordinated. See the criticism

Serious investigation of the economic aspect of such texts in their historical contexts will thus require a serious change in focus to a "wide-angle" lens capable of considering texts and contexts more comprehensively. Moreover, our focus can no longer be confined to theological ideas or "values" or "proof texts" abstracted from the texts, but must be widened to include *the historical political-economic conflict that is being addressed in the text, the historical political-economic action that is being taken,* and *the political-economic practices being pursued.*

Moving beyond Synthetic Constructs That Block Understanding of Texts and Contexts

Recent critical examination of the origins of the texts and contexts that are taken as "biblical" suggests that some of the key assumptions and concepts of biblical studies in general and of New Testament studies in particular block the way to understanding those texts and contexts. The texts now collected in the Hebrew Bible were evidently produced in scribal circles that served the Judean monarchy and temple-state centuries before they were recognized as books of the Bible.[9] It is thus anachronistic to imagine that the political-economic-religious contexts they presuppose and address were "the biblical world."[10] In the ancient world where communication was largely oral and literacy was confined to elite (scribal) circles,[11] even scribes learned and cultivated texts by oral recitation so that they became "inscribed on the tablet of their heart."[12] Written copies of such elite texts were rare, cumbersome, and confined to scribal circles. So it is unlikely that villagers had direct contact with written texts that still existed in different versions in scribal circles. The Gospels were evidently produced in and for communities of ordinary people long before they were canonized in the New Testament by councils of bishops convened by the Roman

---

of structural-functional sociology, which was abandoned by most sociologists after 1970 (Horsley, *Sociology and Jesus Movement*). The texts that became "biblical," however, feature mostly conflicts between the producers and their rulers that sometimes resulted in changes in historical configurations. The legendary narratives of the origins of the people of Israel, for example, tell of the escape (exodus) of the "mixed multitude" of Hebrews subject to forced labor under Pharaoh in Egypt. The ensuing narratives that frame covenantal legal collections tell of the people's attempt to organize a society independent of human rulers who extracted produce. The Gospel stories of Jesus' mission and movement are rooted in this Israelite tradition.

9. Horsley, *Scribes, Visionaries, and Politics*, ch. 6.
10. Ulrich, *Dead Sea Scrolls*, 89–90.
11. Harris, *Ancient Literacy*; Hezser, *Jewish Literacy*.
12. Carr, *Writing on the Tablet*; Horsley, *Scribes, Visionaries, and Politics*.

imperial court.[13]

It became standard long ago to refer to Judean texts, society, and history of the "Second Temple" period (from the Persian Empire to the Roman destruction in 70 CE) as expressions of and evidence for "early Judaism" and to refer to the texts of the New Testament as expressions of and evidence for "early Christianity." Indeed, the subfield of New Testament studies both assumes and explores how the new religion of "early Christianity" originated in and then separated from the older religion of "early Judaism." But these are abstract synthetic constructs that lump together and thus obscure the distinctive texts, figures, movements, institutions, and recurrent conflicts that were the political-economic-religious realities of life in early Roman Palestine and beyond. These historical realities have now been researched and delineated far more precisely and comprehensively than in previous generations when the synthetic constructs were standard.[14] It is now possible to refer fairly precisely to the people of particular areas at particular times, including their movements and revolts; to scribal groups, their political-economic-religious position and support or protest of the high priests; and to the Roman-client rulers in particular areas and times, all in the context of changing historical circumstances and conflicts in Palestine under Roman rule.

It may also be important to avoid another synthetic modern scholarly construct that continues to skew interpretation of New Testament texts. In the late nineteenth and early twentieth centuries Western biblical scholars constructed "Jewish apocalypticism" on the basis of text fragments, figures, and terms extracted from a wide variety of late Second Temple Judean texts (usually labeled "apocalyptic"). It became standard in the field to believe that Jews at the time were caught up in the belief in the imminent end of the world that would unfold according to an "apocalyptic scenario" of key events such

---

13. For a summary of the implications of several separate but interrelated lines of recent research on oral communication and its interface with writing in the ancient world, see Horsley, *Scribes, Visionaries, and Politics*; Horsley, "Oral Communication, Oral Performance"; Horsley, "Can Study Escape."

14. See, for example, Goodman, *Ruling Class of Judea*; Schwartz, *Imperialism and Jewish Society*. Having become concerned over fifty years ago about the discrepancy between the historical diversity and multiple conflicts and complexity, indeed chaos, evident in our textual sources, on the one hand, and the synthetic scholarly constructs with which we attempt to impose order on them, on the other, I devoted decades of research and critical analysis to constructing the complex historical realities of Roman Palestine as comprehensively and precisely as possible. See my "alternative" constructions in the articles behind Horsley and Hanson, *Bandits, Prophets, and Messiahs*; Horsley, *Jesus and the Spiral*, chs. 1–5; *Galilee*; *Revolt of the Scribes*; and *Jesus and the Politics*. The discussions in this article presuppose and depend upon these works and others.

"the last judgment," "the great tribulation," "the resurrection," and, for the early Christians, "the parousia." More careful, critical readings especially of early Judean "apocalyptic" texts (the historical visions in Dan 7, 8, 10–12; and the animal vision in 1 En. 85–90) as they address the looming crisis of the Judean temple-state under Hellenistic imperial rule, conclude that they do not attest such an "apocalyptic" scenario. In these texts, rather, different circles of scribes involved in the temple-state are struggling to understand how the imperial military invasion and economic exploitation of Judea could have happened with "the Most High" still ultimately in control of history.[15] The interpretation of "Judaism" in Hellenistic and Roman Palestine as "apocalyptic" distorts Judean texts and historical movements by imposing a modern synthetic scholarly construct and leads to diversionary debates about whether Jesus was or was not caught up in "Jewish apocalypticism."[16]

Dispensing with the (distorting) synthetic constructs of (early) Judaism and (early) Christianity and Jewish apocalypticism will also enable us to discern how much the Gospels present Jesus' mission and movements as the continuation and fulfilment of the history and cultural tradition of the people of Israel. We thus cannot understand the Gospels without taking into account how they build on, adapt, and continue Israelite popular tradition that we know mainly indirectly from (elite) Judean texts.

Finally, it is essential to avoid the dominant individualism of modern Western culture and of Christian theology that is projected onto Jesus and the Gospels. In the dominant post-Enlightenment cultural atmosphere in which

---

15. For attempts at "deconstruction," see Horsley, *Scribes, Visionaries, and Politics*, esp. chs. 8–9; Horsley, *Revolt of the Scribes*.

16. See the application of the "deconstruction" of "apocalypticism" in Judean texts to studies of Jesus and the Gospels in Horsley, *Prophet Jesus*, chs. 1–4. The shift of terminology from "apocalyptic" to "'millenarian" or the equation of the two terms may be only a further obfuscation of historical movements rooted in Israelite tradition in early Roman Palestine. Toward the beginning of the surge of anthropologists' and historians' fascination with what they labeled "millenarian" movements, John Gager presented an interpretation of the Jesus movement and early Christianity generally on the model of anthropological studies of "millenarian" movements, mainly Melanesian "cargo cults," that burgeoned in the 1960s and 1970s, in *Kingdom and Community*. Like "charisma/charismatic," however, this was yet another imposition of a synthetic, composite social-scientific construct onto diverse historical social movements. In particular, it obscured how different the popular Israelite movements led by Jesus and others that were rooted in the deep Israelite tradition of resistance to domestic and imperial rulers were from "cargo cults" and "nativist" movements that were reacting to the initial wave of European colonial invasion. Also, the nineteenth-century CE peasant movements in Italy and Spain that Hobsbawm studied in *Primitive Rebels* (chs. 4–6) do not appear to have been historically analogous to the cargo cults and other movements being studied by the social scientists at that time.

reality is defined by Reason, defensive Christian interpreters narrowed their scope and "data" to the individual sayings of Jesus. The result has been several versions of a religious "talking head" unengaged in political-economic interaction. The Gospel sources, however, present Jesus embedded in and always engaged in the historical social forms of Galilean and Judean society as a movement gathers around him in oppositional interaction with the rulers (and their representatives) of Roman Palestine. Insofar as the Gospel stories are narrating the interactive mission of Jesus inseparable from the origins of the communities in which they were composed, it is probably impossible to separate the one from the other and from the historical circumstances and forces in which they operated. But this is the case with any historically significant figure.[17] The clear implications are that we consider Jesus-in-interaction together with the movement(s) that resulted from his mission as the stories are told in the Gospel sources.

Historical Development of the Complex Context of Jesus' Mission and Movement(s)

The historical context of Jesus' mission and movement(s) was complex, unstable, and rife with political-economic-religious conflict. This complexity has gone largely ignored, as just noted, because the synthetic modern construct of early Judaism hides the considerable diversity of regional history, the structural political-economic conflict, and the popular and scribal movements of resistance that led the Romans and their client rulers to take repressive action. The most effective way of presenting this diversity, instability, and conflict may be to trace briefly the historical development of the particular political-economic-religious structure and dynamics that are presupposed and attested in the Gospels and contemporary sources. In this way, step by step, it is possible to sketch the complex historical context of Jesus' mission and the resulting movement(s) that were obscured or simply hidden from view by the controlling synthetic scholarly constructs of standard New Testament studies. This survey of the historical development of the complex context of Jesus mission may also serve to at least begin to address the gap, and often disconnect, between study

17. In *Jesus and Empire*, 56–58, I outlined a relational-contextual approach to Jesus-in-interaction, in analogy with the historical figures of Abraham Lincoln and Martin Luther King, that considers five interrelated aspects. We can attempt to understand how, (1) in the particular historical conditions that had created a crisis for the ancient Judean and Galilean people (2) and working out of the Israelite cultural tradition in which those people were rooted, (3) Jesus emerged as a leader (4) by adapting particular social role(s), (5) in interaction with people who responded by forming a movement that became historically significant.

of books of the Hebrew Bible and books of the New Testament.

Over the course of the twentieth century "Old Testament studies" and "New Testament studies" developed into separate subfields of Christian theology. It was simply assumed that there was a centuries-long historical gap between the books of the Hebrew Bible and those of the New Testament. The mainly Judean "noncanonical" scribal texts produced in Second Temple times were classified as Apocrypha or Pseudepigrapha. These were assumed to be expressions of an essentialist synthetic "Judaism." In the five centuries between the rebuilding of the temple and the Roman conquest, however, the Judean temple-state had gone from a tiny territory in the hilly environs of Jerusalem to control of most of Palestine, from Idumea in the south to Samaria and Galilee in the north. The early history of the "Second Temple" period is often obscure because of the limited sources. It is clear, however, that the period involved a diverse regional history and intensifying political-economic-religious conflict, particularly under the Roman military conquests and economic exploitation, along with continuing resistance by popular leaders and movements.

The Base and Structure of the Agrarian Political Economy in Ancient Palestine

The basis of the agrarian political economy in ancient Judea, Samaria, and Galilee, as in virtually any agrarian society, was hundreds of village communities, each comprised of many households.[18] Villagers labored on the land to produce crops and livestock that provided a subsistence living for themselves. Over many generations, villagers had learned how to organize their labor for the optimal use of their land to eke out a subsistence living in ways that required close cooperation, reciprocal aid, and the spreading of risks. Textual and archaeological evidence indicates that village communities periodically (re-)allocated contiguous strips of land shares to the constituent households on the common fields around their nucleated dwellings. Village households also

---

18. A principal reason this has not been discerned is that biblical scholarship, like historical scholarship generally, has not recognized that extant written sources were produced by and represented the interests of the literate elite, who comprised a tiny minority at the top of any agrarian society. Peasants, like women generally, have been hidden from history. Only recently are biblical scholars learning to extrapolate information indirectly from written sources. On the social-economic life and political-economic activities of villagers behind "biblical" texts, see, e.g., Chaney, *Peasants, Prophets*; Knight, *Law, Power, and Justice*, 70–74, 115–56; Boer, *Sacred Economy*, chs. 2–3; Horsley and Hanson, *Bandits, Prophets, and Messiahs*; Horsley, *Galilee*, esp. chs. 6–12; Horsley, "Introduction"; Horsley "Jesus Movements"; Herzog, "Why Peasants Responded to Jesus"; and Wire, "Women's History."

shared a common pasture area beyond the cultivated field(s).[19] Both men and women worked the fields, and combined their long hours of labor at the urgent time of harvest and perhaps in plowing and sowing as well. While some households fared better than others, village communities had customary ways of trying to keep their component household economically viable, e.g., with gleaning rights and interest-free survival loans. Households were patriarchal, under the authority of the senior male.[20] But village communities were acephalos, without hierarchical social organization, with self-governance and cohesion from village assemblies, and with local problems, accidents, and social conflicts handled by the village elders. With their communality of assent, economizing, and enforcement, the village communities, while operating at a subsistence level, had a considerable degree of resilience in adapting to changing conditions and in persisting through difficult circumstances.

Local and imperial rulers living in cities, however, extracted a portion of the villagers' crops to support their own lavish lifestyle, the artisans who served their desires, their scribal and other servants, and, at the imperial level, military forces. They used their power to levy tribute and taxes and their authority to demand tithes and offerings. After yielding up tribute, taxes, and tithes to their imperial and local rulers, some households were unable to feed themselves and forced to take survival loans from neighbors. If their neighbors became unable to provide survival loans, they could be manipulated into debt by their wealthy and powerful creditors who could come to control their labor and even their fields ("woe . . . because they add field to field" [Isa 5:8]; cf. Neh 5:1–13). Interpreters focused on text fragments or on archaeological reports that do not take historical information and broader social patterns into account often miss the basic conflict in this political-economic structure that made it fundamentally unstable. Villagers resisted their rulers' extractions in various ways, and the rulers found further devices by which they could extract produce and labor.

The Emerging Temple-State in Jerusalem as the Local Representative of Imperial Rule

Following the Babylonian destruction of Jerusalem and devastation of the surrounding countryside, *Yehud* consisted of a tiny territory in the hills of

---

19. The concepts of "property" and "ownership" would thus appear not to be applicable to allotted field shares of common village land, but the shares were heritable in multigenerational households.

20. Shafer-Elliot fleshes out the complexities of women's management roles in the household ("Women and Economics").

southern Palestine with a population of perhaps twenty-five thousand people settled mainly in a number of villages. At some point the Persian regime allowed or sponsored a colony of the descendants of the previously deported Jerusalem elite, who claimed to be the true *Yehudim*, to return to the land and rebuild a temple, with the support of Persian governors in command of military forces. In the course of a struggle for power with some of the "big men" in the area, such as the sheikh Tobias in the Transjordan and Geshem the Arab, a priestly aristocracy managed to gain the authority over the tiny territory to gather both tribute to the empire and tithes and offerings to support the temple and priesthood, at least according to accounts in Nehemiah (5:4; 9:35–37; 10:32–39; 12:44; 13:10–13). Under this evolving arrangement at least some of the "Judeans" were ostensibly serving "the god who was in Jerusalem" (Ezra 1:2–4), as directed by their own Judean priestly aristocracy. Sources such as the book of Haggai indicate that the people resisted the demands for revenues and labor to support the building and operations of the temple. Haggai's prophetic harangues sound like what could only be called religious-economic extortion: if you don't render up revenues to support the temple, God will cause your crops to fail (Hag 1:7–11). A succession of imperial regimes, Hellenistic and then Roman, kept the temple-state in place. By early Roman times it had greatly expanded the territory and population over which it had jurisdiction and influence.

Judean (Written) Scribal Texts and the Continuing Cultivation of Israelite Popular Tradition

The structural conflict, hence instability, of Judean society is evident in the texts produced by scribal circles of the temple-state. The (early versions of) books later collected in the Hebrew Bible, however, included legends and stories of how earlier generations of Israelites repeatedly asserted their independence of rulers who were coercing their crops, labor, or both.[21] The paradigmatic legend of the origins of Israel—as a people independent of rulers—was the exodus, led by the paradigmatic prophet Moses. Texts of torah (or teaching) also included the formation of Israel as a distinctive people in the covenant with YHWH through the legendary prophet Moses as a binding mutual commitment that required their exclusive loyalty to their transcendent divine king and their maintenance of justice in social-economic interaction.[22] No mere rules of

21. The relation of popular Israelite tradition and their use and adaptation in scribal texts is discussed in Horsley, "Contesting Authority."

22. Discussed in Horsley, *Covenant Economics*, 17–32.

morality, these were principles of social-economic interaction that protected the people's (economic!) rights to a livelihood. The commandment of exclusive loyalty and that against "bowing down and serving" other gods—and their ruler-regents—in effect prohibited human rulers and their demands for tithes and taxes: implications evident in Jdgs 8, 1 Sam 12. Other commandments prohibited people from striving to take control of or stealing others' resources.[23] Included in the written texts that later became books of the Hebrew Bible are collections of (scribal) adaptations of some of the customs and practices linked with the covenantal principles. These laws and customs extended the supposed protections of people's economic livelihood in the commands or exhortations of lending liberally without interest (e.g., Exod 22:24; Lev 25:36; Deut 15:7–11, 23:19 [the latter prohibition is applicable only to fellow Israelites]), sabbatical cancellation of debts and release of debt slaves (Deut 15:1–2, 12–15), and collective aid for the destitute such as gleaning and leaving the land fallow in the seventh years so that the poor could gather what grew on the land (Lev 25:2–7, Deut 24:21). In the texts later included in the Bible, these law collections were reformulated and reframed to support the centralization of political-economic-religious power in the monarchy and temple-state.[24]

Since literacy was limited to the circles of scribes who served the temple-state, it is unlikely that the villagers had direct contact with the scribal texts that included and adapted these traditions. But the Israelite popular tradition that had been adapted into the scribal texts would have continued to be cultivated orally in village communities that were semi-self-governing, with their elders and village assemblies. Local social-economic interaction continued to be guided by the popular customs and practices and covenantal commandments "underneath" the scribal adaptation of the legal collections that we are familiar with in the Hebrew Bible.[25] Age-old stories of resistance and liberation would have been told regularly, as when the Passover festival was celebrated. As evident in other texts later included in the Bible, memories of earlier resistance and its prophetic leaders inspired subsequent resistance such as that led

---

23. Chaney, *Peasants, Prophets*, ch. 3.

24. Careful critical analysis and exposition of scribal shaping of collections of law in the interest of states in Knight, *Law, Power, and Justice*, esp. chs. 6–7; cf. Knight, "Economics in Israelite Law."

25. See the extensive analysis and discussion in Knight, *Law, Power, and Justice*, chs 2–5. "The population living in the rural villages had a flourishing tradition of customary laws ... [that] lived on in oral form " (96). "The people's customs constituted a body of practices and values into which [each successive] younger generation was socialized ... [Collections of written 'literary laws' were] more the product and possession of the priests and leaders than a shared heritage of the people at large" (52–53).

by the prophets Elijah and Elisha. The covenantal commandments were the criteria on the basis of which later prophets such as Isaiah and Jeremiah pronounced judgment against kings, their officers, and high priests for exploiting the people.[26]

This Israelite popular tradition was distinctive but not unique. It was similar to the popular or "little" tradition that anthropologists and others have discerned and studied in other societies.[27] At the heart of such popular traditions anthropological and historical studies have found core principles and customs of social-economic interaction that, in effect, protecting the people's rights to a livelihood, aimed to maintain the economic viability of each household in village communities. This has been called "the moral economy" of peasant village communities.[28] The popular customs and practices that lie behind or "underneath" the Mosaic covenant, its commandments, and other covenantal laws now included in the books of the Hebrew Bible are indications of the distinctive but similar "moral economy" that continued to function in Judean and other Israelite villages. With sources being scarce we lose track of the Israelite popular tradition in the early Second Temple period, but it clearly became a motivating factor of resistance later in the period.

The book of Nehemiah narrates a political-economic crisis that indicates the continuing function of the ideals of this "covenantal economy" amid the instability of the temple-state as representative of the imperial order in Jerusalem that required intervention by Persian governors such as Nehemiah (with military forces). Under heavy demands for "the king's tax" (tribute paid to the Persian Empire) the people were manipulated into spiraling debt and forced to yield control of their fields and houses and to surrender their children as debt slaves to the Judean nobles and officials. The people appealed to the governor for relief (Neh 5:1–13). Presumably to preserve the empire's economic base in the territory of Judea, Nehemiah forced the nobles and officials to restore the people's houses and fields, along with the produce they had extorted. In doing this he was (at least ostensibly) enforcing the covenantal laws and customs

26. This is the implication of the collection of articles by Chaney, *Peasants, Prophets*; some examples in Horsley, *Covenant Economics*, ch. 5.

27. The best cross-cultural analysis is Scott, "Protest and Profanation." The parallels and differences between the Judean "great tradition" embodied primarily in texts later included in the Hebrew Bible and the Israelite popular tradition that informed popular movements of renewal and resistance, including Jesus, informs Horsley and Hanson, *Bandits, Prophets, and Messiahs*, and the articles behind the book; Horsley, *Jesus and the Spiral*, chs. 3–4. More recent general discussion in Horsley, "Contesting Authority."

28. Scott, *Moral Economy of Peasant*. Applied to Israelite popular tradition, particularly Mosaic covenantal teaching, Horsley, *Covenant Economics*, 35–43.

according to which the religious political economy in Judea was supposed to operate. But he did not relax the demands of the imperial system that still required dues to the temple and the tribute to the emperor that had forced the people into debt in the first place. Even though texts are limited for this period, they indicate that the people faced such crises of debt and survival recurrently. This is indicted in the proverb repeated by the Jerusalem Ben Sira: "The poor are the feeding grounds for the rich" (Sir 13:19).

That the fuller form of the Mosaic covenant along with its commandments continued to be cultivated as the guide and norm for social-economic relations among the people as well as their understanding that the impositions by human rulers were against the will of God is vividly indicated by key texts found at Qumran, especially the Community Rule (1QS). The rule includes instructions for the ceremony of covenant renewal for a new-exodus community in its withdrawal from the rule of the Jerusalem temple-state in which the traditional *sanctions of the blessings and curses* have been transformed into (part of) the new *declaration of deliverance* that provided a basis for the covenantal *commandments* and more specific regulations of community life.[29] That the Mosaic covenant in its fuller form continued to be cultivated in scribal circles where it could provide the political-economic charter for a "breakaway" scribal-priestly group suggests strongly that the covenant form and its commandments continued to function prominently in village communities as well—and could later come to public prominence in John's "baptism of repentance for the remission of sins," which was also symbolically located as a new exodus in the wilderness.

Hellenistic Imperial Invasion and the Hasmonean Takeover of Galilee

The temple-state was kept in place by successive empires as the local representative of imperial rule, with considerable expansion and intensification, along with continuing resistance. While sources for what was happening among the vast majority of people are limited, they are sufficient for the three hundred years under Hellenistic and early Roman imperial rule—from early second century BCE to early second century CE—to warrant two important interrelated generalizations. First, under Hellenistic imperial rule, there was increasing interference and military invasion by the imperial regimes. This continued, indeed escalated, under Roman rule, with military conquest and repeated

---

29. Fuller discussion in Horsley, *Covenant Economics*, 100–103, drawing on Balzer, *Covenant Formulary*; extensive analysis and discussion of what could be called covenantal economic practices evident in the Dead Sea Scrolls in Murphy, *Wealth*.

reconquest. Second, the Israelite peoples, however, having inherited a passion for independence, mounted resistance with increasingly frequent widespread revolts.

Under the Hellenistic regimes the high priestly aristocracy gradually consolidated its command of the temple-state as the local representative of imperial rule and accumulated considerable wealth in the temple. Leading figures at the head of the dominant faction in the aristocracy, Jason and then Menelaus, usurped control by paying ever higher, exorbitant amounts from the temple treasury for the high priesthood to the Seleucid regime that was desperate for resources (2 Macc 4–5). Evidently seeking fuller participation in the imperial political culture, they then transformed Jerusalem into a *polis*: the distinctively Hellenistic form of political economy in which powerful elites dominated indigenous villagers. When the Seleucid emperor Antiochus IV (Antiochus Epiphanes) sent troops to enforce the "reform" against resistance by some scribal groups, widespread popular revolt erupted, which fought the Seleucid army to a standoff with sustained guerrilla warfare (2 Macc 7–15).[30]

The Hasmonean brothers who led the popular ("Maccabean") revolt, who were not of a high priestly family, then arranged with a weakened Seleucid regime to be appointed high priests in a reinstated temple-state. This was evidently the point at which a group of priests and scribes withdrew in protest to the wilderness at Qumran in a new exodus and established a renewed Mosaic covenantal community, deeply informed by the fundamental parts of Judean scribal tradition derived from earlier Israelite popular tradition. The Hasmoneans, after consolidating their power and wealth, hired Greek mercenaries and conquered first the Samaritans to the north, destroying their temple, and then took control of Galilee as well (Josephus, *Ant.* 13.318–319). The Hasmonean high priesthood in Jerusalem thus expanded its rule from a limited area around the city to nearly all of Palestine, including all of the principal areas of Israelite cultural heritage (Samaria and Galilee as well as Judea). For the first time in many centuries the area of Galilee came under Jerusalem rule, although it lasted for only the hundred years prior to the lifetime of Jesus.[31]

According to Josephus, the Hasmoneans forced the inhabitants there to

30. For my own analysis and presentation see further Horsley, *Scribes, Visionaries, and Politics*, ch. 2. There are many and varied constructions of this history, some of which avoid the political-economic aspect, while others downplay the scribal resistance.

31. An attempt to critically reconstruct this history on the limited evidence available in Horsley, *Galilee*, 39–52. Freyne (*Galilee*) and some of the studies based on surface survey archaeology in the 1980s and 1990s were still working with the synthetic construct of "the Jews" and "Judaism" without analysis of the sources for the Hasmonean takeover of Galilee and who the "inhabitants" were.

obey "the laws of the Judeans" (it may be presumed that this meant submitting to taxation by the temple-state). The Hasmoneans, followed by Herod after them, established fortresses in Galilee garrisoned by Judean officers and soldiers (*J.W.* 1.303; for example, at Sepphoris, and probably Gabara [*Life* 246]) to enforce their rule and, presumably, gather revenues).[32] Some of these Judean officers would have been "the power holders in the region" against whom the Galileans revolted sixty years later (*Ant.* 14.450). But there is no good evidence that large numbers of Judeans suddenly flooded into Galilee to become settlers, as is simply assumed by many scholars. Several generations after the Hasmonean takeover of Galilee, Josephus still refers to the Israelite people according to geographical area: the people in or from Judea proper as "the Judeans," the people in Samaria as "the Samaritans," and the villagers in Galilee as "the Galileans."[33] The Galileans, like the Judeans and Samaritans, were people of Israelite heritage. While the Galileans were not (yet) necessarily hostile to Jerusalem rulers, as were the Samaritans, whose temple the Jerusalem rulers had destroyed, it seems likely that they would have been ambivalent at best about the temple and high priesthood as the dominant political-economic-religious institutions.

Roman Imperial Rule in Palestine: Intensification of Exploitation

Roman conquest and imperial rule further complicated the overall political-economic structure and dynamics and intensified the economic circumstances and burdens of the people.

Roman warlords, having already launched their conquest of the eastern Mediterranean, now also conquered Palestine, which had become highly unstable under rival Hasmonean factions. Pompey plundered the considerable wealth that had accumulated in the temple, and confirmed the Hasmonean high priest Hyrcanus as Rome's client ruler in Palestine. The Romans required the subjugated people to render tribute, a principal purpose of imperial conquest, to be collected by the Hasmonean high priesthood. The people, already paying tithes and other dues to the temple and high priesthood, were (again) required to yield up another percentage of their produce to their imperial rulers

32. Fuller discussion, with references, of the Hasmonean and Herodian "administration" of Galilee in Horsley, *Galilee*, 137–44.

33. Occasionally in his accounts of the great revolt in 66–70 Josephus uses "Judeans" with reference to the rebels more generally. Of course, insofar as the Hasmoneans and Herod controlled Galilee by means of several garrisoned fortresses, there were Judeans in Galilee. At one point in the resistance to Herod's conquest of his subjects, Josephus mentions that the Galileans drowned the (Judean) *dynatoi* in the Sea of Galilee (*J.W.* 1.326).

(25 percent every second year, or perhaps every year [Josephus, *Ant.* 14.202–203]).³⁴ Recurrent war between rival Hasmonean factions and the extension of the empire-wide Roman "civil war" into Palestine brought considerable destruction in the countryside, including crops, and further extraction of villagers' economic resources, including a special levy of tribute imposed by the Roman warlord Cassius.³⁵

Wanting to exert far more decisive control over Palestine, the Roman Senate appointed the military strongman Herod as "king of the Judeans" in 40 BCE.³⁶ It took him three years to subdue his subjects, the widespread popular resistance being particularly strong in Galilee. Herod made heavy economic demands on his subjects to fund his extensive building projects and lavish expenditure. In addition to erecting temples in honor of Caesar, he built two new cities named for the emperor, Caesarea as his seaport on the coast and Sebaste (Augustus) in Samaria. In addition, he mounted a massive reconstruction of the temple in grand Hellenistic imperial style, which became known as one of the great wonders of the Roman imperial world. Herod also appointed a succession of his own creatures as high priests, thus expanding the priestly aristocracy that continued as one of the layers of rulers supported by the producers. The funding of all of these grandiose building projects came on top of the expenses of his lavish court, massive military fortresses, and unmatched benefactions to other cities of the empire and gifts to Augustus and others in the imperial family. He did recognize that his exhausted economic base could not survive a famine exacerbated by a drought, and imported grain from Egypt to tide them over to the next harvest and round of extractions (Josephus, *Ant.* 15.299–312).

After Herod's death in 4 BCE, widespread revolt erupted in the major districts of Israelite heritage, Judea, Galilee, and the Jordan Valley and beyond (Perea). In their reconquest (Josephus, *J.W.* 2.66–275; *Ant.* 17.286–295), the Romans exercised the extreme brutality with which they terrorized subjected peoples into submission.³⁷ In systematically suppressing resistance, accord-

---

34. See further Udoh, *To Caesar*, 41–57.

35. Josephus devotes most of *Antiquities*, bk. 14, to these events.

36. Herod had impressed the Roman warlords as the ruthless young military commander of Galilee who had exacerbated the already acute economic distress of the Galileans in the wake of the Roman conquest. He brutally suppressed the bands of brigands continuing the resistance to Roman rule and then ruthlessly collected the special levy of tribute decreed by Cassius (Josephus, *J.W.* 1.204–259; 4.159–160, 271–274).

37. Only recently have Roman historians become more candid about the devastating effects of Roman legions' terrorization of peoples they subjected by slaughter and enslavement of people, devastation of villages, and crucifixion of those viewed as leaders of resistance. See,

ing to Josephus, the Roman legions destroyed the fortress town of Sepphoris in Galilee and enslaved the people, then plundered and destroyed villages, including Emmaus, in a widespread scene of fire and blood through the hill country of Judea. There the warlord Varus sent his soldiers out to round up fugitives and crucified about two thousand of them as supposed leaders of the insurrection. There may thus be at least representative significance in the destruction of villages and the enslavement and crucifixion of Galilean and Judean villagers right at the beginning of the lifetime of Jesus and his followers in the areas of Nazareth and Emmaus, where the Jesus movement apparently spread (Luke 24). The brutal destruction and slaughter of such reconquests left economic devastation of households and villages and collective trauma for survivors in these areas.

After reconquering the Galileans and Judeans, the Romans set different client rulers over separate districts of Palestine. They placed Galilee and Perea under the rule of Herod's son Antipas (reign 4 BCE to 37 CE?), who had been educated at the imperial court in Rome (4 BCE). Within twenty years Antipas built Sepphoris as one capital city and then also built Tiberias along the Sea of Galilee as a second capital city. With less than a quarter of the revenues commanded by his father, he undertook these two massive projects, which would have meant a further intensification of extraction from Galilean villagers. Tax collection would have been far more "efficient" with the ruler of Galilee now located directly in the area, nearly all of the villages of lower Galilee now within (over)sight of one or another of the capital cities.

In Judea, as of 6 CE, the Romans placed the priestly aristocracy in charge of maintaining order and collecting the tribute, and also the tithes and temple dues, only now under appointment and oversight by a Roman governor. During the next several decades the priestly aristocracy became ever more oppressive of their people.[38] They used the surplus wealth building up in the temple to make loans to needy peasants; manipulated them into spiraling debt; and forced them into tenancy, for example, on estates in northwest Judea,[39] meanwhile building ever more lavish mansions for themselves in Jerusalem.[40] Eventually high priestly families even became predatory on their own people, sending strong-armed gangs out to seize grain from the village threshing floors, leaving the ordinary priests as well as the people to starve (Josephus, *Ant.* 20.180–181, 206–207). Later rabbinic texts contain memories of the widespread resentment

---

e.g., Mattern, *Rome and the Enemy*.

38. See the surveys by Goodman, *Ruling Class*; and Horsley, "High Priests and Politics."
39. See esp. Broshi, "Role of the Temple"; and Goodman, "First Jewish Revolt."
40. See Avigad, *Discovering Jerusalem*, 77, 83.

of the high priestly families' rule, in which the economic dimension is clear. For example, in b. Pesahim it is written,

> Woe unto me because of the house of Baithos;
> woe unto me for their lances!
> Woe unto me because of the house of Hanin [Ananus] ...
> Woe unto me because of the house of Ishmael ben Phiabi,
> woe unto me because of their fists.
> For they are high priests and their sons are treasurers
> and their sons-in-law are temple overseers,
> and their servants smite the people with sticks![41]

Economic Pressures on Villagers and Popular Movements of Resistance and Renewal

The eruption of pent-up resentment after Herod's death, however, began a period of several generations in which popular resistance drove the history of Palestine, leading to the collapse of the temple-state, the great revolt throughout most of Palestine, and the brutal Roman destruction of people and their villages in much of the countryside. Set up by the historical development of the previous centuries just outlined, this period of increasingly frequent popular renewal and resistance movements was the immediate context of the emergence of Jesus' mission and movements in Galilee and beyond.

In the face of economic pressures from imperial regimes and their client local rulers, village communities of Israelite and other heritage had been remarkably resilient as well as resistant. At least some of the customs that helped the component families of village communities remain economically viable persisted under early Roman domination. Given the periodic droughts and resultant famine, destruction of villages and killing or enslavement of people by conquering armies, and seizure of family members as debt slaves, the people maintained at least the ideal of community responsibility for the widow, the orphan, and the refugee "resident alien." Rulers periodically cultivated popular support by promising aid for these marginal folks. The practice of allowing the land to lie fallow every seventh year—enabling the destitute to harvest whatever grew in the uncultivated fields—was evidently widely observed, judging from Josephus's accounts of how it figured in famines and in payment of the tribute to Rome (Exod 23:10–11; Josephus, *Ant.* 3.280–284; 12.375–378; 14.202–210; 14.475; 15.5–7). Similarly, the cancellation of debts every seventh year must still have been a widespread practice, at least among villagers and

---

41. b. Pesahim 57a.

perhaps by better-off creditors as well (see just below on the *prosbul* promulgated by Hillel).

The effects of military conquest and the political-economic pressures of multiple layers of rulers, however, were disintegrating families and village communities and their traditional mechanisms of mutual support. Limited by the standard academic separation of economy from politics, historical studies have largely ignored the economic effects of the Roman conquest and reconquest. But the cumulative effect of two or three generations of Roman, Hasmonean, and Herodian devastation and slaughter on household and village life must be taken into account in assessing the largely subsistence economic circumstances of the Galilean and Judean people in the lifetime of Jesus and his movement(s).

Less sudden and more sustained, demands for tribute, taxes, and tithes and offerings from the different layers of rulers left many villagers without enough of their crops to feed their families.[42] Under Herod's regime one of the principal mechanisms of temporary relief was undermined. The scholar-teacher Hillel promulgated the *prosbul* as a device—supposedly to ease credit—to allow creditors to avoid the sabbatical cancellation of debts by placing the records of debts in the hands of a court (m. Sheb. 10:3–7; cf. Deut 15:1–6).[43] This would have led to peasants falling ever more deeply into debt. The cumulative pressures were such that village practices of mutual aid and cooperation could not cope with them. Desperate peasants had borrowed from their neighbors, but those neighbors would have come under ever more stress themselves. Although the particular circumstances would have varied from area to area and village to village, what were already subsistence conditions for many would have deteriorated, with hunger, debts, loss of control over land, and decline into tenancy or increasing dependence on day labor, with the corresponding disintegration of family and village community.

The economic deterioration of the villagers in Galilee and Judea, along with the passion for independence of rulers' extractions deeply rooted in Israelite tradition, would have been a major factor in the widespread popular revolts and resistance movements that were the driving force in the history of early Roman Palestine. Cross-cultural studies of peasants in other times and areas of the world have shown that it is when peasants sense that their subsistence livelihood is threatened, rather than when they have sunk completely into

---

42. Solid analysis with mainly textual evidence in Hanson and Oakman, *Palestine*, 101–25.

43. Good discussion in Goodman, *Ruling Class of Judea*, 57–58. Critical analysis of the rabbinic account in Neusner, *From Politics to Piety*, 14–17.

tenancy and dependency, that they form movements of resistance and mount wider revolts. Just such conditions were developing under the impact of Roman conquest and Herodian and high priestly rule. The lifetime of Jesus and the early development of movements of Jesus loyalists were framed historically by two widespread popular revolts: in 4 BCE, after Herod's death, the eruption of revolt in Galilee, Judea, and the Transjordan from the pent-up resistance; then the great revolt of 66–70 CE, following the steady deterioration of the political-economic order. In between were significant protests and a highly significant series of popular movements of renewal and resistance in the middle of the first century CE.

According to the accounts in Josephus (J.W. 2.56–65; Ant. 17.271–284), the popular revolts in 4 BCE took a distinctively Israelite political-economic form (which is highly relevant to the mission of Jesus, judging from a few Gospel passages).[44] In their revolt villagers in each area acclaimed their leader as a popular "king," a move informed by (evidently) still-cultivated stories of how earlier Israelites had "messiahed" the young David to be their leader in resistance to the Philistines (2 Sam 2:1–4; 5:1–4). The Judean historian Josephus, who despised peasants, especially when they engaged in resistance, focused on their attacks against royal fortresses, palaces, and troops and their raids against Roman supply trains. His accounts, however, also indicate the political-economic agenda of these popular "messianic" movements. In Galilee, he wrote, the movement led by Judas, son of the brigand chieftain Hezekiah, killed by Herod a generation earlier, attacked the royal fortress at Sepphoris (near Nazareth), and took the arms and the goods stored there. These movements were in effect local declarations of independence, an age-old peasant ideal narrated in many stories in Israelite popular tradition, some of which were adapted in the books of Judges, 1–2 Samuel, and 1 Kings. By holding the Herodian troops at bay (before the massive Roman reconquest), these movements and their kings were able to maintain their independent village life free of rulers' extractions for many months and even, in the movement led by the shepherd Athronges in Judea, for three years. Josephus provides a somewhat fuller account of the most significant of these "messianic" movements, led by the popularly acclaimed "king of the Judeans," Simon bar Giora, seventy years later during the great revolt of 66–70 CE. In establishing independent self-rule in much of Judea, he and his movement were evidently striving to reinstitute the

---

44. See further the critical analysis and discussion of Josephus's accounts in Horsley, "Popular Messianic Movements"; Horsley and Hanson, *Bandits, Prophets, and Messiahs*, ch. 3; and Horsley, *Hearing the Whole Story*, ch. 10.

just political-economic relations for which Israelite peasants yearned, including the release of debt slaves (Josephus, J.W. 4.507–510).

Some dissident scribes and Pharisees also mounted significant resistance. As noted above, dissident scribal circles mounted active resistance to the Hellenizing "reform" by the high priestly aristocracy. Continuing conflicts between the high priests and scribal groups who were supposedly servants of the temple-state further complicated the dominant conflict between rulers and ruled. As they faced the increasingly invasive Roman imperial rule, at least a minority of the scribal and Pharisaic guardians of the "great tradition" could no longer compromise the covenantal principles they viewed as the very basis of the people's (social-economic) life under the rule of God. In 6 CE a group that Josephus called "the fourth philosophy," who agreed basically with the views of the Pharisees, organized resistance to payment of the tribute to Caesar, insisting that the people already had God as their lord and master (Josephus, Ant. 18.23).[45] That this group led by a scribal teacher and a Pharisee were willing to organize resistance to the tribute in defiance of Roman rule is evidence that some scribal circles were deeply committed to, indeed ready to die for, the first two Mosaic covenantal commandments that formed the basis of their political-economic life, protecting the people's subsistent livelihood.

Popular resistance became ever more frequent from the end of Antipas's reign in Galilee and from the time of Pontius Pilate in Judea and Samaria, according to the accounts of Josephus, on which we are largely dependent. More or less contemporary with Jesus' mission and movement(s), a series of popular movements emerged in the countryside that took yet another distinctively Israelite social form.[46] In each of these movements people from many villages responded to a prophet who promised to lead a new act of divine deliverance patterned after one of the formative events of Israel. The best known of these was the renewal of the Mosaic covenant led by John the Baptist symbolized by the ritual of baptism, accompanied by sharp prophecy against the injustice of Herod Antipas (Mark 6:16–29; Josephus, Ant. 18.116–119). In addition to a generalization that there were several more of these popular movements (J.W.

---

45. See further Horsley and Hanson, *Bandits, Prophets, and Messiahs*, 190–99. While Israelite popular tradition developed and continued in opposition to rulers and their economic extractions, Israelite scribal tradition included principles and texts that objected to imperial rule, even though the scribes themselves were compromised by it.

46. See further the critical analysis and discussion of Josephus's accounts in Webb, *John the Baptizer*, esp. ch. 10; Horsley, "Popular Prophetic Movements"; Horsley and Hanson, *Bandits, Prophets, and Messiahs*, ch. 4; and of how these movements are pertinent to our understanding of Jesus and the Gospels in Horsley, *Hearing the Whole Story*, ch. 10.

2.259; *Ant.* 20.168), Josephus offers at least a brief account of particular cases (*Ant.* 18.85–87; 20.97–98, 169–171; *J.W.* 2.261–263). The prophet Theudas, in imitation of Moses and/or Joshua, led a large group of villagers out into the wilderness of the Jordan where the waters would be divided, giving them access to the land; again, a movement of renewal patterned after events of the origins of the Israel. Somewhat later in Judea a prophet, who had recently come from Egypt, led followers to the Mount of Olives where they would see the walls of Jerusalem collapse, giving them access to the city, a renewal of the people, and recovery of their land in the mold of the legend of Joshua and the fall of Jericho. Viewing these movements of renewal of Israel as popular uprisings, the Roman governors sent out the military to suppress them.

The mission and movement(s) of Jesus emerged just in this historical context and fit somewhat the same pattern, of a prophet (like Moses or Elijah) leading a renewal of Israel. The mission and movement(s) of Jesus, however, were not caught up in an expectation of a new act of divine deliverance, but focused on the more concrete political-economic-religious renewal of covenantal community in the villages of Galilee and beyond (as should become clear in the discussion below).

Until a generation ago interpreters of Jesus had difficulty imagining that villagers had more than two diametrically opposed options of open revolt or humble acquiescence in their rulers' oppression.[47] To appreciate that villagers were capable of organizing disciplined resistance in which they "held their ground" precisely in asserting—and risking—their economic subsistence it is important finally to attend to the Galilean "peasant strike" in resistance to payment of the Roman tribute (see esp. Josephus, *Ant.* 8.261–288; cf. *J.W.* 2.185–203; Philo, *Leg. ad Gaium* 222–224).[48] The emperor Gaius had ordered his image/statue to be erected in the temple in retaliation for the way Judeans had disrespected his divinity in Alexandria (again note that "politics" and "economics" and "religion" were not separable). As Petronius, legate of Syria, led the Roman troops through Galilee, peasants in many villages refused to plant their fields. They were evidently willing to suffer the consequences of using what little leverage they had: in this case, enduring famine to deny the Romans the tribute by not planting their crops. This was a bold collective action in obedience to the first and second commandments, indicating that the Mosaic

---

47. For further discussion of the various forms of peasant politics (resistance), see Horsley, *Jesus and the Politics*, 36–43.

48. See further the critical analysis and discussion of the sources and the protest in Horsley, *Jesus and the Spiral*, 110–16.

covenant was still operational among Galilean villagers. As Herodian officials pointed out to Petronius in their emergency consultation on how to respond: instead of a harvest from which the Romans could extract their tribute, the result would be "a harvest of banditry," that is, serious political-economic disruption for years to come. Petronius backed off—and was spared suicide by the (un)timely death of Gaius.

The Cumulative Effect: Escalating Political-Economic-Religious Conflict in Roman Palestine

From its foundation under the Persians, there was structural political-economic conflict between the people and the temple and high priesthood as the ruling institutions. The conflict was complicated under the Hellenistic Empires by serious scribal opposition to imperial invasion and further complicated by the Hasmonean high priesthood's conquest of Idumea and Samaria and its takeover of Galilee. The conflict was intensified by the Roman conquest, imposition of Herod's kingship, and more direct Roman rule through the high priesthood in the first century CE, on the one hand, and the many popular movements of renewal and resistance, on the other. In the decades during which the Jesus movement(s) expanded rapidly in Palestine and beyond, the political-economic order further disintegrated until widespread insurrection erupted in Galilee and Judea as well as in Jerusalem in the great revolt of 66–70 CE.[49]

This complex situation of political-economic-religious conflict, with escalating economic pressures on the villagers and their formation of movements of renewal and resistance rooted in Israelite popular tradition, is the context in which the Gospel sources can be read in order to discern the political-economic-religious program of renewal and resistance in Jesus' mission and movement(s).

---

49. It is often claimed that in the time of Jesus' mission and movement, Galilee was generally prosperous and peaceful. Such claims ignore the Galileans' intense opposition to the ruling cities of Sepphoris and Tiberias, as narrated at length by Josephus, that cannot have emerged only suddenly in 66–67 CE. Josephus proudly admits that he and Herodian officers took actions to secure the grain and other resources that had been taken from the villagers in taxes and tribute (*Life* 70–73, 119–120). He also recounts bold actions by Galileans, such as the raid on the royal palace in Tiberias (*Life* 65–66) and an ambush of a convoy under military escort transporting some of the huge quantities of wealth accrued by the ruler of eastern Galilee, Agrippa II, from taxation of his subjects (*J.W.* 2.595; *Life* 126–131). These accounts indicate the economic roots of the revolt in Galilee as well as in Judea. Some of the incidents, moreover, indicate that the Galileans were motivated by their adherence to covenantal principles of economic justice. Critical analysis of Josephus's accounts of the conflicts in Galilee during the great revolt in Horsley, "Power Vacuum."

The Political-Economic Project of Jesus' Mission and Movement(s)

Jesus' mission, his movement(s), and the Gospels that they produced did not stand apart from concrete political-economic life in Palestine, with distinctive religious values and perspectives. They were rather unavoidably embedded in the deepening political-economic-religious conflict between the rulers and the people. Jesus and his movement(s) condemned and actively opposed the ruling institutions and their exploitation of the people as they generated the social-economic renewal of the people in their village communities. As laid out in the Gospels, if we have eyes to see and ears to hear, *Jesus and his movement(s) were engaged in concrete renewal of covenantal community that fostered economic subsistence and justice for component families in opposition to the Roman imperial order in Palestine headed by the high priestly and Herodian rulers.*

Renewal of Covenantal Social-Economic Cooperation in Village Communities

As noted at the outset, recent interpretation of Jesus focused on separate sayings remains limited by its modern individualism and separation of religion from political economy. The Gospels as whole stories, however, present a dramatically different picture, portraying Jesus-in-interaction in fundamental social-economic forms. The Gospel stories, including the speeches of Jesus, present Jesus' mission as the renewal of the people of Israel in its constitutive village communities opposed to and by the Roman and Roman-client rulers.

Generating a Renewal Movement in Village Communities

The Gospels present Jesus' mission as focused on village communities, each comprised of many families. As noted above, these were the fundamental social forms in which people's lives were embedded in Galilee or Judea or any traditional agrarian society. In the early episodes of the Markan story (Mark 1:21, 2:1, 6:6), and their parallels in Matthew and Luke, Jesus seems to have a base in the village of Capernaum, from which he can access other villages in the area that are only a few kilometers apart. Similarly, when he moves into nearby "territories" subject to other Roman-client rulers, he works, for example, "in the villages of Caesarea Philippi." The Gospel stories, moreover, have Jesus going into the "synagogues" of Capernaum and other villages on the Sabbath. Contrary to the standard (but anachronistic) assumption, *synagogai* in the Gospel stories refers not to religious buildings but to village assemblies, the form of local self-governance and community cohesion that gathered at least once a week.[50] Jesus carried out his work in village communities, often when the people were gathered in their assemblies. His mission was directed to whole communities, not just individuals, and he was dealing not just with what we moderns call "religious" matters, but with the more general political-economic-religious concerns of village communities.

Jesus' work in these villages is primarily twofold: He proclaims and teaches about the direct rule (kingdom) of God; and he carries out exorcisms and healings that manifest the direct rule of God. The two are closely related in the Gospel narratives, are directly addressed to the tensions and sufferings of the village communities, and have an economic as well as religious dimension. The teachings will be treated extensively below. Because the exorcisms and healings have been distorted and misunderstood as miracles, however, it is important at least to recognize their social-economic aspect.[51]

The healings and exorcisms are not simply individual interactions between Jesus and someone with a sickness or possessed by a spirit. Sickness and spirit possession affect whole villages, especially component households/families. Paralysis, blindness, spirit possession all mean loss of labor essential to subsistence, which compounds the suffering. Family members or support groups bring sick people for healing. Exorcisms and healings evoke trust (*pistis*) among the people that enables further healing. Jesus sends the healed back into their communities. Some cases of sickness and healing, most clearly the twelve-year-old woman and the woman who has been hemorrhaging for twelve years, are clearly representative of the people of Israel as a whole. The mission of Jesus is bringing renewed life to a people that was nearly dead from hemorrhaging its economic lifeblood.

Jesus' appointment of the Twelve as representative of the people of Israel indicates that what is happening in the direct rule of God and its manifestation is the renewal of the people (as noted above). He commissions his disciples to expand his mission in village communities (Mark 6:7–13 par.; Luke 10:1–16). And his commissioning speeches give several indications that the proclamation and exorcism and healing were addressed to whole communities. The disciples are instructed to stay, in pairs, in one of the households of a village. Insofar as the dwellings in a village were packed closely together, the envoys unavoidably

50. Archaeological explorations have found buildings for the gathering of local assemblies that date mostly to late antiquity, suggesting that there were few or none yet in Galilean villages at the time of Jesus (Horsley, *Galilee*, ch. 10; Horsley, *Archaeology, History, and Society*, ch. 6).

51. See Horsley, *Jesus and Magic*, chs. 9–10; Horsley, *Empowering the People*.

interacted with the other villagers. Their reception or rejection by the village ("place" or "town") is to determine how the envoys respond: i.e., with the peace and healing of the kingdom of God for any and all in the village or by calling down judgment on the whole village. If they are well received, moreover, they are to continue working in that village for a period of time: what today might be called community organizing. Not only are villages the focus of the mission of Jesus and his disciples, but Jesus' project in his proclamation, his healings, and his commissioning the disciples is evidently the political-economic-religious renewal of the people of Israel in their village communities.

That households/families have an integral role in Jesus' mission focused on village communities suggests, contrary to assertions of some recent liberal interpreters, that Jesus and the Gospels were not anti-family.[52] In many episodes of the Gospel stories, households/families are presupposed and renewed. Sick and spirit-possessed people are restored to their families (as noted above). In what seems to be a response to the disintegration of households and villages that was happening as a result of increased economic pressure, Jesus declares that those who do the will of God are his mother and sisters and brothers (Mark 3:31–35; cf. Mark 10:2–45), that is, a renewed village community that can also serve as supportive household/family (which had, in effect, been an aspect of covenantal mechanisms of mutual aid).

Jesus' preaching and healing in many village communities and commissioning disciples to extend his mission in villages is thus Jesus generating a movement. As he proclaims the direct rule of God and manifests it in healings and exorcisms, the word spreads and crowds of people come from other villages in trust (*pistis*) that he can and will heal. He goes on to preach and heal in those other villages to which he sends his disciples, in effect, as a cadre of catalysts who expand and deepen the movement comprised of those village communities. In contrast to the other popular prophets of the renewal of Israel, who

52. In the last several decades, theological liberals (especially the leaders of the Jesus Seminar) have pressed an individualistic interpretation of Jesus and his followers that blocks recognition of the political-economic project of his mission. They took over a construction of Jesus and his followers based on a literalistic reading of isolated individual sayings of Jesus (Theissen, *Sociology*; cf. the criticism in Horsley, *Sociology and Jesus Movement*). In Theissen's construction, Jesus was calling individuals to abandon their families and possessions to pursue an itinerant life that included begging for food. Given the historical circumstances, Jesus would thus have been making life much worse for those abandoned families left without a major contributor of the labor necessary to feed the family; pay tribute, taxes, and tithes; and hold off the creditors, dooming them to debt slavery or worse. The sayings that Theissen and others cite as proof texts (e.g., "whoever does not hate father and mother... cannot be my disciple"), however, are hyperbolic statements of the extreme demands of loyalty to Jesus and his mission.

called people out of their villages to experience a new act of deliverance, Jesus was generating a renewal of the people in their village communities.

Renewal of Covenantal Community

The Parallel Programmatic Covenant Renewal Speeches in Matthew and Luke

According to the Gospels' portrayals, at the center of Jesus' renewal of the people/Israel was his renewal of the Mosaic covenant that for centuries had guided social-economic interaction in the villages.[53] In both Matthew and Luke Jesus begins his mission among the people with a long speech that appears to be programmatic. Particularly striking is Jesus' declaration in the covenant renewal speech in Matthew—"Do not think that I have come to abolish the law or the prophets; I have come not to abolish but to fulfill"—followed by the admonition to keep the covenantal commandments in order to maintain justice (the translation "righteousness" is too weak and individualistic [Matt 5:17–20]). Jesus then exemplifies specifically what he means in what have been called, misleadingly, "antitheses" (Matt 5:21–48). In a patterned series he first cites one of the commandments (of Moses), then intensifies it by moving into the motivation behind keeping the commandment.

Luke has a parallel but shorter speech (still the longest speech in the Gospel) at the beginning of Jesus' mission (6:20–49). Comparison shows that these are speeches of Mosaic covenant renewal.[54] The speeches in Matthew and Luke both contain many references and allusions to covenantal commandments and exhortations that we know from Exodus, Leviticus, and Deuteronomy. They both proceed according to the traditional components of the Mosaic covenantal structure: a declaration of (God's) deliverance; covenantal demands of

---

53. Scholars of Jesus and the Gospels have tended to miss or ignore the prominence, indeed centrality, of Mosaic covenant renewal in the Gospels and Jesus' teaching for several interrelated reasons. Protestant theology identified the message of the Old Testament generally as law and that of the New Testament as gospel. Then New Testament studies developed as a separate subfield from Old Testament/Hebrew Bible studies in which the Mosaic covenant and covenantal laws are central, particularly in the books of Torah. The Christian theological agenda was to discern how different the teaching of Jesus was from Judaism, which was (supposedly) focused on the law, with which the Mosaic covenant was closely interrelated, often virtually synonymous. Jesus interpreters, moreover, as mentioned before, tended to focus narrowly on individual sayings taken out of their contexts in the Gospels, so that they missed the broader cultural patterns evident in Gospel narratives and especially in Jesus' speeches and dialogues. See Horsley, *Jesus and the Spiral*, chs. 8–9; Horsley with Draper, *Whoever Hears You*, ch. 8; Horsley, *Covenant Economics*, ch. 7.

54. Horsley, *Jesus and Empire*, ch. 5; Horsley, *Covenant Economics*, esp. chs. 7 and 10.

exclusive loyalty to God as ruler and of justice in social-economic interaction (in village communities); and sanctions on keeping those demands (e.g., blessings and curses). As in the covenant ceremony prescribed in the Community Rule of the Qumran community that had withdrawn to the Dead Sea wilderness, the sanctioning blessings and curses have been transformed into a new opening declaration of deliverance: "Blessed are you poor, for yours is the kingdom of God/heaven." The original sanction of blessings and curses has been replaced by the double parable of the houses on the rock and the sand (if you keep or do not keep Jesus'"words," that is, his covenantal commands).

In both Matthew and Luke, moreover, the narrative sets up the speeches as renewals of the Mosaic covenant, which in turn set up the rest of the Gospel story and shorter speeches. In Matthew, after Jesus proclaims the kingdom and heals all kinds of sicknesses in village assemblies, leading crowds to come to him from all areas of Israelite heritage (Galilee, etc.), he went up on *the mountain*, as Moses had, and taught his disciples. In Luke, Jesus is up on *the mountain* where he appoints the Twelve as representatives of Israel (undergoing renewal), then goes down where he teaches a great multitude of his disciples.

In the covenantal renewal speeches parallel in Matthew and Luke, Jesus addresses directly the disintegration of village communities under the pressures of Roman imperial rule. The people were evidently blaming themselves for their poverty and illnesses. While the blessings and curses were supposed to function as sanctions to motivate the people to obey the commandments, they had become an explanation of people's fortune or misfortune. If people were suffering sickness, poverty, and hunger, it must be because they or their parents had sinned, that is, broken the covenantal laws and were therefore receiving the curses, as illustrated in the episode of Jesus' healing of the paralytic (Mark 2:1–12). Jesus' response dealt not just with the paralysis but with the people's assumption about its cause. In declaring that the paralyzed man's sins are forgiven, he addressed the debilitating collective self-blame, releasing healing powers that enabled the man to "take up his bed and walk."

Similarly, in the blessings (and curses) with which the covenant speech in Matthew and Luke begins, Jesus first addresses the people's broken spirit, their assumption that their poverty and distress are the result of their having disobeyed the covenantal laws. In the renewal of the covenant, he transforms the blessings and curses into a new declaration of deliverance that addresses precisely the way the people have become dysfunctional. In addressing the people's self-blame and despair, Jesus pronounces God's blessing for the poor and hungry (the blessings are *not* spiritualized in Matthew, contrary to a common interpretation). In the Lukan version, he correspondingly pronounces woes on the wealthy, reminding the villagers that the wealth of the rich derived from their extraction from the crops of the villagers, leaving them poor and hungry.

After declaring the new deliverance in process in the direct rule of God, Jesus presents covenantal demands specifically aimed at overcoming the internal economic and social conflicts that were weakening village communities, threatening their economic viability (Luke/Q 6:27–42). As summarized above, the Roman conquests and demands for tribute, tithes, and taxes by multiple layers of rulers under Roman rule had intensified the economic pressure on the Galilean and other peasants during the several preceding decades. The "moral economy" of the Galilean and other villagers operated according to Mosaic covenantal commandments, customs, and principles aimed at keeping the component households of the village economically viable. Villagers would have been attempting to share their ever-shrinking resources, borrowing from and lending to one another according to the covenantal laws and customs of generous lending at no interest and periodically cancelling debts (Exod 22:25–27; Lev 25:35–37; Deut 15:1–2, 7–8, 12–15). The economic pressures, however, were so heavy that the ability of the people to maintain their commitment to mutual aid had begun to break down.

In restating the demands of the Mosaic covenant, Jesus is focusing on just this disintegration of the village community. He focuses first on economic relations and then on related social interaction in the village. Taken out of the contexts of the covenantal structure and the fundamental social form of the village, "love your enemies" and the associated sayings that Matthew uses in the fifth and sixth "antitheses" of the Sermon on the Mount (Matt 5:38–48) have traditionally been read as commands of non-retaliation against hostile enemies, especially the Roman soldiers. From the context indicated in the content of the sayings, however, it is clear that Jesus is addressing economic and social conflicts in local village life.[55] Lender families, themselves under pressure of the heavy tax burdens, would have been seeking repayment of the loans, but the debtor families would have been unable to pay, leading to local conflicts. Jesus addresses these conflicts with the general principle "love your enemies, do good, and lend" and applies the principle in some typical cases of borrowing and lending that focus the covenant renewal on concrete local conflicts. Since the Matthean version divides the sayings in order to conclude the "antitheses"

55. Thus, in these commands Jesus is not addressing relations with Roman soldiers, who would not have been present in Galilean villages as occupying troops during the rule of Herod Antipas. Those of us looking for a paradigm of nonviolent direct action might well focus on Jesus' confrontation with the rulers and ruling institutions.

with a general principle ("Love your [local] enemies"), we will focus on the Lukan version, which focuses more on concrete economic interaction throughout 6:27–36.

Many villagers would have been indebted to their neighbors, perhaps partly because they had previously aided them with survival loans and become economically vulnerable themselves. The command "If someone sues you for your cloak, let him take your shirt as well" (Luke/Q 6:29) addresses the desperately needy. The implication, of course, was that the debtor would be standing stark naked, embarrassing the neighbor in front of the whole village (Jesus had a sense of humor!—and a sense of how a neighbor could be motivated by threat of local public embarrassment). The reference to the age-old covenant command is unmistakable: "You shall not deal with others as a creditor. If you take your neighbor's cloak in pawn, you shall restore it before the sun goes down, since it is your neighbor's only covering at night" (Exod 22:25–27; Deut 24:10–13).

In these economic commands that adapt the original covenantal commandments, Jesus addresses mainly people in their perpetual role of aiding needy neighbors, insisting that they continue their sharing and generosity (Luke 6:30–36). "To the one who asks from you, give, and from the one who borrows, do not ask back ... But love your enemies, and do good and lend." Having declared the direct rule of God for the people, with its sufficiency for the hungry, Jesus delivers demands for local economic cooperation and sharing that apply traditional covenantal commandments and customs (e.g., Deut 15:7–11) to the economic difficulties of village communities. In the command to "be merciful as your Father is merciful," Jesus calls community members to pattern their generosity on God's generosity. This command also resonates with age-old covenantal tradition, particularly with the similar principle cited in the Levitical scribal collection of customs and laws (Lev 19:2). The principles implicit in these focal cases and the accompanying general exhortation also bear a remarkable resemblance to the third petition in the Lord's Prayer: "Cancel our debts, as we herewith cancel the debts of our debtors."

These commands and rhetorical questions of Jesus that begin with "love your enemies" thus stand directly in the Mosaic covenantal tradition, build on it, and renew the people's commitment to the covenantal demands. The focal instances of lending and borrowing here would have recalled the whole range of such traditional covenantal teachings to the minds of the listeners. To counter the local conflict over borrowing and lending, Jesus thus commands villagers to recommit to the time-honored principles and practices of mutual sharing and cooperation central to covenantal teaching. In an "updating" of the Mosaic covenant, he intensifies the covenantal demands of mutual aid, cooperation, and support, even in the circumstances of intensified economic pressures that probably left most in the village with insufficient resources.

Jesus then speaks to the social disputes that were evidently rooted in the economic conflicts among neighbors in the communities (Luke/Q 6:37–42). "Do not judge and you will not be judged." These instructions are also rooted in the Mosaic covenantal tradition, as can be seen through the window provided by Lev 19:17–18. The appended "parable" and rhetorical questions insist that the people stop accusing one another and return to mutual support in the community.

In accordance with the traditional pattern of the Mosaic covenant, the motivating sanction forms the concluding step (Luke 6:43–49//Matt 7:21–27). Since the blessings and curses had become problematic, inducing people to blame themselves, Jesus tells a double parable of houses built on rock and sand (Luke 6:46–49). The admonitions that precede the double parable (6:43–45) function somewhat similarly to the Matthean intensification or sharpening of the covenantal commandments (Matt 5:20–48), to probe the motivational bases of covenantal behavior. In this regard, Jesus' renewal of the Mosaic covenant stands in a long prophetic tradition that goes back at least as far as Jeremiah's prophecy of the new covenant written on the heart rather than on stone tablets (Jer 31:27–34).

In his covenant renewal speech, Jesus thus addresses economic and social conflicts among households/families under the economic pressures of Roman imperial rule that were disintegrating the fabric of reciprocal economic support that had traditionally held village communities together. The covenant renewal speech, however, was more than mere teaching of economic ethics or values. It was a reenactment of the covenant, in "performative speech," which enacts what it states. In the role of a prophet like Moses, Jesus in community enacted renewed commitment to the practice of mutual support among the component families of the villages. This renewed mutual support, moreover, would have strengthened the solidarity of the community to better withstand and resist the economic pressures from the rulers.

Covenant Renewal in the Markan Gospel Story

Renewal of the Mosaic covenant is also central in the Markan story, although the structural components are not so explicit as in the covenant speeches in

Matthew and Luke.[56] As Jesus is completing his mission of healing and proclamation in the villages of Galilee and beyond, he engages in a series of dialogues, each of which climaxes in a lawlike principle (Mark 10:2–45, followed to an extent by the Matthean and Lukan stories). In the course of the dialogues Jesus cites nearly all of the covenantal commandments, insisting that they must be faithfully observed. The dialogues, moreover, focus on social-economic forms and relations that the Mosaic covenant and covenantal laws and customs were meant to guide and protect: marriage as the basis of households/families that constituted the community, membership in the community, nonexploitative economic relations that the commandments protected, and leadership of the movement (of communities) that was to serve and not dominate. Just as the covenant renewal speeches in Matt 5–7 and Luke 6:20–49 are addressed to the villagers' concrete circumstances of poverty and disintegration of community, so also the covenantal dialogues in Mark are addressed to concrete economic difficulties facing the people.

The Pharisees' question in the first dialogue signals the move into covenantal issues. Two of the six covenantal commandments pertaining to social-economic relations focused on marriage and the family (no adultery and honor father and mother). The command prohibiting divorce and remarriage that concludes this dialogue is one of many indications in the Gospels that Jesus, far from being anti-family, was renewing the household/family, the fundamental (social-economic!) unit of production, consumption, and reproduction in any agrarian society. Presupposed here and evident in later rabbinic discussions, marriage and divorce concerned not merely marital relations, but economic rights, especially for the wife-mother, and the use and the inheritance of the land that was the basis of household/family livelihood. Lax laws on divorce, like the Deuteronomic provision referred to here (Deut 24:1–4, Mark 10:3–4), could enable ambitious men to consolidate their control of land through divorce and remarriage to the detriment of others.[57] Jesus here again (as in Matt 5:20–48) intensified the covenantal commandment on adultery: divorce for the purpose of remarriage is tantamount to adultery. This command reinforces

56. More fully discussed, in connection with the covenant renewal that runs through the Markan story, in Horsley, *Hearing the Whole Story*, ch. 8; and again in Horsley, *Covenant Economics*, ch. 8.

57. Might Jesus and/or those in his movement(s) have been thinking of Herod Antipas, whom John the Baptist had condemned for divorce and remarriage to Herodias, the wife of his brother (Mark 6:17)? See the role of John as prophet summarized by Josephus (*Ant.* 18.106–118), which helps fill in a bit of background to the legend of his imprisonment and beheading in Mark 6. Excellent critical discussion in Webb, *John the Baptizer*, 366–70. Whatever Antipas's motives and expectations, the scheme backfired.

the patriarchal family, including the subordination of the wife. In the historical situation in which families were struggling under economic pressures from their rulers, however, the principal concern of this command would probably have been to reaffirm the economic rights of women in marriage and household in the patriarchal society.

This dialogue about divorce and remarriage should probably be read in connection with Jesus' earlier reaffirmation of covenantal community at the conclusion of the first narrative step in the Markan story. The appearance of Jesus' mother and brothers outside the house (in Mark 3:31–35) sets up his rhetorical question, "Who are my mother and brothers and sisters?" His answer that they are "those who do the will of God"—that is, those who keep the (Mosaic) covenant—suggests that the mission of Jesus aims to renew local covenantal community in ways that would function as a replacement or aid for families that were disintegrating. Is the absence of the patriarchal head of household significant in this conceptualization of renewed familial-covenantal community?

The foil for the next dialogue, stemming from Jesus' blessing of the little children (Mark 10:13–16) is the disciples' discussion about who is the greatest and their rejection of children immediately following Jesus' second announcement that he must be martyred. A reminder that "childhood" is an invention of modern Western society may help in guarding against the frequent sentimentalizing of the principle that one must receive the kingdom of God "like a little child." In a traditional agrarian society, children were the lowest-status members of families and village communities, not necessarily recognized yet as persons. Children hence would have been the opposite of the wealthy and powerful of whom the disciples appear to be thinking in trying to imagine living in the kingdom of God (as in the request of James and John [Mark 10:35–37]). The principle that concludes this dialogue thus has a similar effect to the declaration in the covenant renewal speech in Luke, that the kingdom of God is offered to the poor, as opposed to the wealthy.

It is significant that in the Markan dialogues of renewal of covenantal community the economics of renewal receives the most attention, in a series of three steps (Mark 10:17–22, 23–25, 26–31) beginning with Jesus' interaction with *the rich man*. Though the "man" is not identified further in the Markan story (only Luke 18:18 presents him as "a ruler"), his question identifies him as wealthy. While peasants would be worrying mainly about where the next meal is coming from, only a wealthy person would be looking for "eternal life." Jesus makes a point of walking him (and the audience) through the covenantal commandments that govern social-economic relations. "You shall not defraud" is a pointed substitution for "you shall not covet and seize."[58] Jesus' audience of peasant villagers would have recognized that the only way the man could have gained his wealth was by "defrauding" (other) needy peasants desperate for a loan or day labor when what remained of their crops after taxes and tribute was insufficient to live on. His wealth indicated that he had obviously not been observing the commandments but had been flouting the commandments not to covet and steal. Jesus makes the (wealthy) man questing for "eternal life" into an example of what not to do in the community's economic relations, that is, not to take advantage of one another's need.

In the second step Jesus presents the appropriate renewed covenantal principle: it will be impossible for the wealthy to enter the kingdom. The further statement of the principle, "it is easier for a camel to go through the eye of a needle than for someone who is rich to enter the kingdom of God," is a great example of caustic peasant humor. The hostility of the villagers to the wealthy is not even veiled.

The third step in the focus specifically on covenantal economic relations brings the dialogue directly to bear on the concrete circumstances and project of the communities of the movement in which the Markan story was produced. Peter articulates the puzzlement of the astonished disciples who are wondering, "Then who can be delivered? Look, we left everything and followed you." Jesus' response is one of the key passages in the Gospels that indicates how concretely economic the program of Jesus' mission and movement(s) was in the circumstances in which they lived in the Roman imperial (dis)order in Palestine. Understanding what Jesus is saying enables us to recognize that "and in the age to come eternal life" is a "throwaway" line (mocking the man who was seeking eternal life). The disciples (and Jesus communities) are to anticipate restoration of their families/households as villagers working on their lands. Jesus declares that they will most certainly have economic sufficiency—conveyed in the hyperbole of "a hundredfold." This is to happen "in this time," that is in the future of the movement, but "with persecutions." The rulers in the Roman imperial (dis)order who feel threatened by the resistance of the movement of renewal will be taking measures to suppress them. The renewal of village communities included at its foundation the economic renewal that was happening in the coming of the direct rule of God. Mutual commitment to observing the economic principles of the covenant, in which no one takes advantage of others' circumstances, would result in economic sufficiency for all in the community.

58. Again, see Chaney, *Peasants, Prophets*, ch. 3.

But they were to have no illusions about the continuing political-economic power of the hostile Roman order in Palestine and Syria.

The final dialogue of the series focuses on leadership in the movement that is to be diametrically the opposite of the Roman imperial order. The request of James and John for highest positions of power in the kingdom, following Jesus' third announcement that he must be martyred, is the foil. Jesus' response, which focuses attention again on his impending martyrdom, declares that leadership in his movement is to be just the opposite of the "great ones"/ rulers of the nations (the Romans) who lord it over their subjects, becoming hyper-wealthy as well. The leaders of his movement(s) are to be servants of the movement. In the Markan narrative, and evidently in the Matthean as well, this dialogue includes an economic aspect in Jesus' reference to his own martyrdom, which had become a powerful motivating factor in the expansion of his movement(s). His death would be a ransom for many, "ransom" referring to the covenantal mechanism by which those who had fallen into debt slavery could be ransomed and their land, which had fallen into others' control, be redeemed. It may have been unrealistic, but the story seems to be anticipating that, by energizing the movement, Jesus' martyr death would enable the renewal of community to gain sufficient cooperation that it could redeem debt slaves and families' land. Also, in the Markan narrative, this ransom fits with Jesus' promise at the end of the dialogue on economic life in the renewed community (Mark 10:28–30) that those (the disciples) who left their family and land would receive back (in the hyperbole of "a hundredfold") family and land in this time/age.

Other Episodes of Covenant Renewal

While it is not possible to comment on every episode in the Gospels, it should be noted that a number of other episodes in the Markan Gospel story and/ or in the Matthean and Lukan stories and speeches form parts of the focus on renewing the Mosaic covenant as central to the social-economic renewal of the people of Israel. John's baptism of repentance introduces covenant renewal in the overall Gospel story. Then in the climax of the Gospel story in both Mark and Matthew, Jesus transforms the celebration of the Passover meal he shares with his disciples into a ceremony of covenant renewal (the central symbol of the blood of the covenant in his words refer to the original covenant ceremony on Sinai [Exod 24]), which continued in the communities of Jesus loyalists. Among the speeches parallel in the Matthean and Lukan Gospels (but not in the Markan), Jesus' exhortation to "seek first the direct rule of God" and subsistence food and clothing would take care of themselves presupposes the recommitment to cooperative sharing enacted in the covenant renewal speech.

Some key episodes included only in the Lukan story should disabuse us of the previously standard (and still influential) theological scheme in which Christianity originated in Jesus' criticism or even attack on "the Jewish law." Heard or read in narrative context, moreover, these episodes indicate that the Lukan, Markan, and Matthean Gospels, like the mission of Jesus whose story they tell, were addressed to movements of ordinary people. In the narrative sequence, both the parable of the "good Samaritan" and the story of the obscenely rich man who ignored the plight of the beggar Lazarus, in narrative context, set up elite figures as "straw men."

The parable of the "good Samaritan" follows closely upon Jesus' commission of his disciples to extend his proclamation of the direct rule of God in village communities and his thanksgiving that his "Father" had revealed his renewal of Israel to ordinary folks ("children") and not to "the sages" (the scribal elite) (Matt 11:25//Luke 10:21). Behold! Up pops a scholar of torah/law. Mocking his literacy and learning, Jesus asks what he finds "written" in the torah/law. He answers with what had by late Second Temple times become the standard summary of the torah, the "double" command, the very elaborate command to love God and the almost incidental second, to love neighbor. The torah scholar, who almost certainly did not live in the close social-economic interaction of a village community, naively asks, "So who is my neighbor?" In the parable, the priest and the Levite, staff of the temple-state both presumably well versed in the torah, see the beaten man and pass on by. Astoundingly a Samaritan, despised by the Judeans, especially since the Judean high priests had conquered them and destroyed their temple, came to the beaten man's aid. The parable forces the torah scholar to recognize that it was the Samaritan who responded to the obvious need of the man who proved neighbor to him. The command to "go and do likewise"—respond to people's needs, as in the demands of the covenant renewal speech—is directed through the dense torah scholar to the disciples and hearers/readers of the Gospel story.

Following Jesus' declaration that "you cannot serve God and wealth" and, further, the declaration that the torah and the prophets led to John (presumably his renewal of covenant in the baptism of repentance) after which the direct rule of God is proclaimed, comes the statement that the whole (Mosaic) torah is still in effect (Luke 16:13–18). This stands parallel to the similar statement toward the beginning of the Matthean covenant renewal speech (Matt 5:17–20). The ensuing story of the obscenely wealthy man who utterly ignores the desperate beggar at the gate of his mansion illustrates that social-economic relations should and must be regulated by "Moses and the prophets." The direct rule of God consists in social-economic relations being guided by the covenantal torah of Moses and the pronouncements of the prophets.

As portrayed in the Gospels of Mark, Matthew, and Luke, Jesus in his mission of renewal healed and pronounced the direct rule of God in the villages of Galilee and beyond, households and village communities that were disintegrating under the impact of Roman conquest and the demands of multiple layers of rulers for tribute, taxes, and tithes. The focus of his mission was the renewal of the Mosaic covenant, especially its commandments of no exploitation of one another and its commands and customs of mutual aid and cooperation, even in the circumstances in which all were struggling for subsistence. The promise was that if the people gave priority to "seeking the direct rule of God" (as articulated in the covenantal commandments) and engaged in mutual aid (generous giving to the needy) and cooperation (mutual cancellation of debts), all would have sufficient food and clothing. And this would strengthen the village communities in their efforts to resist the intensified exploitation by their rulers.

Prophetic Condemnation of—and Direct Action against— the Rulers' Control and Extraction

The Gospels also present Jesus' mission as a rejection of and resistance to the high priestly rulers in Jerusalem and their extractions from the people. This has been interpreted—tragically—as opposition to Judaism. What could intelligibly be referred to as Judaism, however, did not emerge until well after the Roman destruction of the temple and high priestly aristocracy in Jerusalem.[59] When something that could more appropriately be referred to as Christianity did develop, some of its texts did blame, reject, and condemn "the Jews." And until recently modern Christian biblical scholarship, as a branch of Christian theology, framed its interpretation of Jesus and the Gospels as opposed to Judaism; some sectors, sadly, still do. The Gospels, however, present Jesus as engaged in the renewal of the people of Israel in proclaiming the direct rule of God and performing exorcisms and healings, starting in the villages of Galilee. The Matthean story even has Jesus instruct the disciples to "go only to the lost

59. In the 1970s, Jacob Neusner, a most distinguished and innovative scholar of rabbinic Judaism, in voluminous publications, encouraged us to speak not of "normative Judaism" but of "formative Judaism" insofar as what most scholars meant by Judaism was basically rabbinic Judaism, which was in the process of formation in the centuries after the destruction of the Jerusalem temple.

sheep of the house of Israel." In the Gospel stories there is no rejection of "the Jews" and no indication of a mission to "the gentiles." The Gospels present Jesus' mission as the renewal of the people of Israel, indeed as the fulfillment of Israelite tradition and history.

On the other hand, the Gospels present Jesus as adamantly opposed to the rulers of Israel, who were appointed and backed by the Romans, and evidently the temple-state they headed, mainly because of their economic extractions from the people. The Gospels' presentation of Jesus' mission fits the historical context of the intensifying conflict between the high priestly rulers and the people in Roman Palestine, as known from Josephus's histories and memories in rabbinic texts, as discussed above. As the dominating political-economic-religious institution in Judea, the temple-state with its high priestly heads, was the face and representative of imperial rule of the (Judean and by the end of the second century BCE the general Israelite) people. The temple itself Herod had rebuilt in grand Hellenistic style, with a Roman eagle over a main gate and daily sacrifices for (the divine) Roma and Caesar. Wealth continued to pile up in the temple, tempting Pontius Pilate, for example, to expropriate some of the sacred treasure known as *qorban* to pay for an aqueduct (Josephus, *J.W.* 2.175–177). The expanded high priestly aristocracy consisted of four principal families, all inherited from Herod, from which Roman governors appointed figures to the high priestly office. And, as noted above, these families had been using their positions of power to considerably expand their own wealth.

Jesus' Conflict with the Pharisees and Scribes

While Jesus' opposition to the rulers in Jerusalem comes to a dramatic climax in his confrontation with the high priestly heads of the temple-state, the Gospel stories present his mission as independent of and objectionable to the temple-state from the beginning. It seems as if his healings and exorcisms— and giving the people authority to forgive one another's sins—might displace the functions of the priests and scribes in temple-system (e.g., sin offerings in the temple [Mark 2:1–12]; stated more explicitly [Matt 9:1–8]). In what became the standard theological scheme of the origins of what developed into Christianit(ies), the scribes and Pharisees were misunderstood as the principal representatives of the supposedly overly legalistic and ritualistic old religion of Judaism. If we consider the Gospels as whole stories, including the speeches of Jesus, it is clear rather that they, in agreement with the Judean historian Josephus (e.g., *Ant.* 13.296–298), present the scribes and Pharisees as the representatives of the Jerusalem temple and its heads: the priestly aristocracy. In the Markan narrative, for example, the scribes and Pharisees "come down from Jerusalem" to condemn Jesus' actions and those of his loyalists. While Jesus' direct confrontation with the high priestly rulers in the temple forms the climax of the Gospel story after his mission in the villages of Galilee and beyond, the opposition to his actions by the representatives of the rulers begins early in the story, as the Pharisees (and the Herodians) plot how to destroy him (Mark 3:6 par.).

In response to their opposition, Jesus declares God's condemnation of the scribes and Pharisees, mainly for their role in the rulers' extractions from the resources that the people need for their own subsistence. The long-standard Christian theological misunderstanding of Jesus as opposed to Judaism and the Jewish law was focused on what is only the rhetoric of Jesus' counterattacks on the scribes and Pharisees. He mocks their focus on particular purity concerns and ritual requirements. But he then zeroes in on their role as representatives of the temple-state and its effects on the people. This can be seen most clearly in three particular episodes in the Gospels.

Both Matthew and Luke include a series of prophetic woes against the scribes (lawyers) and Pharisees, as found in Matt 23 and in Luke 11:37–52.[60] Following a traditional form known from Israelite prophets such as Amos, Isaiah, and Habakkuk, these are indictments for actions that exploit the people followed by declaration of God's judgment. After mocking their cleansing the outside of the cup and dish, he charges that inside they themselves are full of extortion and wickedness. After mocking them for being so scrupulous as to tithe even herbs not clearly subject to tithing requirements, he charges them with neglecting the weightier matters of (covenantal) torah (the law), such as justice and mercy. He indicts them for laying heavy (economic) burdens on people's shoulders and not being willing to alleviate them with (the flick of the pen in) their scribal fingers. These indictments lead to the declaration that the blood of all the prophets killed by their ancestors will be required of "this generation," that is, the scribes and Pharisees and their high priestly patrons.

In the Markan story found in Mark 7:1–13, when the Pharisees and some scribes (again) "come down from Jerusalem" and observe Jesus' disciples eating with unwashed hands, they charge them with not observing "the traditions of the (Pharisaic) elders."[61] Jesus first castigates their laws supplementary to the

---

60. More extensive analysis and discussion in Horsley with Draper, *Whoever Hears You,* 285–91.

61. This and the next paragraph are dependent on the fuller analysis and discussion in Horsley, *Hearing the Whole Story,* 161–76; and *Jesus and the Politics,* ch. 6.

written (scriptural) laws of purity as not being of divine origin. But then he changes the subject from purity to economic subsistence. Jesus charges that by pressing their traditions of the elders, the Pharisees are rejecting the very commandment of God. He focuses on the commandment that was surely the most sensitive to peasants, that is, being able to feed their families. By urging the people to "devote" (*qorban*) a portion of their crops to God, i.e., the temple, the Pharisees cause the people to violate the commandment to "honor your father and mother." That is, Jesus condemns the Pharisees for insisting that the people "devote" to God the economic resources needed locally to feed their families.[62]

At the end of the Markan and Lukan narratives of Jesus' confrontation with the high priests in the Jerusalem temple (Mark 12:38—13:2//Luke 20:45—21:6), Jesus warns, "Beware of the scribes . . . who devour widows' houses [households]." In the immediately ensuing narrative sequence, a widow gives two copper coins to the temple treasury, which is all that remains of her "house"/household, that is, all that remains of her living, which has thus been "devoured" by the scribal staff of the temple-state who were urging the people to support the temple. And this is what leads immediately in narrative sequence to Jesus' announcement that the temple is about to be destroyed.

Jesus' Sustained Confrontation with the High Priestly Rulers of the Temple-State

In all four Gospels the story comes to its climax in Jesus' sustained confrontation with the high priestly rulers and the temple they headed in Jerusalem.[63]

---

62. Unless it is purely a rhetorical device, the location of this episode in Galilee adds another dimension to the Pharisees' urging the people there to "devote" a portion of their crops to God (the temple). After 4 BCE the Romans had appointed Herod Antipas as ruler of Galilee. Presumably the Jerusalem rulers no longer had jurisdiction to impose taxation on Galileans during the lifetime of Jesus and thereafter. Jesus charges suggest that *qorban* was a device by which the Jerusalem temple-state could attempt to continue some economic support from the Galileans, further threatening their economic viability.

63. There is not space here to adequately explain how the Gospel of John also presents Jesus as carrying out a prophetic demonstration against the temple, announcing that it would be (was being) destroyed (John 2:13–22). This is often missed because John has traditionally been taken as a "spiritual" Gospel. The depoliticizing interpretation of the Johannine story according to a standard Christian theological scheme has had particularly tragic consequences insofar as "the Judeans" in John have been taken as a reference to "the Jews" (and Judaism) in general. A careful reading of the Johannine narrative with attention to context (setting), however, indicates that while "the Judeans" sometimes refers to those who live in Judea generally (many of whom the story portrays as responding positively to Jesus), more often the term refers to the heads and staff of the temple-state in Jerusalem, and is synonymous with "the high priests and the Pharisees." In John, Jesus does not oppose "the Jews" and Judaism generally, but the rulers in Jerusalem who head the temple and its

Jesus' direct action against the temple leads the high priests to have him arrested and to hand him over to the Roman governor for execution as a leader of insurrection ("king of the Judeans"). Jesus' prophetic pronouncements against the rulers, moreover, like his woes against the scribes and Pharisees, stand in a deep tradition of Israelite prophets such as Amos, Micah, and Isaiah. In the earliest prophecies attributed to them[64] these prophets had pronounced God's indictment and judgment of kings, their officers, and/or the Jerusalem temple for their economic exploitation of the people. In comparison with the contemporary popular prophets (and kings/messiahs), such as Theudas, Jesus in the Gospels engaged in a bolder and more direct confrontation and condemnation of the rulers and ruling institution in the Jerusalem temple.

In the Gospels Jesus stages his sustained confrontation with the rulers at the Passover festival in Jerusalem, perhaps the principal expression of the irreconcilable contradiction and conflict between Israelite tradition and the Roman imperial order that focused on the rulers' extraction of the people's produce and resources. Passover was the annual celebration of the liberation of the people from political-economic bondage under Egyptian imperial rule. Originally observed in the local family setting, it had long been institutionalized as a pilgrimage festival in the Jerusalem temple, a key concrete as well as symbolic component of economic centralization that extracted resources from the people.[65] For the people, however, Passover remained a celebration of their formative liberation. Under Roman imperial rule, Passover became the occasion for peoples' protest of their current subjugation. Fearing that the celebration by crowds who came in from the villages might get completely out of hand, the Roman governors made a practice of bringing their troops into Jerusalem and posting them on the porticoes of the newly constructed Herodian Temple. But that only exacerbated the symbolic face-off that dramatized the structural political-economic-religious conflict. In the most overt manifestation of the conflict, under the governor Cumanus, when the crowd erupted into protest, the governor unleashed his troops against them (Josephus, *Ant.* 20.105–109;

---

festivals, and who are beholden to the Roman governor. His forcible demonstration in the temple is the first and most dramatic in a series of confrontations with the high priests and the Pharisees. For fuller elaboration of this reading of John, see Horsley and Thatcher, *John, Jesus, and Renewal*, esp. 39–41, 111–12, 122, 127, 161–66.

64. Coote, *Amos among the Prophets*.

65. The centralization of the Passover celebration (and other sacrifices) in the temple required peasants to sell produce for coins and then buy animals (at markup) suitable for sacrifice in the temple and expend other resources required for pilgrimage festival(s) in Jerusalem.

J.W. 2.223–226).⁶⁶ The Gospels place Jesus' confrontation with the rulers precisely in this volatile situation of conflict.

The Gospels' portrayal of Jesus' prophetic demonstration and pronouncements against the temple and high priests is highly significant in yet another way. The crowds at the Passover festival provided a kind of protection for the prophet. In preindustrial capital cities the rulers were hesitant to take direct action against protests and demonstrations lest their repressive action provoke wider protest or prolonged rioting. The Gospels portray Jesus as protected during the day by the crowds that viewed him as a prophet with divine authority, then leaving Jerusalem at night for a hiding place on the Mount of Olives (see esp. the narrative in Mark 11:11, 18–19; 13:3; 14:1–3, 12–17, 26, 43–49; par.).

The sheer number of episodes in the Gospels in which Jesus pronounces God's condemnation of the temple and high priests attests how prominent this was in his mission and for the movements that produced the Gospels.⁶⁷ While it has often gone unnoticed in previous interpretation, the economic dimension is clear and even focal.

Jesus' confrontation with the rulers begins with his forcible *demonstration in the temple,* "overturning tables of the money changers" and "not allowing anyone to carry anything through the temple [courtyard]." This can hardly be construed as a mere "cleansing" of a house of worship from "corruption." He was effectively blocking operations integral to (not "corruptions" of) the functioning of the religious-political economy of the temple. In interpretation of his disruptive action, Jesus recites (appeals to the "written" authority of) an unidentified "prophecy." That it is a combination of lines from two different prophets (what modern scholars recognize from printed editions of canonized books), Isa (56:7) and Jeremiah (7:11), suggests that the prophecy was probably being recited from (oral) popular tradition (not from written scrolls). The second line, "you have made it a bandits' den," would have been an unmistakable reference to Jeremiah's famous prophecy against the temple (7:1–15): God had condemned the temple because, in taking tithes and offerings (and perhaps interest on loans) from the people, its officials were stealing from them, in violation of the Mosaic covenant commandments, confident that their sacred position and space would keep them secure. Thus, they were like brigands who stole from

---

66. On popular protests in Jerusalem, particularly Passover protests, see Horsley, *Jesus and the Spiral,* 34–35, 90–99.

67. The interpretation of Jesus' prophetic action and speech of God's impending judgment of the temple here depends somewhat on earlier analysis in Horsley, *Jesus and the Spiral,* 285–300. See also the insightful discussion emphasizing the economic dimension of the temple and Jesus' prophetic action in Herzog, *Jesus, Justice,* esp. 137–43.

people and then headed for safety to their hideout.[68] Jesus' dramatic disruption of temple business was a symbolic prophetic demonstration, in the tradition of Jeremiah having walked around Jerusalem with an ox yoke on his neck (Jer 27–28). Jesus was symbolically acting out God's condemnation not just of the building (so massively rebuilt by Herod) but of the temple system, because of its exploitation of the people indicated in the reference to Jeremiah's well-known prophecy. The high priests and scribes knew what Jesus had just done: from this point "they kept looking for a way to kill him."[69]

Jesus tells *the parable of the vineyard and tenants as a prophecy against the high priests* (Mark 12:1–12 par.). The vineyard parable builds on a well-known prophecy of Isaiah (5:1–10) that began as an ironic, almost sarcastic "love song" about a vineyard, which turned into a prophetic condemnation of the rulers. In both the historical context of Isaiah and again in that of Jesus, a vineyard was a significant symbol of the dynamics of the political-economic structure in which the rulers used their wealth and power to exploit and impoverish the peasants.[70] The lines of indictment of the rulers in Isaiah's prophecy (5:6) indicate how "a man" went about building a vineyard: by "joining house to house and adding field to field." That is, by manipulating needy villagers into debt, he came to control their fields on which he planted vines—and dug a pit for a winepress, built a storage tower, and hired tenants (perhaps the very peasants whose fields he now controlled). This is just what high priestly figures, and probably Herodian figures as well, had been doing in the hill country of northwest Judea at the time of Jesus, as mentioned above. This process was only too

---

68. The first line of Jesus' prophetic statement, "my house shall be called a house of prayer for all peoples," as indicated by its original context in Isa 56, was part of a prophetic appeal to make the (Second) Temple a center where God could gather the outcasts of Israel and other peoples (Isa 56:8). This would have been virtually the opposite of the actual political-economic-religious function of the temple as known from other sources (Mark 11:17; cf. Jer 7:11).

69. Just as the earlier officers of the temple sought to kill Jeremiah after his oracle pronouncing God's judgment against the temple (Jer 26). That the point of Jesus' action is indeed that God is about to destroy the temple is confirmed from the way the Markan and Matthean narratives frame the demonstration with the analogy of his cursing the fig tree (Mark 11:12–14, 20–24//Matt 21:20–22). Jesus makes the connection in an ominous declaration: "Have faith in God. Truly I tell you, if you say to this mountain [on which the temple stands], 'Be taken up and thrown into the sea,' and . . . trust that what you say will come to pass, it will be done for you."

70. William R. Herzog places interpretation of the parable squarely into this historical context (*Parables as Subversive Speech*, 98–113), which is further sketched out in Horsley, *Galilee*, 132–37, 205–21. The mistranslation of "lord of the vineyard" as "owner of the vineyard," which suggests private property, is a later economic concept that should not be projected onto land tenure in late Second Temple Judea.

familiar to the high priests who were listening to the story about the vineyard; but also to the wider audience of Passover pilgrims who may have lost control of their fields/land and would have silently cheered at the resistance of the tenants and even their scheme to retake control of their fields once the heir was out of the way, as Jesus shifts the focus to the tenants. The high priests, however, knew very well that while they held their positions of power and privilege as regents of God (in the official ideology of the temple-state), instead of producing "justice," they had exploited the people. They would have recognized that they were the analogue of the tenants in the parable. Probably from their own practices, they knew very well what "the lord of the vineyard" would do to such tenants, drew the analogy, and recognized that Jesus had told the parable as a prophecy of God's condemnation of them.[71]

Just as Jesus completes his confrontation with the high priests and scribes in the Gospel stories, he declares that the temple will be destroyed. Then in his trial before the high priestly court he is accused of having declared:

> I will destroy this temple that is made with hands
> and in three days I will build another not made with hands.
> (Mark 14:58 par.)

As he is hanging on the cross he is mocked with the same charge of destroying the temple (15:29). This accusation in the Gospel texts is an adaptation of what would have been a double saying in Israelite prophetic tradition in which the prophet speaks for God (the "I" is God speaking). The prophecy of destruction is clear enough: the temple made with hands would have been the massive edifice rebuilt by Herod (still under construction at great cost at the time of Jesus' mission and the formation of the Gospel story). As for "the temple not made with hands,"[72] the clue to this prophetic statement by Jesus may lie in the parallel to this saying in Gos. Thom. 71, where "house" of God, a

---

71. Christian interpreters, some keying off the cornerstone in the lines from Ps 118, take this parable as an allegory, with the lord of the vineyard as God, "his son" as Jesus Christ, the tenants as "the Jews," and "the others" to whom the vineyard is given as (gentile) Christians. This allegorization is forced; it does not quite work, certainly not in the context of the whole Markan or Matthean or Lukan Gospel story. Certainly, the Lukan narrative does not take the stone as Jesus Christ. This allegory not only became one of the principal textual bases of the Christian doctrine that Christianity had replaced (succeeded) Judaism, but also left Christians with an image of God as a punitive absentee landlord. That the Gospel stories and their parables were not (yet) biblical relativizes their authority claims as "the word of God" so that authoritarian images of God need not be perpetuated.

72. E. P. Sanders argued that this refers to a rebuilt temple in the future (*Jesus and Judaism*). But there was no such tradition, even in scribal texts, of a rebuilt temple; see the critical survey of key Judean texts in Horsley, *Jesus and the Spiral*, 286–92.

synonym for the temple, appears. In Judean scribal texts (e.g., the animal vision in 1 En. 85–90) "the house of God" referred to *the people*, while "the tower" on that house symbolized the temple, which was not to be rebuilt in the future restoration of the people (cf. 1QS 5:5–7, 8:4–10, 9:3–6; 4QFlor 1:1–13, in which the Qumran community understood itself as the temple/house of God). Jesus' prophecy is evidently a declaration that God will destroy "the house of God"—the temple, but rebuild "the house of God"—the people.

Another prophecy of Jesus (Matt 23:37–38//Luke 13:34) is a lament over the impending destruction of the ruling house of Jerusalem because it had exploited rather than protected the "children," a standing image for the villages subject to a ruling city, as in Isa 51:17–18 and Deut 32:11.

These prophecies of condemnation of the high priestly rulers and the temple cannot be reduced to mere "criticism" of "corruption." As earlier in Israelite tradition, prophecies uttered in performative speech were tantamount to announcements of God's (imminent) action. That Judean rulers found them threatening and took repressive action is illustrated by their arrest of that other prophet named Jesus, the son of Hananiah, who similarly pronounced doom on Jerusalem (Josephus, *J.W.* 6.300–309). An important aspect of the (at least temporary) power of these prophecies and especially of the (forcible) prophetic demonstration that blocked temple business, was the authority that Jesus, like John, had among the people who, in the volatile situation in Jerusalem, could generate more widespread resistance (Mark 11:27–33). The high priestly rulers could only take action against the prophet surreptitiously.

Jesus' Opposition to the Roman Tribute

Finally, in recognizing the direct action and ominous prophetic statements in condemnation of the temple-state, we should recognize that Jesus' confrontation against the rulers also takes aim directly at Roman rule, specifically at Roman extraction of the tribute.[73] The Pharisees and the Herodians evidently recognize that his prophetic condemnation of the temple and high priests is also an attack on the Roman imperial order in Palestine. They shrewdly ask him the question that will entrap him: "Is it lawful to pay tribute to Caesar?" Pompey and Caesar had laid Judea under tribute, as discussed above. The tribute was reinstated, certainly by 6 CE, with the high priests responsible for its collection. Meanwhile, Caesar had come to be honored throughout the empire (including by Herod the Great) as divine Lord and Savior. The Judean

---

73. Further analysis and discussion in Horsley, *Jesus and the Spiral*, 306–17.

scribal dissidents whom Josephus calls the "fourth philosophy"—who, according to him, agreed basically with the Pharisees and were led by a Pharisee and a scribal teacher—had organized serious resistance to the tribute in 6 CE. They argued that Israelites could not render tribute to Caesar since they already had a Lord and Master, as noted above. Thus, the Pharisees and everyone else listening to the confrontation knew that it was not lawful, being forbidden by the first two commandments: "no other god" and "do not bow down and serve." The Romans, however, viewed nonpayment as tantamount to insurrection—hence the entrapment of the question. In response to their question, Jesus first tricked the Pharisees into "showing their hand" (they had a coin with Caesar's image). Then, avoiding saying no directly, he skillfully crafted a reply that everyone would have understood: "Give to Caesar the things that belong to Caesar, and to God the things that belong to God." For Israelites, all belonged to God and nothing to Caesar. In this cagy reply Jesus had declared that Israelites did not owe tribute, although the Gospel stories give no indication that he called for active resistance to its payment. Surely Jesus and the loyalists who produced the Gospels knew that active public refusal to pay the tribute would have led the Romans to retaliate with brutal military suppression.

Jesus' Overall Strategy of Opposition to the Roman Imperial Order in Palestine

Jesus' cagy reply to the Pharisees' question as to whether it is lawful to pay tribute to Caesar provides a significant indication of the overall political-economic-religious strategy of Jesus' mission and movement(s) as portrayed in the Gospel stories and speeches: the renewal of the people in recommitment to covenantal sharing and cooperation in their constituent village communities in opposition and resistance to their rulers, but without taking provocative collective action that would evoke brutally destructive Roman military action. Unlike other popular prophets who also led movements in mid-first century CE, Jesus did not summon followers out of their families and villages in anticipation of some fantastic divine act of deliverance like those of old. Contrary to later, especially modern Christian individualistic, interpretation, the teachings of Jesus were not statements of ideals or values for individual "discipleship." Rather Jesus' mission and movement focused on the renewal of the constituent village communities of the people that were beginning to disintegrate under the burdens of intensified extraction of their economic resources by their multiple layers of rulers. Jesus' mission and movement portrayed in the Gospels involved collective action in implementing what might well be called a concrete political-economic program of renewal of those village communities.

In performative speech that enacted what it pronounced, the covenant renewal speeches generated the people's (re)commitment to mutual aid and cooperation in those village communities according to the Mosaic covenantal principles that had long governed local social-economic relations. The assumptions of the Mosaic covenantal tradition were that the people, in their households/families and village communities, had economic rights to a subsistence livelihood and that the community (people) as a whole had responsibility to ensure that they remained economically viable. The mutual aid and cooperation in the covenant renewal, people cancelling their needy neighbors' debts as they petitioned God for cancellation of their debts (in the Lord's Prayer), would have enabled the component families to regain and maintain a subsistence living in the face of the demands for tithes, taxes, and tribute from their rulers. And the renewal of mutual aid and cooperation would have enabled village communities to resist further deterioration due to the extractions of the Romans and their client rulers.

A further key assumption of the Mosaic covenantal tradition was that the people did not owe and should not really yield some of their produce that they needed for support of their families to human rulers, such as kings and high priests, much less to imperial rulers. And again, as in the long Israelite tradition of prophets such as Elijah, Isaiah, and Jeremiah, a key aspect of the broader role of Jesus as the prophet of renewal was to pronounce God's judgment against rulers who exploited the people economically. Again, as in Israelite history and tradition, while rulers feared prophets because of their authority with and support by the people, they were all the more determined to silence them. In the first century CE Roman governors sent out their military forces to suppress their movements and kill the prophets, and Herod Antipas arrested and killed John the Baptist. As indicated in Jesus' prophetic pronouncements against the Jerusalem rulers, he would have known the outcome of his direct confrontation with the rulers. And as is clear from the rapid expansion of the Jesus movements and the Gospels they produced, his execution by crucifixion ostensibly as a leader of insurrection ("king of the Judeans") became the martyrdom that motivated that expansion into villages in other areas and eventually cities as well.[74]

According to the Gospels' portrayal, Jesus' mission and movement(s) evidently had no illusions about the continuing presence and power of the Roman imperial order. Their political-economic-religious strategy, moreover, seems

---

74. For discussion of Jesus' crucifixion as a "breakthrough" event for the movement(s), see Horsley, *Jesus and the Powers*, ch. 8.

to have had a sense of political realism that enabled them not only to survive and spread but also to continue the resistance to the Roman imperial order in Palestine and beyond.

The extensions of Jesus' mission in the movements of loyalists continued to carry out renewal of covenantal community in cooperation and mutual sharing. In the case of the *koinon* in Jerusalem, this was sharing all goods in common (see Acts 2 and 4). These movements continued their resistance to the local rulers, refusing to cease their organizing. The Roman-client rulers (such as the high priests and the Agrippas) and governors and other local officials periodically took repressive measures, and the Jesus movements remained steadfast in their organizing and resistance (Mark 8:34–38, 13:9–11; Matt 10:17–20, 29–33; Luke 12:2–12). But they had sufficient communal solidarity and collective economic staying power to continue the community renewal and resistance to the Roman imperial order that the Gospel story of Jesus' mission exemplified. And they evidently did not engage in any direct collective opposition that would have evoked repressive Roman military action.

* * * * *

Consideration of the economic aspect of the Gospel stories of the interactive mission of Jesus in historical context forces us to move well beyond the domestication of Jesus into a mere "talking head" who uttered pithy sayings about love and justice that reinforce our liberal values. The Gospel stories present Jesus as having discerned concretely what was happening in the Roman imperial order in ancient Palestine, in Galilee and Judea in particular. As indicated in his covenant renewal speech and the Lord's Prayer, he discerned that families/households were being impoverished and village communities disintegrating from the economic extractions (exploitation) of their rulers: the Romans' demand for tribute after they brutally conquered Palestine and the Herodian kings' and the Jerusalem high priests' demand for taxes, tithes, and offerings. This political-economic-religious exploitation was exacerbated by the Herodian and high priestly elite manipulation of needy families into debt at high rates of interest. According to the Gospels' portrayal, Jesus focused his mission precisely in village communities, and commissioned his disciples to expand the mission in villages, first in Galilee and then in the villages of nearby areas. The core of the mission was the renewal of Mosaic covenantal community in mutual aid and cooperation that would restore community solidarity and enable families and village communities to resist their exploitation by the Herodian, high priestly, and Roman rulers. Jesus' mission thus drew deeply on and renewed covenantal community at the center of Israelite (popular) tradition that focused on collective responsibility for keeping each component family economically viable, for example, by ensuring their "daily bread" and the mutual cancellation of debts.

Jesus thus catalyzed a movement of the renewal of the people of Israel in their traditional village communities in opposition to and by their rulers appointed by the Romans. Whether in Jesus' own mission or in its expansion by the disciples and others, the movement(s) soon spread to other peoples subjected to the Roman imperial order. Throughout the Gospel stories but especially in their climactic events, Jesus pronounced God's condemnation of the rulers' (political-religious) economic exploitation and insisted that the communities of the expanding movement(s) maintain their solidarity in resistance to the Roman imperial order whose face was the local political-economic-religious institutions.

Appended Note

This approach to the historical political-economic context and the political-economic agenda evident in the Gospel stories has serious implications for how they are "used" or become "relevant" today—for example, in subsequent volumes in this series. Biblical texts, of course, took on a life of their own in the effective history of their Christian and other reading and usage. If there is some value in and import of attempts at historical readings, then it calls for an appropriate hermeneutics. Such may include the following line of analysis. The texts that were included in the Bible exhibit and address an unstable agrarian political-economic-religious system very different from the also unstable globalized capitalist system in which we live. This makes it inappropriate to apply particular sayings or other text fragments to life today, or to apply theological or "ethical" ideas derived from texts. To say, for example, that the same greed of the wealthy and powerful led to the poverty of the people in ancient Judah/Judea and then again to global capitalism's impoverishment of people today does not explain how the different economic systems "worked." Required instead is an analysis, for example, of how rulers and their officers manipulated the people they overtaxed into mounting debt, took control of their land, and made them into tenants, on the one hand, and a corresponding analysis, for example, of how mega-banks devised subprime mortgages to extract more from marginal home owners and then sliced them into securities which they (over)sold. Such analyses could then inform an attempt to reason through what course of action in response to today's complex crisis may correspond roughly to action or practice in the historical conflict evident in an extended text, such as the Gospel of Mark.

Bibliography

Alcock, Susan. *Graecia Capta: The Landscapes of Roman Greece.* Cambridge: Cambridge University Press, 1993.
Allison, Dale. *Jesus of Nazareth: Millenarian Prophet.* Minneapolis: Fortress, 1996.
Avigad, Nahman. *Discovering Jerusalem.* Nashville: Nelson, 1983.
Balzer, Klaus. *The Covenant Formulary.* Philadelphia: Fortress, 1971.
Boer, Roland. "Production and Allocation in Ancient Southwest Asian Economics." In *Economics and Empire in the Ancient Near East*, edited by Matthew J. M. Coomber, 44–74. Vol. 1 of *Guide to the Bible and Economics*. Center and Library for the Bible and Social Justice Series. Eugene, OR: Cascade Books, 2023.
———. *The Sacred Economy of Ancient Israel.* LAI. Louisville: Westminster John Knox, 2015.
Boer, Roland, and Christina Petterson. *Idols of Nations: Biblical Myth at the Origins of Capitalism.* Minneapolis: Fortress, 2014.
———. *Time of Troubles: A New Economic Framework for Early Christianity.* Minneapolis: Fortress, 2017.
Broshi, Magen. "The Role of the Temple in the Herodian Economy." *JJS* 38 (1987) 31–37.
Bultmann, Rudolf. *Theology of the New Testament.* Translated by Kendrick Grobel. 2 vols. New York: Scribners, 1951.
Carr, David M. *Writing on the Tablet of the Heart: Origins of Scripture and Literature.* Oxford: Oxford University Press, 2005.
Chakrabarty, Dipesh. "Subaltern Studies and Postcolonial Historiography." In *Handbook of Historical Sociology*, edited by Gerard Delanty and Engin F. Isin, 191–204. London: Sage, 2003.
Chaney, Marvin L. *Peasants, Prophets, and Political Economy.* Hebrew Bible and Social Analysis. Eugene, OR: Cascade Books, 2018.
Coote, Robert B. *Amos among the Prophets: Composition and Theology.* 1981. Reprint, Eugene, OR: Wipf & Stock, 2005.
Crossan, John Dominic. *The Historical Jesus: The Life of a Mediterranean Jewish Peasant.* San Francisco: HarperCollins, 1991.
Crossley, James G. *Jesus and the Chaos of History.* Biblical Refigurations. Oxford: Oxford University Press, 2015.
Ehrman, Bart D. *Jesus: Apocalyptic Prophet of the New Millennium.* Oxford: Oxford University Press, 1999.
Freyne, Sean. *Galilee from Alexander the Great to Hadrian: A Study of Second Temple Judaism.* Wilmington, DC: Glazier, 1980.
Gager, John G. *Kingdom and Community: The Social World of Early Christianity.* Englewood Cliffs, NJ: Prentice-Hall, 1975.
Goodman, Martin. "The First Jewish Revolt: Social Conflict and the Problem of Debt." *Journal of Jewish Studies* 33 (1982) 422–34.
———. *The Ruling Class of Judea: The Origins of the Jewish Revolt against Rome. A.D. 566–70.* Cambridge: Cambridge University Press, 1987.
Guha, Ranajit. *Elementary Aspects of Peasant Insurgency in Colonial India.* Delhi: Oxford University Press, 1983.

———, ed. *Writing on South Asian History and Society.* Subaltern Studies 1. Delhi: Oxford University Press, 1982.
Hanson, K. C., and Douglas Oakman. *Palestine in the Time of Jesus: Social Structures and Social Conflicts.* 2nd ed. Minneapolis: Fortress, 1998.
Harnack, Adolf von. *What Is Christianity?* London: Williams & Norgate, 1901.
Harris, William V. *Ancient Literacy.* Cambridge: Harvard University Press, 1989.
Herzog, William R. *Jesus, Justice, and the Reign of God.* Louisville: Westminster John Knox, 2000.
———. *Parables as Subversive Speech.* Louisville: Westminster John Knox, 1994.
———. "Why Peasants Responded to Jesus." In *Christian Origins: A People's History of Christianity,* edited by Richard A. Horsley, 1:47–70. Minneapolis: Fortress, 2005.
Hezser, Catherine. *Jewish Literacy in Roman Palestine.* TSAJ 81. Tübingen: Mohr Siebeck, 2001.
Hobsbawm, Eric J. *Bandits.* London: Weidenfeld & Nicolson, 1969.
———. *Primitive Rebels: Studies in Archaic Forms of Social Movements in the 19th and 20th Centuries.* New York: Norton, 1965.
Horsley, Richard A. "Ancient Jewish Banditry and the Revolt against Rome." *CBQ* 43 (1981) 409–32.
———. *Archaeology, History, and Society in Galilee: The Social Context of Jesus and the Rabbis.* Harrisburg, PA: Trinity International, 1996.
———, and John S. Hanson. *Bandits, Prophets, and Messiahs: Popular Movements at the Time of Jesus.* Minneapolis: Winston, 1985.
———. "Can Study of the Historical Jesus Escape Its Typographical Captivity?" *Journal for the Study of the Historical Jesus* 19 (2021) 1–65.
———, ed. *Christian Origins.* Vol. 1 of *A People's History of Christianity.* Minneapolis: Fortress, 2005.
———. "Contesting Authority: Popular vs. Scribal Tradition in Continuing Performance." In *Text and Tradition in Performance and Writing,* 99–122. BPC 9. Eugene, OR: Cascade Books, 2013.
———. *Covenant Economics: A Biblical Vision of Justice for All.* Louisville: West-minster John Knox, 2009.
———. *Empowering the People: Jesus, Healing, and Exorcism.* Eugene, OR: Cascade Books, 2022.
———. *Galilee: History, Politics, People.* Valley Forge, PA: Trinity International, 1995.
———. *Hearing the Whole Story: The Politics of Plot in Mark's Gospel.* Louisville: Westminster John Knox, 2001.
———, ed. *Hidden Transcripts and the Arts of Resistance: Applying the Work of James C. Scott to Jesus and Paul.* SemeiaSt 48. Atlanta: SBL, 2004.
———. "High Priests and the Politics of Roman Palestine." *JSJ* 17 (1986) 23–55.
———. "Introduction: Unearthing a People's History." In *Christian Origins: A People's History of Christianity,* edited by Richard A. Horsley, 1:1–20. Minneapolis: Fortress, 2005.
———. *Jesus and Empire: The Kingdom of God and the New World Disorder.* Minneapolis: Fortress, 2003.
———. *Jesus and Magic: Freeing the Gospel Stories from Modern Misconceptions.* Eugene, OR: Cascade Books, 2014.
———. *Jesus and the Politics of Roman Palestine.* Columbia, SC: University of South Carolina Press, 2013.

———. *Jesus and the Powers: Conflict, Covenant, and the Hope of the Poor.* Minneapolis: Fortress, 2011.

———. *Jesus and the Spiral of Violence: Popular Jewish Resistance in Roman Palestine.* San Francisco: Harper & Row, 1987.

———. "Josephus and the Bandits." *JSJ* 10 (1979) 37–63.

———. *Jesus in Context: Power, People, and Performance.* Minneapolis: Fortress, 2008.

———. "Jesus Movements and the Renewal of Israel." In *Christian Origins: A People's History of Christianity*, edited by Richard A. Horsley, 1:23–46. Minneapolis: Fortress, 2005.

———. "'Like One of the Prophets of Old': Two Types of Popular Prophets at the Time of Jesus." *CBQ* 47 (1985) 435–63.

———. "Oral Communication, Oral Performance, and New Testament Interpretation." In *Method and Meaning: Essays on New Testament Interpretation in Honor of Harold W. Attridge*, edited by Andrew B. McGowan and Kent Harold Richards, 125–55. RBS 67. Atlanta: SBL, 2011.

———. "The Pharisees and Jesus in Galilee and Q." In *When Judaism and Christianity Began: Essays in Memory of Anthony J. Saldarini*, edited by Alan J. Avery-Peck et al., 117–45. JSJSS 85. Leiden: Brill, 2004.

———. "Popular Messianic Movements around the Time of Jesus." *CBQ* 46 (1984) 471–93.

———. "Popular Prophetic Movements at the Time of Jesus, Their Principal Features and Social Origins." *JSNT* 26 (1986) 3–27.

———. "Power Vacuum and Power Struggle in 66–67 CE." In *The First Jewish Revolt: Archaeology, History, and Ideology*, edited by Andrea M. Berlin and J. Andrew Overman, 87–109. London: Routledge, 2002.

———. *The Prophet Jesus and the Renewal of Israel: Moving beyond a Diversionary Debate.* Grand Rapids: Eerdmans, 2012.

———. *Revolt of the Scribes: Resistance and Apocalyptic Origins.* Minneapolis: Fortress, 2010.

———. *Scribes, Visionaries, and the Politics of Second Temple Judea.* Louisville: Westminster John Knox, 2007.

———. *Sociology and the Jesus Movement.* New York: Crossroad, 1989.

———. *Text and Tradition in Performance and Writing.* BPC 9. Eugene, OR: Cascade Books, 2013.

———. "The Zealots: Their Origins, Relationships, and Importance in the Jewish Revolt." *NovT* 28 (1986) 159–92.

Horsley, Richard A., with Jonathan Draper. *Whoever Hears You Hears Me: Prophecy, Performance, and Tradition in Q.* Harrisburg, PA: Trinity International, 1999.

Horsley, Richard A., and John S. Hanson. *Bandits, Prophets, and Messiahs: Popular Movements at the Time of Jesus.* San Francisco: Harper & Row, 1987.

Horsley, Richard A., and Tom Thatcher. *John, Jesus, and the Renewal of Israel.* Grand Rapids: Eerdmans, 2013.

Horsley, Richard A., et al., eds. *Performing the Gospel: Orality, Memory, and Mark.* Minneapolis: Fortress, 2006.

Joseph, Simon J. *Jesus and the Temple: The Crucifixion in its Jewish Context.* Cambridge: Cambridge University Press, 2016.

———. *Jesus, the Essenes, and Christian Origins.* Waco: Baylor University Press, 2018.

Kazen, Thomas. *Issues of Purity in Early Judaism.* Winona Lake, IN: Eisenbrauns, 2010.

———. *Jesus and Purity Halakah: Was Jesus Indifferent to Impurity.* Rev. ed. Winona Lake, IN: Eisenbrauns, 2010.

Kirk, Alan. *Memory and the Jesus Tradition. The Reception of Jesus in the First Three Centuries 2.* London: T. & T. Clark, 2018.

Knight, Douglas A. "Economics in Israelite Law." In *Economics and Empire in the Ancient Near East*, edited by Matthew J. M. Coomber, 169–93. Vol. 1 of *Guide to the Bible and Economics*. Center and Library for the Bible and Social Justice Series. Eugene, OR: Cascade Books, 2023.

———. *Law, Power, and Justice in Ancient Israel.* Louisville: Westminster John Knox, 2011.

Mason, Steve. *A History of the Jewish War: A.D. 66–74.* Key Conflicts of Classical Antiquity. Cambridge: Cambridge University Press, 2016.

Mattern, Susan P. *Rome and the Enemy: Imperial Strategy in the Principate.* Berkeley: University of California Press, 1999.

Mayer, Emanuel. *The Ancient Middle Classes: Urban Life and Aesthetics in the Roman Empire, 100 BCE—250 CE.* Cambridge: Harvard University Press, 2012.

Morris, Ian, and J. G. Manning, eds. *The Ancient Economy: Evidence and Models.* Social Science History. Stanford: Stanford University Press, 2005.

Murphy, Catherine M. *Wealth in the Dead Sea Scrolls and in the Qumran Community.* STDJ. Leiden: Brill, 2002.

Myers, Ched. *Binding the Strong Man: A Political Reading of Mark's Story of Jesus.* Maryknoll, NY: Orbis, 1988.

Neusner, Jacob. *From Politics to Piety: The Emergence of Pharisaic Judaism.* 1979. Reprint, Eugene, OR: Wipf & Stock, 2003.

Portier-Young, Anathea. *Apocalypse against Empire: Theologies of Resistance in Early Judaism.* Grand Rapids: Eerdmans, 2011.

Roller, Duane W. *The Building Program of Herod the Great.* Berkeley: University of California Press, 1998.

Rostovtseff, Michael. *The Social and Economic History of the Hellenistic World.* 3 vols. Oxford: Oxford University Press, 1941.

Sanders, E. P. *Jesus and Judaism.* Minneapolis: Fortress, 1985.

Schwartz, Seth. *Imperialism and Jewish Society: 200 BCE to 640 CE.* Princeton: Princeton University Press, 2001.

Schweitzer, Albert. *Quest of the Historical Jesus.* Translated by W. Montgomery. London: Black, 1911.

Scott, James C. *Domination and the Arts of Resistance: Hidden Transcripts.* New Haven: Yale University Press, 1990.

———. *The Moral Economy of the Peasant: Rebellion and Subsistence in Southeast Asia.* New Haven, CT: Yale University Press, 1976.

———. "Protest and Profanation: Agrarian Revolt and the Little Tradition." *Theory and Society* 4 (1977) 1–38, 211–46.

———. *Weapons of the Weak: Everyday Forms of Peasant Resistance.* New Haven: Yale University Press, 1985.

Shafer-Elliot, Cynthia. "Women and Economics in Ancient Israel and Judah." In *Economics and Empire in the Ancient Near East*, edited by Matthew J. M. Coomber, 108–27. Vol. 1 of *Guide to the Bible and Economics*. Center and Library for the Bible and Social Justice Series. Eugene, OR: Cascade Books, 2023.

Temin, Peter. *The Roman Market Economy.* Princeton Economic History of the Western World 71. Princeton, NJ: Princeton University Press, 2012.

Theissen, Gerd. *Sociology of Early Palestinian Christianity.* Translated by John Bowden. Philadelphia: Fortress, 1978.

Udoh, Fabian E. *To Caesar What Is Caesar's: Tribute, Taxes, and Imperial Administration in Early Roman Palestine (63 BCE—79 CE)*. BJS 343. Providence: Brown Judaic Studies, 2005.

Ulrich, Eugene. *The Dead Sea Scrolls and the Origins of the Bible*. Grand Rapids: Eerdmans, 1999.

Webb, Robert L. *John the Baptizer and Prophet: A Socio-Historic Study*. 1991. Reprint, Eugene, OR: Wipf & Stock, 2006.

Wire, Antoinette Clark. "Women's History from Birth-Prophecy Stories." In *Christian Origins: A People's History of Christianity*, edited by Richard A. Horsley, 1:71–93. Minneapolis: Fortress, 2005.

4. Imaginings of Jesus and the Economic Questions of His Day

JAMES CROSSLEY

Introduction

The quest for the economy of Roman Galilee and Judea is tied up with the mainstream quest for the historical Jesus. As we will see, the resulting Jesus of scholarship will depend on questions of how economically oppressed the people were—or were not—according to a given scholar. Nevertheless, it is fair to say that scholarship has typically downplayed notions of class and class conflict. As I have argued in detail elsewhere, the questions posed by Socialist and Communist thinkers of the late nineteenth and early twentieth centuries were once taken seriously in New Testament studies, but with the Russian Revolution, the rise of the Soviet Union, and the Cold War, materialist or revolutionary questions—and indeed social-scientific questions more generally—were at best found on the fringes of academic debate.[1] While these questions may simply be ignored, sometimes they were polemically attacked. In his historical Jesus book from 1956, Günther Bornkamm provided a discussion of the parallels between Bolshevism and Jesus through their respective takes on eschatology. Predictably, Bornkamm concluded that there were profound, incompatible differences.[2] Similarly, in an appendix discussing the Sermon on the Mount, Bornkamm dismissed the ideas of "Kautzky and others," and the argument that Jesus was a revolutionary of the lower classes who wanted to

1. Crossley, "First World War."
2. Bornkamm, *Jesus of Nazareth*, 102.

create a new socioeconomic order.³ This fear of Marxism and revolutionary ideas would recur in scholarship into and beyond the 1970s.⁴ We might think of the reception of S. G. F. Brandon or Richard Horsley—both major historical scholars in their own right—and how their Marxist, Marxian, or revolutionary portrayals of Jesus have not been welcomed into the mainstream and, in the case of Brandon, even brought about a mainstream (and somewhat conservative) reaction.⁵

Overt critiques of such works have partly given way to another response now typical in an age of neoliberalism and postmodernity—the appropriation of the language of "radicalism" and "subversion" while maintaining the ideological status quo and avoiding materialist struggles.⁶ Today, there are numerous anti-imperial and anti-capitalist Jesuses that have become a normative part of scholarly discourse. Whatever the motivations, beliefs, and practices of individual scholars to one side, it is difficult to see how the contemporary subfield of radical historical Jesuses is having any significant oppositional political impact—and of course we never expect it to! John Dominic Crossan and Marcus Borg may have produced edgy liberal Jesuses, but one significant ideological function is a channel to the lucrative liberal church audiences.⁷ N. T. Wright may repeatedly tell us how dangerous and subversive his Jesus is, whether pre- or post-resurrection—not least in the face of tyrants—but his books also sell extremely well in comfortable Anglo-American markets.⁸ We need only contrast the political impact of strands of liberation theology that have a Jesus dedicated to socioeconomic liberation in contexts that have faced serious peasant

---

3. Bornkamm, *Jesus of Nazareth*, 223.

4. Crossley, *Why Christianity Happened*, 3–22; Friesen, "Poverty in Pauline Studies," 323–37.

5. For classic treatments, see, e.g., Brandon, *Jesus and the Zealots*; Horsley, *Jesus and the Spiral*. For the major reactions against Brandon, see, e.g., Bammel and Moule, *Jesus and the Politics*. For critical assessment of the history of the revolutionary Jesus in scholarship, see, e.g., Bermejo-Rubio, "Jesus and Anti-Roman Resistance"; Elliott, "Jesus, Temple, and Crowd."

6. Crossley, *Jesus and the Chaos*; Myles, "Fetish for Subversive Jesus." On the broader cultural phenomenon, see, e.g., Fisher, *Capitalist Realism*; Cremin, *Capitalism's New Clothes*.

7. E.g., Borg, *Conflict, Holiness, and Politics*; Borg, *Jesus, a New Vision*; Crossan, *Historical Jesus*. For contextualization of such scholarship among church audiences, see King, "Author, Atheist, Academic Study."

8. Wright, *Jesus and the Victory*; cf. Wright, *Resurrection of the Son*, 737: "In the real world ... the tyrants and bullies (including intellectual and cultural tyrants and bullies) try to rule by force, only to discover that in order to do so they have to quash all rumours of resurrection, rumours that would imply that their greatest weapons, death and deconstruction, are not after all omnipotent."

exploitation and the brutal effects of imperialism of the sort that might form the backdrop for a historical Jesus book. This is not to say Borg, Crossan, or Wright should or should not be writing books that provide serious challenges to power and class. Instead, we should be suspicious of claims that these works are subversive or the like. We should view these popular, "radical" historical Jesuses as performing our anti-capitalism and radicalism for us, allowing us to consume books about Jesus with impunity.[9]

This chapter pushes a different agenda. My influence on liberation theology will be minimal at best, but I think it is still possible to do justice to a materialist tradition in understanding the economic context of Jesus' Palestine without succumbing to the neoliberal rhetoric of "subversion" or the like. What this piece seeks to do is to return to questions about historical change and historical materialism raised by the British Marxist historians of the twentieth century in order to understand why the Jesus movement emerged when and where it did, and how we may understand notions of class and class conflict in their economic settings and in relation to modes of production. To do this, the following considers one of the most standard issues in historical Jesus research: the idea of Jesus as a millenarian or apocalyptic figure. I will look at how apocalypticism and millenarianism should be seen as vehicles for socioeconomic agitation and how such issues of class can be seen as a motor of historical change in the world of the historical Jesus. To accomplish this task, some of the definitional issues relating to apocalypticism, millenarianism, and socioeconomic agitation must be considered.

Apocalypticism, Millenarianism, and Pre-Political Agitation

I will not offer another technical or definitive definition of *apocalyptic* or *apocalypticism*, or indeed *millenarianism*, as they might have been understood in the first century. Rather, I want to use such language in the general sense of the expectation of impending destruction and radical transformation of the social, economic, and political order, typically believed to involve supernatural intervention and their human agent or agents, with prophetic figures claiming access to the truth of divine revelation. This general definition of millenarianism reflects a phenomenon common in the first century, at least as we can gather from Josephus and other Jewish literature of the time, and would include figures such John the Baptist and Theudas. The option of such apocalypticism or millenarianism provided an esoteric language that could function as a means of rallying sociopolitical discontents. This could involve apocalypticism "from

9. Here I paraphrase Fisher, *Capitalist Realism*, 12.

above," such as in the elite scribal traditions of Jewish literature and their particular discontents, or apocalypticism "from below," such as the popular movements described by Josephus. This would not have been a neat distinction, of course, with "above" and below" interacting and influencing one another, sometimes with shared interests and enemies, sometimes with their own specific concerns.

It is these kinds of millenarian tendencies that were described (among other things) as *pre-political* by Eric Hobsbawm in his analysis of precapitalist forms of social agitation and how they adapted (or not) with the arrival of capitalism, particularly in southern Europe and Latin America.[10] For Hobsbawm, the phenomena of rural banditry (including the more benevolent Robin Hood-type) and peasant millenarianism were important examples of "pre-political" resistance in the sense that they were effectively *precapitalist* forms of resistance. This does not mean that such movements showed no interest in politics and political engagement (on the contrary). Rather, Hobsbawm argued, these phenomena were pre-political in the sense that they had to come to terms with a new world and be absorbed into more organized and bureaucratized resistance to capitalism, such as Socialist or Communist parties. Some pre-political rebels could have once provided some defence against a world of unjust princes, tax collectors, and landlords, while millenarians could promise a dramatic new world free from injustices of the present order. Indeed, it is this hope for a radical transformation that could feed into revolutionary politics of the twentieth century, Hobsbawm claimed.

Some of the specifics of Hobsbawm's argument have been strongly critiqued, and some academics are not fond of his ideas about historical development and progression, while his interests do not stretch further back than the influence of medieval forms of resistance on the modern world. Moreover, the cultural peculiarities of millenarianism from different times and places do not come through strongly in Hobsbawm's argument. But whatever the merits or otherwise of such critiques, the general point about pre-political peasant rebellion in the form of banditry or millenarianism remains useful and relevant for understanding the economic context of Palestine, not least because it helps us guard against historical anachronism. Concerns about anachronism should be obvious (and are indeed common), but historical Jesus studies will often provide arguments about Jesus' relevance for today with the "apocalyptic Jesus" also

---

10. E.g., Hobsbawm, *Primitive Rebels*, 503–5; "Social Banditry"; "Peasants and Politics"; "Peasant Land Occupations."

functioning as a cipher for the interests of Christian theology.[11] Readers may or may not find relevance for today from this essay but that is not the point I wish to make. As a historian, I want to retain Hobsbawm's emphasis by stressing that the material interests of millenarianism at the time of Jesus belonged to a precapitalist way of life that attempted to address injustices—perceived or otherwise—in an agrarian economy and in ways we might find strange, unusual, or weird. I understand the ongoing relevance of Jesus more in line with Hobsbawm's point about the importance of millenarianism for understanding modern socialist and revolutionary movements in the sense that they would drain the cultural and religious weirdness from millenarianism.

This is the sort of argument that was crucial to the historical materialism of the British Marxist historians such as Hobsbawm, Dona Torr, A. L. Morton, Christopher Hill, E. P. Thompson, and Rodney Hilton. Their influence is often praised in terms of pioneering history from below. Certainly, this is cause for praise, but what is often lost is their historical materialist agenda and how to explain changing means of production and the emergence of capitalism from feudalism, including the ways in which apocalypticism functioned as a medieval form of agitation.[12] This interest in changing epochs and means of production was extended further back to the ancient world in the work of Geoffrey E. M. de Ste. Croix. The questions associated with Ste. Croix have recently reemerged in scholarship of Christian origins about whether a slave economy, unfree labor, the tributary system, or some combination of these, made up the dominant mode of production in the ancient world.[13] These issues are too vast for a proper assessment here. Nevertheless, what we can say is that in the eastern Mediterranean, as may be expected in more advanced agrarian societies, the town-countryside relationship formed one crucial part in economic production, which in turn helps us understand localized class conflict and disruptions.

We will return to these issues below. But what I would stress first is that apocalypticism and millenarianism should be seen as phenomena long predating their medieval use. Indeed, we know that apocalypticism and millenarianism were common in the first century (and indeed inspired medieval uses). As Richard Horsley and John S. Hanson showed decades ago, the interrelated phenomenon of banditry discussed by Hobsbawm was likewise prominent in

---

11. Arnal, *Symbolic Jesus*.
12. Hilton, *Bond Men Made Free*.
13. Ste. Croix, *Class Struggle*; Boer, "Marxism and Spatial Analysis"; Galbraith, "Interpellation, Not Interpolation"; Boer and Petterson, *Time of Troubles*.

first-century Palestine.[14] Such banditry could take on different forms. The classic definition of "social banditry"—namely, those outlawed by the ruling classes, championed by the peasantry, upholders of traditional values and morality, fighters of injustice—is a phenomenon certainly attested in the first century. Stories of such social bandits, some of whom set themselves up as alternative kingly figures, are recounted by the first-century historian Josephus and may have come down to him (and us) as idealized stories. But whatever the realities behind the stories, they were live ideas present in the first century. Josephus has examples of the common cliché of the popularity of the social bandit among the peasantry. Villages could be a safe place to hide for bandits who robbed the representatives of Rome, with villagers refusing to give them up (Josephus, *J.W.* 2.228–231; *Ant.* 20.113–117). A bandit called Eleazar ben Dinai was active in the mid-first century and managed to resist capture for twenty years before he, his followers, and numerous peasant supporters were crucified, according to Josephus (*Ant.* 20.121, 160–161; *J.W.* 2.253). At the beginning of the Jewish revolt against Rome in 66 CE, debt records in Jerusalem were a target for bandits (*J.W.* 2.427–448).

Bandits could also be seen as arbiters of local justice settling localized disputes and vendettas, perhaps at times close to gangsterism (Josephus, *J.W.* 2.232–235; *Ant.* 20.118–119, 232–235). As this may suggest, first-century Jewish bandits were not always remembered as Robin Hood has typically been today. In plenty of instances they were understood to engage in basic theft without any indication that they were robbing the rich to give to the poor. A famous example is from the parable of the good Samaritan where the victim was beaten, stripped, and left for dead by bandits (Luke 10:30), which reflects a sensible enough sentiment known from elsewhere that it is best to be armed when travelling (*J.W.* 2.125). Nevertheless, rural robbery can also tell us something about the socioeconomic options open to people. We know, for instance, that famine, unusually heavy taxation, and bad harvests were known to cause a rise in banditry in the first century (*Ant.* 18.269–275; cf. 16.271–272)—in some cases there was simply no other option for survival—and that people involved in banditry could be remembered as (former) slaves, shepherd, soldiers, sailors, as well as people more generally designated destitute and poor (*Ant.* 17.270–284; *J.W.* 2.60–65; 5.58–85; *Life* 66, 175, 372). Yet bandits were not always so concerned with their roots, and Roman officials in the build-up to the Jewish revolt could use them and bribe them as hired muscle or allow banditry while taking a cut from their spoils (*J.W.* 2.272–276; *Ant.* 20.255–257).

---

14. Horsley and Hanson, *Bandits, Prophets, and Messiahs*.

Millenarians and prophets were not necessarily bandits in the sense of violence in the here and now—if God was going to intervene, then perhaps there was not always the need for physical violence by humans in the present. But some, such as the popular prophet "the Egyptian," could combine the expectation of supernatural intervention with violent subversion such as the overthrowing of Jerusalem (Josephus, *J.W.* 2.259–263; *Ant.* 20.169–171; Acts 21:38). Josephus gives us further indication that such categories could be blurred in his presentation of the mid-first century, particularly in the build-up to the Jewish revolt against Rome. In an extended discussion of prophets, bandits, and the violent *sicarii*, he argued that those with "divine inspiration" for "revolutionary changes" could lead crowds "out into the desert under the belief that God would there give them tokens of deliverance." But he further added that such prophetic types and bandits made an alliance, inciting revolution, promoting political independence, threatening to kill those who submitted to Roman domination, looting the houses of the wealthy, and burning villages (*J.W.* 2.254–265). Whatever the realities behind these recollections, it is clear that Josephus could view the categories of "prophet" (or false prophet, for Josephus) and "bandit" as representing similar and interrelated concerns.

Jesus and Pre-Political Agitation

Indeed, it was the very blurriness of such categories that provided a way for having Jesus executed, at least according to some of the earliest memories of his death as a violent bandit. It is claimed that the "whole cohort" were called in to deal with Jesus (Mark 15:16) and he was crucified between two bandits (Mark 15:27). Jesus the millenarian could easily be confused (deliberately or not) with a violent bandit or subversive from the perspective of Roman power and thus provide a reason for his execution. And Jesus was not the only such millenarian of his time to receive brutal treatment. John the Baptist and Theudas, for instance, were both killed as seditious threats, irrespective of whether either would have taken arms against the political rulers (Josephus, *Ant.* 18.116–119; 20.97–98; Acts 5:36).

That Jesus was also remembered as an apocalyptic or millenarian prophet in the earliest traditions and perceptions has been shown on numerous occasions.[15] This sort of apocalypticism overlapped with the class interests we may associate with a social bandit and should also be seen as an integral part of

15. Among recent defences of this well-known position, see, e.g., Allison, *Jesus of Nazareth*, 78–94; Allison, *Constructing Jesus*, 85–97; Fredriksen, *Jesus of Nazareth*, 78–89; Frey, "Apokalyptik als Herausforderung"; Casey, *Jesus of Nazareth*, 212–26.

understanding the historical Jesus, or at least the earliest perceptions of him. For instance, the kingdom-related themes of an eschatological reversal of rich and poor, the stark opposition of wealth and poverty, and sayings about God and Mammon are found across the Synoptic tradition, including independent tradition and different forms (e.g., Mark 10:17–31; Luke 6:20–26//Matt 5:3–12; Matt 6:24//Luke 16:13; Luke 14:12–24//Matt 22:1–14; Luke 4:18; 12:13–21; 16:19–31; cf. Gos. Thom. 64). There are also closely connected themes across the Synoptic tradition such as those concerning debt (e.g., Luke 12:57–59//Matt 5:25; Luke 6:35; 16:1–8; Matt 5:40–42; 6:12; 18:23–35), those without food, clothing, drink, and community (Matt 25:31–46; Luke 6:20–21), and opposition to wealth, fine clothing, and eating well (e.g., Matt 11:8//Luke 7:25; Matt 6:25–34//Luke 12:22–31; 6:24–25; cf. 1 En. 98:2, 102:9–11). Whether this takes us back to the historical Jesus cannot be said with any degree of certainty. It is entirely possible that such interests in stark economic inequality could have been created at any point in the tradition or found in a range of cultural contexts. Moreover, such clichéd language could have been imported into the tradition any time after Jesus' death. However, the sheer amount and concentration of such themes in independent sources and forms strongly suggests that this was a theme inherited by the Gospel writers.

We should further add that Jesus was perceived to be representative of class-based agitation. Chris Keith has shown just how problematic Jesus' class status was understood in terms of literacy.[16] Perhaps most importantly for our purposes, his approach shows how ideas concerning Jesus' trade and social standing shift from being a manual worker in Mark 6:3 through to being an elite scribal figure in Luke 4:16–30. In Mark 6:3, Jesus returns to Nazareth and teaches in the synagogue. The amazement of the people present is because of his trade as a *tektōn* (an artisan, often translated as *carpenter*, but covers a wider range of work). This label does not seem to be a problem for Mark, but Matthew transfers the label to Joseph (Matt 13:55), which suggests a distancing of Jesus from his trade. One obvious reason for this was that *tektōn* was not seen as a properly elevated label for one teaching in a synagogue, and especially problematic for Matthew in his arguments against the heirs of the scribes and Pharisees towards the end of the first century (Matt 23).[17] Luke substantially

16. Keith, *Jesus against Scribal Elite*.

17. Matthew was likely writing towards the end of the first century in dispute or competition with other Jewish groups of his time who inherited the legal traditions of the Pharisees of Jesus' time. These groups, it is typically argued, were part of emerging rabbinic Judaism, which would write down or codify legal traditions associated with the Pharisees and related groups or individuals.

rewrote this story (Luke 4:16–30). He omits the reference to *tektōn*, has Jesus as "Joseph's son," and, tellingly, now has Jesus read from the scroll of Isaiah.

The question of whether the historical Jesus was literate enough to read extensively from Jewish Scriptures is a question for another time. However, what is clear is that the post-Markan Gospel tradition attempts to explain that Jesus was sufficiently educated to be active in the synagogue by downplaying his role as a rural manual worker. Elite assumptions at least would suggest to them that the more likely option was that Jesus was not deemed of a suitable status and was perhaps perceived or assumed to be illiterate in the earliest tradition. But there is more to it than Jesus' status in terms of class. The reason why some people might have expected Jesus to remain a *tektōn* for the rest of his life was because of an ideological imagining of the world that mystified the realities of economic production. Sirach 38:24–34 reveals assumptions about the division of labor in maintaining social order:

> The wisdom of the scribe depends on the opportunity of leisure . . . How can one become wise who handles the plough, who glories in the shaft of a goad, who drives oxen and is occupied with their work, and whose talk is about bulls? . . . So too is every artisan [*tektōn*] and master artisan who labours by night as well as by day . . . So too is the smith sitting by his anvil, intent on his iron work . . . So too is the potter sitting at his work and turning the wheel with his feet . . . All these rely on their hands and all are skillful in their own work. Without them no city can be inhabited . . . Yet they are not sought out for their council of the people, nor do they attain eminence in the public assembly. They do not sit in the judge's seat, nor do they understand the decisions of the courts; they cannot expound discipline or judgement, and they are not found among the rulers. But they maintain the fabric of the world, and their concern is for the exercise of their trade. How different the one who devotes himself to the study of the law of the Most High!

Even in this heavily romanticized reading of the world where manual workers should know their place, Sirach knows the underlying reality that rural labor keeps the world running and aristocrats in their lavish lifestyles.

Galilean Economy and Class Conflict

Here we can return to questions of modes of production and historical materialism in the ancient world, albeit on a more modest scale than proposed by Ste. Croix. As noted above, the town-countryside relationship in an agrarian society of the sort we find in the Levant was an important part of economic production and contributed to localized class antagonisms. The elites in urban centers maintained the tributary system and their lifestyles by extracting surplus from the villages in the surrounding countryside, as implied in Sir 38:24–34.[18] Where conflicts and disturbances can arise is when urbanization projects get introduced into a rural economy and this involves changes in demands on rural labor. This is precisely what was happening in Galilee as Jesus was growing up. There were well-known projects at this time: the massive expansion of the Jerusalem temple in Judea, the rebuilding of Sepphoris in Galilee after it was razed in 4 BCE, and the building of Tiberias around 19 CE. Sepphoris was, Josephus notes, "situated in the heart of Galilee, surrounded by many villages" (*Life* 346) and "the ornament of all Galilee" (*Ant.* 18.27; *J.W.* 2.511). Among these surrounding villages was Nazareth, about an hour's walk away. Nazareth would have contributed labor and surplus for the ornamentation of Sepphoris and the luxurious lifestyle of the elites further enabled by (mild) commercializing activities, as John Kautsky's approach to economic change has shown.[19] With the development of the water system, including from around the time of Antipas, Sepphoris would also have dominated water resources in the area.[20]

Again, this should not be seen merely as some abstract theorizing. It is of some significance that there was a full-scale revolt against Rome in 66–70 CE, accompanied by reports of great hatred levelled at Sepphoris and Tiberias (e.g., *Life* 30, 39, 66–68, 99, 374–384). A different form of witness to the upheavals in Galilee is from the Gospel tradition and the multiply attested theme of the fragmentation of households (e.g., Mark 3:20–22, 31–35; 10:29–30; Matt 8:22//Luke 9:60; Matt 10:34–36//Luke 12:51–53//Gos. Thom. 16:1–4; Matt 10:37//Luke 14.26). It may also be significant that Jesus was remembered as moving around regularly, returning just once to Nazareth in Mark (6:1–6), which was understood to be problematic. Moreover, these traditions include tensions with Jesus' own family and the creation of an alternative one, which appears to mimic gendered roles in the household, with a particularly large

---

18. The literature on the economic setting of Palestine in relation to the Jesus movement is vast. For a selection see, e.g., Schüssler Fiorenza, *In Memory of Her*; Horsley, *Jesus and the Spiral*; Moxnes, *Economy of the Kingdom*; Fiensy, *Social History of Palestine*; K. C. Hanson and Oakman, *Palestine*; Freyne, "Herodian Economics in Galilee"; Crossan, *Birth of Christianity*; Stegemann and Stegemann, *Jesus Movement*; Carter, *Matthew and the Margins*; Herzog, *Prophet and Teacher*; Crossley, *Why Christianity Happened*; Fiensy, *Jesus the Galilean*; Myles, *Homeless Jesus*.

19. Kautsky, *Politics of Aristocratic Empires*, e.g., 278–303, the influence of which is clear throughout Crossan, *Birth of Christianity*.

20. Freyne, *Jesus, a Jewish Galilean*, 46–4.

father figure looming (cf. Matt 23:9).[21]

While there is a long scholarly tradition that has pointed out how crucial this background is to our understanding of the emergence of the Jesus movement and the economics of the time, there has been another influential scholarly tradition that has tried to downplay ideas about class conflict. E. P. Sanders claimed that "the lack of uprisings also indicates that Antipas was not excessively oppressive and did not levy exorbitant taxes . . . he undertook large building projects that helped reduce unemployment. Galileans in Jesus' lifetime did not feel that things most dear to them were seriously threatened: their religion, their national traditions and their livelihoods."[22] More recently, scholars such as Morten Hørning Jensen and Helen Bond have developed this argument, likewise claiming that archaeological evidence suggests that Galilee under Antipas was relatively stable economically and not unduly oppressed.[23] Bond further contrasts those who use social-scientific approaches and Josephus with archaeological scholarship, which, she argues, commonly portrays "a relatively tranquil setting."[24]

These arguments are not without merit; they are a helpful counter to the more vulgar popular notions of class conflict. But this is why a more nuanced notion of class conflict is needed. Archaeology itself cannot tell us everything either. Evidence of widespread material damage would doubtlessly be particularly helpful in understanding any discontents. Yet in the absence of such evidence it does not necessarily follow that there were not significant discontents—indeed we simply cannot know much about widespread perceptions of the economic situation in Galilee from the archaeological evidence.[25] The framing of the debate in terms of an unambiguous rise or fall in the standards of living is not always helpful. Unrest does not necessarily have to be a product of an unambiguous fall in the standard of living or elites exploiting people more than usual. Theoretically, major social and economic changes (like two urban projects) could lead to a range of reactions. Some might have materially benefitted,

---

21. For discussion, see, e.g., Moxnes, *Putting Jesus*; Crossley, *Jesus and the Chaos*, ch. 5. It is difficult to support the claim by Loader that Mark 3:20–22, 31–35, and 6:1–6 are not only "a new family, a new system of belonging" but that in this "new system women are no longer defined as mother or spouse. They are people" (*Sexuality and Jesus Tradition*, 58). The gendered labels may be fictionalized but they do not disappear.

22. Sanders, *Historical Figure of Jesus*, 21.

23. Jensen, *Herod Antipas in Galilee*; Jensen, "Herod Antipas in Galilee"; Bond, *Historical Jesus*, 75–77; Bond, "Response."

24. Bond, "Response," para. 5.

25. But cf. Berlin, "Romanization and Anti-Romanization."

while some might not, some might have been opportunistic, some might have accepted the changes willingly even if against their material interests, while others might have been furious. The classic materialist point (usually ignored in debates about the economics of Galilee) is that in the case of material rises in the standard of living there can also be antagonisms between classes. This may be because of further demand being made after improvements in life and ongoing unequal distribution of resources remaining.

There is good evidence for something like this more complex scenario in Galilee while Jesus was growing up, as Josephus's description of the building of Tiberias indicates. Some people benefitted from land gifts, while others were removed from land with little choice:

> The new settlers were a promiscuous rabble, no small contingent being Galilean, with such as were drafted from territory subject to him [Herod Antipas] and brought forcibly to the new foundation. Some of these were magistrates. Herod accepted as participants even poor men who were brought in to join the others from any and all places of origin. It was in question whether some were even free beyond cavil. These latter he often and in large bodies liberated and benefited imposing the condition that they should not quit the city, by equipping houses at his own expense and adding new gifts of land. (Josephus, *Ant.* 18:36–38)

The idealized claims made by Sanders and others about how Herodian urbanization projects would have increased employment overlooks the differing results among the populace. While some benefitted materially from these changes, labor and materials still had to be produced while land was being acquired or reallocated. This would have further meant that peasants and artisans faced increased demands on their time and labor, as well as the possibility of land dislocation, to make way for the changes. In such settings, the creation or perpetuation of landless peasants, day laborers, indebtedness, banditry, and destitution was very real.[26] Given that such themes appear to have been inherited by the Gospel writers (see above), then such emphases were most likely to have been generated (at least in part) by the changes in land use, dislocation and labor in Galilee relating to the rebuilding of Sepphoris and the building of Tiberias, as well as what was happening more broadly in Palestine as a result of the extensive additions to the Jerusalem temple.[27]

In more advanced peasant or agrarian empires and societies, agitation,

---

26. Stegemann and Stegemann, *Jesus Movement*, 112.
27. Crossley, *Jesus and the Chaos*, 68–71.

dissent, and discontent did not always move beyond specific localized concerns. Thus, it has regularly been argued, the dissemination of ideas was often (but not exclusively) due to assistance coming from outside the peasantry, to which we should add similar types in the form of intellectuals or religious specialists.[28] Indeed, Sarah Rollens has argued that the perpetuation of the Jesus movement in Galilee owed much to scribal or administrative "middling" roles in Galilee.[29] Rollens was working with those responsible for collecting Q material, including the shift from the historical Jesus, or rather the earliest perceptions about him. Given that Jesus is far less likely to be understood in the scribal sense, this is also why it is important to think of alternative intellectuals or religious organizers. Here I am developing a heuristic model based on a cross-cultural observation concerning individuals who are authorized to mediate between humanity and the divine.[30] These may be official priestly figures who broadly support the status quo and have official authorization to do so but could also cover those who stand outside the official system and utilize traditions of wealth redistribution to address the material needs of the lower orders. This type of specialist can critique the status quo and its ideological ordering of the world through personal access to divine authority while gaining further authorization from groups with different material interests from the elites. In terms of the first century we may think of bandit leaders or popular prophets like Theudas or John the Baptist, who could envisage a more wide-ranging vision of a new world order beyond localized peasant discontent.

Jesus, too, should be seen in this context, not least because his authority was remembered as coming directly from God and deemed problematic enough for questions to be raised about it (e.g., Mark 1:23–27, 2:10, 3:22–30, 6:1–6, 11:27–33; Matt 12:28//Luke 11:20). But what we also know about the early tradition was that Jesus comes across as a millenarian figure preaching the end of days and a dramatic new vision for the world, which would involve reversals in wealth and privilege. This should be seen as one expected response to the socioeconomic changes taking place in Galilee as he was growing up—in other words, a reaction to changing material interests and class conflicts. This was never realistically going to do much about political power or transform the world in any obvious way. But this very naivety, and the need for dramatic superhuman intervention in the world, points to the enormity of challenging

---

28. A classic treatment is Hilton, "Peasant Society."

29. Rollens, *Framing Social Criticism*.

30. A classic treatment of this issue (which I develop here) is Lenski, *Power and Privilege*, 263–65.

the economic and political system. And this potential points to the possibilities of mobilizing on a broader and more threatening scale, as indeed happened in the revolt again Rome. The changes in Galilee had thrown up issues of millenarianism, divine authority, human authority, dramatic transformation gender, households, wealth, poverty, etc., which would then have to be dealt with in different—sometimes contradictory—ways by the Jesus movement and Christianity. In other words, the economic changes taking place in Galilee should be seen as of importance not only for the emergence of the historical Jesus but also of the movement that would follow in his name.

Concluding Remarks

A cross-cultural understanding of the historical Jesus can help us understand the socioeconomic context of Roman Palestine—and vice versa. Furthermore, discussions of class conflict, tensions over changes in production and land use, and historical change also help us understand longer-term changes and the emergence of a new movement in its own right.

While our scale may be more modest, a parallel can be made with some of the British Marxist historians who attempted to explain the emergence of the emergence of capitalism. Christopher Hill understood the seventeenth-century civil wars as a bourgeois revolution paving the way for longer-term capitalist development. As part of this "revolution," Hill famously gave much attention to radical developments "from below," all of which would have to be dealt with or domesticated.[31] This "world turned upside down" provided a context for unheard-of radical claims concerning democracy, sexuality, theology, God, education, millenarianism, and so on. Hill's work may have long gone out of fashion, but the general point that this "world turned upside down" fed into longer-term changes, suppression, and/or developments in science, theology, literature, politics, democracy, philosophy and so on—all to be taken up in the Enlightenment—remains an important one that is echoed in more recent scholarship.[32] We may similarly think of the emergence of the Jesus movement and later Christianity as owing something to the contexts of chaotic social upheaval. This upheaval contributed to shifts in, and explosions of, ideas and thinking (whether revolutionary, reactionary, creative, culturally bizarre, peaceful, violent, accidental). In turn, these ideas may have huge long-term impacts, be clamped down almost immediately, or have potential unrealized.

31. Hill, *World*.
32. Braddick, *God's Fury, England's Fire*, xxv; Hughes, *Gender and English Revolution*, 2, 29.

This is why it is important to think about the building projects in agrarian societies, like Roman Palestine, and how they contributed to ideas about rich and poor, gender and sexuality, kingdoms and imperialism, and so on, and how they opened up discussions that would ultimately contribute to the development of Christianity as it eventually became the religion of empire. If we want to understand Christian origins, we cannot do so without understanding the socioeconomic situation of Roman Palestine.

Bibliography

Allison, Dale C., Jr. *Constructing Jesus: Memory, Imagination, and History*. London: SPCK, 2010.

———. *Jesus of Nazareth: Millenarian Prophet*. Philadelphia: Fortress, 1998.

Arnal, William E. *The Symbolic Jesus: Historical Scholarship, Judaism and the Con-struction of Contemporary Identity*. London: Equinox, 2005.

Bammel, Ernst, and C. F. D. Moule, eds. *Jesus and the Politics of His Day*. Cambridge: Cambridge University Press, 1984.

Berlin, Andrea M. "Romanization and Anti-Romanization in Pre-Revolt Galilee." In *The First Jewish Revolt: Archaeology, History, and Ideology*, edited by Andrea M. Berlin and J. Andrew Overman, 71–87. London: Routledge, 2002.

Bermejo-Rubio, Fernando. "Jesus and the Anti-Roman Resistance: A Reassessment of the Arguments." *Journal for the Study of the Historical Jesus* 12 (2014) 1–105.

Boer, Roland. "Marxism and the Spatial Analysis of Early Christianity: The Contribution of G. E. M. de Ste. Croix." *Religion* 41 (2011) 411–30.

Boer, Roland, and Christina Petterson. *Time of Troubles: A New Economic Framework for Early Christianity*. Minneapolis: Fortress, 2017.

Bond, Helen K. "Response: Historical Jesus, Epistemic Modesty." Syndicate, Nov. 23, 2015. https://syndicate.network/symposia/theology/jesus-and-the-chaos-of-history/.

———. *The Historical Jesus: A Guide for the Perplexed*. Guides for the Perplexed. London: T&T Clark, 2012.

Borg, Marcus J. *Conflict, Holiness, and Politics in the Teachings of Jesus*. Harrisburg, PA: Trinity, 1998.

———. *Jesus, a New Vision: Spirit, Culture and the Life of Discipleship*. San Francisco: HarperSanFrancisco, 1992.

Bornkamm, Günther. *Jesus of Nazareth*. Translated by Irene McLuskey et al. New York: Harper, 1960.

Braddick, Michael. *God's Fury, England's Fire: A New History of the English Civil Wars*. London: Penguin, 2008.

Brandon, S. G. F. *Jesus and the Zealots*. Manchester: Manchester University Press, 1967.

Carter, Warren. *Matthew and the Margins: A Religious and Socio-Political Reading*. Maryknoll, NY: Orbis, 2000.

Casey, Maurice. *Jesus of Nazareth: An Independent Historian's Account of His Life and Teaching*. London: T&T Clark, 2010.

Cremin, Ciara. *Capitalism's New Clothes: Enterprise, Ethics and Enjoyment in Times of Crisis*. London: Pluto, 2011.

Crossan, John Dominic. *The Birth of Christianity: Discovering What Happened in the Years Immediately after the Execution of Jesus*. Edinburgh: T&T Clark, 1989.

———. *The Historical Jesus: The Life of a Mediterranean Jewish Peasant*. New York: HarperOne, 1993.
Crossley, James G. "The First World War, the Russian Revolution, and the Fate of Social-Scientific Approaches to the New Testament and Christian Origins." Scriptural Traces. In *The First World War and the Mobilization of Biblical Scholarship*, edited by Andrew Mein et al., 225–40. New York: Bloomsbury, 2020.
———. *Jesus and the Chaos of History: Redirecting the Life of the Historical Jesus*. Biblical Reconfigurations. Oxford: Oxford University Press, 2015.
———. *Why Christianity Happened: A Sociohistorical Account of Christian Origins*. Louisville: Westminster John Knox, 2006.
Elliott, Neil. "Jesus, the Temple, and the Crowd: A Way Less Travelled." In *Class Struggle in the New Testament*, edited by Robert J. Myles, 15–52. Minneapolis: Fortress, 2018.
Fiensy, David A. *Jesus the Galilean: Soundings in a First Century Life*. Piscataway, NJ: Gorgias, 2007.
———. *The Social History of Palestine in the Herodian Period: The Land Is Mine*. Lewiston, NY: Mellen, 1991.
Fisher, Mark. *Capitalist Realism: Is There No Alternative?* Winchester, UK: Hunt, 2022.
Fredriksen, Paula. *Jesus of Nazareth, King of the Jews: A Jewish Life and the Emergence of Christianity*. New York: Knopf, 2000.
Frey, Jörg. "Die Apokalyptik als Herausforderung der neutestamentlichen Wissenschaft. Zum Problem: Jesus und die Apokalyptik." In *Apokalyptik als Herausforderung neutestamentlicher Theologie*, edited by Michael Becker and Markus Öhler, 21–94. WUNT 2/214. Tübingen: Mohr Siebeck, 2006.
Freyne, Sean. "Herodian Economics in Galilee: Searching for a Suitable Model." In *Galilee and Gospel: Collected Essays*, 86–113. WUNT 125. Tübingen: Mohr Siebeck, 2000.
———. *Jesus, a Jewish Galilean: A New Reading of the Story*. London: T&T Clark, 2004.
Friesen, Steven J.. "Poverty in Pauline Studies: Beyond the So-Called New Consensus." *JSNT* 26 (2004) 322–61.
Galbraith, Deane. "Interpellation, Not Interpolation: Reconsidering Textual Disunity in Numbers 13–14 as Variant Articulations of a Single Ideology." *Bible & Critical Theory* 10 (2014) 29–48.
Hanson, K. C., and Douglas E. Oakman. *Palestine in the Time of Jesus: Social Structures and Social Conflicts*. 2nd ed. Minneapolis: Fortress, 2008.
Herzog, William R., II. *Prophet and Teacher: An Introduction to the Historical Jesus*. Louisville: Westminster John Knox, 2005.
Hill, Christopher. *The World: Radical Ideas*. London: Temple Smith, 1972.
Hilton, Rodney. *Bond Men Made Free: Medieval Peasant Movements and the English Rising of 1381*. London: Routledge, 2003.
———. "Peasant Society, Peasant Movements and Feudalism in Medieval Europe." In *Rural Protest: Peasant Movements and Social Change*, edited by Henry A. Landsberger, 67–94. London: Palgrave Macmillan, 1974.
Hobsbawm, Eric. *Bandits*. London: Weidenfeld & Nicolson, 1969.
———. "Peasants and Politics." *Journal of Peasant Studies* 1 (1973) 3–22.
———. "Peasant Land Occupations." *Past & Present* (62) 120–52.
———. *Primitive Rebels: Studies in Archaic Forms of Social Movement in the 19th and 20th Centuries*. Manchester: Manchester University Press, 1959.
———. "Social Banditry." In *Rural Protest: Peasant Movements and Social Change*, edited by Henry A. Landsberger, 142–57. London: Palgrave Macmillan, 1974.

Horsley, Richard A. *Jesus and the Spiral of Violence: Popular Jewish Resistance in Roman Palestine*. Philadelphia: Fortress, 1993.
Hughes, Ann. *Gender and the English Revolution*. London: Routledge, 2012.
Jensen, Morten H. "Herod Antipas in Galilee: Friend or Foe of the Historical Jesus?" *Journal for the Study of the Historical Jesus* 5 (2007) 7–32.
———. *Herod Antipas in Galilee: The Literary and Archaeological Sources on the Reign of Herod Antipas and Its Socio-Economic Impact on Galilee*. WUNT 2/215. Tübingen: Mohr Siebeck, 2010.
Kautsky, John H. *The Politics of Aristocratic Empires*. Chapel Hill: University of North Carolina, 1982.
Keith, Chris. *Jesus against the Scribal Elite: The Origins of the Conflict*. Grand Rapids: Baker Academic, 2014.
King, Rebekka. "The Author, the Atheist, and the Academic Study of Religion: Bourdieu and the Reception of Biblical Criticism by Progressive Christians." *BSR* 41 (2012) 14–20.
Lenski, Gerhard E. *Power and Privilege: A Theory of Social Stratification*. New York: McGraw-Hill, 1966.
Loader, William. *Sexuality and the Jesus Tradition*. Grand Rapids: Eerdmans, 2005.
Moxnes, Halvor. *The Economy of the Kingdom: Social Conflict and Economic Relations in Luke's Gospel*. Overtures to Biblical Theology. 1988. Reprint, Eugene, OR: Wipf & Stock, 2004.
———. *Putting Jesus in His Place: A Radical Vision of Household and Kingdom*. Louisville: Westminster John Knox, 2003.
Myles, Robert J. "The Fetish for a Subversive Jesus." *Journal for the Study of the Historical Jesus* 14 (2016) 52–70.
———. *The Homeless Jesus in the Gospel of Matthew*. Sheffield: Sheffield Phoenix, 2014.
Rollens, Sarah E. *Framing Social Criticism in the Jesus Movement: The Ideological Project of the Sayings Gospel Q*. WUNT 2/374. Tübingen: Mohr Siebeck, 2014.
Sanders, E. P. *The Historical Figure of Jesus*. London: Penguin, 1993.
Schüssler Fiorenza, Elisabeth. *In Memory of Her: A Feminist Theological Reconstruction of Christian Origins*. New York: Crossroad, 1983.
Ste. Croix, G. E. M. de. *Class Struggle in the Ancient Greek World: From the Archaic Age to the Arab Conquests*. London: Duckworth, 1981.
Stegemann, Ekkehard W., and Wolfgang Stegemann. *The Jesus Movement: A Social History of Its First Century*. Edinburgh: T&T Clark, 1999.
Wright, N. T. *Jesus and the Victory of God*. Vol. 2 of *Christian Origins and the Question of God*. Philadelphia: Fortress, 1997.
———. *The Resurrection of the Son of God*. Vol. 3 of *Christian Origins and the Question of God*. Minneapolis: Fortress, 2003.

5. Women and Economics in the Roman World

CAROLYN OSIEK

Introduction

The undervaluation of women's labor is a constant in most cultures, not excluding our own. Until recent years, there has been substantial neglect of the acknowledgment of women's participation in the economy and property ownership. To the extent that domestic labor in the context of house and family is expected to be performed only or mostly by women, to the same extent their work will not be measured or valued, even though it is a vital contribution to the economy.

In the study of Mediterranean antiquity, the social sciences have more recently given some attention to cultural factors, but women in economic life remain understudied. Even among traditional economic studies of the Roman world, acknowledgment of the role of gender in the differentiation of work is only slowly being recognized. Some studies have been done on specific populations, but little on overall perspectives.[1]

As is widely recognized, and discussed by Hirth in this series, the ancient economy was embedded in social systems, the three major ones closely entwined with each other: family, religion, and politics. Whether the whole system functioned as a market economy or one closely regulated by political power

---

1. Saller, "Women, Slaves," 185–87. Some examples of study of small groups include Susan Treggiari and Walter Scheidel (Saller, "Women, Slaves," 187n9).

is debated,[2] but its economic life was in some ways highly gender specific, and in other ways, not at all.

Family and Household

The idealized household was the basis of economic life, a center of production as well as consumption, though market expansion and the availability of more and different resources through trade considerably weakened that ideal over time. Though not from the Roman period or setting, the description of the valiant wife in Prov 31 is worth reading to get a sense of how an ancient Mediterranean household was expected to function and the administrative role expected of the mistress of the house, while her husband is occupied with public political life.

Women's traditional work included processing and production of food; weaving, sewing, and production of clothing; birthing and child care; and education of girls for specifically feminine work and roles. See, for example, the exhortation to older women to be educators of younger women to their traditional family roles in Titus 2:3–5.

The idealized Roman family was patriarchal and androcentric in both nuclear and extended units, with senior male authority invested in the one holding *patria potestas* over all women, minor boys, and even adult sons, married householders in their own right. The so-called "household codes" of the New Testament (Col 3:18—4:1, Eph 5:21—6:9, partially 1 Pet 2:18—3:7 and elsewhere) echo this philosophy. This often-expressed ideal of domestic harmony served to reinforce patriarchal dominance over everyone else in the household, and distinguished between the indoor life of the home as the woman's proper sphere, and the outside public life of politics and commerce as the male world (e.g., Philo, *Spec.* 3.169–70). This expressed ideal totally ignored the actual presence of women in so-called public space. For example, the exclusion of women in the public speeches of Peter and Paul in Acts is deliberate. Not only do the speakers address the hearers with the grammatical convention of masculine pronouns for a gender-mixed group, but they begin with the exclusive masculine term *andres*, demonstrating that the ideal of the public sphere as that of men knowingly excludes such women, necessarily present in trade and market, as undeserving of being addressed (e.g., Acts 2:14, 5:35, 7:2, 13:16,

---

2. Temin argues for a market economy, in spite of the prevalence of slavery in the processes of production, because Roman slavery was an open and highly varied system, with high expectation of manumission and, therefore, positive incentive (*Market Economy*, 124–38).

17:22, 22:1). Nevertheless, when helpful to the narrative, women as converts are explicitly mentioned, for example, in Athens, some elite women join the cause (Acts 17:4), and at the end of the speech, a woman named Damaris (Acts 17:34).[3]

As articulated early and often, the security of the state depended on the sacred values of home and hearth: as goes the family, so goes the state—a not unfamiliar argument in more recent times. In reality, wealthy upper-class women had the luxury of not having to be engaged in the daily work of economic survival, but other women were of necessity present in wide areas of public life, contributing to the economy as vendors and in service roles. On the other hand, in Roman urban life, a great deal of both civic political negotiations and economic and business transactions took place in the homes of elite men, what would have been considered, in today's thinking, "private" space. Notions of what was appropriate economic activity for elite families circled around landownership, therefore, farming. By extension, ownership of businesses that remained somehow associated with land were tolerated as acceptable—mining, brick production, etc.—while participation in trade and crafts was considered beneath the dignity of the elite.

Notions of "public" and "private" were complex and not at all like those of the modern West with its separation of business and private life. Issues of property ownership and commercial production were considered part of the "private" sphere, while politics and civic responsibility were "public" activities. Moreover, any attempt to distinguish one from the other was often unclear.[4]

The economics of marriage were not as simple as the idealization. For those adhering to Roman law, traditional Roman marriage *cum manu*, with legal authority over the bride, transferred her and her property from her family of origin to her husband's *familia*, that is, his personal domain, including persons and property. The evidence suggests that this practice went out of customary use in the early empire, replaced by marriage so-called *sine manu*, in which the bride retained membership in her original *familia*, including inheritance rights. This change probably developed to prevent alienation of property owned by a woman's own *familia*, otherwise lost to it with dowry in marriage. The result was the odd arrangement by which the bride lived in a different social unit, that of her husband, than the one in which she was socially and financially embedded,

---

3. Many years ago, a Greek guide with whom I was talking at the Areopagus assumed that Damaris was a prostitute, probably what the contemporary local church thought of her for being out and about in the public space of the Areopagus.

4. Savunen, "Women in Urban Texture," 1–3; Osiek et al., *Woman's Place*, 3–4; Cooper, "Closely Watched Household."

her family of origin. At the same time, however, she obtained greater economic autonomy over her own property brought into the marriage, because it did not belong to her husband. In practice, therefore, in many functioning family units, women held a great deal of economic power, especially as owners of property brought into the marriage. Wife and husband were not supposed to will property to each other, since it was meant to stay in their own *familia*. In practice, however, this stricture was often ignored.

Roman laws about marriage and property rights directly affected those with Roman citizenship, which was certainly an increasing number as generations moved on in the early empire, because of wide practices of manumission. Nevertheless, the majority of marriages were probably not legal Roman marriages of two Roman citizens (*justum connubium*), but *concubinatus*, marriages of noncitizens, recognized as marriage for most purposes, following local customs and other marriage traditions. To what extent non-Roman citizens observed Roman marriage laws and customs is unknown. Later Constantinian legislation, in the interest of Christian teaching on the indissolubility of marriage, sought to return to the unification of property in marriage under male control. The result in those later years was some loss of property rights and control for married women.

The ideal household in the surviving literature is that articulated in the New Testament household codes: father, mother, children, and slaves, all under the control of the *paterfamilias*. In the census records of Roman Egypt, however, more information about living situations is preserved than from anywhere else, and the purpose of the census is economic: taxation. In preserved records, a household (*oikia*) can be a conjugal couple with or without children, a group of multiple or extended families, unmarried siblings, single parent with children, or even a solitary person.[5] Though the typicality of Egyptian information for elsewhere in the empire is debated,[6] household organizations like these are probably reflective of the wider situation. Life expectancy in Roman Egypt hovered in the mid-twenties when the high rate of infant mortality was factored in; in the low forties for those who survived to age five.[7] Marriage patterns at first marriage were generally of older men, in their late twenties, marrying younger

---

5. Bagnall and Frier, *Demography of Roman Egypt*, 57–66.

6. Bagnall and Frier, *Demography of Roman Egypt*, 171–73. Their general conclusion is affirmative.

7. Bagnall and Frier, *Demography of Roman Egypt*, 87–90. Thirty-five percent of female deaths occur under one year old. Excluding those under five years old, the average is 42.4 years. These numbers closely resemble the results from other studies elsewhere, particularly imperial Rome, where there is enough surviving funerary information to study.

women in their late teens. This information from Egypt matches what is known elsewhere, especially from the funerary inscriptions of the city of Rome.

Women as Household Managers

Throughout the period, women of higher social status held a good deal of authority in their own household and were expected to exercise it. The common model is of the conscientious and capable household manager as *custos*, who sees to all the servile population and their work, while her husband is abroad or at least out of the house, occupied in civic responsibilities. The model usually presumes careful and benevolent supervision by the husband, older and more experienced but not directly involved. Responsibilities of the wife include care of children, oversight of food production and acquisition, and all the other economic aspects of the well-functioning household, as well as personnel management of the slave members of the household and looking to their welfare, including explicitly the care of sick slaves. For example, Xenophon's *Oeconomicus*, read by such later figures as Cicero, Philodemus, and Galen, instructs the young husband how to instruct his even younger wife in household management. Indirectly, it lays out the responsibilities expected of wife managers. This arrangement is reflected in such New Testament sources as 1 Tim 5:14 and Titus 2:4–5, where young widows are to remarry and be good household administrators. In spite of the difference in age and status between husband and wife, such manuals often speak of a partnership (*koinōnia* or *societas*) between the two, all the while upholding the traditional subordination of wife to husband.[8]

While the idea in household treatises is that the teaching on household management comes from husband to wife, in reality the practical aspects of running a household devolved upon women and would have been taught by mothers to daughters. These treatises of male-centered ideals nevertheless reveal not only expectations of wife managers but actual responsibilities. The models all presume a nuclear family with a slave household, an *oikia* in Greek or *familia* in Latin. As we have seen, the census records from Egypt, the only place where such records have been preserved to any number, suggest that the nuclear family is not the only social grouping that qualifies as a household for census purposes, and this probably reflects actual demography more realistically. Women were managers not only of the nuclear household (*oikia*) with

---

8. Other examples include Ps.-Aristotle, *Oeconomica*; the Pythagorean Letters; and Plutarch, *Advice*. See discussion in Osiek et al., *Woman's Place*, 144–52; Saller, "Women, Slaves," 190.

husband in charge, but also of their own households as head, especially in cases of widowhood without remarriage. One famous example from the elite classes known from the literature is Cornelia mother of the Gracchi, who in widowhood refused remarriage and was heavily involved in the education and political advancement of her sons, then withdrew to her private villa, where she invited guests of her choice. Another example is Ummidia Quadratilla, known to Pliny the Younger, who did not approve of the way she ran her household and chose the dinner entertainment (Pliny, *Ep.* 7.24.5).

This demographic reality has been closely studied in recent years from the perspective of early Jesus groups who would have met for their sacred meals and other rituals in domestic settings. Some sources portray women leading a variety of different religious rituals, both at home and in other venues.[9] Such New Testament passages as those naming Phoebe (Rom 16:2–3) and other women leaders in Rom 16, and the narrative of the householder Lydia (Acts 16), suggest that they are independent leaders of their households. Some references explicitly acknowledge a household (*oikos*) belonging to them, e.g., Nympha[10] (Col 4:15) and Tavia (Ign. *Smyrn.* 13.2).[11] The marital status of women disciples in the Gospels is not very clear. Only Joanna (Luke 8:3) and Mary wife of Clopas (John 19:25) are clearly identified as married, yet it is generally said of the group of women in the Gospels that they provided *diakonia* for the group of disciples, in this context, material support and maybe more; see below (Matt 27:55, Mark 15:41, Luke 8:3).

Women as Property Owners, and in Trades and Crafts

In the case of the majority of inhabitants, those who earned their living by trades and crafts, entire modest households worked together, male and female, free and slave alongside each other. The missionary couple Prisca and Aquila are examples of husband and wife working together in a craft and trade. It is not necessarily to be supposed that they were the only ones in their workshop. Indeed, Paul joins them at some points, but they may have had other free or

---

9. Many good examples in Alikin, who cites examples of women in religious leadership roles in their own homes ("Women as Leaders," 222–28).

10. This name could possibly be masculine, or the pronouns altered to be understood as masculine (Alikin, "Women as Leaders," 229–30).

11. Careful reading of the sources suggests that the main location of meetings of Jesus followers would have been in private houses, though certainly other venues were used (Adams, *Earliest Christian Meeting Places*; Oakes, "Nine Types of Church"). Last and Harland cite evidence of *collegia* meeting in storehouse, stable, room in a temple, and rented movable locations (*Group Survival*, 78).

slave helpers working alongside them (Acts 18:1–3). In cases in which husband and father was present in the household, surviving documentation usually focuses on him. Likewise, funerary commemorations that specify the craft or trade of the deceased will name the man alone, even though his wife was just as involved in the business.[12]

Yet there is sufficient evidence of independent women owners and managers of businesses such as brick manufacturing, perfume production, weaving and selling material, for example, and others attested, some from one very well-preserved site, Pompeii, to show that women were also involved in buying and selling property and running trade and businesses, participating independently in the economy. Some estimate that Roman women may have owned as much as 40 percent of property.[13]

The wealthy freeborn son of a freedman, Lucius Caecilius Iucundus, was an *argentarius*, a sales agent or auctioneer in Pompeii. Among his 153 business records for private customers, fifteen women had hired him for sixteen different property sales, including the sale of slaves. Women recorded loans to one another with contract restrictions and objects left as security, in one case a pair of earrings.[14]

Freeborn Julia Felix owned a property complex near the amphitheater in Pompeii that included two possible single residences (*domus*), a garden with pond and elegant dining rooms (*cenacula*), a bath complex (*balneum*), and a food shop and dining area (*taberna*). At the time of the eruption, she was leasing out various parts of it for a period of up to five years, and may have been living with a small household in one of the residential units. She independently rented or leased parts of her property for profit.

Two women of Pompeii, Vibia and Caesia Helpis, were in production and sale of both fish sauce (*garum*) and wine. Gavia Severa was apparently a producer and merchant of perfume, an *unguentaria*; six amphorae with ingredients for perfume bore inscriptions with her name in house VII.7.5 at Pompeii. Other women seem also to have been involved in the wine trade, as attested by amphorae bearing their names. Another woman named Laturnia Januaria was a *calcaria*, of unsure meaning but having something to do with production and/or sale of lime or plaster. Holconia and Attia Calliste operated a brick factory that produced brick stamps bearing both of their names; Holconia probably belonged to one of the leading families, and Attia Calliste may have been

12. Lovén, "Women, Trade, and Production."
13. Cooper, "Closely Watched Household," 6.
14. Savunen, "Women in Urban Texture," 72.

her freedwoman.[15] Lydia, the merchant of purple cloth (*porphuropōlis*)[16] in Philippi, can be understood in this context (Acts 16:14–15, 40). As with many both men and women in the same situations, her house was a center of both production and circulation of goods. Some of the women known from these Pompeian inscriptions were probably freedwomen. Their particular social situation and their contribution to the economy will be discussed below.

Elsewhere, for example, first-century Antiochis of Tlos in Lycia erected her own statue of herself with recognition of the city's gratitude for her medical arts. Eutychias of second-century Mysia self-identified as one of the fullers, the business of cleaning wool garments, and provided from her own funds a tomb for herself, her parents, and her children, with no mention of a husband.[17]

Trade and religious associations of merchants and craft people (*thiasoi, eranoi, collegia*) have long been studied for their similarity to early groups of Jesus followers. Voluntary members contributed regular donations to a common fund for mutual benefit, including a regular common meal, religious ritual, and often provision of funds for burial. These groups had definite elements in common with what we know of early Jesus groups, and have long been studied with this in mind. The evidence for participation of women in such groups is thin but not unknown. Some such groups, known by their monuments and inscriptions, list no women among their members, but others do include small numbers of women. In the few cases where there is only one, it is possible that she is not a regular member, but the patron of the organization (for more on women patrons, see below). However, in the forty-four associations listed in one study on women in the associations, in the period first century BCE to third century CE, nineteen had some women on their membership list. All the women are listed in their own name, not as wives of male members. In two cases, membership is 100 percent female; probably there the religious devotion, not a common trade, draws them together, though it is not impossible that they also share a trade or craft. In others, female membership ranges from a small number to nearly half. Whatever drew the male members seems also to have drawn the female ones on the same terms.[18]

An occupation with economic impact that was predominantly female

---

15. Savunen, "Women in Urban Texture," 80–95, 102; Osiek, "Growing Up Female," 10, 17–19.

16. Either the very expensive fabric made from murex shells and affordable only by the wealthy, or a plant-based dark color that was easier to produce and less expensive—or both.

17. Bain, *Women's Socioeconomic Status*, 72–74.

18. Last and Harland, *Group Survival*, 189–92.

was prostitution. It is not clear to what extent free women participated, though certainly they did, presumably self-employed, joining the classes of women considered to be without honor. Prostitutes were forbidden to wear the *stola*, the formal dress of the honorable matron. Many workers in prostitution, however, were enslaved. The sources do not allow an adequate whole assessment of their legal status. Another role with economic consequences was performed uniquely by women: wet nursing. Male physicians debated the benefits of mothers nursing their own children, which was regarded as virtuous, yet apparently, many were not willing or able. Working slave mothers may have been sent back to work prematurely. Male authors satirize freeborn women who do not wish to be so limited for such a long time. Tacitus, for one, lamented that the practice of nursing one's own baby was becoming something of the past (*Dialogue* 28:4–5). While extended households may frequently have had someone on staff to do it, wet nursing was also something of a business, regulated by contracts. Such documents usually specify a limited time, ranging from six months to three years, during which time the wet nurse was under contract not to engage in sexual intercourse so as not to become pregnant. Not only did free women hire out in this role, but slave women were also contracted out by their slaveholders, with little choice in the matter. Some discussions in the medical sources favor someone with a larger frame and medium-sized breasts, and a preference for a well-educated Greek-speaking woman so that the baby will be sensitized to learn good Greek.[19]

Enslaved Women

Enslaved women appear and are taken for granted in the New Testament. They are among the enslaved household members who are to obey their master as to the Lord (Col 3:22–25, Eph 6:5–8). They are among slaves who are bidden to suffer in silence even when beaten (1 Pet 2:18–25). They also appear as characters: the *paidiskē* (girl) of the high priest's household staff who recognizes Peter in the passion narrative (Matt 26:69–71, Mark 14:66–69, Luke 22:56, John 18:17); the housemaid Rhoda in the house of Mary, mother of John Mark, who conforms to the stereotype of the "running slave" (Acts 12:13–15); and especially the unnamed slave woman with more than one owner (perhaps business partners or a couple) whose gift of prophecy is lucrative for them until Paul exorcises her (Acts 16:16–18). Not to be forgotten is the wife of the indebted steward who will be sold along with him and their children if his master does not have mercy (Matt 18:25).

19. Osiek et al., *Woman's Place*, 64–65, 100.

Roman society was heavily invested in slavery, and the extent to which this institution affected the economy is debated but was certainly significant. Slavery was widely, though not exclusively, used in mines, construction, and agriculture. In the kinds of urban, mostly domestic, slavery that concern us here, there was strong motivation on the part of the enslaved to perform well in order to advance toward manumission. Closely studied inscriptional evidence indicates a high expectation of manumission around age thirty, or by testamentary action of a deceased slaveholder, in a society in which life expectancy was not high. Additionally, some slaves were able, probably by conducting a small business on the side, to accumulate a modest amount of money, known as a *peculium*, toward the purchase of freedom.[20]

Most evidence indicates a preponderance of males in the enslaved population, for a number of reasons: abandonment of unwanted children probably left more girls than boys to die, and heavy labor in agriculture, mining, trade, and construction favored males. Even the preponderant evidence for household staff, other than private attendants to women, is of males. This would pose problems for maintaining an adequate slave population; without enough females, the numbers could not be maintained, and projected models presume a continual new supply from military conquest and other sources, including abandonment and rescue of newborns. By contrast, two-thirds of listed slaves in the Egyptian census records are female. A different pattern of practice in Egypt is unlikely. This difference may mean that the Egyptian records reflect more accurately actual household practice.[21]

Most large households encouraged female slaves to reproduce. The many years that it takes to raise children to an age to be able to contribute by their labor was an economic disadvantage, perhaps outweighed by the social advantage of familiarity and loyalty instilled in the *verna*, the household slave raised in the same *familia*, by contrast to the difficulties of socializing newly enslaved adults into the household. Slaves often lived in their own family groups, as evidenced by epitaphs that describe their relationships. Though slaves could not legally marry, they still often used marital terms for each other in their funerary commemorations. This presupposes some kind of stable family life for many, though of course they could be separated at any time by the will of

20. One enslaved woman of Pisidia, Auxilia, slave of Telemachos, was even able to build a tomb for her two sons from her *peculium*. She was still a slave when she dedicated it. This is undoubtedly not an isolated example (Bain, *Women's Socioeconomic Status*, 155).

21. The sources of slaves are much debated. For further references to the general discussion, see Osiek et al., *Woman's Place*, 100, 217; Saller, "Women, Slaves," 188n10. On Egypt, Bagnall and Frier, *Demography of Roman Egypt*, 48–49, 71.

the slaveholder. The very fact that many could afford these commemorations while still being slaves suggests an interesting complex of financial relationships between slaves and slaveholders.

In keeping with the usual discounting of women's labor, the work of the slave woman, the *ancilla*, the Latin equivalent of the Greek *paidiskē*, is frequently not taken seriously in Roman literature. Female slaves are usually classified as slaves who do not work. All the domestic work of food processing, child rearing, and house management was done primarily by female slaves, and simply not counted as true labor. *Ancillae* attending the mistress of the house were considered not working, though the *materfamilias* of an elite household was expected to be surrounded by a bevy of attendants, each with a distinct role in her clothing, coiffure, and makeup. In spite of the wide evidence for women owning and conducting certain kinds of businesses, the available information suggests in general a gendered pattern of those occupations that are more likely to feature slave, freed, and freeborn working side by side. Domestic service and "skilled service" dominate for women.[22]

Prostitution, legally recognized and controlled by urban authorities, engaged both slave and free, in what balance it is impossible to know. The bodies of slaves, as well as their marketable skills, belonged to the slaveholder, who was free to use them as he or she wished. Hiring out a slave in a brothel was a source of income. Since slaves were considered to be without honor, there was little social stigma attached, though sometimes a contract for the sale of a female slave specifies that she cannot be used for prostitution. Both female and male prostitutes were available, though by far the majority were female.

A further ramification of the presumed lack of honor for slaves was that, aside from the economic aspects of formal prostitution, slaves were vulnerable to sexual exploitation, either by their owners or by anyone to whom the owner granted access. Violation of a slave without the owner's permission was a transgression of property rights. The children of female slaves followed the legal status of their mother, so no matter what the legal status of the father, a slave mother produced a slave child: an economic gain for the woman's master or mistress. Sexual use of slaves carried no particular ethical disapproval except in circles like that of the Stoic Musonius Rufus, not because of the rights or feelings of the slave, but because he rejects the double standard by which the freeborn adult male can indulge but would not tolerate the same from his wife. Even this consideration is rare in ancient thinking. In view of this general

---

22. Perry, *Gender, Manumission*, 43–51; Saller, "Women, Slaves," 193–95, drawing on work of Treggiari and Joshel.

presumption in the Roman world, it is not clear how those who joined the Jesus groups in the cities of the empire would have understood expressions of the expectation of chastity (e.g., 1 Thess 4:3–7; 1 Cor 6:13–20, 7:1–7), over against exhortations to slaves to "obey your masters in all things" (Eph 6:5–8, Col 3:22–25, 1 Tim 6:1–2, Titus 2:9–10, 1 Pet 2:18–25). Would sexual exploitation of one's own slave, not generally disapproved of, be included or not?

Most attention in this research goes to the urban setting, and far less is known about rural life. Certainly there were free small farmers, but also large estates owned by the elite. There, mostly slaves worked the fields. Treatises on agriculture meant for these elites give only passing reference to female slaves. Employment of women in direct agricultural work was limited, but not unknown. More common was "indoor" work of domestic service that kept the estate functioning, though perhaps at times of greatest demand, such as the harvest, all who were capable joined in the field work. It is uncertain to what extent stereotypical gender roles would be applied. In his treatises on agriculture, Columella discusses the role of the *vilicus*, the slave supervisor of the agricultural work. In book 12, he gives a description of his wife, the *vilica*, her ideal qualities and her responsibilities. Her role is to supervise the work of the house and to care for sick members of the household, the *familia*. She is responsible for stores and supplies of everything needed by the rest. Her role is therefore fairly well described, but all the female workers whom she supervises, who carry on the whole domestic infrastructure, are taken for granted. For those who have read some of the Greek and Roman treatises on household management, much of this sounds familiar. There, it is the wife of the male householder who has these responsibilities. Here, the author snipes at the *matron*, wife of the estate owner, as incapable of doing this work because of her indolence.[23] Such treatises by elite estate owners are of course idealized. To what extent on actual estates the *materfamilias* carried out these responsibilities herself, and to what extent the *vilica* was the real person in charge, no doubt varied, but the unusual attention given by the author to this role suggests that the responsible, capable *vilica* was critical.

Most of the literature that contains information about slaves and slaveholders, including the household codes of the New Testament, assumes male slaveholders of both male and female slaves. It should not be forgotten that this is not about two distinct classes of persons, owners and slaves. Rather, the whole system was very flexible. Freed persons could and did become slaveholders, and

23. Perry, *Gender, Manumission*, 48–52; Saller, "Women, Slaves," 197–99, on Columella, *De re rustica* 12.1–6.

then patrons of their freed slaves. Women were equally slaveholders of both male and female slaves, and then patrons of their freed slaves. The opening line of the second-century Christian composition the Shepherd of Hermas situates the social status of the male writer: he was an abandoned child fostered and raised as a slave by an unnamed man, who then sold him to a woman named Rhoda in Rome. In the next line, he restores his relationship with her after many years, implying that he was later freed by someone else, as he would have remained in necessary connection with her as her freedman (Herm. Vis. 1:1). He is a freedman at the time of writing, for he has his own household (*oikos*), with wife and grown children.

Freedwomen

The Roman institution of slavery was relatively "open," at least for those enslaved in urban and domestic contexts, that is, the possibility of manumission to become freed persons with or without full Roman citizenship,[24] was relatively high, so high in fact that in the early years of the reign of Augustus, a series of laws were enacted, some of them regarding marriage and others on the process of manumission. The Lex Aelia Sentia of 4 CE prohibited a slave from being manumitted under the age of thirty, and an owner to manumit below the age of twenty—a good indication that manumissions were happening on a large scale. The exception, however, was manumission of a female slave *matrimonii causa*, to be married to her former owner. This, too, seems to have been happening widely; the allowance for marriage at a lower age would encourage the birthing of more citizens.

That there was anxiety about low birthrates among citizens is also suggested by another law, the Lex Pappia Poppaea of 9 CE that gave freedom from *tutela*[25] to freeborn women who produced three children that survived to one year of age, and to freedwomen who produced four. In the same spirit a few years later, the agriculturist Columella reported that he gave exemption from work to a slave mother of three children, and manumission to one who had

---

24. Laws about the status of freed persons are complicated; see Perry, *Gender, Manumission*, 53–67.

25. A legal restriction on minors meant for their protection, requiring the consent of the guardian (*tutor*) for business transactions that would affect family property; extended in theory to all adult women, considered to be perpetual minors needing guardians. Because a woman's property came from her own *familia*, not that of her husband, the guardian was usually a male member of her family of origin. Little is known about how it may have functioned—or not—when women owned and operated businesses.

more than three.[26] These regulations reveal a number of things. One is concern about low levels of population in the empire at that time. Another is the casualness with which *tutela* of adult women seems to have been taken at this point, that dropping it could be a reward for childbearing. It must not have been taken very seriously in the general population, perhaps only in the case of wealthy elites with much property to lose for their family of origin. The requirement that the children still be alive at one year is indication of the high levels of infant mortality across the population.

In this society that valued female honor in the form of sexual propriety, the freedwoman (*liberta*) was in a complicated situation. She had come from slavery, where no honor was to be attributed to her and she was, as it were, free for the taking, within the limits of a slaveholder's property rights. Now she was part of the free female population, about which there were some expectations with regard to honor, critical for her reputation. If properly manumitted by a Roman citizen, she was fully a citizen before the law, included among the *matres familias*, respectable matrons, yet she was held in suspicion in freeborn society because of her origins, and, along with her freedman counterparts, socially questionable. In much of the literature, freedmen and freedwomen are considered second-class citizens.[27] Only in the next generation would society to some extent forget their servile origins.

Though clearly not a middle class in modern terms in this highly stratified society, yet the social group of freedmen and freedwomen with newly acquired Roman citizenship was the most upwardly mobile group in the imperial population. They were not hindered by elite prejudices about the appropriateness of banking and business. Some became quite wealthy and were deeply resented by traditional landed elites with their vast properties and little economic agility. Petronius's famous character Trimalchio in the *Satyricon* is the satire of this situation: exaggeratedly wealthy but hopelessly ignorant of what is expected of the educated and refined gentleman. The first freed generation were not eligible to participate in local elected magistracies, but by the second generation, servile origins were often forgotten or brushed aside. Nevertheless, some imperial freedmen rose to powerful positions, for example, Narcissus and Pallas, freedmen of Claudius. Pallas's brother Felix, as procurator of Judea, appears in Acts 23–25. Paul in Acts contrasts his Roman citizenship by birth with the military tribune in Jerusalem who purchased his freedom (Acts 22:27–28).

Freed persons were not completely independent, however. The former

---

26. *De re rustica* 1.8.19. From what kind of work she is exempted is not clear.
27. Perry, *Gender, Manumission*, 9–22, 131–33.

owner was now patron and *tutor* to the freedwoman, in a society that relied on patronage for its social functions. While the specifics of patronage at large in the society were voluntary, the patronage relationship of freed to former owner was codified by law. The freed person owed two things to his or her patron, summed up by modern scholars as *obsequium et operae*.[28] The former could be understood as loyalty and support, especially in time of possible need. The latter meant a certain amount of free labor owed to the patron, agreed upon in the document of manumission. The law specified that in the case of freedwomen, such work could not be anything degrading or that would compromise their dignity, for example, prostitution.

Not all marriages of newly freed women were to their former owner, however. Such marriages could happen with anyone other than members of the senatorial class. Sometimes a slave couple from the same household, for example, having been manumitted, would marry, now able to produce freeborn children and to acquire property that could be willed to them. In cases in which a freedwoman married someone other than her patron, a conflict of loyalty would ensue; she owed it to two different men, often with deep affection for both. This conflict is apparent in some funerary commemorations.[29]

It is not known how many female slaves gained their freedom and went on to pursue business interests. The predominant occasions in which manumission might be expected for a female slave were testamentary manumissions in the will of a deceased slaveholder, or marriage with her previous owner. Inscriptional evidence indicates that such marriages of slave woman with male slaveholder were not unusual, and not particularly frowned upon for citizens below the senatorial class. Manumission for marriage in the other direction, of male slave and female slaveholder, was not so common and not readily accepted socially, reflecting a common pattern of gender prejudice, by which a woman marrying up was regarded favorably but a man marrying a woman of a higher social status was not.

There is some evidence of "sacral" manumissions, by which a slave was freed in a temple by a fictive transfer of ownership to the god who resided there. This practice probably provided some income to the temple. The custom seems to have been taken up by both Judeans and Jesus followers as well. For example,

28. For details of the legal discussion, see Perry, *Gender, Manumission*, 69–95.

29. In the inscriptions of the city of Rome in the imperial period, strong majorities (seventy-one of eighty-two) of freedwomen commemorating both patron and husband (two different men) put patron first. In their descriptions of themselves, strong majorities (seventy-six of ninety) identify themselves first as freedwoman of their patron, then as wife (Perry, *Gender, Manumission*, 96–128).

the first-century enslaved woman Helpis was one of four slaves manumitted in a synagogue in the Bosporus; she is to be free of any claim by the manumitters' heirs, but must remain under the guardianship of the community. In Ign. *Pol.* 4.3, the recipient is exhorted not to let slaves expect to be freed at community expense, suggesting that this has become a custom in communities of Jesus followers, but not one of which Ignatius approved.[30]

Because so much information has been preserved from the city of Rome, attention tends to focus there, but all urban centers had similar dynamics. Because of the open practice of manumission, numbers of Roman citizens and other freed persons were present in all of them, and therefore in communities of Jesus followers. Lydia of Acts 16, a seemingly independent merchant of dyed cloth with her own household, fits the pattern. Her name is that of a geographical area in the province of Asia, far from where she presides. She is most likely thought to be a freedwoman with a successful business of her own.

Women Participants in the Patronage System

The practice of patronage in the Roman world can be understood as an informal, unequal relationship involving reciprocal exchange and responsibilities for the benefit of both parties. Except for the formal legal arrangements that ensued from manumission, discussed above, it was voluntary in the sense that it was an informal social relationship not prescribed by law. That is not to say that often it probably arose out of economic necessity or need for social connections on the part of the client.

Women as well as men exercised their power of patronage. One of the most important levels of patronage involved politics and political appointments. From this system, women were excluded as direct participants. They did not participate in the *cursus honorum* of appointment to the highest civic offices. Women were not eligible for elected local public offices, nor did they have the power of vote for those offices. Their indirect influence, however, could be wielded even there through their exercise of social and economic power. Every patronage relationship had at least some economic aspect. Clients expected direct gifts from their patrons, and it was essential to the role of patron to act with generosity and even largesse toward one's clients. Clients also expected access to economic as well as social advantages through the power and connections of their patrons. The exercise of patronage was intricately linked to the smooth running of the economy.

30. Bain, *Women's Socioeconomic Status*, 100–165.

One of the intriguing examples of direct political pressure exerted by women was their participation as *rogatores* in *programmata*, public endorsement of candidates running for civil office in the city, still to be seen on the walls of Pompeii. There is no reason to think this form of public endorsement was unique to Pompeii, only that, thanks to the unique way in which the city was destroyed, the information has been preserved there. Though these endorsements have long been studied, there is little consensus on context. We do not know, for example, if they were posted only on one's own property or elsewhere, who paid for them, or what was the relationship between endorser and endorsed. For the most part, endorsers are otherwise unknown now; they are not the elites or known leaders of the city, whose names appear frequently on dedicatory inscriptions. Of the surviving endorsements, 14.5 percent are by women alone, while 16 percent of the total are done by more than one person, and some also include women. One possibility is that they reflect ongoing patronage relationships, from either direction; the endorser may be patron or client of the endorser.[31] They may be in some cases the exercise of *obsequium* by freed persons to their patron. The endorsers are for the most part not known to be distinguished figures; in fact, three were probably barmaids.[32] While most of the endorsing women in these graffiti are certainly not otherwise socially powerful figures in the city, women would not have engaged in such endorsements if their endorsements were not judged to be credible and effective.

In some cities, especially in Roman Asia Minor, women held titles of appointed civic office and public priesthoods. In previous scholarship, it was often assumed that men who held the same offices actually exercised their power, but for women the titles were purely honorary. A better conclusion is that these positions were often honorary, equally for men and women, and that there is no reason to assume a double standard. For example, one of the principal duties of a public priest was to offer sacrifice at civic rituals, often of a large animal such as an ox. The rather naïve supposition was that a woman would not have the strength to make the kill. But of course, elite males did not engage in the direct killing, either, leaving that to lesser agents, probably slaves. The priest or priestess presided over the ritual.

While gender roles remained a source of discrimination for women, higher status prevailed. Status spoke more loudly than gender. A higher-status woman, especially a wealthy one with available resources, could have access to more social and economic power than a lower-status man. Whether man or

31. Savunen, "Women in Urban Texture," 34–47.
32. Savunen, "Women in Urban Texture," 41.

woman, public lavishness was expected of the wealthy. One of the most frequent examples of this kind of patronage by women was sponsorship of public works. Mamia, from a leading family of Pompeii and a public priestess, built a temple in the city *sua pecunia*, from her own money, and was buried at city expense in a prominent place outside the Herculaneum Gate because of her civic benefaction.[33] In Casinum, not far from Rome, Ummidia Quadratilla, already mentioned above as an independent household leader, was commemorated by her town for building its amphitheater and temple *sua pecunia*. The widow Atalante of Termessos in Pisidia was honored by her city for her public gifts and priesthoods and for providing grain to the people in time of need; for all this, the city awarded her a bronze statue and a gold crown.[34]

Claudia Metrodora in mid-first century on the island of Chios was both a Roman citizen and a citizen of Chios. She was commemorated with three civic decrees for providing public banquets and public baths. Though born illegitimate, she was adopted by a prominent citizen and became very involved with a leading family. She held the title of *agōnothetēs* (president and defrayer of expenses for the public games), *gymnasiarch* (superintendant of training of athletes), twice *stephanephoros* (crown bearer, one of the highest civic honors), and *basileia* of the federation of thirteen Ionian cities. Her brother Claudius Phesinus was a prominent contemporary figure in Ephesos.[35]

Tata of second-century Aphrodisias was priestess for life of Hera and twice of the imperial cult. Like Claudia Metrodora, she once held the rank of *stephanephoros*, one of the highest civic honors, and provided oil for athletes and banquets for the public with entertainment, importing the best performers in the region. Yet she is hailed in the inscription for her appreciation of the traditional feminine virtues of honor and chastity.[36]

Like Claudia Metrodora, Junia Theodora of first-century Corinth appears to have been a Roman citizen of Greek heritage. She held multiple citizenships of Rome, Corinth, and at least one city in Lycia, part of the Roman province of Asia. Though she apparently resided in Corinth, she was honored in Lycia as civic patron. Her patronage in Corinth took the form of individual assistance for citizens of her home region. Reinscribed on a single funerary stele, found in secondary use near Corinth, were five public attestations. The assembly of Lycians had bestowed on her a gold crown, and the cities of Myra,

33. Savunen, "Women in Urban Texture," 52–63.
34. Bain, *Women's Socioeconomic Status*, 112–15.
35. Kearsley, "Women in Public Life," 198–201.
36. Alikin, "Women as Leaders," 226–27.

Patara, and Telmessos had also honored her. More significantly, the Lycian *koinon* in Corinth, the assembly or organization of Lycian emigrants there, had honored her for her *prostasia*, leadership and patronage. They expressed their gratitude for the ways in which she sheltered Lycian refugees, assisted them in personal and business affairs, and used her influence on their behalf with Roman officials. The key position of Corinth for trade between the Roman East and Italy prompted the formation of groups of resident aliens for business purposes, and Junia Theodora was in an ideal position to benefit and provide mutual benefit to her fellow Lycians. There is no reference to any family connections in the information about her in the inscriptions. Her heir was one Sextus Julius, otherwise unknown. She seems to have been an independent and sufficiently wealthy woman to perform this function.[37]

These are some of many examples of the ways in which women in the Roman world participated in and contributed to economic life outside the domestic sphere.

Another frequent form of patronage by women as well as men was of private associations, whether commercial or religious. One such woman from a leading Pompeian family is well known to anyone who studies the people of Pompeii. Eumachia, a public priestess, was also patron of the fullers' guild. Her father was probably the Lucius Eumachius known as an exporter of wine from amphora stamps in many areas of the Mediterranean. In her own name and that of her minor son, Numistrius Fronto, she erected for the fullers at her own expense, a gallery, portico, and cryptoporticus on the front of their building in a prominent location in the forum, and dedicated them herself to *Concordia* and *Pietas Augusti*, demonstrating her loyalty to Roman authority. In gratitude, they erected a statue of her in the building. It depicts her as a matron with right hand on the *stola* in which she is wrapped, in the traditional gesture of female modesty. Eumachia was mistress of a large household in Pompeii and built an extensive funerary monument, the largest tomb complex in Pompeii for the members of her *familia*, including slaves and freed persons, outside the Nucerian Gate, on one of the roads leading into the city. Yet while her whole household were buried there, she herself was given civic honors and buried elsewhere, in a tomb paid for by the city, just outside the Herculaneum Gate.[38]

37. Kearsley, "Women in Public Life," 191–98. These and other examples in Bain, *Women's Socioeconomic Status*, 97–117; Osiek et al., *Woman's Place*, 194–219.

38. Osiek et al., *Woman's Place*, 204–5. Provision of burial space for the extended household was of key importance, and in succeeding centuries, for Christians it would later take the form of developing such burial complexes by extension for members of the church community. The beginnings of several Roman catacombs bear the names of the original female

This pattern of patronage extended to religious associations. Pompeia Agrippinilla was priestess and patron of a large Dionysiac group of worshipers near Rome, who dedicated a statue to her. Sergia Paulina hosted a burial society in her house in Rome. Patronage of religious groups included synagogues. Tation in second-century Smyrna was rewarded for her synagogue patronage with a gold crown and a seat of honor. Rufina, also in Smyrna, held the title *archisynagōgos*, leader of the synagogue, a title held by a number of others, both male and female, in the synagogue inscriptions across the area.[39]

The Galilean women who provided funds for Jesus and his disciples did something similar (Luke 8:2–3, Mark 15:40–41, Matt 27:55–56). Modern art and biblical interpretation tend to cast them as faithful followers, completely dependent on Jesus. In reality, they were funders of the mission, without whose patronage the movement could not have continued. While some may have had immense gratitude to Jesus for favors received, for example, Mary Magdalene healed of some kind of mental anguish (Luke 8:2), it was not their dependence on him but his on them that meant that the group of disciples could keep going.

In this context are to be found other female figures in positions of patronage in the first years of the Jesus movement. Chloe of 1 Cor 1:11 was a head of household, some of whose members belonged to the Jesus group and sent a report to Paul of dissent in the local groups. She probably was not a follower herself, since the reference in 1 Corinthians does not include her, but only unnamed others who are associated with her. Hers is probably an example of a householder with members, both those related by blood or marriage and those enslaved and freed, who belong to the *familia*.

Later, Ignatius, on his way to his destiny in Rome, names two women of Smyrna, Tavia and Alce, sending greetings to the household (*oikos*) of Tavia, praying that she will hold firm in faith and love. He also greets two men, Daphnos and Euteknos, along with Alkē, "whose name is dear to me" (Ign. *Smyrn.* 13:2). Tavia and Alkē were probably well-placed women with their own houses and disposable wealth and influence that they could dispense as they chose. The leading women of Thessalonica attracted to the preaching of Paul also fit this pattern (Acts 17:4).

Eminent among the women of this group is Phoebe, *prostatis* of Paul and many others and *diakonos* of the gathering of believers in Cenchrae, the eastern seaport of Corinth (Rom 16:1–2). She is often compared to Junia Theodora (see above), active in Corinth at about the same time, honored by her fellow

---

property owners: Domitilla, Priscilla, and Comodilla.

39. Bain, *Women's Socioeconomic Status*, 120–21.

Lycians for her *prostasia*, which consisted especially in hospitality and commercial and legal assistance with connections, networking, and access to city officials. This is consonant with Paul's acknowledgment of her patronage for himself and others. Her role then would be to receive him for lodging, introduce him to influential figures in the city and the Jewish community, and be leader of the assembly, whereby she hosted and presided over regular meetings of the community. We do not know the ethnicity of this woman referred to with a single Greek name. She would not necessarily have to be Jewish to have connections with the local synagogue; patrons were not always members of the ethnic group concerned. Cenchrae was an important port city about six miles from Corinth; without the reference, we would not have known of the existence of a group of Jesus believers there. The journey would have taken several hours on foot, so it is unlikely that the members there were regularly part of such groups in Corinth itself.[40]

Besides her role as patron, Phoebe also bears the title *diakonos*. Little is known of the content of this role in the earliest years of the Jesus movement. The semantic domain of *diakonia* in wider usage ranges from service to agency and official representation. In the well-known narrative of Acts 6, projected back from later years but often idealized as the source of the office of deacon in the early church, *diakonia* is both the preaching and teaching that the Apostles do (*diakonia* of the word [Acts 6:4]), what might be called spiritual leadership, and table service or presidency of the assembly (Acts 6:2). There are also unnamed persons in Philippi who hold the title, but whose role is uncertain (Phil 1:1). Whatever Phoebe's role as *diakonos*, it had the characteristic of spiritual leadership. The fact that she was bearing Paul's letter to Rome and that he introduced and commended her there may mean that hers was also the function of agency or representation: she represented the Jesus groups of the Corinth region to the communities in Rome.

Conclusion

As in most societies, the economic contributions of women and their labor went underreported in the Roman world and, thus, in early Christianity along with it. The domestic labor of female slaves was not considered "work" for purposes of economic calculations, to say nothing of the domestic work of free wives and mothers. Couples and families working together at trades

40. For further discussion of Phoebe, see Bain, *Women's Socioeconomic Status*, 102–11; Osiek, "*Diakonos* and *Prostatis*." For more, wider examples of women presidents of assemblies, see Alikin, "Women as Leaders."

were usually considered under the leadership of the male head only. Profiles in Roman patronage often focus on elite men involved in political struggles. Women's public patronage in cities—gifts of public banquets, buildings, and memorials—has more recently received closer attention, as has their patronage of smaller and unofficial religious and commercial groups. When searched for, the evidence is abundant that, as in every economy, women were active contributors and sustainers.

Bibliography

Adams, Edward. *The Earliest Christian Meeting Places: Almost Exclusively Houses?* LNTS. London: T&T Clark, 2013.

Alikin, Valeriy A. "Women as Leaders in the Gatherings of Early Christian Communities: A Sociohistorical Analysis." In *Stones, Bones, and the Sacred: Essays on Material Culture and Ancient Religion in Honor of Dennis E. Smith*, edited by Alan H. Cadwallader, 221–40. ECL. Atlanta: SBL, 2016.

Bagnall, Roger S., and Bruce W. Frier. *The Demography of Roman Egypt*. Cambridge Studies in Population, Economy and Society in Past Time 23. Cambridge: Cambridge University Press, 1994.

Bain, Katherine. *Women's Socioeconomic Status and Religious Leadership in Asia Minor in the First Two Centuries CE*. Emerging Scholars. Minneapolis: Fortress, 2014.

Cooper, Kate. "Closely Watched Household: Visibility, Exposure and the Private Power of the Roman 'Domus.'" *Past and Present* 197 (2007) 3–33.

Kearsley, R. A. "Women in Public Life in the Roman East: Junia Theodora, Claudia Metrodora and Phoebe, Benefactress of Paul." *TynBul* 50 (1999) 189–211.

Last, Richard, and Philip A. Harland. *Group Survival in the Ancient Mediterranean: Rethinking Material Conditions in the Landscape of Jews and Christians*. London: T&T Clark, 2020.

Lovén, Lena Larsson. "Women, Trade, and Production in the Urban Centres of Roman Italy." In *Urban Craftsmen and Traders in the Roman World*, edited by Andrew Wilson and Miko Flohr, 200–19. Oxford Studies on the Roman Economy. Oxford: Oxford University Press, 2016.

Oakes, Peter. "Nine Types of Church in Nine Types of Space in the Insula of the Menander." In *Early Christianity in Pompeian Light: People, Texts, Situations*, edited by Bruce W. Longenecker, 23–58. Minneapolis: Fortress, 2016.

Osiek, Carolyn. "*Diakonos* and *Prostatis*: Women's Patronage in Early Christianity." *HvTSt* 61 (2005) 347–70.

———. "Growing Up Female in the Pauline Churches: What Did She Do All Day?" In *Early Christianity in Pompeian Light: People, Texts, Situations*, edited by Bruce W. Longenecker, 3–22. Minneapolis: Fortress, 2016.

———. "The Politics of Patronage and the Politics of Kinship: The Meeting of the Ways." *BTB* 39 (2009) 143–52.

Osiek, Carolyn, et al. *A Woman's Place: House Churches in Earliest Christianity*. Minneapolis: Fortress, 2006.

Perry, Matthew J. *Gender, Manumission, and the Roman Freedwoman*. Cambridge: Cambridge University Press, 2013.

Saller, Richard. "Women, Slaves, and the Economy of the Roman Household." In *Early Christian Families in Context: An Interdisciplinary Dialogue*, edited by David L. Balch and Carolyn Osiek, 185–204. Grand Rapids: Eerdmans, 2003.

Savunen, Liisa. "Women in the Urban Texture of Pompeii." PhD diss., University of Helsinki, 1997.

Temin, Peter. *The Roman Market Economy*. Princeton Economic History of the Western World 71. Princeton and Oxford: Princeton University Press, 2013.

6. Urban Economy and Economics Relationships in the Roman Empire and Pauline Assemblies

Warren Carter

Introduction

With respect to urban economies in the Roman Empire, C. R. Whittaker observes correctly that "the study of cities is only an imperfect way of studying the operations of power in society."[1] Michael Mann identifies economic power as one of four societal sources and organizations of power along with the ideological, political, and military.[2] For some time this operation of economic power in the cities of the empire has been understood primarily as the preserve of the elite in exploitative relationship over the countryside. The interaction has been styled as "parasitic" whereby the urban center, dominated by the powerful and wealthy, benefitted by siphoning off and consuming rural production while offering little in return.[3]

More recently, this operation of power has been increasingly rethought to suggest much more diverse, complex, and interactive operations of power and to recognize a greater range of economic structures, agents, and beneficiaries.[4] Yet these recognitions have also acknowledged the large percentage of

---

1. Whittaker, "Theories of Ancient Cities," 22.
2. Mann, *Sources of Social Power*, 1:22–28, esp. 22–25; on Rome's "legionary economy," 1:250–300.
3. Finley, *Ancient Economy*, 110–18.
4. For example, among others, Scheidel and Reden, *Ancient Economy*; Manning

the ever-present "poor" who struggled to survive in the "Roman system of economic inequality."[5] It is axiomatic to observe that describing poverty is easier than defining it.[6] While poverty concerns deprivation, establishing criteria to define or measure poverty in the Roman world with any precision is very difficult whether, for example, in terms of a minimal level of resources needed to sustain life, or levels of calorific needs, or size of living space, or social stratification whereby anyone who was not identified as "rich" was poor. Sources for the ancient world do not offer documented surveys nor clear notions of what was necessary for subsistence. They do offer upper-level prejudices toward and stereotypes about the poor as well as evidence that most of the population knew degrees of poverty.

What, then, were the economic structures and practices of the cities in which the assemblies addressed by Paul's letters existed?[7] How may we understand the ways in which members of these assemblies participated in these economic structures?

This essay is divided into four sections. The first sketches the changing understanding of power in the empire's urban economic structures. The second section considers some specific urban situations to illustrate their structures of power. The third section takes up the debate about the socioeconomic levels of early Christ believers in order to locate their modes of participation in urban economic structures. The fourth section considers an economic survival strategy shaped by a goal of socioeconomic well-being. It hardly needs to be said that scholarly debate concerning these issues is extensive and complex; the discussion here can be partial at best with an emphasis on urban economic structures, societal strata, and survival strategies.

It has generally been estimated that in the first and second centuries CE some 80 to 90 percent of the population of the Roman Empire worked the land, with 10 to 20 percent of the population living as city dwellers.[8] The larg-

---

and Morris, *Ancient Economy*; Hitchner, "Advantages of Wealth"; Scheidel, *Cambridge Companion*.

5. To modify the description of Garnsey and Saller, *Roman Empire*, 125. Whittaker suggests three sesterces per day as the wage for an unskilled laborer while Cato the Younger had property valued at four million sesterces and yielding an income of 550–650 sesterces per day ("Poor," 278). On Pliny the younger's wealth, Duncan-Jones, *Economy of Roman Empire*, 17–32; Scheidel, "Economy and Quality."

6. Whittaker, "Poor," 274–90.

7. My wording here reflects recent feminist emphases on decentering Paul and recognizing that these assemblies had voice and life apart from Paul. Ease of expression will require on some subsequent occasions that I identify them as "Pauline assemblies."

8. Hopkins, "Economic Growth, 37; Chandler and Fox suggest 650,000 in 100 CE (3000

est urban population by far was Rome with a population of perhaps near a million;[9] Alexandria, Antioch, and Ephesus each held between two to three hundred thousand, with Carthage about the same.[10] Most urban areas, though, comprised, to varying degrees, smaller populations: Pergamum near one hundred and eighty thousand,[11] Corinth and Sardis perhaps around one hundred thousand or somewhat smaller,[12] Lugdunum (London) perhaps around forty thousand,[13] Ostia at twenty-five thousand, Pompeii at fifteen thousand,[14] and Philippi around ten to fifteen thousand.[15] The 80–90/10–20 farm to city percentages indicate the enormous importance of ownership of land and its production as a source of wealth. Yet the percentages may also suggest that urban areas were independent of rural areas, and that cities were, economically, not very significant. Neither notion is correct.

The Economic Role(s) of Ancient Cities

The economic structures and interactions of first-century CE cities in the Roman Empire have been much debated. Numerous studies have examined practices of production, distribution, consumption, labor, and markets.[16] Moses Finley's notion of the consumer city has dominated the discussion.[17]

The "consumer city" model was an ideal type borrowed from Max Weber. It emphasized the role of cities as political and social centers of power over surrounding territory under the control of urban elites. These elites asserted cultural values of socioeconomic entitlement, which created an exploitative

---

Years, 81, 303).

9. Morley, "Population Size," 29–36.

10. Duncan-Jones suggests more than 300,000 for Alexandria with Carthage and Antioch comparable (*Economy of Roman Empire*, 260–61); Hopkins, 300,000 ("Economic Growth," 38); Chandler and Fox, 400,000 for Alexandria (c. 100 CE) and 200,000 for Ephesus and Antioch (*3000 Years*, 81). For Carthage; Chandler and Fox are confusing, suggesting 200,000 on one page (*3000 Years*, 81) but 90,000 on another (303).

11. Duncan-Jones claims about 180,000 (*Economy of Roman Empire*, 261); Chandler and Fox suggest between 120,000 and 180,000 (*3000 Years*, 81).

12. Chandler and Fox suggest 100,000 for both (*3000 Years*, 81); D. Engels suggests 80,000 to 85,000 for Corinth (*Roman Corinth*, 32–33, 85).

13. Chandler and Fox, *3000 Years*, 303.

14. Erdkamp, "Urbanism," 244.

15. Oakes, *Philippians*, 45–46.

16. In addition to the literature cited elsewhere in this chapter, see chapters on "production," "distribution," and "consumption" (Scheidel et al., *Cambridge Economic History*, 543–618); Scheidel, *Cambridge Companion*.

17. Finley, *Ancient Economy*; Finley, "Ancient City."

economic relationship with rural areas transferring agricultural production to the city by taxation and rents.[18] Ancient consumer cities were said to contrast with medieval cities, which, for Weber, were "producer cities," politically independent from rural aristocracy, economically independent through trade, manufacturing, and services, and involved in mutual interaction with the countryside. Ancient consumer cities, by contrast, were considered not to be independent. They were entangled with the countryside in parasitic interactions. They did not reciprocate rural production, with the model placing little value on urban artisan production.

The consumer city model was part of Finley's view of the ancient economy based in and reflective of particular "institutions, power structures, and ideologies" enacted by elite control.[19] Elites controlled agricultural and rural production as well as urban areas that were not generative but were underinvested and underdeveloped in manufacturing and commercial activity, without technological developments, and lacking profit-directed growth and long-distance or interregional trade in non-luxury items. This model of the ancient city in parasitic relationship to "the countryside" rejected other models: a producer or commercial city,[20] a service city,[21] or the city in a market economy.[22]

Finley's "consumer city" model has raised numerous questions and has been examined for both its comprehensiveness and even its validity as an explanatory model. The discussion has raised questions about the usefulness of one ideal model to articulate complex socioeconomic and political realities and diverse urban systems; the model's representation of cities as non-generative by being inattentive to urban artisan production;[23] its denial of technological innovation;[24] its setting of urban and rural areas in antithetical or oppositional—rather than cooperative—interaction; its inability to embrace archaeological

18. Corbier, "City Territory and Taxation."
19. Morley, "Cities in Context," 43.
20. Mattingly and Salmon, *Economies beyond Agriculture*, 82–83.
21. D. Engels, *Roman Corinth*.
22. Temin, *Roman Market Economy*.
23. Hawkins, "Manufacturing."
24. For example, Kevin Greene engages in a point-by-point refutation of Finley's arguments, detailing, for example, technological developments in food production from agricultural products (grape and olive pressing, mechanical grain mills; selective breeding; iron tools ploughs and sickles), the use of water-powered technologies in mining; increased ceramic production; the development of glassblowing ("Technological Innovation"). Andrew Wilson examines developing technologies in water-lifting devices, the water-powered grain mill, and the use of water-power in mining (gold, silver, lead, copper) ("Machines, Power"). See also Kron, "Food Production."

evidence concerning urban levels of production and export; its neglect of local, regional, and long-distance trade for both supplying urban areas and as markets for its production; its dismissal of the role of urban elites in funding both agricultural and commercial endeavors.[25]

Thus Nicholas Purcell, for example, underscores the overlap of and interaction between city and countryside when he observes that "cities in antiquity were territories as well as urban nuclei."[26] Urban and rural areas were interconnected economically. Peregrine Horden and Purcell speak of "the dissolution of 'the town' into a less arbitrarily bounded, and rapidly mutable, area of inquiry."[27] These observations suggest more cooperative economic interactions between cities and rural areas involving food supply, markets, labor, manufacturing, and other services. Cities benefitted from rural production, markets, and labor while also processing raw materials and providing manufactured goods along with markets, labor, infrastructure, and services for the benefit of rural areas. Wealthy landowners frequently lived, at least for part of the time, in cities and were involved in their commercial activities—often through funding trade and production[28]—while "many people living in towns worked the land," especially in smaller towns.[29] Interregional trade, such as that which supplied grain for Rome, or pottery for cities such as Carthage, Berenice, Ostia, and London,[30] and attested extensively by shipwrecks,[31] linked urban and regional areas. Peter Temin has emphasized the importance of market economies involving—for example—food supplies, labor, land ownership, and financial intermediation.[32]

Taking account of these links between urban and rural areas and the emphasis on market economies, David Mattingly proposes a model comprising three-interlocking economies:[33]

1. The *imperial economy* stretching across the empire and beyond, focused on supplying resources to Rome, the army, and provincial administra-

25. Horden and Purcell, *Corrupting Sea*, 105–22; Wilson, "Urban Production," 232–34.
26. Purcell, "Urbanism," 583.
27. Horden and Purcell, *Corrupting Sea*, 112.
28. Wallace-Hadrill, *Houses and Society*, 11–121; Wallace-Hadrill, "Elites and Trade."
29. Erdkamp cites the large numbers of agricultural tools and implements found in Pompeii and indicates the involvement of townsfolk in agricultural work in the town's hinterlands ("Urbanism," 246).
30. Fulford, "Economic Independence," 62–66; on amphorae, Peacock and Williams, *Amphorae and Roman Economy*.
31. The catalogue of Parker, *Ancient Shipwrecks*, 16–22; 31–35.
32. Temin, *Roman Market Economy*, 95–189.
33. Mattingly, *Imperialism, Power, and Identity*, 125–45, esp. 138–40.

tors. Its mechanisms involved a census to catalogue resources, land confiscation and allocation, the levying of tax and tribute, exploitation of natural resources, and distribution.

2. *Extraprovincial economies* centered on interregional trade (including agricultural staples) across custom zones of goods not involved in the imperial economy.

3. *Provincial economies* concerned local market systems involving rural production and manufacturing activity.

The evaluation of the "consumer city" model, then, has highlighted complex and diverse urban economic systems involving various economic agents. It is fair to say that increasingly discussion has recognized that the economies of ancient urban areas do not fit the one model offered by Finley. Urban economies are, in Horden and Purcell's language, "sites of shifting, overlapping ecologies."[34] Elites do not exercise power alone and are not the sole beneficiaries. So too are traders, artisans, financiers, unskilled workers, and agricultural workers as the following discussion will show. Yet the "Roman system of economic inequality,"[35] marked by various power structures as well as systemic poverty and deprivation for many, will also emerge.

Case Studies of Urban Economies

I assess Finley's proposal and the recent post-Finley discussion by sampling analyses of seven urban areas across the empire, diverse in location and structures. The first three cities to be addressed are located in North Africa (Leptiminus, Timgad, and Sabratha), the second two in modern-day Greece (Philippi and Corinth), and the final two in modern-day Italy (Pompeii and Rome).

The City of Leptiminus

Archaeological work at Leptiminus (Tunisia) has established that some of the city's residents were involved in manufacturing, reciprocal trade with the hinterlands, and long-distance trade. Finley's model minimalized the contribution of these economic activities and agents.[36] Kilns of considerable size and capacity, as well as "finds of wasters and discards show that pottery for

---

34. Horden and Purcell, *Corrupting Sea*, 108.
35. Garnsey and Saller, *Roman Empire*, 125.
36. I am following Mattingly et al., "Leptiminus," 82–84.

local consumption (coarsewares) and for export (*amphorae*) was produced."[37] Leptiminus-produced amphorae were "widely distributed in the western Mediterranean region, and particularly common at Rome and Ostia, but also reaching the eastern Mediterranean and Britain" conveying "fish products . . . and olive oil."[38] Such levels of production and widespread distribution throughout the Mediterranean region indicates that production far exceeded Finley's claim of urban "petty commodity production" for local consumption.[39] Remains of fermentation tanks confirm significant levels of fish-processing activity. The exports of olive oil and fish products undermine Finley's view of self-sufficient towns and indicate long-distance trade in agricultural staples.

In addition, "two types of ironworking activity" involved "smelting of iron from raw ore" and "smithing floors" for working metal into usable forms.[40] The smelting required the import of iron ore from overseas, and the smithing activity indicates the city possessed the necessary technology and manufacturing to supply its hinterland with needed metal products. This activity undermines Finley's claims of the city's parasitic exploitation of the hinterland offering it nothing in return.

Further, the harbor's trading activity generated additional economic activity in providing employment for sailors as well as in the servicing of ships and their crews through maintenance, loading, unloading, and storing materials, providing supplies, entertainment and hospitality. In addition to the city providing services, there are also features here of what Weber identified as a merchant or *entrepôt* city whereby groups profited from the importing of foreign materials and the exporting of local production. Mattingly et al. also argue that elites derived income from ownership of landed estates as well as from financing some of the above activities. They conclude that Finley's "consumer model" is simply not adequate for the complexity of this urban economic situation, and they evoke models of a producer and commercial city.[41] Power is not restricted to elite circles. Successful artisans, traders, financiers—comprising a middling group—exercised some forms and levels of economic power.

---

37. Mattingly et al., "Leptiminus," 76.
38. Peacock and Williams, *Amphorae and Roman Economy*, 153–57.
39. Finley, *Ancient Economy*, 194.
40. Mattingly et al., "Leptiminus," 79–80.
41. Mattingly et al., "Leptiminus," 82–84.

The City of Timgad

Andrew Wilson's discussion of second- to fourth-century CE textile production in Timgad in Algeria highlights at least seventeen, and perhaps as many as twenty-two, fulling (and dyeing?) operations in workshops in the city's northeast quarter.[42] The key archaeological evidence identifies in each facility one to six "terracotta treading tubs and concrete vats" that signify fulling and perhaps dyeing activity.[43] Fulling removed fats and grease from the fibers by trampling them in an alkaline solution combining elements of soda, dilute urine, and water. The cloth was then beaten, washed, and dyed. Vats and treading tubs were therefore essential fixtures for this production. Also evident in the town are two cloth markets attested by an inscription.

Noting twice as many fulling operations in Timgad as Pompeii, along with several cloth markets, Wilson argues that this large-scale economic enterprise produced a volume of textiles beyond the town's own needs. Wilson suggests it may well have drawn supplies from transhumant pastoral activity to the north of the town and produced, for beyond the town's own market, blankets and cloaks perhaps for the nearby legionary headquarters at Lambaesis.[44] Along with other possible North African sites, Timgad demonstrates, so Wilson argues, that Finley's claim that consumer towns engaged only in "petty commodity production" is vastly understated. Again, various economic agents—a middling group of successful artisans, traders, financiers as well as lower-level manual workers—exerted and benefitted from different forms and levels of economic power.

The City of Sabratha

Wilson also examines the commerce and industry of Roman Sabratha, a town of perhaps ten thousand on coastal Libya.[45] Foremost in the town's exports was salted fish. Wilson draws attention to sixteen sites comprising some forty-five to forty-nine vats that resemble those of other North African and Spanish sites for salting fish. Alternating layers of salt and gutted fish were compressed in the vats and after a period of time (perhaps six weeks), the salted fish was packed into amphorae for export. Wilson sustains his claim that this was a significant export industry in Sabratha by attempting to quantify the levels of production.

42. Wilson, "Timgad and Textile Production," 237–41.
43. Wilson, "Urban Production," 237–38.
44. Wilson, "Timgad and Textile Production," 280–87.
45. Wilson, "Commerce and Industry."

He writes, "If each batch took an average of six weeks, and the total number of vats was only double the number excavated, annual production could have totaled sixteen thousand amphorae of salted fish."[46] This level of production far exceeds the needs of the town's population. Three further factors suggest export activity. The availability of fresh fish along with other food products rendered salted (preserved) fish unnecessary for the local market. And, clearly, fish is salted to preserve it for export and transportation. Moreover, fish guts were used to make the fish sauce, or *garum*, for export.

Wilson's emphasis on fish salting exists alongside other economic activity in the town. Olive oil production from the surrounding territory was important.[47] Wilson also notes the presence of crushed sea snail shells (*Murex trunculus*) and the presence of some small masonry tubs that may well indicate their use to produce purple dye for dyeing cloth or wool (from locally raised sheep). Pottery, plaster, and glass manufacture also contributed to the local economy. Peacock and Williams note that Algerian-produced amphorae were found in Sabratha as well as in Alexandria, Benghazi, Switzerland, and England.[48] Such distribution indicates Sabratha's participation in extensive interregional trade. This observation along with Wilson's arguments show Sabratha does not conform well to Finley's depiction of a self-sufficient consumer city. And the discussion highlights numerous agents exercising economic power in the town.

The City of Philippi

In Acts 16:12, Philippi is referred to as a "leading city of the district of Macedonia and a Roman colony." Roman veterans, settled in 42 BCE by Antony and after Actium in 31 BCE, controlled much of the extensive land surrounding the town as well as the town's politics. Philippi's population was comprised predominantly of non-Romans, including Greeks and Thracians. Oakes calculates that perhaps 3 percent comprised the Decurian elite; 37 percent service, craft-working, and trading interests; 20 percent slaves (domestic or working in trades with their owners); 20 percent peasant or colonist farmers who commuted from town in order to work either their own or rented land in the immediate vicinity of the town; and 20 percent poor persons who lived below subsistence level.[49] These figures and the geography of the town suggest that

---

46. Wilson, "Urban Production," 247.
47. Mattingly, "Oil for Export."
48. Peacock and Williams, *Amphorae and Roman Economy*, 171.
49. Oakes, *Philippians*, 45–54; Oakes, "Economic Situation"; Bakirtzzis and Koester, *Philippi*.

one of its main economic functions was interactive and mutually benefitting with the surrounding territory, supplying and being supplied by its agricultural production. The town provided a market for agricultural goods and food, while artisans produced products that farmers did not produce themselves. More successful traders and artisans comprised a middling group, along with lower-level manual workers. Because of its location on the east-west Via Egnatia,[50] its very large *territorium* which produced agricultural products, and its proximity to the port of Neapolis, a further economic function involved regional and interregional trade in goods. Philippi was a market and trading center.[51]

The City of Corinth

In a controversial—and in places somewhat romanticized—study of Roman Corinth, Donald Engels rejects the "myth of the consumer city" and proposes instead the model of the "service city."[52] His proposal constructs a city that closely interacts with the countryside, that is funded to a significant degree by peasant productivity, and that provides significant services, especially for trading sectors. He finds Finley's consumer city model generally unsustainable. Towns with a population exceeding ten thousand people did not have access to sufficient surrounding land within a walking distance of six kilometers to supply their needs for food and other products. Rents from land could have supported at most only 10 to 20 percent of the eighty thousand to eighty-five thousand people who comprised Corinth's population.[53] Such urban-rural interaction was crucial since there was no cultivated land within the city "except for a few garden plots."[54]

Likewise, Engels contests the view that peasants had a minimal surplus of

---

50. This important west-east road, estimated to be about seven hundred miles in length, spanned the Roman provinces of Illyricum, Macedonium, and Thrace. It started in the west in the port city of Dyrrachium, traversed the area north of the Adriatic Sea (including Thessalonica and Philippi), and ended in the east in Byzantium.

51. Diodorus Siculus 16:8 mentions gold and silver mines exploited by Philip II of Macedonia in the fourth century BCE.

52. D. Engels, *Roman Corinth*, 121–42.

53. D. Engels, *Roman Corinth*, 32–33, 83; summary, 121–22. Mary E. Hoskins Walbank proposes a much lower population range of twenty thousand to fifty thousand ("Foundation and Planning," 106).

54. D. Engels, *Roman Corinth*, 27–28. This claim is contested. James Wiseman argues that agricultural production in the larger Corinthia exceeded trade and manufacture (*Land of Ancient Corinthians*, 9, 12–13). And Guy R. Sanders argues urban Corinth contained fertile and well-watered land that supplied agricultural products for export ("Urban Corinth," 15).

2 percent of production after taxes and rents. He argues for a tax rate of about 20 percent, which means peasants would have had a significantly higher posttax and rent surplus of 30 to 50 percent, which allowed them to purchase various services and goods available in and/or produced by Corinth.[55] Engels asserts, then, that Corinth was a market economy,[56] providing a market for peasants' agricultural surplus and for goods and services peasants themselves could not produce. Corinth's residents purchased food since they mostly earned a living from manufacturing of imported goods (lamps and pottery, bronze and marble sculpture, perfume making, etc.). Like Keith Hopkins, Engels emphasizes Corinth's manufacturing activity, which produced jobs, goods, and income to purchase goods and services. In turn, peasants purchased from Corinth items that were not produced by smaller villages and the countryside such as pottery, cloth and clothing, metal products, and farm equipment. Landlords required luxury skills (e.g., painters, sculptors) and items.[57] Hence much of Corinth's population was involved in and earned its income from manufacturing, trading, and service activities.

The "primary services" the city provided for itself and for smaller towns, villages, and the countryside included "religious, educational, cultural (entertainment) and judicial activities," as well as secondary services such as food, temporary lodging, public baths, etc.[58] In addition to these, because of its strategic location, the city provided services for merchants, travelers, and tourists accessing the port of Corinth.[59] Seaborne commerce brought food and raw materials (e.g., marble and metal) into Corinth, and visitors who arrived for various entertainments—such as religious festivals and games—required food and accommodation. Merchants and their crews required support services such as markets, supplies, and repairs, as well as considerable labor for loading and unloading goods, for hauling cargo across the *diolkos* or road crossing the isthmus,[60] for warehouses, transport on land involving animals, leatherworkers for harnesses, wagons, rope making and repair, cloth sacks and ceramics for

---

55. D, Engels, *Roman Corinth*, 41.
56. D. Engels, *Roman Corinth*, 25, 48.
57. D. Engels, *Roman Corinth*, 47–50.
58. D. Engels, *Roman Corinth*, 43; see also 125.
59. D. Engels, *Roman Corinth*, 50.
60. The *diolkos* refer to the limestone-paved road near Corinth, some four to five miles in length, that enabled boats and goods to be moved overland across the isthmus. Its advantage was that ships avoided the somewhat hazardous trip around the Peloponnese Peninsula. Tolls and taxes benefitted Corinth.

materials, and financial services such as banking and insurance.⁶¹ The city provided infrastructure and commercial facilities that employed many.⁶²

Considering these complexities found within relationship that existed between urban and rural areas, Engels concludes:

> The classical city was not parasitical but was maintained to a large extent through the voluntary exchange of the peasant's agricultural surplus for urban goods and services... The nature of the city attracted many peasants and tenant farmers, as well as travelers and tourists, to participate in its social, economic, and cultural affairs.⁶³

The country, whether nearby or further afield, supplied resources for urban subsistence and manufacturing, and the city reciprocated with manufactured products and services. Engels recognizes that among many different kinds of cities, Corinth was a large commercial city that provided a vast array of goods and services to inhabitants, country people, merchants, and travelers. Contra Finley, Corinth and other cities were fundamentally about providing services and not just collecting rents from exploited peasants.⁶⁴

Engels's proposal provides a very different model of a city and its service interactions with the surrounding countryside. His model is complex in foregrounding the diverse services a city might offer, in decentering claims of exclusive elite power, and in highlighting numerous economic agents. His proposal has generated considerable debate. Several, including Daniel Tompkins and Andrew Wilson, argue that Engel "underestimates the role of local production for export, and of merchants operating out of Corinth itself,"⁶⁵ thereby neglecting a key contrast with Finley's "consumer" city. Whittaker thinks the figure of 50 percent for rural surplus (a key economic driver in Engels's scenario) is far too high.⁶⁶ Wilson suggests that Engels's "service city" utilizes aspects of Weber's merchant city, or *entrepôt*, that involves groups deriving profits from importing materials and exporting locally produced goods.

61. D. Engels, *Roman Corinth*, 57.
62. D. Engels, *Roman Corinth*, 58–62.
63. D. Engels, *Roman Corinth*, 128.
64. D. Engels, *Roman Corinth*, 129. Engels's contribution is significant though marked by a somewhat romantic view of the levels of the comfort of first-century Corinth while underplaying well-established urban challenges involving poverty, disease, food insecurity, and social stratification.
65. Wilson, "Urban Production," 233; and Daniel Tompkins's important review in *Bryn Mawr Classical Review*.
66. Whittaker, "Theories of Ancient Cities," 12–14.

While Engels's contribution significantly diversifies understandings of the operation of economic power through various agents, he nevertheless operates with a somewhat romantic view of the levels of comfort in first-century Corinth, overstating the rural food surplus and underplaying well-established urban challenges for its poorer inhabitants involving poverty, disease, food insecurity, and social stratification. I will return to the challenges of the urban poor (disease, food insecurity, housing etc.) below.

The City of Pompeii

What might one of the empire's most studied towns contribute to understandings of urban economies? Walter Moeller rejected Finley's consumer city model and constructed Pompeii's economy more in terms of a producer city. He argued that the town's economy centered on textile production derived from the surrounding area's sheep farming.[67] He posited that the town's textile business was economically rational in its production structure and primarily export-oriented. In Moeller's construction, Pompeii's wool craftsmen exercised considerable political—as well as economic—control in the city.

Willem Jongman countered much of Moeller's political and economic analysis. Jongman argued that the area surrounding Pompeii could not supply the quantity and quality of wool required to sustain an export business, no archaeological evidence supports a large enterprise of fulling/dyeing, and a prominent political rule in the town by fullers cannot be sustained. He concludes that Pompeii cannot be identified as a producer city, but with small-scale artisan production for local elites, it is best understood in terms of Finley's consumer city.[68]

Without intending it, Jongman's reference to small-scale artisan production pointed a way ahead to a different model of Pompeii's economic structures of power. Ray Laurence argues that the consumer city model, utilized by Jongman, "marginalized small-scale production in the city"[69] and that Jongman underestimated the cumulative level of production from numerous small-scale commercial and manufacturing workshops "that nevertheless produced a large volume of goods."[70] This production meant the town participated in extensive trade networks with cities in Italy and elsewhere in the empire. As a result, imported products such as pottery items (lamps, amphorae, tableware) existed

67. Moeller, Wool Trade.
68. Jongman, Economy and Society, 155–86, esp. 158.
69. Laurence, Roman Pompeii, 62.
70. Laurence, Roman Pompeii, 66.

in the town alongside local production. For example, amphorae produced in Pompeii have been found in "Italy, Sicily, France, Spain, and parts of North Africa," while amphorae produced in such diverse areas as Spain, Tripolitania in North Africa, the Aegean, Crete and southern Greece have been found in Pompeii.[71] Such production and involvement in trade was facilitated by Pompeii's strategic location on the Bay of Naples, and linked with other towns of Campania. Pompeii functioned as an *entrepôt* for the Sarno river valley with good river access to the towns of the hinterland. Such activity and networks indicate that Pompeii enabled economic life in its hinterlands rather than functioning as a parasitic "consumer city" exploiting the hinterland for the benefit of a few elites.

Laurence identifies the powerful role played by traders (*negotiators*) as economic agents in facilitating trade "by bringing goods from one location and selling them in another."[72] Traders bought products in small lots from producers in Pompeii and transported them elsewhere in the empire, particularly, but not exclusively, Rome. Successful traders, with artisans comprised a middling group and shared economic power with the town's elites (who owned considerable agricultural holdings yet resided in the town for at least part of the year). These economic agents were clearly interested in profit, as the words "Hail, profit" (*salve lucru*) at the entrance to a house articulate.[73] Andrew Wallace-Hadrill underscores the roles of the town's elites in this economic activity:

> As private patrons, partly of freeborn clients, but most conspicuously of freedmen, [urban elites] were drawn into advising and supporting traders. As candidates for office . . . they benefitted from the support of groups of traders . . . [who] could represent themselves as having sufficiently powerful group-identity to be worth cultivating for commercial disputes. Both as patrons of freedmen engaged in trade and as property owners drawing rents from the lease of stores and shops, a substantial portion of the urban elite must have derived at least part of their income from trade, even if they did not actually run businesses.[74]

We could add that urban spatial arrangements ensured artisan production, trade, and elite interaction. Private houses renting space for apartments, shops (depending on location) and workshops (carpenters, potters, weavers, metal

---

71. For example, and by no means comprehensive, Peacock and Williams, *Amphorae and Roman Economy*, 85, 93–94, 166, 173, 177.

72. Laurence, *Roman Pompeii*, 66.

73. *Corpus Inscriptionum Latinorum* X.874 (also 875).

74. Wallace-Hadrill, *Houses and Society*, 121.

workers, etc.), bakeries, fulleries, blacksmith shops, taverns and food counters, etc., facilitated elite contiguity to, investment in, and income from commercial enterprise. Moreover, commercial market gardens, vineyards, orchards, and the gardens of larger houses within the city such as that of Julia Felix (an orchard) or Euxinus (a vineyard) supplied fruits, vegetables, wine, and medicinal plants for household use and sale in markets.[75]

Such discussions do not construct Pompeii as a monolithic "consumer city" with elites exercising all economic power. Rather, Pompeii emerges as an urban space of diverse and vibrant economic activity involving producing, consuming, and trading, all while embracing numerous economic agents in facilitative interaction with its hinterland, and also in active interregional trade.

The City of Rome

Rome, with a population of nearly a million, has been called the "arch consumer,"[76] often constructed as an insatiable "parasite-city"[77] that consumed products from throughout the empire and offering no goods or services in return. Yet as the following discussion shows, several observations indicate Rome's economic structures were much more complex and diverse, and its economic agents much more varied, as befits a city of its size.

The city's food supply evidences its power and reach in drawing crop production from around the empire, once the city outgrew the ability of its immediate environs to supply sufficient food.[78] Paul Erdkamp rightly observes that feeding the city "tested the logistical, economic and organizational abilities of the Roman world to its limits."[79] Greg Aldrete and David Mattingly observe that "one of the most impressive achievements of the Roman Empire was simply the fact that . . . it managed to sustain and supply its capital city, which had a population of around one million people."[80]

75. Ciarallo, *Gardens of Pompeii*, 41–50. The pioneering work was Jashemski, *Gardens of Pompeii*; also Cooley, *Pompeii*, 97–112; Laurence, *Roman Pompeii*, 64–68.
76. Horden and Purcell, *Corrupting Sea*, 111.
77. Finley, *Ancient Economy*, 125, 130.
78. Among many others, Sirks, *Food for Rome*.
79. Erdkamp, "Food Supply of Capital," 262.
80. Aldrete and Mattingly, "Feeding the City," 171. Steven Friesen affirms from his survey of isotopic investigations of skeletons that "for average inhabitants of the Roman Empire . . . cereals (esp. wheat and barley) supplied about 70 to 75 percent of the caloric intake" with "olives, wine, vegetables, legumes and other plants" supplying the rest. Isotopic study shows that adults consumed more protein than children, and that urban residents had a more enriched diet than rural residents, but thus far evidence does not establish consistent correlations between diet and gender and socioeconomic status ("Embodied Inequalities," 14).

The diet of common folks required large supplies of grain,[81] supplemented by legumes, vegetables, olive oil, wine, meat, and fish. Elites enjoyed considerably more variety from luxurious and exotic foods.[82] Imports supplied grain from the Italian peninsula, and especially from Egypt, northern Africa, Sicily, and Sardinia; Spain, North Africa, and Asia Minor supplied olive oil;[83] Spain and Gaul wine. Ships transported this production to Rome. Grain was procured by several means. Erdkamp argues that "most of the grain supplied to Rome was state-owned, and hence the authorities needed the services of ship owners who transported grain rather than of grain merchants who supplied it."[84] According to Erdkamp, the grain itself was state owned. First, it was procured either from taxation in which a percentage of the crop was handed over by provincial producers, or a certain percentage of the crop was handed over it as rent for the use of imperially owned land. To enact what Mattingly calls the imperial economy, the state contracted with owners or financiers of ships to transport grain to Rome.[85] Second, Erdkamp claims that the state owned grain because it bought it from landowners. Third, Erdkamp finds that elites and/or merchants also bought and sold surplus grain on the market and transported it to Rome.[86] Finley argued that grain was procured by both methods of levy (tax, rents) and purchase,[87] and Temin recognizes, against Erdkamp, that a grain market—or, more accurately, many interconnected and interdependent wheat markets—existed around the Mediterranean, which facilitated the purchase and shipping of grain to be sold in Rome.[88] Olive oil seems to have been similarly produced, procured, and transported to Rome through the efforts of traders, as were other food and material supplies.

The state supplied infrastructure such as port facilities at Ostia (developed by Claudius, and extended by Trajan). Also required were state and/or elite-funded warehouses (*horrea*) for storing supplies in Puteoli, Ostia, and

81. Estimates of quantities per year are more than 150,000 tons (Erdkamp, "Food Supply of Capital," 263); 150,000 to 300,000 tons (Temin, "Market Economy," 176); "237,000 metric tons of wheat" (Aldrete and Mattingly, "Feeding the City," 193).

82. Dalby, *Empire of Pleasures*, 243–57.

83. Mitchell, "Olive Cultivation," 93, 98; Mattingly, "First Fruit."

84. Erdkamp, "Food Supply of Capital," 272.

85. For discussion of Cato's funding of shipowners (Plutarch, *Cato the Elder* 21:5–6), Temin, "Market Economy," 175–76; Pleket, "Urban Elites and Business."

86. Pleket, "Rome," 15–16.

87. Finley, *Ancient Economy*, 198–99.

88. Temin, *Roman Market Economy*, 29–65; 97–113; also Garnsey, "Grain for Rome," 119–21, 127–28.

Rome. Supplies were unloaded in Puteoli and transported overland by carts or unloaded at Ostia and brought up the Tiber River in barges towed by animals and/or men.[89] This unloading, transporting, and warehousing of sacks and amphorae, as well as other resources for the city such as building supplies (bricks, timber, marble, etc.[90]), provided vast employment—as well as significant unemployment, especially during the winter months of November to March, when little produce was moved. Professional bakers milled grain and baked it as bread. The well-known Eurysaces operated a very sizable and profitable bakery.[91] Other workshops, some funded by wealthy freedmen, produced a wide range of goods.

Distribution of food and other goods constituted a thriving and diverse retail business in essentials and luxuries involving shops (*tabernae*), markets, fairs, auctions, and street hawkers and peddlers.[92] Goods and services were purchased by money transactions (rather than barter), an indication, as Peter Temin highlights, of a market economy. A labor market also operated. Temin highlights that "some of the work . . . was done for wages and some under the duress of slavery";[93] the latter does not preclude a labor market in which "free urban workers were able to change their economic activities."[94]

While elites, traders, some artisans, and financiers did very well as a middling group, others in the city did not benefit well from this economic activity. Instigated in 123 BCE, a dole made a monthly ration of grain available, which male citizens of Rome could purchase.[95] Subsequently, in 58 BCE the purchase price was abolished, and recipients and eligibility requirements were regularly revised over subsequent centuries, thereby ensuring supply for some and resulting in significant sections of the population (very poor, *peregrini* or foreigners, and some slaves) remaining food insecure, vulnerable to varying supplies, quality, and prices—with limited options if grain was unavailable and/or prices increased—and restricted by unstable incomes from varying employment.[96] In fact, as Peter Garnsey writes, "For most people, life was a perpetual struggle

---

89. Tuck, "Tiber and River Transport"; on roads, Laurence, "Traffic and Land Transportation."
90. Graham, "Counting Bricks."
91. Petersen, *"Baker."*
92. Holleran, *Shopping in Ancient Rome.*
93. Temin, "Market Economy," 173.
94. Temin, "Market Economy," 174.
95. Erdkamp, "Food Supply of Capital," 264–67.
96. Whittaker, "Poor," 272–73.

for survival."[97] Unsanitary and overcrowded living conditions,[98] numerous life stressors,[99] diseases of deficiency (e.g., malnourishment, rickets, bladder stones, eye diseases) and diseases of contagion from lack of immunity (diarrhea. dysentery, etc.) inevitably afflicted many.[100] Whittaker appeals to "better-documented ages" to formulate a profile of the Roman population. Estimates for thirteenth-century Florence, for example, indicate that 70 percent of households had "consumption needs greater than their incomes." Estimates for fifteenth- to eighteenth-century preindustrial European cities suggest "4 to 8 percent of the population were incapable of earning a living ... another 20 percent were permanently in crisis through price fluctuations and low wages, and another 30 to 40 percent were small artisans, petty officials or shopkeepers who might temporarily ... fall below subsistence levels."[101] If these figures are on target—and I will return subsequently to further attempts to identify the numbers of the destitute in Rome and other urban areas—at least half of the urban population had little economic power and inadequate resources to sustain their lives.

It would be too simplistic to style Rome as only a parasitic consumer city. The above description points to a complex urban economy that also stimulated economic activity, especially through trade, financing, and manufacturing in supplying this huge market.[102] A frequently quoted passage from Revelation, commonly understood to construct Rome as a city consuming luxury goods, points to this greater complexity. Revelation 18 catalogues exotic goods that "merchants of the earth" brought to Rome:

> Gold, silver, jewels and pearls, fine linen, purple, silk and scarlet, all kinds of scented wood, all articles of ivory, all articles of costly wood, bronze, iron, and marble, cinnamon, spice, incense, myrrh, frankincense, wine, olive oil, choice flour and wheat, cattle and sheep, horses and chariots, slaves— and human lives. (Rev 18:11–13)

Richard Bauckham has helpfully identified geographical locations across the Roman Empire that produced these luxury items, as well as the dominant ways

---

97. Garnsey, *Food and Society*, xi.
98. Scobie, "Slums, Sanitation, and Mortality."
99. Toner, *Popular Culture*, 54–91.
100. Garnsey, *Food and Society*, 43–46; Scheidel, "Germs for Rome."
101. Whittaker, "Poor," 276.
102. Pleket, "Rome," 17–31.

in which wealthy elites used them in Rome.[103] Such observations reinforce the stereotype of Rome's elite as the consumer of the empire's "dainties and splendor" (Rev 18:14b).

But often not noticed is the passage's testimony to various market economies and the involvement of diverse economic agents.[104] "Merchants of the earth weep and mourn" at Rome's demise because "no one buys their cargo anymore" (18:11) and "shipmasters and seafarers, the sailors and all whose trade is on the sea . . . wept and mourned" because "all who had ships at sea grew rich by her wealth" (18:19). These groups of merchants, shipmasters, and seafarers lament because Rome's (imagined) destruction means the loss of their markets and profits. Sources such as inscriptions ("Profit is happiness"), biographies (Plutarch's description of Cato the Elder's underwriting of ships [*Cato the Elder* 21:5–6]), and literary fictions (Trimalchio's boasts of his huge profit margins from trade) attest the importance of profits for this merchant/trade group.[105]

Also unnoticed in the discussion of Rev 18 are the extensive urban economies of artisanal production and retail activity that the mourning of the traders assumes. While some products came to Rome in finished form (for example, dyed fine linen from Miletus, Thyatira, Laodicea, Hierapolis), other items were processed in Rome where artisans turned gold into ceiling decoration, or silver into plating for households items, or precious stones and pearls into jewelry, or ivory or costly woods into carved items, or marble into construction material. These items were not for export but for local markets. And along with the manufacture of elite items existed the manufacture of items for the daily life of common folks. Significant in the Rev 18 passage is that what is usually seen as evidence for Rome's insatiable consumption of exotic goods also attests the existence and importance of networks of production and retailing in the city.

Another frequently quoted passage indicates a further dimension of the city, what Horden and Purcell identify as *rus in urbe*, the countryside in the city, comprising "large open spaces—uncultivated, agricultural land, or orchards—in even the largest and apparently most crowded of Mediterranean cities."[106] Suburban areas produced food within and for the larger urban area. Neville Morley identifies developments in the *suburbium*'s "agricultural practice:

---

103. Bauckham, "Economic Critique of Rome."

104. Paterson, "Trade and Traders," emphasizing the role of markets in trade and links between trade and empire.

105. *CIL* 10:875; cited in Shelton, *As the Romans Did*, 135. See also Petronius, *Satyricon* 76:3–9; Meijer and Van Nijf, *Trade, Transport and Society*.

106. Horden and Purcell, *Corrupting Sea*, 110–12.

a greater degree of orientation towards the market, with specialization in a particular set of crops [expensive perishables: fruit, certain vegetables, dairy products] and more intensive cultivation."[107] Dionysius of Halicarnassus observes:

> If anyone wishes to estimate the size of Rome by looking at these suburbs he will necessarily be misled for want of a definite clue by which to determine up to what point it is still the city and where it ceases to be the city; so closely is the city connected with the country, giving the beholder the impression of a city stretching out indefinitely. (*Roman Antiquities* 4:13)

As seems typical for many cities and towns, urban and rural boundaries were porous and fluid, with the city producing some of its own food supplies and supplying goods and services for its suburban areas. Robert Witches observes that "gardens [*horti*] and groves penetrated the city, whilst urban-style building spilled into the countryside."[108] Larger villas and small farms or market gardens "intensively produced food and luxuries for the urban market," even while pottery, bricks, and marble found in archeological investigations attest that so-called rural areas availed themselves of goods, skills, and services originating and produced in the city to display "a 'metropolitan' style of consumption."[109] Claire Holleran observes the production from market gardens that passed through the profiteering hands of numerous "middlemen" before being sold in Rome.[110] Research into brick production in the Tiber Valley, upriver from Rome to Orte, indicates a number of brickmaking works.[111] Some were oriented to the Roman market with access to transportation, warehousing, and consumer building projects; some were oriented to Tiber Valley needs. Jean-Jacques Aubert draws attention to the key role of business managers—whether independent craftsmen or agents acting on behalf of absentee entrepreneurs—in running economic enterprises such as retail, real estate/estates, workshops, garment production, and traders/shippers.[112] Emanuel Mayer identifies successful artisans and merchants who supplied urban markets with various products as comprising an economically and culturally influential "ancient middle

---

107. Morley, *Metropolis and Hinterland*, 83, 86.
108. Witcher, "(Sub)urban Surroundings," 212.
109. Witcher, "(Sub)urban Surroundings," 214; see also Purcell, "Roman *Villa*."
110. Holleran, *Shopping in Ancient Rome*, 95–97, 182–83.
111. Graham, "Of Lumberjacks and Brick Stamps."
112. Aubert, "Fourth Factor."

class,"[113] while Jean Andreau highlights the contribution of elite financiers and professional bankers in facilitating business transactions.[114] The city's economy and economic agents are much more complex than an emphasis on consumption allows, and economic power is not confined to elites.

Taking a wider geographical perspective, Neville Morley has examined the interaction between Rome and the rest of Italy to argue for economic interdependence between "metropolis and hinterland." Part of his argument is to reject a view of independent, isolated, and self-sufficient town-country units and to set Rome and the rest of Italy "in the context of larger urban systems" of production and consumption in which various parties benefitted.[115] Puteoli and Ostia clearly benefitted from their roles in supplying Rome's needs, but also developed their own market economies.[116] Various large estates and small peasant farmers throughout the peninsula sold surplus produce to traders and in local markets, from which Rome also drew resources including "staples like wine and oil; fruit, vegetables, and meat; wool, wood, and other raw materials."[117] Towns throughout Italy—Capua, Mediolanum, Patavium, Pompeii, Beneventum—functioned as market centers for surrounding areas in providing employment, goods, and services, as well as drawing traders who facilitated commerce with much broader markets including Rome.[118]

Conclusions from Case Studies

The seven urban vignettes given here provide several insights into urban economies and their personnel. One of these insights is the complexity of urban market economies, another is their variety, a third is the porous nature of urban-rural interactions, and a fourth is the recognition of micro- or regional economies. One model based on an urban-rural polarity of consumption and production does not fit all scenarios. The "consumer city" model proposed by Finley is too simplistic and lacks explanatory power to account for these diverse and fluid realities. While all cities consume rural production, styling the interaction as parasitic is not justified. The vignettes discussed above attest

113. Mayer, *Ancient Middle Classes*.
114. Andreau, *Banking and Business*.
115. Morley, "Cities in Context," 45.
116. Janet DeLaine counters the "better-known picture of state control" in Ostia by sketching its diverse and complex private and civic commercial activities and transactions, including the roles of individual traders, entrepreneurs, and businessmen ("Commercial Landscape of Ostia").
117. Morley, "Cities in Context," 47–48.
118. Morley, *Metropolis and Hinterland*, 108–83.

that cities provided markets, services, employment, and goods for rural areas just as rural areas provided food, resources, markets, and labor for urban areas. And frequently urban production surpassed local needs so that products were traded around the empire. Nor, then, was urban-countryside interaction the only dynamic of urban economies. Both intra- and interregional interactions were also vital.

Participating in these structures and practices of economic power, of course, are people, a hierarchy or spectrum of economic agents who make the system work and who work the system. Landowning elites produced, financed, traded, and consumed products. A small but significant middling group comprised some artisans with larger workforces of poorer workers,[119] interregional traders and merchants,[120] and wholesalers and financiers[121]—some of whom were freed persons. This middling group made a good living in producing and moving significant quantities of goods either for elite consumers or for small farmers who produced food but needed supplies of other household goods. Some freed persons contributed in "intellectual and artistic professions" such as "professors, writers, physicians, architects, painters, sculptors, actors"; they owned sizable landholdings, and functioned as traders, wholesalers, professional bankers and financiers.[122] Other artisans, including some freed people, and both men and women, produced on a much smaller scale and struggled to survive around or below subsistence level,[123] as did small shopkeepers, and those with only their labor to offer in producing and transporting goods.[124] Morley identifies three features of this latter group: their vulnerability especially to food shortage, their exclusion from social frameworks, and their sense of shame and envy of those with better circumstances.[125] Non-elite workers of the land, whether owners of small areas, renters, or waged day laborers, comprised a "highly variegated group" of peasants who existed near subsistence and participated in local or regional markets, selling produce and purchasing what they could not produce.[126] Slaves existed across the spectrum but especially in lower

---

119. Morel, "Craftsman," 216–23, 242; for example, Eurysaces the baker in Rome; Petersen, "Baker."
120. Giardina, "Merchant."
121. Andreau, *Banking and Business*.
122. Andreau, "Freedman," 177, 188–89.
123. Morel, "Craftsman," including women (223–25) and poor workers (233).
124. Kehoe, "Contract Labor.:
125. Morley, "Poor in the City," 32–36.
126. Kolendo, "Peasant," 212.

levels,[127] while others—the physically or psychologically broken and socially isolated—struggled at the very bottom of the economic structures with few resources or means of procuring them. Such an economic hierarchy of inequality reflected and effected economic power at work.[128] It is important to note that even with the recognition of a range of economic activities—including market economies and some entrepreneurial activity—benefits were not equally distributed; there was no widespread "trickle-down" effect that alleviated the varying degrees of poverty experienced by most. Rather, most people worked hard with limited resources for minimal returns that did not substantially distance them from subsistence existence.

These conclusions cohere with that of Keith Hopkins who—while recognizing the value of the "consumer city" model—acknowledges that "ancient towns served other functions" and that the "weakness of the ideal type ... is that it replaces complexity with over-simplification."[129] Mattingly et al recognize "a great range of urban forms, some more productive, some more rural, some more commercial, some thriving market centers, some with a more socially embedded economy. Archaeologists have tended to be more skeptical that a single model could encompass the reality of all the towns of the Roman world."[130]

Christ-Believing Assemblies: Socioeconomic Levels and Participation

Considering what is known about the nature of urban economics in the Roman Empire, where might we find the Christ-believing assemblies addressed by Paul's letters in the complex, diverse, and in part vibrant economic structures and personnel of such cities? It would be fair to observe that Pauline scholarship has generally been much more interested in Paul than in the assemblies that he addressed, in his theology more than their bodies, and in his ideas more than their economic experiences and structures. Nevertheless, some scholars have been keen to locate these assemblies' Christ believers in the empire's socioeconomic structures.[131]

---

127. Thébert, "Slave," 170; Scheidel, "Slavery."

128. See further below in sect. 3 for analysis of societal inequalities in the work of Friesen, Oakes, and Longenecker.

129. Hopkins, "Economic Growth," 75.

130. Mattingly et al., "Leptiminus," 76.

131. For discussion, Holmberg, *Sociology and New Testament*, 21–76.

The Findings of Engels, Kautsky, and Deissmann

Friedrich Engels (1820–95) saw the early assemblies as comprising the economically powerless and deprived. Not surprisingly, Engels noted some significant

> points of resemblance with the modern working-class movement. Like the latter, Christianity was originally a movement of oppressed people: it first appeared as the religion of slaves and emancipated slaves, of poor people deprived of all rights, of peoples subjugated or dispersed by Rome. Both Christianity and workers' socialism preach forthcoming salvation from bondage and misery; Christianity places this salvation in a life beyond, after death, in heaven; socialism places it in this world, in a transformation of society. Both are persecuted and baited.[132]

Engels elaborates those afflicted with "bondage and misery" as "those who have nothing to look forward to from the official world or have come to the end of their tether with it,"[133] who are "struggling against the whole world,"[134] "the 'labouring and burdened,' the members of the lowest strata of the people . . . for [whom] paradise lay lost behind them"[135]—for whom the only way out was "recompense and punishment in the world beyond, namely heaven and hell."[136]

Significantly, while Engels sees the earliest Christians as emerging from the poorest and the enslaved in the Roman world, he does not offer a systematic or detailed analysis of the empire's urban economic structures. And while his discussion recognizes Roman oppression in the form of slavery, and also deep class resentment against the wealthy, he does not see early Christianity addressing material and political deprivations and structures in any programmatic way that offers any prospect for socioeconomic transformation. The only rescue takes the form of escape into a future heavenly life.[137]

In Karl Kautsky 1908 work, *Ursprung des Christenthums* (translated into English in 1925 as *Foundations of Christianity*), he positions his discussion of

132. F. Engels, "History of Early Christianity," 316; "religion of the slaves and the oppressed" (F. Engels, "Anti-Dühring," 145); "the religion of the slaves, the banished, the dispossessed, the persecuted, the oppressed" (150); "its disciples among the poor, the miserable, the slaves, and the rejected and [it] despises the rich, the powerful and the privileged" (F. Engels, "Bruno Bauer," 196); "the enslaved, oppressed, and impoverished" (F. Engels, "History of Early Christianity," 335).

133. F. Engels, "History of Early Christianity," 322.

134. F. Engels, "History of Early Christianity," 330.

135. F. Engels, "History of Early Christianity," 334.

136. F. Engels, "History of Early Christianity," 336.

137. Engel's discussion does not engage the Pauline communities; his focus is on the book of Revelation.

"primitive Christianity" in the context of his economic analysis of the Roman Empire, which emphasizes elite wealth based in slave labor. With superlative adjectives, Kautsky reconstructs a system marked by a binary:

> The most colossal and intoxicating accumulation of wealth and power in a few hands; with the most abundant accumulation of the greatest misery for slaves, ruined peasants, craftsmen and lumpenproletarians;[138] with the crudest class contradictions and bitterest class hatred—[that] ended with the complete impoverishment and despair of the entire society. All of this left its mark on Christianity.[139]

Accordingly, for Kautsky, "Christianity was in its initial stages a movement of the propertyless"[140] and, quoting Friedländer at length, of "the poor and lowly ... the lower classes ... the lowest groups ... simpletons and slaves, women and children ... the uneducated and crude and peasant-like men ... little people, artisans and old women."[141] Kautsky identifies the movement as proletarian, by which he means the urban poor and uneducated. He identifies four features of the "proletarian character of the community: class hatred against the rich, communistic organization, contempt for labor, and destruction of the family." He cites 1 Cor 1:26–27 to support his claim of low status (though without any nod to the now commonplace recognition of some wealthy and powerful within the community) but mentions Paul again only in relation to family and sexual relations.[142]

Like Engels, Kautsky works with a broad economic binary of the very rich and the poor. His analysis of economic power is more developed than Engels's in emphasizing the importance of slave labor and elite land ownership, but he gives almost no attention to urban structures of manufacturing and trade. And like Engels, he offers little attention to the realities of poverty. The communities associated with Paul receive limited attention.

Adolf Deissmann offers a somewhat mixed economic analysis. In his influential *Light from the Ancient East*, he emphasizes "the close inward connexion between the gospel and the lower classes":[143] the biblical writings comprise "a book of peasants, fishermen, artisans, travelers ... of the village and the town ...

---

138. Those who are disenfranchised by their society but not engaged, or interested in, revolutionary action.

139. Kautsky, *Foundations of Christianity*, 59.

140. Kautsky, *Foundations of Christianity*, xiii.

141. Kautsky, *Foundations of Christianity*, 273–74.

142. Kautsky, *Foundations of Christianity*, 272, 276–300.

143. Deissmann, *Light from Ancient East*, 394.

of the people and the peoples ... of the weary and heavy-laden."[144] Christianity rose "from the workshop and the cottage ... the lower ranks of society ... the humbly situated."[145] He makes his argument, however, not primarily on the basis of any economic analysis of the ancient world but on the basis of a philological analysis of similarities between the New Testament texts and recently discovered nonliterary (non-elite) texts.

However, in his book on Paul, Deissmann describes the Pauline communities in more diverse terms as embracing a cross section of society. He identifies "Paul and his companions" as overwhelmingly "men and women from the middle and lower classes" (citing 1 Cor 1:26–28), and recognizes both poverty in the Macedonian churches (2 Cor 8:2) as well as some "fairly well-to-do Christians."[146] Strangely, in this study, Deissmann discusses the language, geography, and papyri of "Paul's world," but does not locate Paul's assemblies in relation to any analysis of the political and economic structures of the empire and its urban centers.[147]

Several similarities mark the work of Engels, Kautsky, and Deissmann. All three recognize, at least in wide-lens perspective, the hierarchical structure of the Roman Empire, including a fundamental economic binary of the powerful wealthy and powerless poor. Yet none of them pursues a detailed analysis of the economic roles and structures of cities in the imperial system. They recognize that the early Christian movement draws primarily from the powerless poor, though Deissmann recognizes the presence of both the "middle and lower classes." Yet despite this societal recognition, none understands the Pauline communities to be committed to addressing the socioeconomic conditions of the powerless poor. Engels pays little attention to Paul or the here-and-now of his communities. Kautsky identifies class hatred whereby the poor hated the rich but does not identify any program to address the needs of the poor, and likewise pays little attention to Paul himself. Deissmann notes some sympathies with the poor and with relief activity in 1 Corinthians, but his emphasis falls on spiritualized "riches in Christ" and his attention often focuses on the "types of souls among the ancient non-literary classes" more than on their somatic, economic, and societal conditions.[148]

144. Deissmann, *Light from Ancient East*, 392.

145. Deissmann, *Light from Ancient East*, 395. Deissmann thinks Kautsky was right to "link Primitive Christianity with the ranks of the people" but finds Kautsky's materialistic approach and disregard for Jesus and Paul unconvincing.

146. Deissmann, *Paul*, 241–44.

147. Deissmann, *Paul*, 27–51.

148. Deissmann, *Light from Ancient East*, 290–300.

Further Attempts at Understanding the Economics of the Pauline Assemblies

In a 1977 book, revised and republished in 1983, Abraham Malherbe declared that in relation to "the social level of early Christians . . . a new consensus may be emerging . . . quite different from the one represented by Adolf Deissmann." Malherbe saw this consensus comprising the recognition of "a higher status of early Christians" with the Pauline assemblies embracing a cross section of society.[149] In his influential *The First Urban Christians* (1983), Wayne Meeks supported the consensus that Malherbe was claiming.[150] Meeks sought to sustain the claim of a cross section of society present in the Pauline assemblies with prosopographic evidence[151] and "indirect evidence" comprising references to money matters in Paul's letters. Meeks concludes that "people of several social levels are brought together" in Paul's congregations though missing from the assemblies are "the extreme top and bottom" societal levels."[152] While the multifeatured notion of social status[153] dominates the discussion, urban economic power structures—as with Malherbe's discussion—receive little attention.

Not everyone, though, is convinced by this new consensus. Justin Meggitt rejects the claim of a societal cross section by arguing first for a strictly binary understanding of the empire's economic structures whereby most of the empire's subjects, "the non-elite, over 99 percent of the Empire's population, could expect little more from life than abject poverty." Meggitt insists that there were "few economic differences between those that found themselves outside of the rarefied circles of the elite."[154] Moreover, he argues that the Pauline assemblies participated in and reflected these circumstances. Meggitt writes that "The Pauline Christians, *en masse*, shared fully the bleak material existence that was the lot of more than 99 percent of the inhabitants of the Empire."[155] Discussing a number of texts, especially from 1 Corinthians, he contests any

---

149. Malherbe, *Social Aspects*, 45–59, esp. 31, 41. Malherbe cites the work of Judge, *Social Pattern*, 59, interpreting 1 Cor 1:26–28 as indicating the Corinthian community included "well-to-do persons." See also Judge, "Early Christians"; and Judge, "St. Paul."

150. Meeks, *First Urban Christians*, 51–73, esp. 52–53, 73. In addition to Judge and Malherbe, he appeals to Theissen, *Social Setting*.

151. Meeks, *First Urban Christians*, 55–63.

152. Meeks, *First Urban Christians*, 73.

153. Meeks lists "power, occupational prestige, income or wealth, education and knowledge, religious and ritual purity, family and ethnic-group position and local-community status" (*First Urban Christians*, 54).

154. Meggitt, *Paul, Poverty, and Survival*, 7.

155. Meggitt, *Paul, Poverty, and Survival*, 99; see also 50, 75, 153.

economic reading of 1 Cor 1:26–27; particularly, though not exclusively, he engages Gerd Theissen's work; and he finds no persuasive evidence for wealthy groups or individuals in the assemblies, including Erastus.[156] Paul's groups reflect and fully participate in the economic misery, deprivation, life at subsistence level, and limited opportunities that marked the lives of 99 percent of the population. While Meggitt rightly draws attention to Pauline scholarship's neglect of poverty in the Roman Empire and in the assemblies addressed by Paul, and also sets his discussion in an analysis of the empire's economy, his discussion remains unconvincing for at least two major reasons. One is that his argument concerning the Pauline assemblies employs a simplistic binary of the very wealthy and "the lived reality of the other 99 percent of the population."[157] The binary allows no room for gradations of poverty or the presence of any middling group that, though not wealthy, might have gained some level of economic resources and security through trade and manufacturing (as we saw in the previous discussion of cities in the Roman world).

Furthermore, Meggitt's discussion of the Roman economic system with its emphasis on "mass urban destitution"[158] is limited by being informed by the primitivist perspective, notably the work of Moses Finley and his supporters. As the discussion above has shown, recent work has found this approach to be inadequate. Accordingly—influenced by this deficient economic model—Meggitt rejects a market economy and economic rationalism; underscores the primacy of agriculture (though undeveloped); regards urban industry or manufacturing as insignificant, small scale, and concerned only with local demand; styles trade as "essentially primitive"; does not recognize technological advance or the role of entrepreneurs; and asserts that economic activity in Paul's context lacks a "clear work-ethos." According to Meggitt, no means or motivation for economic growth existed since urban manufacturing and trade were of little account: only a binary of those born with wealth and those born into poverty can exist, with no means of changing it and no "mid-range economic group" possible.[159] This does not appear to be the case.

The preceding discussion on urban areas indicates that Meggitt significantly understates the role of trade, levels of production from many small workshops, export activity of goods around the Mediterranean, the existence of market economies, and the presence of middling groups. Some urban residents,

---

156. Meggitt, *Paul, Poverty, and Survival*, 101–54.
157. Meggitt, *Paul, Poverty, and Survival*, 13.
158. Meggitt, *Paul, Poverty, and Survival*, 52.
159. Meggitt, *Paul, Poverty, and Survival*, 41–53, esp. 45, 47, 49.

and possibly/probably some members of Pauline assemblies, benefitted from their participation in such economic activities and accumulated some, though not excessive, wealth, which means that there were distinctions across society. And his brief reference to the grain dole in Rome feeding 150 thousand, or a fifth of the more "economically successful of Rome's population," undermines his claims of "few economic differences" in the 99 percent.[160] The result is that Meggitt's claims of an undifferentiated 99 percent both misrepresent both Roman urban populations and also distort any analysis of Pauline assemblies.

Steven Friesen's Findings on the Social Structures of the Pauline Assemblies

Steven Friesen is also not convinced by Malherbe's and Meeks's claims of a new consensus, though for different reasons. First Friesen contests Malherbe's assertion that there is a new consensus whereby "members of [Paul's] assemblies represented a cross-section of society." He argues, correctly, that this view did not emerge toward the end of the twentieth century. Malherbe is "factually wrong" to claim this new consensus as recent since Deissmann (at least in his book on Paul) argued for this view in 1912.[161]

Second, Friesen argues that the real change across twentieth-century scholarship on Paul since Deissmann has been the rendering invisible of political concerns and poverty, the elevation of the complex, multivariable, and elusive notion of "status," and the removal of discussions of "oppression, injustice and poverty."[162]

Third, contrary to Meggitt's claim of an undifferentiated 99 percent, Friesen proposes a graduated "poverty scale" to measure "poverty in cities of the empire" and to describe "the economic resources of Paul's congregations."[163] Friesen identifies seven socioeconomic levels and assigns percentages for each level:[164]

PS 1, Imperial elites	The imperial dynasty, Roman senatorial families, a few retainers, local royalty, a few freed persons	0.04 percent of the population

160. Meggitt, *Paul, Poverty, and Survival*, 51–52.

161. Friesen, "Poverty in Pauline Studies," 325. Friesen does not recognize the differences in Deissmann's discussion in *Light from Ancient East* and *Paul* that I note above.

162. Friesen, "Poverty in Pauline Studies," 331–36.

163. Friesen, "Poverty in Pauline Studies," 337.

164. Friesen, "Poverty in Pauline Studies," 341, 347, for percentages.

PS 2, Provincial elites	Decurial families, some freed persons, some retired military officers	1 percent
PS 3, Municipal elites	Most decurial families, wealthy men and women who do not hold office, some freed persons, some retainers, some veterans, some merchants	1.76 percent
PS 4, Those with moderate surplus resources	Some merchants, some traders, some freed persons, some artisans (especially those who employ others), and military veterans	7 percent?
PS 5, Economically stable persons living near subsistence level (with reasonable hope of remaining above the minimum level to sustain life)	Many merchants and traders, regular wage earners, artisans, large shop owners, freed persons, some farm families	22 percent?
PS 6, Those living at subsistence level (and often below the minimum level necessary to sustain life)	Small farm families, laborers (skilled and unskilled), artisans (esp. those employed by others), wage earners, most merchants and traders, small shop or tavern owners	40 percent
PS 7, Those living below subsistence level	Some farm families, unattached widows, orphans, beggars, disabled, unskilled day laborers, prisoners	28 percent

On this basis, Friesen draws three conclusions about Paul's assemblies. First, the letters do not attest to the presence of anyone from the top three levels. Second, only a few (perhaps two, and perhaps up to seven of the named persons in Paul's letters) belong to levels 4 and 5. Third, the majority, including Paul, belong to levels 5 through 7.[165] That is, just as "the overwhelming majority of the population under Roman imperialism lived near the subsistence level" (levels 5 through 7), so too did members of Paul's assemblies.[166]

Friesen's contribution is considerable, providing much-needed nuance to the discussion about both the Roman imperial economy and the Pauline assemblies. His seven-level scale recognizes gradations within vague and generalizing terms such as "elite" or "upper class" and "the poor." In response, however, John Barclay laments the lack of data to sustain such an analysis and doubts that "we

---

165. Friesen, identifies Gaius (Rom 16:23), Chloe (1 Cor 1:11), Phoebe (Rom 16:1–2), Erastus (Rom 16:23), Philemon (Phlm 22), Prisca and Aquila (1 Cor 16:19) ("Poverty in Pauline Studies," 352–57).

166. Friesen, "Poverty in Pauline Studies," 343; larger discussion, 348–58.

will ever be able to reach more than tentative and imprecise conclusions."[167] On the other hand, Peter Oakes finds Friesen's discussion limited in its focus on resources rather than behaviors and on the difficult notion of subsistence. More positively, Oakes thinks "sociological measures of poverty" that attend to deprivations and necessities offer a fruitful way ahead.[168]

Peter Oakes's Approach to Understanding Economic Status within the Pauline Assemblies

Subsequently, Oakes developed a different approach to identifying the economic resources, levels, and practices of the Pauline assemblies. He foregrounds not subsistence levels or calorie consumption but size of living space to construct four readings of Romans based in the living-working conditions and levels of four imagined non-elites who might inhabit space in the Insula of the Menander in Pompeii. He constructs "Sabina" as a very poor freedwoman who works with her husband as an artisan stoneworker. "Iris" is a barmaid and slave who is subjected to sexual exploitation. "Primus" is a middle-aged male slave whose menial work comprises stoking the fire for the boiler in the household bathhouse. Finally, the best resourced (though not elite) of the quartet is Holconius, who is a cabinetmaker with some means and who hosts the assembly of believers (about thirty persons) in his larger space.

Oakes develops this scenario in three ways. First and most significant for our purposes, he builds a "space distribution" model on the basis of a correlation between house size/living space and income. His assumption is that those with more income will rent a larger space. On this basis he estimates the following percentages of the population in Pompeii rented this amount of living space:[169]

Space Occupied (square meters)	Percentage of Population
1,000 and above	2.50
600–999	2.00
300–599	10.50
200–299	7.00
100–199	11.00
0–99	67.00

167. Barclay, "Poverty in Pauline Studies," 365.
168. Oakes, "Constructing Poverty Scales," 369–71.
169. Oakes, *Reading Romans*, 46–68, esp. 61. I have modified the presentation of Oakes's table, by combining figures for 600–999 and 300–599.

Oakes notes that the bottom category of his table contains those of very little or no income (slaves, dependents living in someone else's house, the homeless), and that the percentages closely resemble those of Friesen's scale (3 percent in PS 1–3, 68 percent in PS 6–7, approximately 29 percent in PS 4–5).[170]

Second, through several computations, Oakes develops a profile of a "model craftworker house church" led by a craftworker from an approximately three-hundred-square-meter "house," comprising several other householders and households from smaller living spaces, some freed persons, slaves, and some homeless people. He suggests that twenty-five of the forty members have either a living space of either under one hundred square meters or no space at all.[171]

Third, Oakes then reads sections of Romans through the economic eyes of his four characters. Chapter 12 of Romans shapes a household community in ways that depart from some societal practices. Primus, who struggles with the injustice of his situation, finds good news in the proclamation of God "punishing his oppressors and improving his position" with a new status.[172] Sabina finds good news in the promise of help for endurance and the hope of eternal life.[173] Iris finds redemption from her sexual exploitation and the tensions of embodied Christian life.[174] Holconius, a gentile, is challenged to accept Jews as well as gentiles along with poorer people in his house church.[175]

Oakes's reconstruction is very suggestive. It is not clear, however, whether or not Oakes imagines readers of Romans from higher economic levels and how their location might impact their readings of the letter. We should also observe that by setting up a house church under the leadership of Holconius, the occupier of the largest space in Oakes's model, Oakes reinscribes the structure of dominant economic power that pervades the societal hierarchy and suggests that only those with some economic resources and living space could host a meeting of believers.

Bruce Longenecker appreciatively affirms the "significant heuristic potential" of Friesen's poverty scale[176] in declaring it "helpfully heuristic and un-

---

170. Oakes, *Reading Romans in Pompeii*, 66.
171. Oakes, *Reading Romans in Pompeii*, 69–97, esp. 85, 87, and 96 (modified for Rome).
172. Oakes, *Reading Romans in Pompeii*, 133.
173. Oakes, *Reading Romans in Pompeii*, 137–43.
174. Oakes, *Reading Romans in Pompeii*, 143–49.
175. Oakes, *Reading Romans in Pompeii*, 150–74.
176. Longenecker, "Exposing the Economic Middle," 244.

avoidably preliminary," and "generally helpful and constructive."[177] Longenecker questions Friesen's nomenclature of a "poverty scale" and prefers that of "economic scale." The heart of his critique, though, concerns the size of the middling groups in Friesen's scale, highlighting Friesen's dependence on Finley's construction of ancient economies.[178] While Friesen seeks to replace a binary of rich and poor with some gradations (*pace* Meggitt), his scale remains, in Longenecker's view, effectively a binary between a small percentage in the top three levels (PS 1–3, 3 percent) and a very large percentage in the bottom three levels (PS 5–7, 90 percent). PS 4 comprises a very small middle group (7 percent). Longenecker sees this binary and the absence of any significant middle group as reflecting Friesen's expressed debt to Finley's views. With Finley's denial of significant manufacturing production, technological advance, entrepreneurial activity, and widespread trade, middling groups cannot emerge or be established.

Longenecker, however, appeals to the more recent work by classicists noted in the discussions above to argue—contrary to Finley—that significant production by some artisans, expanding trade involving traders, and improving technologies produced substantial economic benefits for a middling group comprising wealthy freedmen, traders, and some artisans. Consequently, Longenecker argues that Friesen's low percentage for PS 4 (7 percent)—reflective of the Finleyan binary economic model—needs revising upwards to recognize a significant middling group.[179] Accordingly, and aided by arguments about a spectrum of housing, Longenecker proposes an "economic scale" with revised percentages:

ES 1–3	3 percent	Friesen, 3 percent
ES 4	17 percent	Friesen, 7 percent
ES 5	25 percent	Friesen, 22 percent
ES 6	30 percent	Friesen, 40 percent
ES 7	25 percent	Friesen, 28 percent

Longenecker populates his ES 4 group with not only Friesen's collection of "some merchants, some traders, some freed persons, some artisans (especially

177. Longenecker, "Exposing the Economic Middle," 251.

178. Friesen, "Poverty in Pauline Studies," 338–39; Longenecker, "Exposing the Economic Middle," 254–55.

179. Longenecker, "Exposing the Economic Middle," 255–59; for a similar rejection of a binary construction and support for a significant middling group, Scheidel, "Stratification, Deprivation, and Quality."

those who employ others) and military veterans," but also adds *apparitores* (magistrate's scribes/messengers),[180] and economically successful *Augustales* (freedmen) to propose a more substantial middling group. He argues that adding ES 5 to an expanded ES 4 means a reduction in the numbers of those who experienced life-threatening poverty, though at least 55 percent remain in this peril (ES 6–7).

In his subsequent book-length study, Longenecker revises two percentages slightly, decreasing ES 4 to 15 percent, but increasing ES 5 to 27 percent.[181] He also offers an economic profile of Paul's assemblies, arguing that three of those named in Paul's letters (Erastus, Gaius, and Phoebe) belong to ES 4; three (Stephanas, Philemon, Crispus) belong to ES 4 or 5; and two (Prisca, Aquila) belong to ES 5 or 6, as do most of the assemblies, with some also from ES 7.[182] He cautiously proposes that an assembly may have comprised five members from ES 4 (10 percent), twelve from ES 5 (25 percent), and thirty-three from ES 6–7 (65 percent), suggesting that the assemblies did not exactly mirror societal economic gradations but tended more toward the greater presence from poorer societal members (ES 6–7).[183]

Longenecker's attention to the importance of his expanded middling group, identified in section 2 above, receives support from two particular discussions, one concerning society and one concerning the assemblies. As noted above, Mayer's 2012 study of *The Ancient Middle Classes* argues in part from housing decorations (wall painting, furniture, sculpture) and tombs for the emergence of a successful "commercial urban middle class" of urban businessmen (traders and craftsmen) with its own forms of cultural expressions. This middling group existed between wealthy landowners and the various gradations of the poor; operated through a *"taberna* economy" by conducting commercial activity in taverns, shops, etc. around agoras; and supplied urban markets with a range of products.

Sociologist Rodney Stark—rejecting the argument that material deprivations fuel new religious movements—argues that "religious movements typically are launched by the privileged classes . . . (and that) Christianity also began as a movement of the privileged."[184] Influenced in part by the work of E. A. Judge and Gerd Theissen, and appealing to 1 Cor 1:26–28, Stark examines the

---

180. Longenecker, "Exposing the Economic Middle," 264; see also Purcell, *"Apparitores."*
181. Longenecker, *Remember the Poor*, 53.
182. Longenecker, *Remembering the Poor*, 220–58, 267.
183. Longenecker, *Remember the Poor*, 294–97.
184. Stark, "Early Christianity," 2.

NT writings to establish the "social position" of the early Christian movement and concludes that while early Christianity attracted "lower-class converts," it "substantially *over*-recruited the privileged."[185] Though he is not careful to define the parameters of the term "privileged," Stark accounts for this interest on the basis of the quest of the privileged for "self-realization" in which "dissatisfied upper classes ... depressed by materialism ... initiate supernatural solutions to their thwarted existential and moral desires."[186] Stark's discussion seems too one-sided to be fully convincing, but it does highlight the importance sociologically of those with some resources in fuelling new religious movements.

Conclusions on the Economic Locations of the Pauline Assemblies' Members

The above discussion has provided both some clarification and some obscurity. Some clarity has emerged about the nature of the Roman economy. Meggitt's claims of a Finley-shaped binary comprising a few very wealthy (1 percent) and a vast-majority poor (99 percent) seem unsustainable and collapse before an emerging recognition of gradations among both the wealthy and the poor, along with the recognition of a more sizable middling group. But just what this means for understanding the economic activity of the early Christian movement is not immediately clear. Does the movement reflect these economic levels (Friesen), or does it have its own contours within those structures (Longenecker)? The appeal to oft-referenced 1 Cor 1:26–28 supports both those who argue for a cross section of society and those who claim a movement dominated by poorer societal members. The language of "not many" certainly does not mean "not any," and there seems to be universal agreement that the language does not reference levels 1 to 3 on the Friesen-Longenecker scales. The "not many," then, seem to reflect level 4 and perhaps level 5. And likewise, there seems to be agreement that while folks from level 7 are present in the assemblies, the majority (the many) belong to levels 6 or 7 and perhaps level 5. If these conclusions are on target, the so-called "cross section" is more closely defined as levels 4 through 7 with a weighting to levels 5 through 6 or 7. In other words, the assemblies may span some 70 percent of society but are weighted more to the lower than the upper levels, where economic struggles comprised daily experience.

---

185. Stark, "Early Christianity," 7; larger discussion, 2–12.
186. Stark, "Early Christianity," 13–14.

An Economic Survival Strategy

In the light of the above discussions that have identified the "Roman system of economic inequality" marked by a considerable spectrum, a middling group, and systemic poverty and deprivation, and that has suggested a likely location of most members of the Pauline assemblies within these economic structures (levels 4 through 6), does the eschatological thinker Paul offer any economic strategies for survival in the time before the eschatological completion of the divine purposes (1 Cor 15:20–28)? Meggitt mentions four economic strategies: self-sufficiency, almsgiving, hospitality, and mutualism, and he argues that only the last receives any endorsement from Paul.[187] Friesen mentions three "topics to explore . . . the Lord's Supper as a meal shared among the poor, Paul's manual labor as a refusal to commodify his apostolic calling . . . and the Jerusalem collection as a form of economic redistribution," all of which failed, he notes, as churches became participants in the system of inequality.[188] Space permits a consideration of only the Jerusalem collection here (1 Cor 16:1–4, 2 Cor 8–9, Gal 2:10, Rom 15:25–27).[189]

Meggitt argues that economic mutualism or mutual interdependence in the form of shared material support among believing communities expressed their theological solidarity "in Christ." It provided an alternative strategy to patron-client economic relations (which Meggitt regards as overrated and overemphasized in contemporary scholarship). Such relations rarely embraced the poor because they had nothing to offer the wealthy. Meggitt sees the Jerusalem collection as one expression of this mutualism whereby the collection of material supplies from Paul's churches for the Jerusalem poor would be reciprocated with material (not spiritual) gifts in the future.[190]

Friesen argues along somewhat similar lines. Like Meggitt, he rejects discussions of the collection that see it "in terms of patronage (Joubert) or as a redefinition of patronage (Harrison) but rather sees it as an alternative to patronage, one that functions to subvert the values of patronage and euergetism—in which wealthy individuals gave to the community in exchange for honors and/or status—by depicting an alternative mode of benefaction."[191]

---

187. Meggitt, *Paul, Poverty, and Survival*, 155.

188. Friesen, "Paul and Economics," 51–52.

189. I leave aside Paul's use of metaphors drawn from urban, manufacturing, business and rural life. Williams's *Paul's Metaphors*.

190. Meggitt, *Paul, Poverty, and Survival*, 157–61, 166–75.

191. Friesen, "Paul and Economics," 45–49; citing with approval Downs, *Offering of the Gentiles*, 240; contra Harrison, *Language of Grace*; Joubert, *Paul as Benefactor*.

Friesen elaborates this alternative act of benefaction in relation to three economic factors. First, the contributor was communal, from several groups, not from a single wealthy benefactor who gained much honor from the act and secured hierarchical structures; second, the contributor comprised people with limited resources who lived around subsistence level, giving a little and progressively building up the fund, not from the surplus of the wealthy; third, the act comprised economic redistribution aimed at economic equality, not a "public largesse that diverted attention from the daily exploitation of the majority."[192] Friesen sees such mutuality as fundamental to different economic relations.

Sze-kar Wan identifies further dimensions in this economic act involving ethnic and anti-imperial layers. Wan writes, "In bringing Jewish and Gentile congregations together, the collection symbolized an emerging universalizing society that came with its own economic principles and bases for structuring life in that society."[193] The collection symbolized the inclusion of gentiles in "the metanarrative of Israel," while simultaneously rejecting "Jewish ethnic exclusiveness" that might exclude gentiles or make gentiles adopt Jewish customs or identity markers. Likewise, in constructing this universalizing society, its "narrative stood in opposition to and criticism of all Roman imperial political, social and cultural hegemonic forces, expressions and institutions including the patronage system."[194] Wan sees the act of taking the collection to Jerusalem as evoking the eschatological and cosmic scenario of Isa 60 in which "the wealth of the nations" comes as tribute to Zion; it is a resistive act that "proclaims an all-encompassing sovereignty, to which all empires, including the Roman Empire, must pay obeisance." It relativizes and cripples "the world-governing scope of the colonizers."[195] By soliciting the collection from multiple assemblies, he destabilizes the power of patronal structures to bind a client to a particular patron.[196] Wan helpfully recognizes ethnic and imperial dimensions in the act but does not notice the reinscribing of imperial ways in this cosmic and ethnic vision of divine sovereignty.

Evidence for such "mutualism" or alternative and subversive communal benefaction also exists elsewhere in Paul's letters, in his emphasis on the identity of his addressees as members of one body in relationship with other members of the body (Rom 12; 1 Cor 12). This identity is expressed in the sharing

192. Friesen, "Paul and Economics," 49–51.
193. Wan, "Collection for the Saints," esp. 196.
194. Wan, "Collection for the Saints," 196.
195. Wan, "Collection for the Saints," 207.
196. Wan, "Collection for the Saints," 213–14.

of food when the assembly gathers (1 Cor 11:17–22). It is also expressed in commands concerning how assembly members are to treat one another as "members of one another" (Rom 12:5). Members are to love one another and outdo one another in showing honor (Rom. 12:10; 13:8; 1 Thess 3:12, 4:9), to live in harmony with one another (Rom. 12:16; 15:5), to not pass judgment on one another (14:13), to welcome one another (15:7), to instruct one another (15:14), care for one another (1 Cor 12:25), to serve one another (Gal 5:13), to not bite and devour one another (5:15), to not provoke or envy one another (5:26), to bear one another's burdens (6:2), to comfort one another (1 Thess 4:18), to encourage one another (5:11), and to be at peace with one another (5:13).[197] Such "one-anotherness" surely embraces all of the interactions within the assemblies, not just "spiritual interactions" but also economic matters such as financial circumstances and the practical sharing of resources, not only by those with a little surplus but also by those with scarcely enough to survive.

In constituting a different socioeconomic experience of mutual beneficence, such commands and the daily practices that they signify, moreover, created the possibility of some improved physical well-being, or at least some protection against or relief from an urban economic system that "failed to deliver longer lives and better bodies to" more than half its inhabitants."[198] The assemblies addressed by Paul were far too small and insignificant to effect any structural change to imperial urban economics, yet all faced the challenge to thrive—or simply to survive—within it. In a series of chapters, influenced by the work of Amartya Sen and rejecting quests for an elusive per capita GDP, Walter Scheidel wants to focus attention on markers of the quality of life that urban economies might or might not have produced. Scheidel writes, "There is little point in studying the Roman economy unless doing so gives us some idea of how it benefitted, or failed to benefit, the inhabitants."[199] In his view, its failures, more than its benefits, are especially evident, attested by a short and decreasing life expectancy comprising "twenty to thirty-five years," and by nutritional and health factors that have left their mark on skeletal remains.[200] This failure permeates the whole demographic spectrum, including the elite and the middling sectors; "health, even more so than income, is a critical factor

---

197. In non-Pauline letters, Eph 4:2, 25, 32; 5:21; Col 3:9, 13; 2 Thess 1:3.

198. Scheidel, "Physical Well-Being," esp. 330.

199. Scheidel, "Economy and Quality," 603. See also Scheidel, "Stratification, Deprivation, and Quality."

200. Scheidel, "Physical Well-Being," 321–29; similar to Duncan-Jones, *Structure & Scale*, 103–4.

in human well-being."²⁰¹ Scheidel concludes that "it appears that the imperial economy did not generally enhance biological living standards."²⁰² The nurturing of pragmatic, beneficial, caring "one another" interactions within and among the assemblies that Paul addresses, including the making available of economic resources, offers the possibility of an alternative structure based not on elite power but mutually shared resources. However, such a program faces a fundamental recognition by economic studies (especially within the formalist school) that *homo economicus* is primarily concerned with self-preservation and advantage.²⁰³

Conclusion

The members of the Christ-believing assemblies addressed by Paul participated in the urban economic structures of the Roman Empire. How to name those structures has been much debated. The prevailing model of a parasitic or "consumer city" has been evaluated and challenged from various perspectives. The discussions have demonstrated considerable complexity and variety in urban economies that are involved in interactive relationships with rural areas, that provide markets, services, employment, manufacturing, labor, and goods, and that participate in interregional trade. Urban areas constituted a hierarchy or spectrum of economic agents, from landowning elites who also financed some artisans and traders; through middling-level successful traders, financiers, and artisans; to low-level artisans, shopkeepers, land workers, unskilled laborers, and slaves. Such an economic hierarchy of inequality reflected and effected economic power at work.

Several attempts (Whittaker, Friesen, Oakes, Longenecker) have sought to bring some precision to defining this spectrum, replacing Finley-informed binary models with a recognition of gradations of both the wealthy and the poor and including a significant middling group of some resources. The assemblies addressed by Paul participated in these economic structures and practices. There is some agreement that they did not include people from the wealthiest levels but did include folk from middling and especially poor levels. While we cannot identify the specific economic roles of particular believers, we have some sense of the types of jobs and roles that were available, as well as the successes and rewards of some and the suffering and struggles of others. There is also

201. Scheidel, "Economy and Quality of Life," 603. See also Scheidel, "Stratification, Deprivation, and Quality."
202. Scheidel, "Physical Well-Being," 330.
203. This point is well made in Shim, "Re-Reading Luke's Gospel Economically."

some recognition of at least a proposed alternative economic practice of mutual benefaction among members of these assemblies that contests dominant imperial economic structures as well as individual self-interest. Whether members embraced and practiced this proposed economic alternative is not clear.

Bibliography

Aldrete, Greg, and David Mattingly. "Feeding the City: The Organization, Operation, and Scale of the Supply System for Rome." In *Life, Death, and Entertainment in the Roman Empire*, edited by David S. Potter and David J. Mattingly, 171–204. Ann Arbor: University of Michigan Press, 1999.

Andreau, Jean. *Banking and Business in the Roman World*. Key Themes in Ancient History. Cambridge: Cambridge University Press, 1999.

———. "The Freedman." In *The Romans*, edited by Andrea Giardina, 175–98. Chicago: University of Chicago Press, 1993.

Aubert, Jean-Jacques. "The Fourth Factor: Managing Non-Agricultural Production in the Roman World." In *Economies beyond Agriculture in the Classical World*, edited by David Mattingly and John Salmon, 90–111. Leicester-Nottingham Studies in Ancient Society. New York: Routledge, 2001.

Bakirtzzis, Charalambos, and Helmut Koester, eds. *Philippi at the Time of Paul and after His Death*. Harrisburg, PA: Trinity International, 1998.

Barclay, John. "Poverty in Pauline Studies: A Response to Steven Friesen." *JSNT* 26 (2004) 363–66.

Bauckham, Richard. "The Economic Critique of Rome in Revelation 18." In *The Climax of Prophecy: Studies in the Book of Revelation*, 338–83. Edinburgh: T&T Clark, 1993.

Chandler, Tertius, and Gerald Fox. *3000 Years of Urban Growth*. Edited by H. H. Winsborough. New York: Academic, 1974.

Ciarallo, Annamaria. *Gardens of Pompeii*. Rome: Bretschneider, 2000.

Cooley, Alison. *Pompeii*. London: Duckworth, 2003.

Corbier, Mireille. "City Territory and Taxation." In *City and Country in the Ancient World*, edited by John Rich and Andrew Wallace-Hadrill, 211–39. Leicester-Nottingham Studies in Ancient Society. New York: Routledge, 1991.

Dalby, Andrew. *Empire of Pleasures: Luxury and Indulgence in the Roman World*. New York: Routledge, 2000.

Deissmann, Adolf. *Light from the Ancient East: The New Testament Illustrated by Recently Discovered Texts of the Graeco-Roman World*. Rev. ed. New York: Harper & Brothers, 1927.

———. *Paul: A Study in Social and Religious History*. New York: Harper & Brothers, 1957.

DeLaine, Janet. "The Commercial Landscape of Ostia." In *Roman Working Lives and Urban Living*, edited by Ardle MacMahon and Jennifer Price, 29–47. Oxford: Oxbow, 2005.

Downs, David. *The Offering of the Gentiles: Paul's Collection for Jerusalem in Its Chronological, Cultural, and Cultic Contexts*. WUNT 248. Tübingen: Mohr Siebeck, 2008.

Duncan-Jones, Richard. *The Economy of the Roman Empire: Quantitative Studies*. Cambridge: Cambridge University Press, 1974.

———. *Structure & Scale in the Roman Economy*. Cambridge: Cambridge University Press, 1990.

Engels, Donald. *Roman Corinth: An Alternative Model for the Classical City*. Chicago: University of Chicago, 1990.

Engels, Friedrich. "Anti-Dühring." In *On Religion*, edited by Karl Marx and Friedrich Engels, 145–51. Classics in Religious Studies 3. Repr., Chico, CA: Scholars, 1982.
———. "Bruno Bauer and Early Christianity." In *On Religion*, edited by Karl Marx and Friedrich Engels, 194–204. Classics in Religious Studies 3. Repr., Chico, CA: Scholars, 1982.
———. "On the History of Early Christianity." In *On Religion*, edited by Karl Marx and Friedrich Engels, 316–47. Classics in Religious Studies 3. Repr., Chico, CA: Scholars, 1982.
Erdkamp, Paul. "The Food Supply of the Capital." In *The Cambridge Companion to Ancient Rome*, edited by Paul Erdkamp, 262–77. Cambridge Companions to the Ancient World. Cambridge: Cambridge University Press, 2013.
———. "Urbanism." In *The Cambridge Companion to the Roman Economy*, edited by Walter Scheidel, 241–64. Cambridge Companions to the Ancient World. Cambridge: Cambridge University Press, 2012.
Finley, Moses. "The Ancient City: From Fustel de Coulanges to Max Weber and Beyond." *Comparative Studies in Society and History* 19 (1977) 305–27.
———. *The Ancient Economy*. Rev. ed. Berkeley: University of California Press, 1999.
Friesen, Steven. "Embodied Inequalities: Diet Reconstruction and Christian Origins." In *Stones, Bones, and the Sacred: Essays on Material Culture and Ancient Religion in Honor of Dennis E. Smith*, edited by Alan Cadwallader, 9–31. SBL Early Christian Literature 21. Atlanta: SBL, 2016.
———. "Paul and Economics: The Jerusalem Collection as an Alternative to Patronage." In *Paul Unbound: Other Perspectives on the Apostle*, edited by Mark Given, 27–54. Peabody, MA: Hendrickson, 2010.
———. "Poverty in Pauline Studies: Beyond the So-Called New Consensus." *JSNT* 26 (2004) 322–61.
Fulford, Michael. "Economic Interdependence among Urban Communities of the Roman Mediterranean." *World Archaeology* 19 (1987) 58–75.
Garnsey, Peter. *Food and Society in Classical Antiquity*. Key Themes in Ancient History. Cambridge: Cambridge University Press, 1999.
———. "Grain for Rome." In *Trade in the Ancient Economy*, edited by Peter Garnsey et al., 118–30. Berkeley: University of California Press, 1983.
Garnsey, Peter, and Richard Saller. *The Roman Empire: Economy, Society, and Culture*. Berkeley: University of California Press, 1987.
Giardina, Andrea. "The Merchant." In *The Romans*, edited by Andrea Giardina, 245–71. Chicago: University of Chicago Press, 1993.
Graham, Shawn. "Counting Bricks and Stacking Wood: Providing the Physical Fabric." In *The Cambridge Companion to Ancient Rome*, edited by Paul Erdkamp, 278–96. Cambridge Companions to the Ancient World. Cambridge: Cambridge University Press, 2013.
———. "Of Lumberjacks and Brick Stamps: Working with the Tiber as Infrastructure." In *Roman Working Lives and Urban Living*, edited by Ardle MacMahon and Jennifer Price, 106–24. Oxford: Oxbow, 2005.
Greene, Kevin. "Technological Innovation and Economic Progress in the Ancient World: M. I. Finley Re-Considered." *Economic History Review*, n.s., 53 (2000) 29–59.
Harrison, James. *The Language of Grace in Its Graeco-Roman Context*. WUNT 172. Tübingen: Mohr Siebeck, 2003.

Hawkins, Cameron. "Manufacturing." In *The Cambridge Companion to the Roman Economy*, edited by Walter Scheidel, 175–94. Cambridge Companions to the Ancient World. Cambridge: Cambridge University Press, 2012.

Hitchner, R. Bruce. "'The Advantages of Wealth and Luxury': The Case for Economic Growth in the Roman Empire." In *The Ancient Economy: Evidence and Models*, edited by J. G. Manning and Ian Morris, 207–22. Stanford, CA: Stanford University Press, 2005.

Holleran, Claire. *Shopping in Ancient Rome: The Retail Trade in the Late Republic and the Principate*. Oxford: Oxford University Press, 2012.

Holmberg, Bengt. *Sociology and the New Testament: An Appraisal*. Minneapolis: Fortress, 1990.

Hopkins, Keith. "Economic Growth and Towns in Classical Antiquity." In *Towns in Societies: Essays in Economic History and Historical Sociology*, edited by Philip Abrams and E. A. Wrigley, 35–77. Past and Present Publications. Cambridge: Cambridge University Press, 1978.

Horden, Peregrine, and Nicholas Purcell. *The Corrupting Sea: A Study of Mediterranean History*. Oxford: Wiley-Blackwell, 2000.

Jashemski, Wilhelmina. *The Gardens of Pompeii, Herculaneum and the Villas Destroyed by Vesuvius*. 2 vols. New Rochelle, NY: Caratzas Brothers, 1993.

Jongman, Willem. *The Economy and Society of Pompeii*. Amsterdam: Gieben, 1991.

Joubert, Stephan. *Paul as Benefactor: Reciprocity, Strategy, and Theological Reflection in Paul's Collection*. Tübingen: Mohr Siebeck, 2000.

Judge, E. A. "The Early Christians as a Scholastic Community." *JRH* 1 (1960–61) 4–15, 125–37.

———. *The Social Pattern of Christian Groups in the First Century*. London: Tyndale, 1960.

———. "St. Paul and Classical Society." *JAC* 15 (1972) 19–36.

Kautsky, Karl. *Foundations of Christianity*. Translated by Henry F. Mins. New York: Russell, 1953.

Kehoe, Dennis. "Contract Labor." In *The Cambridge Companion to the Roman Economy*, edited by Walter Scheidel, 114–30. Cambridge Companions to the Ancient World. Cambridge: Cambridge University Press, 2012.

Kolendo, Jerzy. "The Peasant." In *The Romans*, edited by Andrea Giardina, 199–213. Chicago: University of Chicago Press, 1993.

Kron, Geoffrey. "Food Production." In *The Cambridge Companion to the Roman Economy*, edited by Walter Scheidel, 156–74. Cambridge Companions to the Ancient World. Cambridge: Cambridge University Press, 2012.

Laurence, Ray. *Roman Pompeii: Space and Society*. 2nd ed. New York: Routledge, 2007.

———. "Traffic and Land Transportation in and near Rome." In *The Cambridge Companion Ancient Rome*, edited by Paul Erdkamp, 246–61. Cambridge: Cambridge University Press, 2013.

Longenecker, Bruce. "Exposing the Economic Middle: A Revised Economy Scale for the Study of Early Urban Christianity." *JSNT* 31 (2009) 243–78.

———. *Remember the Poor: Paul, Poverty, and the Greco-Roman World*. Grand Rapids: Eerdmans, 2010.

Malherbe, Abraham. *Social Aspects of Early Christianity*. 2nd ed. Philadelphia: Fortress, 1983.

Mann, Michael. *The Sources of Social Power*. 3 vols. Cambridge: Cambridge University Press, 1986–93.

Manning, J. G., and Ian Morris, eds. *The Ancient Economy: Evidence and Models*. Stanford, CA: Stanford University Press, 2005.
Mattingly, David. "First Fruit? The Olive in the Roman World." In *Human Landscapes in Classical Antiquity: Environment and Culture*, edited by John Salmon and Graham Shipley, 213–53. Leicester-Nottingham Studies in Ancient Society. London: Routledge, 1996.
———. *Imperialism, Power, and Identity: Experiencing the Roman Empire*. Miriam S. Balmuth Lectures in Ancient History and Archaeology. Princeton, NJ: Princeton University Press, 2011.
———. "Oil for Export: A Comparison of Libyan, Spanish, and Tunisian Olive Oil Production in the Roman Empire." *JRA* 1 (1988) 33–56.
Mattingly, David J., and John Salmon, eds. *Economies beyond Agriculture in the Classical World*. Leicester-Nottingham Studies in Ancient Society. New York: Routledge, 2001.
Mattingly, David J., et al. "Leptiminus (Tunisia): A 'Producer' City?" In *Economies beyond Agriculture in the Classical World*, edited by David J. Mattingly and John Salmon, 66–89. Leicester-Nottingham Studies in Ancient Society. New York: Routledge, 2001.
Mayer, Emanuel. *The Ancient Middle Classes: Urban Life and Aesthetics in the Roman Empire, 100 BCE—250 CE*. Cambridge: Harvard University Press, 2012.
Meeks, Wayne. *The First Urban Christians; The Social World of the Apostle Paul*. New Haven, CT: Yale University Press, 1983.
Meggitt, Justin J. *Paul, Poverty, and Survival*. SNTW. Edinburgh: T&T Clark, 1998.
Meijer, Fik, and Onno van Nijf, eds. *Trade, Transport and Society in the Ancient World: A Sourcebook*. Routledge Revivals. New York: Routledge, 1992.
Mitchell, Stephen. "Olive Cultivation in the Economy of Roman Asia Minor." In *Patterns in the Economy of Roman Asia Minor*, edited by Stephen Mitchell and Constantina Katsari, 83–113. Swansea: Classical of Wales, 2005.
Moeller, Walter. *The Wool Trade of Ancient Pompeii*. Leiden: Brill, 1976.
Morel, Jean-Paul. "The Craftsman." In *The Romans*, edited by Andrea Giardina, 214–44. Chicago: University of Chicago Press, 1993.
Morley, Neville. "Cities in Context: Urban Systems in Roman Italy." In *Roman Urbanism: Beyond the Consumer City*, edited by Helen Parkins, 42–58. New York: Routledge, 1997.
———. *Metropolis and Hinterland: The City of Rome and the Italian Economy: 200 B.C.—A.D. 200*. Cambridge: Cambridge University Press, 1996.
———. "The Poor in the City of Rome." In *Poverty in the Roman World*, edited by Margaret Atkins and Robin Osborne, 21–39. Cambridge: Cambridge University Press, 2006.
———. "Population Size and Social Structure." In *The Cambridge Companion to Ancient Rome*, edited by Paul Erdkamp, 29–44. Cambridge Companions to the Ancient World. Cambridge: Cambridge University Press, 2013.
Morris, Ian. "Foreword." In *The Ancient Economy*, by Moses Finley, ix–xxxvi. Rev. ed. Berkeley: University of California Press, 1999.
Oakes, Peter S. "Constructing Poverty Scales for Graeco-Roman Society: A Response to Steven Friesen's 'Poverty in Pauline Studies.'" *JSNT* 26 (2004) 367–71.
———. "The Economic Situation of the Philippian Christians." In *The People beside Paul: The Philippian Assembly and History from Below*, edited by Joseph A. Marchal, 63–82. ECL. Atlanta: SBL, 2015.
———. *Philippians: From People to Letter*. Society for New Testament Studies Monograph Series 110. Cambridge: Cambridge University Press, 2001.

———. *Reading Romans in Pompeii: Paul's Letter at Ground Level*. Minneapolis: Fortress, 2009.

Parker, A. J. *Ancient Shipwrecks of the Mediterranean and the Roman Provinces*. British Archaeological Reports International Series 580. Oxford: BAR, 1992.

Paterson, Jeremy. "Trade and Traders in the Roman World: Scale, Structure, and Organisation." In *Trade, Traders, and the Ancient City*, edited by Helen Parkins and Christopher Smith, 149–67. New York: Routledge, 1998.

Peacock, David P., and David Williams. *Amphorae and the Roman Economy: An Introductory Guide*. Longman Archaeology Series. London: Longman, 1986.

Petersen, Lauren Hackworth. "The Baker, His Tomb, His Wife, and Her Breadbasket: The Monument of Eurysaces in Rome." *Art Bulletin* 85 (2003) 230–57.

Pleket, H. W. "Rome: A Pre-Industrial Megalopolis." In *Megalopolis: The Giant City in History*, edited by Theo Barker and Anthony Sutcliffe, 14–42. New York: St. Martin's, 1993.

———. "Urban Elites and Business in the Greek Part of the Roman Empire." In *Trade in the Ancient Economy*, edited by Peter Garnsey et al., 131–44. Berkeley: University of California Press, 1983.

Purcell, Nicholas. "The *Apparitores*: A Study in Social Mobility." *Papers of the British School at Rome* 51 (1983) 125–73.

———. "The Roman *Villa* and the Landscape of Production." In *Urban Society in Roman Italy*, edited by Tim J. Cornell and Kathryn Lomas, 151–79. London: UCL Press, 1995.

———. "Urbanism." In *The Oxford Handbook of Roman Studies*, edited by Alessandro Barchiesi and Walter Scheidel, 579–92. Oxford Handbooks. Oxford: Oxford University Press, 2010.

Sanders, Guy R. "Urban Corinth: An Introduction." In *Urban Religion in Corinth: Interdisciplinary Approaches*, edited by Daniel Schowalter and Steven Friesen, 1–15. HTS 53. Cambridge: Harvard University Press, 2005.

Scheidel, Walter, ed. *The Cambridge Companion to the Roman Economy*. Cambridge Companions to the Ancient World. Cambridge: Cambridge University Press, 2012.

———. "Economy and Quality of Life." In *The Oxford Handbook of Roman Studies*, edited by Alessandro Barchiesi and Walter Scheidel, 593–609. Oxford Handbooks. Oxford: Oxford University Press, 2010.

———. "Germs for Rome." In *Rome the Cosmopolis*, edited by Catharine Edwards and Greg Woolf, 158–76. Cambridge: Cambridge University Press, 2003.

———. "Physical Well-Being." In *The Cambridge Companion to the Roman Economy*, edited by Walter Scheidel, 321–33. Cambridge Companions to the Ancient World. Cambridge: Cambridge University Press, 2012.

———. "Slavery." In *The Cambridge Companion to the Roman Economy*, edited by Walter Scheidel, 89–113. Cambridge Companions to the Ancient World. Cambridge: Cambridge University Press, 2012.

———. "Stratification, Deprivation, and Quality of Life." In *Poverty in the Roman World*, edited by Margaret Atkins and Robin Osborne, 40–59. Cambridge: Cambridge University Press, 2006.

Scheidel, Walter, and Sitta von Reden, eds. *The Ancient Economy*. New York: Routledge, 2002.

Scheidel, Walter, et al., eds. *The Cambridge Economic History of the Greco-Roman World*. Cambridge Histories—Ancient History & Classics. Cambridge: Cambridge University Press, 2007.

Scobie, Alex. "Slums, Sanitation, and Mortality in the Roman World." *Klio* 68 (1986) 399–433.

Shelton, Jo-Ann, ed. *As the Romans Did: A Sourcebook in Roman Social History*. Oxford: Oxford University Press, 1997.

Shim, SeungWoo. "Re-Reading Luke's Gospel Economically: Aspects of a Market Economy and Economic Rationality in Luke's Gospel." PhD diss., Brite Divinity School at TCU, Fort Worth, TX, 2016.

Sirks, Booudewijn. *Food for Rome: The Legal Structure of the Transportation and Processing of Supplies for the Imperial Distributions in Rome and Constantinople*. Amsterdam: Gieben, 1991.

Stark, Rodney. "Early Christianity: Opiate of the Privileged?" *Faith & Economics* 54 (2009) 1–18.

Temin, Peter. "A Market Economy in the Early Roman Empire." *JRS* 91 (2001) 169–81.

———. *The Roman Market Economy*. Princeton Economic History of the Western World 71. Princeton, NJ: Princeton University Press, 2013.

Thébert, Yvon. "The Slave." In *The Romans*, edited by Andrea Giardina, 138–74. Chicago: University of Chicago Press, 1993.

Theissen, Gerd. *The Social Setting of Pauline Christianity: Essays on Corinth*. Edited and translated by John H. Schütz. Philadelphia: Fortress, 1982.

Tompkins, Daniel. "Review of Donald Engels, *Roman Corinth: An Alternative Model for the Classical City*." *Bryn Mawr Classical Review* 1 (1990) 11.

Toner, Jerry. *Popular Culture in Ancient Rome*. Cambridge: Polity, 2009.

Tuck, Steven. "The Tiber and River Transport." In *The Cambridge Companion to Ancient Rome*, edited by Paul Erdkamp, 229–45. Cambridge Companions to the Ancient World. Cambridge: Cambridge University Press, 2013.

Walbank, Mary E. Hoskins. "The Foundation and Planning of Early Roman Corinth." *JRA* 10 (1997) 95–130.

Wallace-Hadrill, Andrew. "Elites and Trade in the Roman Town." In *City and Country in the Ancient World*, edited by John Rich and Andrew Wallace-Hadrill, 241–72. Leicester-Nottingham Studies in Ancient Society. London: Routledge, 1991.

———. *Houses and Society in Pompeii and Herculaneum*. Princeton, NJ: Princeton University Press, 1994.

Wan, Sze-kar. "Collection for the Saints as Anticolonial Act." In *Paul and Politics: Ekklesia, Israel, Imperium, Interpretation*, edited by Richard A. Horsley, 191–215. Harrisburg, PA: Trinity International, 2000.

Whittaker, C. R. "The Consumer City Revisited: The *Vicus* and the City." *JRA* 3 (1990) 110–18.

———. "Do Theories of Ancient Cities Matter?" In *Urban Society in Roman Italy*, edited by Tim J. Cornell and Kathryn Lomas, 9–26. London: UCL Press, 1995.

———. "The Poor." In *The Romans*, edited by Andrea Giardina, 272–99. Chicago: University of Chicago Press, 1993.

Williams, David J. *Paul's Metaphors: Their Context and Character*. Peabody, MA: Hendrickson, 1999.

Wilson, Andrew. "Commerce and Industry in Roman Sabratha." *Libyan Studies* 30 (1999) 29–52.

———. "Machines, Power, and the Ancient Economy." *JRS* 92 (2002) 1–32.

---. "Timgad and Textile Production." In *Economies beyond Agriculture in the Classical World*, edited by David J. Mattingly and John Salmon, 271–96. Leicester-Nottingham Studies in Ancient Society. New York: Routledge, 2001.

---. "Urban Production in the Roman World: The View from North Africa." *Papers of the British School at Rome* 70 (2002) 231–73.

Wiseman, James. *The Land of the Ancient Corinthians*. Studies in Mediterranean Archaeology 50. Gothenburg: Aström, 1978.

Witcher, Robert. "(Sub)urban Surroundings." In *The Cambridge Companion to Ancient Rome*, edited by Paul Erdkamp, 205–25. Cambridge Companions to the Ancient World. Cambridge: Cambridge University Press, 2013.

7. An Alternative Society of Local Communities among Peoples Subject to the Roman Empire

RICHARD A. HORSLEY[1]

Introduction

Until recently Paul was understood in New Testament studies as the great hero of individual faith in the emergence of Christianity as a supposedly more universal and spiritual religion from the supposedly more parochial Judaism that was focused on legalistic obedience to the law. Trained in New Testament studies as a subdivision of Christian theology, scholars treated Paul's letters as theological treatises from which they could cite text fragments to attest certain theological doctrines such as Christology and soteriology. Deeply embedded in the modern Western separation of religion from political-economic life, Paul scholars imposed this separation onto the ancient world in general and onto Paul and his letters in particular. Paul was also understood as a social conservative, usually illustrated by one of his few statements about slavery. According to the standard interpretation, Paul had advised slaves to remain in the situation in which they were called, since supposedly he was concerned with only religious life, not social-economic relations.

Read more critically in recent decades, however, Paul's letters give a very different picture of the apostle, his mission, and the letters' function in that mission. In recent decades interpreters of Paul have begun to recognize that

---

1. Unless otherwise indicated, Scripture quotations in this chapter are from the author's translation.

religion was not separate from political-economic life. Paul and his coworkers were not "preaching" just about religious life. They were excitedly proclaiming that the climax of history had begun with the crucifixion and resurrection of Christ and would be gloriously fulfilled with Christ's parousia in "the day of the Lord."

Paul borrowed some of the central concepts and symbols of his proclamation from the Roman imperial order under the rule of Caesar in order to oppose it. The *gospel*, inscribed on massive monuments throughout the empire, proclaimed Caesar as the *Lord* and *Savior* who had brought *salvation* and *peace and security* to the world. Paul's proclamation of his alternative *gospel* that Christ was now *Lord and Savior* meant that Caesar's rule had been "overruled" by that of Christ. "The rulers of this age," who did not understand the secret plan of God in working precisely though their actions, had crucified Christ (1 Cor 2:6–8). But in the resurrection God had vindicated him, exalting him as the new, heavenly ruler, the true *Lord* (1 Cor 2:6–8, 15:1–28). At the "coming" of Christ in "the day of the Lord," the Roman imperial world, in which the wealthy imperial and local elite exploited, impoverished, and enslaved subject peoples, would be terminated and the kingdom of God finally be realized.

The time in between the crucifixion-resurrection and the parousia was the period of Paul's and other's urgent mission to expand the movement into new communities among subjected peoples in the empire. Paul's urging the communities of subjected peoples to persist in their *loyalty* (*pistis*, *fides*) to Christ, meant that they could no longer have *loyalty* to Caesar.[2] It seems evident from Paul's letters that the assemblies of Christ loyalists were forming communities that at least Paul understood as an alternative, inter-people society whose *politeuma* (social-political order)—already established in heaven with/by their *Lord*—would descend with him from heaven in the final realization of the kingdom of God (Phil 3:18–21).

Early twentieth-century interpreters of Paul and his letters have devoted considerable attention to the political-religious dimension of the Roman imperial world and the relation of the Pauline mission to it. But little attention has been given to the economic dimension, which was not separable from the political and religious dimensions in a movement of fledgling local communities in cities of the Eastern Empire. The agenda of this article—avoiding the

---

2. The term *pistis/fides* is usually translated in English Bibles and in New Testament scholarship by "faith/belief." In the Roman imperial world in which Paul worked and formulated letters, however, *pistis/fides* meant loyalty, usually to a lord or a political regime, especially to Caesar and to Roman imperial rule. Thus, the term "Christ believers" should be replaced by "Christ loyalists" or "Jesus loyalists."

standard assumption in New Testament studies that Paul's letters contain theological teaching with occasional ethical implications—is to discern the concrete economic aspects of the struggles of those newly established alternative communities.

It is important first to sketch the broader political-economic-religious context in the Roman imperial order in which the Pauline mission happened, perhaps as a response to it. Then attention will be devoted mainly to an investigation into the ways in which the Pauline mission sought to generate an alternative society "in but not of" the Roman imperial order. Since the movement that Paul and his coworkers started continued to develop, we can then trace the different lines of its development: on the one hand, in the deutero-Pauline letters but also, on the other hand, in what appears as a far less accommodationist way in other texts. Finally, we can examine indications in a few texts that some of the communities of Jesus loyalists took the more radical economic step of sharing their resources in common, particularly to aid the needy so that all had enough.

The Political Economy of the Roman Empire

Interpreters of Paul have been heavily dependent on scholars of the Hellenistic-Roman world for their understanding of the context of Paul's mission and letters. Nothing has been more bewildering than the variety of differing views on what is meant by "economics" or "the economy" and the different, often opposed, reconstructions of "the Roman economy."

A generation ago Moses Finley and others had laid out how ancient cities were economically dependent on the countryside, increasingly on land controlled by the wealthy living in the cities but farmed by tenants or slaves.[3] Informed by how Karl Polanyi was rethinking premodern economies, Finley also recognized that while trade was important particularly for luxury goods for the elite, the ancient economy was not dominated by "the market" and "trade," that is, it was not proto-capitalist. In the last few decades, however, as neoliberal economic theory and practice came to dominate not only in the West but in a globalized capitalist economy,[4] a new generation of Roman historians revived neoclassical economic theory, as exemplified in recent books on *The Roman Market Economy* and *The Ancient Middle Classes*.[5] In these neoclassical

---

3. Finley, *Ancient Economy*.

4. Recent criticism as it pertains to biblical studies in N. Elliott, "When Bridges Fail Us," 208–10.

5. Temin, *Roman Market Economy*; Mayer, *Ancient Middle Classes*. While balanced by

constructions, the Roman economy appears to have been proto-capitalist after all.

Neoclassical economics, however, abstracts "the economy" from society. Indeed it assumes that "the economy" is something in itself, an independent entity operating according to its own laws, such as that of "supply and demand."[6] In the Roman Empire, however, as in any empire or society in any historical circumstances, concrete *economic realities were embedded in networks of social-political-religious power relations* that were often complex and full of conflict, whether in the Roman Empire as a whole or in the particular cities where Paul and his coworkers generated new communities. The concepts and generalizations in which "economics" is discussed do more to hide than illuminate the conflictual relations. For example, to conclude from recently unearthed archaeological evidence of urban artisan production that economic structures and personnel were "complex, diverse, and vibrant" does not ask, much less investigate, the exploitative relation between those artisans and their "patrons" or "landlords." Application of models of social-economic stratification does not even ask, much less investigate, who was exercising power in what forms over whom in the urban and urban-and-rural network of (changing) power relations. To discuss a "labor market" in which "free urban workers" found work stops short of inquiring about the masses of people who had been thrown off the land. In Italy, for example, large numbers of peasants were displaced by slave labor on large estates during several decades of Roman conquests and enslavement of subjugated people (including in Judea and Galilee).[7] These displaced people joined the mass of "surplus" population in Rome.

The recent focus on Rome as having had a *market* economy that achieved a considerable degree of "integration" through "the expansion of trade" imagines "the economy" as somehow separate from "the state." But this analysis ignores the historical reality that the Roman imperial state stood not only at the apex

---

more critical articles, many of the essays in Scheidel's synchronic *Cambridge Companion to the Roman Economy* work with the controlling concepts of "market," "money and prices," even "economic integration through the expansion of trade and markets." The reversion to neoclassical economic theory is interwoven with much more extensive and detailed research into economic matters, relying heavily on archaeological investigations. Much of the evidence available is from cities and pertains to local production, for example, of ceramics and trade. See the essay by Carter in this volume for references to and summaries of some of this research. Many of these studies lack historical perspective, do not consider the overall Roman imperial political-economic structure, and revive neoclassical economics uncritically.

6. For the intellectual history that defined the economy as an independent entity, see Boer and Petterson, *Idols of Nations*.

7. Hopkins, *Conquerors and Slaves*.

but at the center of the Roman imperial economy.[8] It is puzzling to read an argument (based on a limited set of data) that Rome had a unified wheat market[9] when, according to extensive historical sources, the Roman imperial state was extracting huge quantities of grain from Egypt and other areas of the empire that it had conquered. One of the central concerns of the imperial state was the food supply for the Roman populace and army, which would have been a significant part of the imperial economy.[10] More than one emperor fixed food prices and subsidized the shipping enterprises contracted to transport grain from Egypt and elsewhere, whether in the building of ships or in compensation for losses (Tacitus, *Annals* 2:59, 89; 15:18.2, 39.2; Suetonius, *Claudius* 18–19). Augustus had even established a grain dole for the citizens of the metropolis (*Res gestae* 15). Most of the grain supply for Rome, for the army, and for the urban elites and their underlings was expropriated in the form of taxes and tribute from previously conquered peoples. One effect of this drain on producers in the provinces such as Egypt was to make it more difficult for them to maintain a subsistence living.[11] There evidently was an expansion of long-distance trade (as well as of local trade) in "commodities" in the early empire. Such trade, however, was primarily for the lifestyle of the wealthy in Rome and the other cities of the empire (see the list in Rev 18:11–14). The economy of the Roman Empire was not a market economy but a *political economy* that was based not on "supply and demand" (a modern notion) but on "demand and supply," that is, demand by the imperial state and its wealthy urban elites and supply coerced from subject peoples, tenants, and slaves.

Indeed, the percentage of goods needed to supply the empire that was produced by slaves was so great—especially in Italy but also in the other areas—that some critical scholars have characterized the Roman imperial economy as a slave economy.[12] Slavery was such a prominent reality in the Roman imperial political economy that slave relations affected every other aspect of the society and culture.[13] Ironically, the practice of emancipation was instrumental in the maintenance of the slave system. It was frequent enough that masters'

8. "The dominant force in the Roman economy," as explained by Morley, "Economy and Economic Theory," 12.

9. See Temin, *Roman Market Economy*.

10. Garnsey and Saller, *Roman Empire*. This remains the most comprehensive critical analysis and presentation of the Roman imperial economy, recognizing how economic structures and power relations were embedded with imperial political and cultural life.

11. Scheidel, "Real Wages."

12. Most important is the magisterial study of Ste. Croix, *Class Struggle*.

13. Critical discussion in Boer and Petterson, *Time of Troubles*, ch. 4.

promises and slaves' hopes for eventual emancipation helped to motivate their obedience and acquiescence. Even when emancipated, slaves became "freed persons" who were generally still dependent on their former owners, often continued as members of the larger household, and were socially despised as former slaves.

Treatments of "the Roman economy" have often been presented synthetically and synchronically—somewhat analogous to the synthetic Hellenistic urban culture that New Testament studies previously thought provided the context of Paul's mission and letters. But ancient Rome had a long and changing history. Already in the second century BCE Roman warlords and their armies were building an empire around the eastern Mediterranean. In the last few decades, moreover, Roman historians have become far more candid about the brutality of Roman conquest. The slaughter and enslavement of conquered people and the destruction of their villages, and even cities, were clearly major factors in the political economy, particularly in the devastated areas. Roman historians have also brought attention to the distinctive historical differences between the various cities and areas of the empire, including in ancient Greece and Asia Minor. These initiatives help provide a more precise picture of political-economic-religious relations in the cities and areas in which Paul and his coworkers focused their mission—and one that should replace the picture of the synthetic Hellenistic culture that was supposedly everywhere.[14]

In the same year that the Romans annihilated the city of Carthage (146 BCE) they also utterly destroyed the classical city of Corinth and enslaved its populace. For a century it lay in ruins until Julius Caesar established a Roman colony on the site, sending army veterans, freed slaves, and other unwanted "surplus population" from the city of Rome that the patricians were finding difficult to control. As the principal hub of shipping and communications between Italy, the Aegean, and points eastward, Corinth grew in size, with displaced people from diverse backgrounds including people who had been enslaved. At Philippi two successive colonies of Roman army veterans were established in 42 and 30 BCE. The previously conquered indigenous Thracians (and/or "Greeks") were pushed off their lands by the Roman colonists and subordinated to the now predominantly Roman politics and political culture of the city. Slaves (or other dependents) were brought in to work the estates of the Roman veteran families.

Distinctive as they were in their origins as Roman colonies in the first century BCE, Philippi and Corinth shared many of the key developments of the political-religious economy of Greece (and Asia) generally. While the

14. Laid out, in reliance on key works of Roman historians, in Horsley, *Paul and Empire*.

Roman metropolis extracted huge quantities of grain from conquered peoples, particularly Egypt, other cities of the empire depended largely on their own countryside (*chora*) for food.[15] Exploitation of both agricultural producers and urban populations by the wealthy urban elite was intensified and consolidated under Roman domination. The political economy of the Roman Empire was dominated by an alliance between the imperial court and the local and provincial wealthy elite.[16] The imperial court placed them in charge of tax collection and favored them in every way. By gaining control of more and more land, they steadily expanded their wealth and local power, and as land tenure became less secure, small-scale cultivators disappeared.[17]

In the generations preceding the Pauline mission in Macedonia and Achaia many people were evidently being forced off their land and into the cities in hopes of eking out a living.[18] Some wound up far from their origins in search of a living. Some of the people in any of these cities—probably many in Corinth—would have been displaced people, uprooted from their ancestral homes and homelands, having lost supportive family and village community with their familiar customs. Recent efforts to quantify and stratify the "income" of the (freeborn urban) population of the empire (on the basis of limited evidence) draw sobering estimates of the huge gulf between the tiny percentage of the extremely wealthy and powerful and the poverty of the vast majority, with nearly 90 percent living at or below subsistence and only 8 to 10 percent having a moderate surplus.[19] Also, some of the people on the land and certainly in the cities would have been slaves, although it is difficult to know what portion of the population—it would have been far less than in Rome and the Italian

15. "Agricultural production must always have constituted the lion's share of ancient activity" (Alcock, *Graecia Capta*, 109).

16. A common historical observation; see Alcock, *Graecia Capta*, 77.

17. For results from archaeological surface surveys that have confirmed textual indications, see Alcock, *Graecia Capta*, 71–72. For thorough analysis and discussion of the long-term process by which the magnates of Greek cities steadily increased their wealth and power by taking over people's land and forcing them into dependent tenancy and the continuation of this process in the alliance between the imperial court and the urban elite in the Roman imperial order, see Ste. Croix, *Class Struggle*. Drawing on Ste. Croix, Boer and Pettersen, in *Time of Troubles*, lay out a comprehensive critical overview of the long historical process by which the colonate emerged as the dominant political-economic form in late antiquity.

18. Many references in Apuleius, *Metamorphoses*; see further Alcock, *Graecia Capta*, 107.

19. See especially Friesen, "Poverty in Pauline Studies"; Scheidel and Friesen, "Size of the Economy." Some strive to expand the stratum of moderately well off, perhaps to reestablish the credibility of a "middle class" in the cities of the empire; see Longenecker, *Remember the Poor*.

peninsula—were freedmen/women (or their descendants), who remained dependent on their former owners.[20]

Much of the recent discussion of "Paul and economics" has continued and refined earlier discussion of the social stratification of the members of the assemblies that Paul and his coworkers catalyzed in the "social world" of Greek cities.[21] This, however, only perpetuates the structural-functional sociological approach that had been abandoned by social scientists in the 1960s. Borrowing this approach enabled New Testament scholarship to avoid recognition of significant historical change and especially serious (structural) political-economic conflict.[22] It is important in understanding Paul's mission and letters in the Roman imperial context to move beyond social-economic stratification to appreciation of who had what forms of power over whom, and what forms of economic exploitation were employed. Also, simultaneous with the recent recognition that the historical context and opposition of Paul was the Roman imperial order (and not "Judaism") was the recognition of the dramatic changes that Rome had imposed and evoked in the cities into which Paul carried his mission, as noted just above.

What held the Roman imperial economy together city by city, especially in the Greek East, was not an imperial bureaucracy and the army, but the elaborate honors to Caesar.[23] It may be difficult for comfortable people in the modern Western countries to appreciate just how destructive and unsettling the chaos was that was left in the wake of the Roman civil war fought for over a decade by rival Roman warlords and their armies. Octavian's great victory over the "dark" forces of Marc Anthony at Actium thus evoked intense relief and gratitude among the elite of the cities in Greece and Asia over the *peace*

---

20. One of the effects of the recent debates about social-economic stratification of the population of the empire has been to distract attention from the presence and situations of slaves and freed persons in the cities, and the situations of slaves/slavery and other forms of non-free labor in the countryside, such as tenants on large estates.

21. For example, some of the essays in Blanton and Pickett, *Paul and Economics*, attempt to further refine Longenecker's mitigating adjustment of Friesen's "poverty scale" based on data for social-economic stratification. Friesen's work was a sharp criticism and "correction" of the social stratification analysis in Meeks, *First Urban Christians*, which in turn depended heavily on Theissen, "Social Stratification." Cf. the criticism and more critical approach suggested in Horsley, "Paul's Shift," 90–99.

22. For criticism of applying structural functional sociology to New Testament texts, see J. Elliot, "Social-Scientific Criticism"; Horsley, *Sociology and Jesus Movement*, 35–39, 156–65; and N. Elliott, "When Bridges Fail Us," 213–15; and "Diagnosing an Allergic Reaction," 2, 7–8.

23. See esp. Price, *Rituals and Power*; and Zanker, *Power of Images*; summarized and abridged in Horsley, *Paul and Empire*, chs. 3–5, 7.

and security that Caesar Augustus had brought them. In cities such as Ephesus, Philippi, Thessalonike, Athens, and Corinth, the wealthy magnates sponsored the building and funding of temples and monuments grouped around newly constructed temples to the emperor, the *Lord* and *Savior* of the world. Statues of the emperor were placed in those temples, and rituals to the emperor were performed in other public arenas such as the theaters. Festivals and (Caesarian) games were held in honor of the emperor. The presence of the emperor came to pervade public space, and honors to the emperor came to structure the annual calendar. People who lived in the religious-political economy of these cities were literally surrounded by images and rituals of the divine Caesar, *son of god, Lord* and *Savior,* who had brought *salvation* to the world. By participating in these honors and festivals the people were expressing their loyalty (*pistis*) to their Lord and Savior. There could not be a more vivid illustration of how religion was inseparable from political economy and of how political-economic power relations were legitimated and mediated through the central symbols and rituals exhibited in the built environment and the annual rhythm of public life.

These elaborate honors to the emperor were funded and led by the wealthy men of each city, who held not only the city priesthoods and civic offices but also the highly coveted imperial priesthoods in those cities.[24] Through these civil-religious offices, as well as by their wealth, they wielded political-economic power in the cities and provinces. The wealthy elites' sponsorship of such public buildings, services, festivals, and other acts of "beneficence" generated much of the work on which the populace hovering at subsistence had become increasingly dependent.[25] As a further antidote to the hunger of the poor, and probably with an eye to preventing social unrest, the wealthy also regularly sponsored public banquets or other distribution of food. Such actions, memorialized in decrees and inscriptions honoring local *euergetai*, consolidated the rule of the wealthy in city life and contributed to the acceptance of the new political-economic-religious order.[26] The council (*boule*) of the elite

---

24. Alcock, *Graecia Capta*, 163; Richard Gordon, "Veil of Power: Emperors, Sacrificers, and Benefactors," in Horsley, *Paul and Empire*, 132–37.

25. Alcock, *Graecia Capta*, 114.

26. While some of the urban poor may have been pulled into patronage networks of wealthy figures, thus increasing the latters' political-economic power, the extensive pyramids of patronage that developed in Rome, filled with people forced off the land or otherwise socially and economically adrift, were probably not duplicated in Corinth and other Greek cities. See Horsley, *Paul and Empire*, pt. 2, esp. 94–95. For the extensive patronage networks in Rome, see Saller, *Personal Patronage*.

in Greek cities now held effective control; having been left without a voice, with the decline of the city assembly (*ekklesia*), the people were effectively controlled by the local imperial order.

Despite their political domination and economic vulnerability, the people in the cities of the empire were remarkably resilient. As noted above, many had been displaced from their socioeconomic origins in some way. Yet among those displaced, indigenous language and culture and even aspects of social structure persisted underneath the dominant Hellenistic-Roman political-economic-religious forms in some of the cities around the eastern Mediterranean. While also involving degrees of adjustment, the formation and persistence of religious-ethnic communities in the Greek cities (e.g., the "synagogues" of Judeans in the diaspora) were one possible form of resisting more complete assimilation into the local and wider imperial order.[27] In the narrative of Paul's and his coworkers' mission in the book of Acts, they habitually begin by speaking in the local assembly of Judeans in a given city or town; a conflict develops, and Paul's faction splits off. Despite this being a repeated scheme in the narrative, it is possible that the Pauline mission built on already existing networks and communities. In Philippi, on which Roman warlords had twice imposed colonies of Roman veterans, the Philippians pushed out of their homes and lands may well have had continuing indigenous networks and identity over against the dominant new Roman ethos of the city, which Paul and his coworkers could mobilize into a community of Christ loyalists.

In recent decades interest has increased in "associations," variously called *collegia*, *familia*, *synodoi*, *thiasoi*, etc., as analogies or even models for the assemblies (communities) that developed from the mission of Paul and his coworkers.[28] Given the origins of this mission in a movement of renewal of Israel based in villages and in village and town *synagogai*, it seems more likely that Paul and his coworkers were adapting the form of the Judean and Galilean synagogues/assemblies in which the movement(s) had originated during and after the mission of Jesus.[29] In the cities of the empire, especially once the assemblies became viable and relatively stable communities over a period of decades, they may have resembled the "associations." Key aspects of such associations provided

---

27. This possibility, exemplified perhaps by the Jewish/Judean communities/synagogues in Alexandria or Rome, has not been adequately investigated, perhaps largely because of the lack of sources.

28. A very helpful critical review of the "models" that scholars suggest for the communities Paul and coworkers catalyzed is Adams, "First-Century Models." On *collegia* etc., see collection of source material in Ascough et al., *Associations in Greco-Roman World*.

29. Discussed in Horsley, "Paul's Assembly in Corinth."

communal economic self-help, such as periodic feasts, funerals, and in times of need, possible low-interest loans. Membership in a *collegium*, however, was costly, involving expenditures, including entrance fees, periodic dues, and ad hoc contributions. Such resource pooling could help members alleviate poverty in difficult times. But such associations "had the effect of obstructing the poorest from accessing support networks, resources, and work opportunities."[30]

Considering how important slavery was in production in the Roman imperial order, including in households with only a few slaves, note should be taken of the steady and widespread resistance by slaves.[31] Earlier New Testament interpretation, following classical historians, underestimated slave resistance—in arguments that ancient slavery was generally benign and/or that slaves were acquiescent if not content with their lot. The sources on which they depended, of course, were from the elite, who were involved, directly or indirectly, in slave ownership. Slaves themselves, like peasants, left no written accounts that can be used to balance the slave owners' views. Elite sources do, however, regularly indicate various forms of slave resistance and the measures slave masters and imperial or local authorities took to suppress or retaliate against such resistance. And these indications open toward recognition of various "hidden" forms of resistance by slaves who knew that open defiance or revolt would be suicidal.

Pretense—or at least the grudging performance—of acquiescence and obedience was one way slaves might lessen potential cruelty and brutality from their masters, even while they might have been slowing down or sabotaging production in the household. That slaves ran away was a direct "withholding" of their labor as well as a challenge to the slave masters' authority. Literary sources are rich with references to *fugitivi* and to professional "slave catchers," suggesting that slaves running away was a familiar phenomenon. Plays entitled *Fugitivi* and *Captivi* characterize slaves as likely to run away. City-states made treaties with the specific purpose of extraditing fugitive slaves. In his *Res gestae*, Caesar Augustus boasts that following his victory in the Roman civil war he had returned thirty thousand slaves to their masters for punishment—but not mentioning that he had simply crucified another six thousand for whom no master could be found.[32] Fugitive slaves themselves formed bands of brigands in remote areas (e.g., Athenaeus, *Deipnosophistai* 6.265d–266e). Given the conditions of their servitude, in which slaves were dispersed onto smaller or larger farms in Italy and Sicily (and elsewhere), it is amazing that they could organize

30. See the broader survey and critical assessment in Liu, "Urban Poverty," esp. 44–49.
31. More fully discussed in Callahan and Horsley, "Slave Resistance."
32. Caesar Augustus, *Res gestae* 25; Dio Cassius 49.12.5.

widespread revolts. Best know are the massive revolts in the late republic (135–34 BCE, 104 BCE, and 74–73 BCE), but revolts were more frequent than usually acknowledged. These revolts are also significant because of the social-political forms in which slaves organized themselves, such as copying indigenous forms of kingship derived from the areas of their origin, such as Syria. Extensive slavery in Rome, Italy, and the provinces and cities of the empire, and continuing enslavement of tens of thousands, for example, in Judea and Galilee (in 52 and 4 BCE and 70 CE), who were sent to Roman slave markets, created pressures from below and motivation to participate in forms of resistance.

Paul's Agenda for the Assemblies of an Inter-People Alternative Society

Only in the last twenty years or so have historical interpreters begun to recognize that Paul's mission was not opposed to "Judaism" but rather to the Roman Empire. Until recent decades, theological New Testament studies sought its Christian identity through interpretation of the letters that Paul wrote in his mission to "the gentiles" and his supposed break with "Judaism." What could intelligibly be referred to as Judaism, however, had not developed yet historically. As used with reference to late "Second Temple" times, "Judaism" is an abstract synthetic construct that hides both a diversity of social phenomena, movements, and the structural political-economic-religious conflict in Roman Palestine and a diversity of religious-ethnic communities of Judeans in various cities of the empire. Similarly, what could intelligibly be called "early Christianity" and its "New Testament" had not yet emerged historically. Applied to the time of Paul and the Gospels, these are abstract and synthetic constructs that hide the diverse "Jesus movements" that existed, some of which produced texts that became stabilized and incorporated into the New Testament at a much later time.

The "Gospels" and the letters of Paul later included in the New Testament evidently were addressed to and probably produced in different movements (communities) of Jesus– or Christ loyalists that developed from Jesus' mission in Galilee (and beyond) and his crucifixion (and vindication/resurrection) in Jerusalem. The early narratives in the book of Acts recount the movement led by Peter and other disciples of Jesus based in Jerusalem that expanded into the towns and cities of Palestine-Syria and beyond. Like those addressed by most of the Gospels, this movement understood the mission of Jesus and his crucifixion (and vindication/resurrection) as the fulfillment of the tradition of Israel, indeed as the fulfillment of history that had been running through (the history of) Israel and not through (the history of) Rome. Early on, several figures from communities of Judeans in the diaspora, apparently on pilgrimage to Jerusalem, joined the expanding movement. Saul (Paul) was among these (Greek-speaking) "Hellenists."

Other, non-Israelite peoples subject to the Roman Empire were soon eager to join the movement. Claiming a dramatic commissioning as an apostle from "a revelation of Jesus Christ" (Gal 1:15–20), Paul had pushed himself forward in the leadership of the rapidly expanding movement of the renewal of Israel in opposition to and by their Roman-client rulers. Yielding to Cephas as the leading apostle to "the circumcised," Paul claimed leadership of the expansion of the movement among the other peoples in the cities of Asia Minor and Greece.[33] In contrast with Jesus and his envoys, who had worked to revitalize existing village communities already embedded in Israelite tradition, Paul and his coworkers attempted to catalyze new communities of people in cities of the Eastern Empire. The generation of these "assemblies" was an audacious project to establish new communities that embodied alternative social-economic relations in the hostile context of the Roman imperial order established in cities of the Greek East.

When Paul and his coworkers moved on after working for many months in a given city to begin catalyzing another fledgling community in another city, Paul sent letters to the newly established assemblies, responding to questions and conflicts and urging them to maintain their loyalty to their new Lord and their solidarity as a community. Paul's letters were previously read as theological treatises from which Christian doctrines or values could be derived. In recent years, however, interpreters have recognized that Paul's letters focus mainly on the affairs of particular communities and their relations with the larger cities in which they had formed. Interpreters have only begun to ask what the political-economic situation was in each city where an assembly had come together, whether and how Paul and his coworkers addressed that situation, what economic issues may have arisen in or for the assembly, and what Paul and his

---

33. The term "the gentiles" in dichotomy or opposition to "the Jews" is thus historically misleading and carries a good deal of Christian ideological baggage. In Paul's letters the Greek term *ta ethne* usually refers to the *other peoples* besides Israel. The translation "nations" is also misleading insofar as it carries modern and contemporary connotations back into Roman antiquity. Nations were created in modern Western Europe from the top down, in the nineteenth century (e.g., Germany and Italy). Critical discussion in Anderson, *Imagined Communities*. In the mid-twentieth century, European imperial governments imposed "nation" status on different peoples; e.g., Nigeria is comprised of several peoples, such as the Yoruba and the Ibo. More recently peoples of distinctive regional identity such as the Scots and Welsh have struggled about whether they are "united" under the United Kingdom dominated by the English.

coworkers were urging the assembly to do in the context of the broader Roman imperial (dis)order.

The "Pauline" letters in the New Testament that scholars believe Paul himself produced (Romans, 1–2 Corinthians, Galatians, Philippians, 1 Thessalonians, and Philemon) will be the basis of analysis of the mission of Paul and his coworkers. The "deutero-Pauline" epistles (2 Thessalonians; Colossians; Ephesians; and what are called "the Pastorals," 1–2 Timothy and Titus) offer access to one of the ways in which the movement generated by Paul developed in the ensuing generations. But it will be important to note other ways in which the Pauline tradition was developed.

The Assemblies as Local Communities in an Alternative Society

In attempting to understand the political-economic-religious agenda laid out in Paul's letters it is necessary to take into account a factor not usually considered in investigation of historical economic relations. New social movements sometimes initiate innovative changes in local social-economic relations and challenge the dominant power relations, even though they may not make much of an impact on the overall political-economic system. These innovations may be responses to the intensification of dominant power relations, and may be driven by a vision of a dramatically different political-economic-religious life, an alternative to the dominant system.

In his letters, particularly those to the Galatians and Romans, Paul struggles to explain that the communities that have come together from among other peoples subjected to the Roman Empire are an extension of the people of Israel. They did not become "ethnically" Israelite/Judean, much less convert to Judaism, which did not yet exist. But in the crucifixion and resurrection of Jesus Christ these people had become heirs of the promise to Abraham that all peoples would receive blessing through his "seed" (Gal 3–4); they were now being "grafted into" the main trunk that was Israel as a historical people (Rom 11:17–24). The movement of the nascent assemblies that he had catalyzed was the fulfillment of the tradition and history of Israel. The implication was that in the context of the Roman Empire—where everyone assumed that history was running through Rome—Paul was making the audacious claim that the nascent assemblies he and coworkers were catalyzing were extensions of a history that had been running through the people of Israel.

To appreciate how Paul's "gospel" of Christ's crucifixion, resurrection, and parousia may have resonated with and motivated subject peoples in cities such as Philippi, Thessalonica, and Corinth to join and continue in fledgling counter-imperial communities it may help to review how that gospel addressed their life circumstances. These peoples who had been subjugated by Caesar were variously slaves or freed slaves and displaced people living around the subsistence level in an environment that was pervaded by the presence of the imperial Lord and Savior. These peoples were regularly reminded of their subjugation by the imperial ideology and rituals and images of power that established distinctions between citizen and noncitizen, conqueror and conquered, free and slave.[34]

The counter-imperial gospel Paul preached focused on the crucifixion of Jesus by "the rulers of this age" (Roman officials). The assemblies lived their personal and community lives under the symbol of the crucifixion. And that crucified figure of abject humiliation had become their Lord and was imminently to come, as the direct rule of God would finally be realized (on earth) and the *politeuma* of the alternative society descend with their crucified Lord from heaven (1 Cor 15:12–28, Phil 3:19–21). These interrelated successive images are all juxtaposed in the early (pre-Pauline) hymnic "creed," presumably recited regularly in community gatherings (Phil 2:5–11). Christ had taken the form of a slave, obedient to the point of death, even death on a cross. It was the crucified Christ who had been exalted as Lord (1 Cor 2:6–8). In Galatians Paul appeals to what he hoped would be the performative effects of his (and others') preaching before the communities of the movement: "It was *before your eyes* that Jesus Christ was publicly exhibited as crucified!" (Gal 3:1). As Paul's letters became Scripture, the imperial images that Paul borrowed to oppose the imperial order could easily be co-opted to again reinforce imperial political-economic-religious structures.[35] But Paul evidently hoped that the performative effect of his gospel could reverse or at least effectively oppose "the sedimented effects" of the imperial images of conquest, enslavement, and domination in the nascent communities of subjected peoples that could now embody just and caring social-economic relations as they awaited the final actualization/realization of their *politeuma*.[36]

34. These were also distinctions between who could and could not be tortured in the Roman Empire, in which the principal instrument of torture was public crucifixion, mainly of slaves and subject peoples (provincials) who resisted their subjugation.

35. Paul may have hoped that he and the nascent "assemblies" were breaking free of the structures of kyriarchal domination. But as Neil Elliott notes, from his reading of Jameson, *Political Unconscious*, 17–102, "the liberating impulses arising from the collective imagination, or 'political unconscious,' are limited and channeled by the dominant ideology of the power structure" ("Ideological Closure," 151–54).

36. See Butler, *Excitable Speech*, 147. On how Paul attempts to reverse the effects of the imperial ideology, see now Nasrallah, "You Were Bought."

We have rarely if at all inquired specifically into the economic circumstances and practice of the assemblies as evident in Paul's letters. It has recently become clearer that Paul, his coworkers, and fledgling assemblies encountered serious political opposition in Philippi, Thessalonica, and Corinth, judging from his discussions in letters to the assemblies there (1 Thess 1:2–3, Phil 1–2), and these would have had economic effects. His and his coworkers' "shameful mistreatment" in Philippi, for example, led Paul to anticipate that he might soon suffer martyrdom. Only in the context of these official and unofficial attacks on the communities and their members can the implications of some of Paul's statements and the economic dimension of the assemblies be understood.

Thessalonians and Philippians

As Paul mentions at several points in 1 Thessalonians, the assembly had suffered and endured serious persecution that had persisted for some time (1:2–10; 3:1–5, 6–10), so that they became an example of loyal endurance to all the loyalists in Macedonia and Achaia. Paul and his associates had also encountered "great opposition" in Thessalonica (2:2). The account of their work in Thessalonica in the book of Acts (17:1–9) confirms that they evoked political repression. The report of jealous opposition from "the Judeans" is suspect as a standard theme in the book of Acts. But the report that the political authorities of Thessalonica were concerned that Paul and his coworkers were acting "against the decrees of Caesar" in saying that there is "another emperor named Jesus" (that is, instead of Caesar) fits what Paul said in several of his letters to other communities. Evidence of such "decrees" and of Thessalonian coins make it highly likely that Paul and the community he had generated were seriously attacked by the authorities for their apparent opposition to the imperial order. The city was unusually active in its honors to Caesar, including ceremonies at the temple to Caesar, and the "politarchs" of the city were evidently charged with enforcing loyalty to the emperor, which would have been important in ensuring the cities' continuing "peace and security" under Roman imperial rule.[37] As part of his closing exhortation to perseverance in 1 Thess (5:1–11), Paul suggests that the urban elite who are trusting in the (imperial ideology of) "peace and security" established by Caesar, including those who enforce it, are making war on the community, whom he exhorts to put on the protective armor of "the breastplate of loyalty and love and for a helmet the hope of (concrete) salvation/well-being."

37. Discussed in Donfried, "Imperial Cults of Thessalonica"; and the research of Holland Hendrix on which he relies.

Paul's immediately preceding reassurance to the community about "those who have fallen asleep," which he has "by the word of the Lord," that is, by a direct revelation from Christ, suggests that some members have been martyred in the officials' attacks. Following the paradigmatic martyrdom and vindication/resurrection of Christ, whom Paul refers to as "the first fruits of the resurrection," those who have fallen asleep will also be resurrected to join their Lord. The scenario featuring vindication/resurrection in "the clouds of heaven" derives from a long Judean tradition—standardly referred to as *apocalyptic*—that we recognize from Dan 7 and 11–12. Paul's version in "the word of the Lord" is also patterned after, and is perhaps a mocking of, the visit (parousia, "coming") of the emperor to a city in which all of the residents poured forth from the city in a ceremonial precession to greet their "Lord" and "Savior."

It is difficult to imagine that the members of the Thessalonian assembly under severe persecution could maintain even a subsistence economic livelihood. Many, if not most, people in the cities were directly or indirectly dependent on the wealthy and/or powerful in some way. It seems that Paul's exhortations to "abound in love for one another" (3:12) and to love all the Christ loyalists, clearly addressed to the whole community, suggest that they aid one another economically. The further exhortations "to live quietly and mind your own affairs" (4:9–10), suggest keeping some separation from others in the city. And the admonition "to work with your own hands . . . and be dependent on no one" (4:11–12) and, especially, the "do good to one another" (5:15) imply some sort of taking care of one another economically. This love and mutual aid, moreover, is not just a desirable "value" that Paul recommends. Given the persecutions they were undergoing, the "doing good to one another" and "abounding in love for one another" refer to measures of concrete mutual aid, practices in which they are already engaged and that he urges them to continue.[38]

His Letter to the Philippians Paul sends from where he has been arrested and imprisoned, presumably for his activities that at least seemed to the authorities to be subversive of the Roman imperial order. In his keen anticipation of possibly becoming a martyr for his resistance to the imperial order (in the image of dying and being vindicated in exaltation to the heavens [Phil 1:19–23]), he stands in the tradition of the "Enoch" scribes and the *maskilim* two centuries earlier who were being martyred for their resistance to the Seleucid regime's enforcement of the Hellenizing imperial order (1 En. 90:6–19; 104:2–6; Dan

---

38. While it seems unlikely that Paul knew much of the teaching of Jesus, such practices of mutual aid in communities ("love your enemies, do good, and lend") were the core of the covenant renewal in the mission of Jesus; see discussion in ch. 3 of this volume.

11:32–35; 12:3).[39]

With a clearer sense of the context of Paul's mission in Philippi and elsewhere, it is important not to perpetuate the depoliticizing translations of this letter. The (N)RSV of Phil 1:27–29 (and other passages) has been easily construed as exhortation to apolitical Christian pietism. The language, however, is literally political-economic in this passage that presses the Philippians to collectively resist those who oppose them: "Operate politically [*politeuesthe*] in a way worthy of the gospel of Christ [their alternative to the gospel of Caesar as Lord] ... striving side by side with one mind [in solidarity] for the loyalty [*pistis*] of/to the gospel, in no way intimidated by those who oppose you." Paul further suggests that they have been granted the privilege of suffering for Christ, hinting at possible martyrdom like his own (Phil 1:29, 2:15–17). His and their commonwealth (*politeuma*, in the sense of shared governance for the common social-economic good) is in heaven, whence they are expecting a Savior, that is, their alternative Lord, who is in the process of subjecting the imperial order (3:20—4:1).

Does the conduct of their own separate politics in resistance to the imperial order in Philippi also include an economic dimension? The letter includes no reference to economic aid of one another. But Paul expresses appreciation that the Philippians have been sending aid to him again while he is imprisoned, as they had more than once during his mission in Thessalonica (Phil 4:15–19). That they were sending economic aid to Paul suggests that there had been at least some economic aid to one another in the community.

Corinthians

In discussion of 1 Corinthians, it is important to confront head-on the focus on social stratification that has dominated interpretation of the "social world" of Paul's assemblies and diverted attention from economic power relations in the Roman Empire. Particularly influential has been a literalistic reading of 1 Cor 1:26: "If Paul says that there were not many in the Corinthian congregation who were wise, powerful, and wellborn, then this much is certain: there were some."[40] The logic of that statement, of course, is faulty. More important is the broader cultural context and a sense of the rhetoric of Paul's argument in 1 Cor 1:10—4:13. Terms such as "wise, powerful, and wellborn," had long since become widely used metaphorically as standard discourse among philosophers,

---

39. Critical analysis of texts and discussion in Horsley, *Revolt of the Scribes*, chs. 4–5.
40. Theissen, "Social Stratification," page number unavailable.

particularly the Stoics: a discourse shared by the Wisdom of Solomon and elaborated by Philo of Alexandria.[41] In this discourse, not the political-economic power holders but (only) the *sophos* (wise person) was truly "wise," "powerful," and "nobly born"—and, to go on to 1 Cor 4:8, also "rich," "king," and "honored." Paul's argument (from 1:10—4:21) is laced with steps that are loaded with irony and/or sarcasm (e.g., 1:26–31, 4:8–13). Paul is mocking people who were suddenly claiming exalted spiritual status.[42] Indeed, most of Paul's long arguments that comprise 1 Corinthians are evidently addressed to several people whose boasting of their status as "spirituals" (*pneumatikoi*) Paul believes was disrupting the unity of the assembly: In 1 Cor 1:10—4:13 he mocks their claims of exalted spiritual status. In 8:1—11:1 he counters their claim that their enlightened theology makes "all things permissible to them." In 12–14 he urges them to use their special spiritual gifts for the benefit of the whole community. And in 1 Cor 15 he insists on the collective resurrection of the body to counter their view of the immortality of the soul/spirit freed from the prison of the body. First Corinthians does not give evidence of different social-economic statuses/strata, but of several people who are excited about attaining high *spiritual* status.

First Corinthians does, however, offer good evidence for what Paul was insisting on as the political-economic practices of the Corinthian assembly both within the community and in its relations to the larger imperial order in Corinth.[43] First, it is worth noticing that the overall *ekklesia* in Corinth was not a religious cult, but a nascent social movement consisting of several cells (centered in Corinth but extending into the surrounding Achaia) some of which were based in the households of persons who probably provided the leadership, such as Stephanas, Gaius, possibly Crispus, Chloe, and, in the suburb of Cenchreae, Phoebe. Some members of these households may have been slaves or freed slaves (e.g., "Cloe's people" [1 Cor 1:11]; and "Lucky" and "the Greek," who accompanied Stephanas in traveling to see Paul in Ephesus [16:15–18]).

In 1 Cor 5–6, more explicitly than in other letters, Paul insisted that the assembly conduct its own affairs autonomously, in complete independence of "the world."[44] This did not mean cutting themselves off completely from con-

41. For more on this, see Horsley, *Wisdom and Spiritual Transcendence*, esp. chs. 1–2.

42. All investigated in a series of articles (based on a 1971 dissertation), later collected in Horsley, *Wisdom and Spiritual Transcendence*; laid out in commentary form in Horsley, *1 Corinthians*.

43. Some of the following points and arguments were first articulated in Horsley, *1 Corinthians*.

44. The previous projection of "church-state" relations (separation) on these arguments

tact with outsiders, including the immoral, the greedy, and those who might steal—presumably the insiders were attempting to recruit outsiders into an expanding movement. Not only were they to maintain group discipline, in contrast with the injustice of the dominant society, but they were to handle their own disputes in independence of the established courts, which were "unjust" (6:1). Courts in the Roman Empire were instruments of exploitation of the poor by the wealthy. That Paul's list of unjust outsiders features the economic injustices of coveting and theft suggests that the issue over which one member of the assembly had taken another to civil court was economic (perhaps "defrauding," which may have been via the court [6:7–8]). The rhetorical question, "Do you not know that the saints will judge the world," indicates that it was a standard teaching the Corinthians knew well.

Paul and his coworkers had evidently been teaching that the individual assemblies and the larger movement of assemblies were an alternative society, the beachheads of the new age, and were to act as such in handling their own affairs, including economic issues, in independence of the established order. Although the immediate context concerns issues of marriage and sexual relations, the general statement in 7:29–31—"from now on let those who mourn be as though they were not mourning ... and those who buy as though they had no possessions, and those who deal with the world as though they had no dealings with it. For the present form of this world is passing away"—would have powerfully enforced the insistence on the political-economic independence of the assembly.

Paul's next argument, in 1 Cor 8:1—11:1, deals with how political-economic relations are inseparable from religious ceremonies. In the course of the argument he focuses on slogans of several "spiritual" or enlightened Corinthians, especially that "all things are lawful/permissible for me," quoted in 6:12 and again in 10:23 as Paul moves to the conclusion of this argument. He begins with a "correction" (really a rejection) of their (Hellenistic Judean) enlightened theology that, since there is no God but one, the gods of the city and empire have no real existence (but are mere "idols"). Religion in the ancient Roman world was not primarily a matter of personal belief. Religious ceremonies were the way social-political-economic relations were constituted. As noted above, statues, temples, and shrines to the emperor, located in the center of public space, and citywide festivals played important roles in the cohesion of the empire as well as local urban society under the domination of the sponsoring elite.

---

of Paul is anachronistic, and results in exegesis almost the diametric opposite of what Paul is arguing. See older commentaries, such as Conzelmann, *First Corinthians*.

Sacrifices were integral to, in fact, constitutive of community life in the Roman world at every level, from households to guilds and associations to citywide celebrations and imperial festivals.

Paul does not side with, but rebukes the *gnosis* of the enlightened Corinthians who have developed a "strong consciousness" that "idols (of gods) do not really exist" and hence, no longer obsessed with traditional Judean food codes, they have the authority/liberty (*exousia*) to eat meat offered to idols in temples. In an awkward aside to their slogan (1 Cor 8:5b) he insists that "in fact there are many gods and many lords" (in those temples and shrines and festivals and associations). His argument climaxes in 1 Cor 10:14–22, with 10:23—11:1 as a conciliatory afterthought and summary of the implications of his argument. This is not, as some modern theological interpreters suggested, a "sacramental realism," but a political-economic realism that Paul shared with both the unenlightened majority of ancient Greeks and Romans and the "biblical" tradition of unenlightened Israelites/Judeans. In 10:1–13 Paul insists that biblical traditions not be taken as symbols of spiritual realities (spiritual food/drink/rock), but as references to events that had happened to Israelites after their liberation from oppression in Egypt—hence a warning about collective discipline and solidarity. In 10:14–22 Paul insists on the exclusivity of the assembly of Christ loyalists. In the Lord's Supper the cup is "a sharing [*koinonia*] in the blood of Christ" and the bread is a "sharing [*koinonia*] in the body of Christ." The Corinthian addressees would already have known (as Paul reminds them in 1 Cor 12) that "body" was a well-established political-economic-religious metaphor for the "body politic" of the citizen-body of a city-state, and by analogy the "body politic" of their assembly. But Paul insists on the exclusivity over against the dominant society in which many overlapping social bonds were established in sacrifices to multiple gods. It was simply impossible and forbidden for members of the body of the assembly established and perpetuated in the cup and table of the Lord to partake also in the cup and table of gods, that he now denigrates as "demons."

Paul insists that eating "food offered to idols" was not an issue of ethics, but of "building up" the assembly of saints over against the networks of power relations by which the imperial society was constituted. He insists on political-economic-religious solidarity over against the dominant society that was constituted precisely in such banquets and "sharing" with the gods. For members of the new alternative community in Corinth, this meant cutting themselves off from the very ceremonies by which their previous social economic relations in the established order were maintained.

Paul's discussion of his own example of *not* accepting economic support from the Corinthians (in 1 Cor 9) indicates one way in which the Corinthian and other assemblies were engaged in economic cooperation and collaboration: the support of the apostles and their coworkers who were organizing and teaching among them to build up the communities of the movement(s). As illustrated in the agrarian images that authorized the practice (not muzzling the ox, included in the authoritative Torah of Moses, and the worker worthy of sharing in the harvest) that Paul cites, it had been the practice from the outset of the movement(s) that the envoys of Jesus who traveled and worked in local communities were supported economically by them. And as illustrated in Jesus' instructions to the envoys, "remain in the same house, eating and drinking whatever they provide; do not move from house to house" (Luke/Q 10:7), the support was modest—necessarily so since the communities, whether villages in Galilee or the assemblies in Thessalonica or Corinth, were comprised of people living near the subsistence level (like the vast majority of people in the empire). As we know from the Didache (The Teaching of the Twelve Apostles) 11–12, in the decades after Paul's mission, traveling apostles and prophets became a serious burden on such communities of meager resources, and the movement had to establish criteria for such support.

Paul's motives for declining support in principle (or at least from the Corinthians) may have been several. He may have felt self-conscious or embarrassed as someone of previously adequate means who had joined a movement of marginal people. The reasons he gives in 1 Cor 9:15–23 are credible—he was defensive about his commissioning and his legitimacy as an apostle, as indicated again in 1 Cor 15:8–10—and/or he did not want to be a burden on people living mostly at a subsistence level. His acceptance of aid from the Philippians may have been a special case insofar as Paul's own situation there, like that of the Thessalonians themselves, was unusually precarious (Phil 4:15–16, 1 Thess 1–2, 2 Cor 8:1–2); but it makes him appear inconsistent.

Paul's Stance toward Slavery and Slaves' Status in the Assemblies

Slavery was central to the political economy of the Roman Empire in which Paul and his coworkers conducted their mission. The "Pauline" letters later became part of the Holy Scriptures that carried divine authority for subsequent Western Christian history, including the history of slavery in European and American history. It is thus important to deal critically with slaves and slavery in Paul's letters, mission, and assemblies.

The "canonical Paul" has been understood as an advocate of slavery. If Paul himself was the "author" of Colossians and Ephesians and the Pastoral Epistles, he clearly accepted and supported the slaveholding patriarchal family that was a cornerstone of the Roman imperial order. Slaveholders and advocates of slavery in European and American history claimed the canonical Paul as scriptural authority for the institution, although abolitionists also appealed to Paul in arguing against the institution. It will be important to deal with the deutero-Pauline letters produced by some disciples of the apostle as a determinative influence on later interpretation of Paul in a subsequent step of this article. Perhaps under that influence, even many (perhaps most) interpreters of Paul who accept only the seven letters as "authentic" view him as a political-social conservative hesitant to challenge the established order. Interestingly, they base this view on one of the rare references to slaves/slavery in Paul's letters, focusing on an uncertain reading of 1 Cor 7:21 as their proof text, along with a traditional reading of the brief Letter to Philemon.

Once it is recognized that Paul and his coworkers were anticipating the termination of the Roman imperial order, the previous debates about whether Paul opposed or supported slavery seem beside the point. In the final fulfillment of the kingdom of God, slavery would be terminated along with less extreme forms of domination and exploitation. That slave relations were pervasive in Roman imperial society, however, was one of the key factors in the background to the intense expectation of freedom in Paul's letters: in the Christ events people had been delivered from "slavery" and brought into the freedom of the children of God (Rom 8, Gal 3–5). The question is whether and in what way anticipation of the end of slavery may have affected slave relations in the communities of the alternative society Paul and his coworkers were catalyzing, which were still living in the Roman imperial order in which slavery was central and slaves were under the coercive domination of their masters.

In his main argument in Galatians, Paul cites a "baptismal formula" that addresses three of the principal divisions and power relations in the Roman world (including Hellenistic and Judean society):

> You are all children of God.
> For as many as were baptized into Christ
> have put on Christ.
> There is neither Judean nor Greek
> There is neither slave nor free
> There is no "male and female"
> For you are all one in Christ Jesus. (Gal 3:26–28)

In the slaveholding kyriarchal family that was foundational for the political economy of the Roman world, women were subordinated to their husbands (*kyrioi*, "lords"), and slaves lived and worked under the total domination of their masters (*kyrioi*, "lords"). In the Eastern Empire where Hellenistic culture was still dominant, "Greeks" were privileged and often despised Judeans and Syrians and other subject peoples as suitable for little more than laboring or slavery. In the expansion of the movement of Christ loyalists, however, in which history was understood as moving through Israelite tradition instead of Roman imperial dominance, this rank or precedence was reversed.

Standard older interpretation of Paul, still assuming the separation of religion from concrete political-economic life, understood the baptismal formula and Paul as referring only to spiritual life and/or the future in the final fulfillment of the kingdom of God following "the day of the Lord." Such interpretation had not yet discerned that this baptismal formula had been the pronouncement, in "performative speech" that effected what it pronounced, of the dramatic and powerful ritual drama (with the disrobing, immersion, re-emergence, and re-robing) that (evidently) all members of the assemblies of Christ had undergone as the ceremony by which they had joined the community/movement of Christ. It is clear from Paul's adamant overall argument in Galatians (which continued with confused and confusing "rhetorical overkill"), however, that Paul understood, and was insisting, that his addressees in Galatia recognize that the "no longer Judean or Greek" was concretely realized for those who were "in Christ," that is, in the communities of the movement.

But can we conclude that Paul also understood the other two social relations of domination to have been socially transcended in the assemblies of Christ? It should be noted that the formulation of the line pertaining to women and men is not symmetrical with the other two lines: it is "no longer 'male and female,'" clearly a reference to the creation of people in Genesis, "male and female [God] created them" (1:27). If this phrase was understood as a reference to patriarchal marriage, then the baptismal formula evidently meant that such patriarchal marriage has been significantly relativized in the communities of Christ loyalists (although it is difficult to discern how marriage suddenly became egalitarian, given how people had been socialized). But what about "slave and free"?

Although the ideal of and exhortation to "freedom" is strong in Paul's letters, his references to slavery and slaves are very few.[45] This makes it all the

---

45. It may be important to recognize that the term *doulos/oi* has different meanings in Paul's letters and the Gospels and related texts that derive from the different

more striking that the standard older view that Paul was a social conservative, standing solidly behind the established order politically-economically, is based primarily on a rare and highly debatable reference to slavery (1 Cor 7:21–23). The baptismal formula in Gal 3:28 indicates that some members of the assemblies were slaves or former slaves. Interpreters have also taken Paul's references to "Cloe's people" and "the household of Stephanas" in 1 Corinthians (1:11, 16; 16:15–17, in which "Lucky" [Fortunatas] and "the Greek" [Achaicus] could have been typical slave names) as indications that those households included slaves. His brief exhortation in 1 Cor 7:21–24 assumes that some members of the Corinthian assembly had been slaves when they were brought into the community. Like women, who might have been wives of husbands who also joined the community or of husbands who did not, the slaves might have been enslaved to men or women who joined the community or to men or women who did not. If Chloe's people and "Lucky" and "the Greek" were slaves we can only speculate whether they were emancipated when Cloe and Stephanas and they joined the assembly. It seems likely that, with no other options for a subsistence living, they would have remained in the household even if they were freed (and we can imagine that the dynamics in the household interaction may not have changed all that much).

The standard reading of the principal "proof text" by which Paul was taken as a conservative supporter of the institution of slavery is highly questionable in a number of ways.[46] First, the conservative interpretation projected

---

political-economic-religious systems in the historical background. See the analysis and discussion in Horsley, "Slave Systems"; Callender, "Servants of God(s)"; and Wright, "*Ebd/Doulos*." The one meaning, dominant in Greek texts of the Roman Empire, was the chattel slavery that became institutionalized in ancient Athenian and other Greek societies and expanded considerably in the Roman Empire. This is the meaning in the "baptismal formula" in Gal 3:28 and in Paul's statements in 7:21–24. On the other hand, in the ancient Near East in general and in Israelite/Judean society, all people were understood as "servants of God/the gods," and some had a special calling or rank or office as "servants of God." Kings, such as David; priests; and prophets were "servants" of God in this special sense. Ordinary people were then also "servants" of the king as well as of God, and depending on their relationship of debt or other subordination might be "servants" of their (land)lords, etc. (for which the term "debt slave" is often used). Such relationships appear in several of the parables in the Gospels; considering the political-economic-cultural background, it is unclear why the NRSV opted to translate *doulos/oi* consistently with "slave(s)" and not according to the literary and social context and cultural tradition. When Paul refers to himself as "*doulos* of God/Christ" he evidently means "servant of God/Christ" commissioned as an apostle, just as the prophets had been specially commissioned. He does not regularly refer to Christ loyalists in general as "*douloi* of God/Christ." The occurrence of the phrase in 1 Cor 7:21–24 must be determined from context. See the fuller analysis and discussion in Horsley, "Paul and Slavery."

46. On these key points, see further the critical discussion of 1 Cor 7:21–24 in Horsley, *1 Corinthians*.

a peculiar translation and reading of Paul's argument when he comes to slaves. Paul's statement in 1 Cor 7:21 involves a rhetorical omission of an object in the last, imperative clause: "rather use [it]!" (*mallon chresai*). In the appropriate way of reading the Greek, the implied object for the slave to "use/make use of" would be supplied from the closest preceding clause that begins with a strong adversative to being a slave. "But indeed if you can gain your freedom..." This is what the RSV translation committee did, in a break with the traditional interpretation: "But if you can gain your freedom, avail yourself of the opportunity." Ironically, the NRSV committee reverted to the pro-slavery (mis)reading of the Greek that filled in the missing object from three clauses before: "Were you a slave when called?"

Second, the standard conservative reading does not attend to the context of Paul's overall argument in 1 Cor 7. Paul begins this argument in the letter addressing an inquiry from the Corinthians about what the "spirituals" evidently took as an implication of their spiritual transcendence with regard to marriage and sexual practice (their slogan, "It is well for a man not to touch a woman" [7:1]). With the threat of *porneia* in mind, he then gives advice or a "word of the Lord" to people in different kinds of situations or relationships (7:2–16). Then he states a general rule for all of the assemblies: "Let each of you lead the life that the Lord has assigned," and proceeds to apply the rule to the fundamental social relationships addressed by the baptismal formula (7:18–20). In further illustrating his rule, just as it seems to apply to variations on marriage and sexual relations, it applies well to Judeans and Greeks, the circumcised and the uncircumcised. When he comes to slave and free (slavery), however, he realizes that he must qualify the general rule in a major way (before restating the rule in 7:24). "Were you a slave when called? Do not be concerned about it. *But if* indeed you are able to become free, rather use (it)." Seize the opportunity! He then follows up with a confirmation. "For whoever was called in the Lord as a slave is a freedperson of the Lord . . . You were bought with a price. Do not be(come) slaves of humans." Following Paul's argument carefully thus shows that Paul makes a significant exception to his general rule of remaining in one's situation for slaves who have an opportunity to become free.

Third, that Paul is making an exception to his general rule in 1 Cor 7:21–23 follows the pattern of his foregoing argument on marriage and sexual relations. In 1 Cor 7:5a, 9, 11a, 15, and again in 29, he makes exceptions to his main exhortations, advice, commands, or counsel in his respective treatments of different kinds of relationships.

Fourth, despite the efforts of those who produced the deutero-Pauline letters to represent Paul as supporting slavery, his statements in 1 Cor 7:21 continued to be understood to urge slaves to take the opportunity to become free. The fourth-century theologian John Chrysostom, whose influence contributed to the establishment of the proslavery interpretation, knew that this statement had been understood in the opposite sense.[47]

Given these and other considerations, there is thus no basis for the interpretation of 1 Cor 7:21 as an indication that Paul was advocating that slaves continue in their slavery. In 1 Corinthians Paul was advocating that the nascent assembly operate as independently as possible from the dominant order of "this world." That slaves should seize an opportunity to become free fits with other ways that the assembly should treat the conditions of the Roman imperial order, of which slavery was a foundational reality, "as if not" in attempting to be an alternative society.

Interpretation of the brief Letter to Philemon has been dominated by the assumption that Onesimus was a slave, evidently a runaway slave, and even a runaway slave who was a thief. Operating on the assumption that he was a slave, interpreters then find other characterizations of Onesimus in the letter that "fit" his slave role, such as being a "child" (v. 10), being "useful" (v. 11), and being "of service" (v. 13). Although none of these characterizations necessarily indicate that he was a slave, the net effect is to confirm the assumption. Some interpreters who follow along in this traditional assumption then find in Paul's subtle argument that he was an active advocate of emancipation of a slave in one of the communities he helped catalyze.[48]

In the ongoing debate over the interpretation of this letter, Allen Callahan has delivered the most telling criticism of the assumption that Onesimus was a slave and the interpretation based on that.[49] He argued that a careful critical reading of the Greek text (as established by text critics) reveals that it contains

---

47. Harrill, *Manumission of Slaves*, 77–78. In his earlier, exegetical writing Martin Luther broke with the traditional interpretation, drawing the implications for the serfs of his day, reassuring them that they were not to interpret Paul to mean that they should remain in their servitude. But in his vociferous later reaction to the Twelve Articles of the Peasants in Swabia and the German peasant revolt, he reverted to the traditional interpretation. Luther, *Works*, 28:42–43, 46:146–47.

48. Petersen, *Rediscovering Paul*; Winter, "Paul's Letter to Philemon." For references to the numerous recent studies of slavery in the Greco-Roman world, of Paul and slavery, and of Paul's Letter to Philemon, see the extensive notes in Marchal, "Usefulness of an Onesimus." Many of these studies seem to assume that Paul's statements and relations would have fit into the slave relations and slave-owning and slave-using culture attested in references from texts produced by the slave-owning elite.

49. Callahan, *Embassy of Onesimus*; and "Paul's Epistle to Philemon."

no clear indication that Onesimus was a slave, much less a runaway. The term "slave" (*doulos*) appears only in v. 16. There it is preceded by the term *hos* (as [if]), which indicates a virtual, not an actual, state of affairs or relationship. The sense can be discerned in v. 17, where Paul asks Philemon "to receive him as (you would) me" (*hos eme*), and in v. 14, where Paul wants Philemon's good deed to be voluntary, and "not as though by constraint" (*hos kata anagken*). In the key clause in v. 16, Paul thus hopes that Philemon will have Onesimus back "no longer as if a slave, but more than a slave, a beloved brother." The letter could most easily be read on the assumption that Onesimus was an estranged brother of Philemon. (Had the latter been treating his brother "as if he were a slave"?) Callahan's further thorough investigation of the manuscript tradition and the reception history of the letter finds that until the fourth century it was ignored or considered insignificant or even non-Pauline. Then in the late fourth century, primarily in the works of John Chrysostom, appears the stereotyped runaway-slave-who-stole-his-master's-belongings reading stated explicitly against charges that Christianity was "the subversion" of the social order, specifically taking servants away from their masters. The debate continues; but after Callahan's critical reading of the text and survey of the reception history it would be difficult to revert to the assumption that Onesimus was a slave and the interpretation of the letter as evidence that the assemblies were not concerned that some of their members were slaves.

It may be disappointing to some that Paul did not make some unequivocal statement of condemnation of the institution of slavery. We can assume, but cannot know for sure, that he had in mind that slavery would be terminated along with the whole dominant imperial "world that was passing away." It seems clear that in the performative speech of the ritual baptism by which people joined the assemblies the relations of "slave and free"—like the relations of "Judean and Greek" and the traditional patriarchal marriage understood as ordained in the "male and female" of the creation story—were transformed in the communities of Christ (at least in Paul's understanding). In the appropriate reading of 1 Cor 7:21, far from telling slaves to remain in their situation, Paul urged them to seize an opportunity to become free. The text of the brief Letter to Philemon is sufficiently unclear and susceptible of different readings that it seems unreliable as a basis for conclusions about whether and when emancipation occurred in slave relations in the assemblies that Paul and his coworkers catalyzed.

The Collection for the Poor in the Jerusalem Community

At the end of 1 Corinthians and at points in most other letters Paul focuses on the most striking economic aspect of the movement, one that is unprecedented and perhaps unique in antiquity: the collection for the poor among the saints in Jerusalem.[50] The collection was evidently connected with, indeed had its origin in, the practice of sharing goods in common in order to aid the needy in the early community of Jesus loyalists in Jerusalem, as portrayed in the accounts in Acts (2:44–45, 4:32–37). Within a few years the practice had been extended to other communities. During a period of severe famine in Palestine, the community in Antioch had sent aid (*diakonia*) to the Jerusalem community for distribution to the poor, which was delivered by Saul and Barnabas, according to the account in Acts (11:27–29). This would have been the precedent behind what was extended in the agreement Paul and Barnabas had made with James, Peter, and John (Gal 2:9–10) that they should "remember the poor" as they expanded the movement among other subjected peoples. This meant that from the outset of Paul's mission the newly formed communities of "the (other) peoples" would be sharing some of their resources horizontally, in contrast with the usual vertical flow of resources in the Roman Empire to rulers, landowners, and creditors.

Paul had evidently been giving instructions about the collection to the communities that he and coworkers catalyzed, from Galatia though Macedonia to Corinth. As he writes to the Corinthians: "You should follow the directions I gave to the assemblies of Galatia: On the first day of every week, each of you is to put aside and save whatever extra you gain (earn), so that the collections need not be taken when I come (back)" (1 Cor 16:1–2). The further instructions Paul gives the Corinthians indicates that he had developed an ambitious plan for how he would implement the collection (1 Cor 16:3–4; 2 Cor 8, 9). After the amount had accumulated week by week (for well over a year), then the Corinthian and other assemblies would choose delegates to accompany Paul in taking the gift to Jerusalem.

In two subsequent short letters to the Corinthians (1 Cor 8, 9) he pressed them insistently about the collection. He first uses the Macedonians as an example to the Corinthians. Despite their "severe ordeal of affliction" and their "extreme poverty" they had been eager to "share in this service [*koinonia tes diakonias*] to the saints" (2 Cor 8:1–4). It seems clear that the people in these assemblies must have been living close to subsistence but nevertheless, with a

---

50. Helpful summary of previous interpretation of the collection in Kloppenborg, "Paul's Collection for Jerusalem," 307–11. Recent theological treatments are Joubert, *Paul and Benefactor*; and Downs, *Offering of the Gentiles*.

good deal of persuasion, accepted the collection as an obligation. Not wanting to put pressure on the Corinthians to give what they did not have in relief of others, Paul suggested they seek a balance between their "present abundance" and the "need" of the folks in Jerusalem (2 Cor 8:9–14). He further grounded his appeal by quoting from the story of God's provision of manna to the desperately needy Israelites in the wilderness who shared among them, so that no one had too much and no one had too little. Paul urged that the Corinthians' contributions to the collection would be a further expression of their "love," which consistently in the letters means concrete care and sharing (e.g., 1 Cor 13). Again, citing Israelite tradition in 2 Cor 9, Paul draws a homology between the justice of God, which means giving to the poor, and ("the harvest of") the justice of the Corinthians in giving to the collection. The service of the poor folks in the Jerusalem community by the Corinthians and other peoples, moreover, is a manifestation of "obedience to the confession of the gospel of Christ." That is, the concrete results of the gospel of Christ were the communities of the movement that had an economic dimension, and that included the sharing of resources with other communities in need.

As he heads toward Spain after completing his mission in the Greek cities and writes to the Romans, Paul continues to conceive of the collection in terms of what the peoples involved in the movement share in common. The peoples other than Judeans now share in common "the spiritual things" that originated with the Israelites (Judeans), and are obligated to share in common "the material things" with the poor in the Jerusalem community. For Paul at least, the economic and the spiritual dimensions of the movement that he was devoted to expanding were inseparable. In the collection for the poor in Jerusalem the local assemblies of the movement shared economic resources (albeit quite limited) across considerable distances. The movement of assemblies had an inter-people ("international") economic dimension that was virtually the opposite of the centralizing tributary political economy of the empire.

* * *

In sum, although it was limited by the Christ loyalists' own marginal existence, the counter-imperial inter-people alternative society that Paul thought he was building did indeed have an economic dimension with some distinctive features. The *ekklesiai* were still within the Roman imperial order. But in significant ways they opposed and resisted it in their own practices, although probably not to the degree that Paul wanted. In cases where they were under attack locally, some sort of cooperation and mutual aid would have been necessary in order to survive. Paul urged them to mind their own affairs in community solidarity and separation from the established political-economic-religious order. In what was the most striking aspect of the alternative society Paul hoped they might embody what would have been unique in the Roman or any other imperial order. The sharing of resources among marginal subject peoples in the collection for the poor in Jerusalem was the diametric opposite of the vertical flow of resources to the urban elite and the imperial Lord and Savior.

The Deutero-Pauline Letters—and Other Developments of the Pauline Legacy

The deutero-Pauline letters produced by Pauline disciples display a dramatic difference from the "authentic" letters of Paul with regard to slavery as well as other issues. Critical analysis has determined that Colossians and Ephesians are probably at least a generation later and that the Pastoral Letters are two or three generations later than the letters that were integral in the mission of Paul and his coworkers. The communities addressed are now comprised of (at least some) slaveholding kyriarchal families/households that were basic to the overall Roman imperial order. Also, more families in these assemblies are relatively more comfortable than living close to the subsistence level. First Timothy even addresses some who are "rich," and accordingly instructs them to be "rich in good works, generous, and ready to share" (6:17–18). In the Pastorals there now appears a hierarchy in the communities, with deacons, elders, and bishops, who are to be honored and obeyed.

These deutero-Pauline letters include what have been called "household codes," which give admonitions for the basic component relations within families, for example, to wives to be subject and obedient to husbands, who are to love their wives. Slaves now come under constraint and obligation to masters that are above and beyond those of slaves in non-Christian households, insofar as their masters' authority is now also that of their heavenly Lord (Col 3:18–25, Eph 5:21—6:9, 1 Pet 2:18–25, 1 Tim 6:1–2, Titus 2:9–10).[51]

> Slaves, obey your earthly masters with fear and trembling . . . as you obey Christ . . . as slaves of Christ. Render service with enthusiasm, as to the Lord and not to men and women. (Eph 6:5–8)

Slave masters are asked only to stop threatening their slaves, since they have the same Master in heaven (6:9).

It has been recognized in recent decades that the Pastoral and other

---

51. See further the chapter by Osiek in this volume; and Osiek et al., *Woman's Place*.

deutero-Pauline letters were not the only continuation of Paul's legacy and at the time probably not the dominant line of development. Rooted in and descended from parallel and often rival "apostolic" missions, communities of Christ loyalists developed in different ways contingent on different regions and influences. From the early second century (two generations after Paul's mission) there is considerable evidence from the former Pauline mission area ranging from Antioch in Syria, Smyrna in Asia Minor, Corinth in Greece, to Rome for the use of common funds of the communities to aid widows, orphans, the destitute, and to emancipate community members who were slaves.[52] A letter from the "Christian" community in Rome to that in Corinth refers to voluntary enslavement as an example of noble self-sacrifice as if it were familiar as a frequent practice. "We know that many among ourselves have given themselves to bondage that they might ransom others; many have delivered themselves to slavery, and provided food for others with the price they have received for themselves" (1 Clem. 55:2). Another, somewhat later communication from the community at Rome exhorts (perhaps the better-off?) members "to minister to widows, to look after orphans and the destitute, and to redeem from distress the servants of God" (Herm. Mand. 8:10) and "instead of lands, to purchase afflicted souls and to look after widows and orphans" (Herm. Sim. 1:8).[53] At mid-second century, Justin Martyr attests the same tradition and practice among "Christian" assemblies: a fund supplied mainly by the better-off members was used to "support orphans and widows and those in want and those who are in chains" (1 Apol. 67.6).

Further attestation of the same practices is supplied by its sharp prohibition. Ignatius, the bishop of Antioch (later martyred), expresses the standard concern to provide concrete aid to the widow and orphan, the distressed and imprisoned (Ign. *Smyrn.* 6:2). But he also has some pointed instruction for his fellow bishop Polycarp regarding slaves, which resembles that in the Pastorals.

> Do not be haughty to slaves, either men or women, yet do not let them be puffed up, but let them rather endure slavery to the glory of God, that they may obtain a better freedom from God. Let them not desire to be made free from the common fund, that they not be found the slaves of desire. (Ign. *Pol.* 4:3)

Further, the fourth-century Apostolic Constitutions, which contains much earlier material and is usually located in Antioch/Syria, attests the deliverance of

---

52. Callahan, *Embassy of Onesimus*, 89–90.
53. Osiek, *Shepherd of Hermas*, 371–73.

slaves and captives by drawing on the common fund (4.9.2; cf. 5.1–2). It also comments that the only reason for Christians to be found at public meetings was "to purchase a slave and save a soul" (2.62.4). These references to the practice among "Christian" communities of buying members out of their slavery by drawing on a common fund are made all the more credible by evidence that Jewish congregations and some associations engaged in the same practice.[54]

It would appear that many of the communities descended from Paul's mission and other missions came to act on the fundamental principles of their loyalty to Christ, such as articulated in the baptismal declarations of social relations to be embodied in the assemblies. Common funds of the communities were established for the purpose of aiding the destitute, widows, and orphans, and of purchasing members out of slavery. It may well be that the prohibition of this practice by a bishop such as Ignatius, who with fellow bishops such as Polycarp was trying to consolidate ecclesial power in the monarchic episcopate, was motivated by the concern to make the nascent "Christian" assemblies appear less subversive of the Roman imperial order based in the kyriarchal slaveholding households.

All Things in Common: Sharing of Resources and Aid to the Poor

The letters of Paul are the earliest texts in the New Testament. They have also been the most decisive for Christian theology and ethics, particularly in Protestant churches. Insofar as the deutero-Pauline letters were included in the New Testament Scriptures, moreover, the canonical Paul has been the most problematic, both in historical influence and for critical interpretation. Yet not only in the various ways that the Pauline legacy was developed, but also in the New Testament and in related texts not included in the canon there is a considerable diversity of economic practice. It is evident in most of these texts that they addressed a movement or community(ies) and were probably products of those communities. Thus, what is often referred to as "early Christianity" was by no means unitary, but diverse communities and movements, probably in somewhat different areas and with different emphases. Prior to the wider recognition of this considerable diversity of texts and movements—and rooted in an acceptance of the narrative in the early chapters of Acts as a credible representation of history—New Testament scholars believed that most of these branches of "Christ believers" or "Jesus movements" developed from or broke off from the community that formed in Jerusalem following the resurrection

54. P.Oxy. 1205 = *CPJ* 3:473; Harrill, *Manumission of Slaves*, 167–68, 174–77.

and bestowal of the Spirit. It is clear from Paul's own account that he and his mission did branch off from the Jesus/Christ movement based in Jerusalem (Gal 1–2). But this is probably not the case for most of the other texts and movements that appear to have emerged independently of the early community in Jerusalem.

"All Things in Common" and Aiding the Needy in the Early Jerusalem Community

In their conviction that religion was separate from political-economic life and reacting with remorse over Christian complicity in the Jewish Holocaust, Christian scholars assumed that, like Jesus himself, Jesus' followers were faithful "Jews" for whom the temple was the holy place of worship (in their synthetic construct of "Judaism"). One of the key decontextualized proof texts on which they relied was the historic mistranslation (in the KJV and still in the RSV) that the believers were "day by day attending the temple together" (Acts 2:46). The sense of the text, however, is not that the early Jesus loyalists in Jerusalem were "attending the temple" (like attending church or synagogue today), but that they were spending much time together in the temple courtyard. This was the central public space in Jerusalem after Herod's massive reconstruction of the temple and the Jesus loyalists were probably gathering there to attract attention and to recruit. Translators, moreover, appear to have missed the connotations of key Greek terms applied here to the (Jesus) loyalists. They were "all together" (*epi to auto*) in the sense of *the assembly* of Israel (*yahad* in Hebrew, for which *epi to auto* is used in the Septuagint, the Greek translation of Judean Scriptures [Acts 2:44]). Similarly, the term *homothumadon* in the phrase translated "they spent much time *together*" also suggests that they were the true *assembly* of Israel (*yahad*, for which *homothumadon* was also used in the Septuagint).

The broader context in the narrative of Acts, however, indicates that the Jerusalem community and its leaders continued Jesus' conflict with the (Roman-client) high priestly rulers. And the immediate context (Acts 2:44–47, 4:32–37) indicates that a central and distinguishing aspect of the Jerusalem community was its common possession of goods and distribution according to need.[55] The main point in the immediate narrative context is: "All who had become loyal were together and had all things in common [*eichon hapanta koina*]; they would sell their possessions and goods and distribute the proceeds to all, as any had need" (Acts 2:44–45). Then, following the observation about "spending time in

---

55. For a critical review of dismissive previous interpretation and an argument for trusting the historical core of the account of sharing of goods in the Jerusalem community, see Bartchy, "Community of Goods."

the temple," comes the account that "they broke bread from house to house and ate their food with glad and generous hearts" (Acts 2:46; evidently eating communally in small groups, as houses were quite small). Several episodes later a fuller statement of the community's economic practice appears:

> The whole group of those who had become loyal were of one heart and soul, and no one said that any possessions/goods were his/her own [*idion einai*)] but that all things were theirs in common [*autois panta koina*] . . . There was not a needy person among them, for as many as possessed lands and houses sold them and brought the proceeds of what was sold. They laid it at the apostles' feet, and it was distributed to each as any had need. (Acts 4:32–35)

Establishment New Testament scholars, who are generally socially and politically conservative, dismissed these accounts as romanticizing and utopian.[56] The narratives of the origins of the movement in Jerusalem in Acts are idealizing, to be sure. Yet it is evident in the continuing narrative in Acts that there was some such sharing of goods and distribution to the needy more or less from the outset. As more and more Hellenistic Judeans, evidently in the city as pilgrims, joined the movement, their leaders complained that their widows were being neglected in the daily distribution (*diakonia*, service) (Acts 6:1–6), a confirmation that such distributions were happening.[57]

To understand this "communism" of goods and distribution to the needy that is often dismissed as utopian and impractical we need to explore why it was necessary and the background of the practice in Israelite tradition. Who comprised the community of Jesus loyalists in Jerusalem? At the core were at least several of "the twelve" disciples, headed by Peter. There may also have been others who had come up to Jerusalem with Jesus in his prophetic confrontation with the high priests in the temple. These people had left behind whatever economic base they had previously in Galilean villages. In their excitement from the "breakthrough" constituted by Jesus' confrontation with the high priestly rulers in the temple and his ensuing martyrdom, they may well have recruited others, either Jerusalemites or others from outside, including some from Judean villages nearer to the city. Some of these may also have left

---

56. Critical discussions of the language of the Hellenistic ideal and arguments for the economic practices of the Jerusalem *koinon* in Draper, "Social Milieu and Motivation"; and Bartchy, "Community of Goods."

57. According to the narrative in Acts this became the occasion for the movement to develop further infrastructure, with seven appointed from the "Hellenists" to be "servers" (deacons) in order to free up the "apostles" for prayer and preaching (i.e., recruiting?).

their previous economic base, but others were still in possession of resources. The Acts narrative mentions in particular the Levite Joseph (Barnabas), who sold a field he possessed and donated the proceeds, and the couple Ananias and Sapphira, who sold some property but donated only a portion of the proceeds (Acts 4:36–37, 5:1–11).

It may help interpreters to allow for some real practice that is indicated by the supposedly idealizing language to recognize that such sharing of goods was not unprecedented in Roman Palestine. As the Hasmonean strong men maneuvered to assume the high priesthood in Judea, a group of priests and scribes, evidently seriously committed to what they understood as the central exodus– and Mosaic covenantal traditions of Israel, withdrew into the wilderness of Judea at Qumran, near the Dead Sea. They established a new exodus and renewed covenant community, considering that they were the true/faithful *yahad* (assembly) of Israel. As indicated in their Community Rule, the Qumran community/*yahad* required that members share all things in common. Those who remained committed to the covenant were to go through major steps of trial and approval. Upon entry into the community, if they were accepted after a two-year trial period, they were to hand over their possessions and earnings, which would then be merged with the common goods (1QS 5:1–3, 6:18–24). It is noteworthy that, like the Jesus loyalists who formed the Jerusalem *koinon*, those who joined the Qumran community had left whatever economic base they had previously (which for priests and scribes was presumably in the Jerusalem temple-state).

In sharing their resources in common and aiding the needy, the members of the Jerusalem community were following—and dramatically intensifying—the Israelite tradition they were familiar with in their Galilean and Judean village communities. As known from the adaptations of early Israelite (village) customs (and practices) in the scribal collections of laws and customs in Exod 21–23, the "Holiness Code" in Leviticus, and Deuteronomy, Israelite village communities had traditional ways of cooperation and mutual aid that enabled component families to remain economically viable.[58] These practices included customs such as gleaning and leaving fields fallow every seven years so the needy could harvest the produce, liberal lending to the needy at no interest, and cancellation of debts every seven years. The overarching "social-economic contract," the general Israelite "moral economy," was summarized and focused in the Mosaic covenant between God and the people, and between the people and

---

58. Careful, critical examination of Israelite "Law in the Villages" in Knight, *Law, Power, and Justice*, ch. 5.

their neighbors. The "Ten Commandments" were in effect rules or principles that guided economic relations in agrarian communities.[59]

As explained in the third chapter of this volume, the center of Jesus' renewal of the people of Israel was his renewal of the Mosaic covenant. And the center of his covenant renewal was a restatement and intensification of the demands for mutual aid and community cooperation amid the difficult circumstances imposed by the Roman imperial order in Palestine. The communal sharing of resources and aiding the needy were an intensification of the traditional Israelite covenantal principles, demands, and customs in the new circumstances of having left behind their previous economic bases in village communities and the formation of a new community of Jesus loyalists in Jerusalem, where they were attempting to expand the movement of the renewal of Israel (against the exploitative rulers). The claim in the Acts narrative that "there was not a needy person among them" (4:34) suggests that they were (supposedly) realizing the ideal articulated in the covenant torah of Deuteronomy (15:4) that in (the *yaḥad* of) Israel there should not be a needy person if the people were keeping the covenant.

The "Hellenists," who presumably had come from diaspora communities in other cities of the empire, would have been familiar with the Mosaic covenantal traditions that required aiding the needy. Some of them may well have held some economic resources insofar as it would have required some means to make the journey to Jerusalem and to support themselves during their stay.

A standard explanation among New Testament scholars for various ethical stances and behavior among "early Christians" has been that they were caught up in an apocalyptic fervor, expecting that the end of the world was at hand. Such an expectation, however, does not appear anywhere in the narrative of Acts about the community of Jesus loyalists in Jerusalem and their sharing all things in common. Their orientation is indicated probably by the speeches given by Peter that led to his and others' arrest and imprisonment and the speech by Stephen that led to his martyrdom. The Jerusalem community was evidently acting in the conviction that the mission of Jesus, the prophet like Moses, climaxing in his crucifixion and his vindication by God as the messiah designate, had begun the renewal of Israel, in fulfilment of prophecies and of the promises to Abraham.

As the movement rapidly expanded from the Jerusalem community to

---

59. For an application of the cross-cultural study of the "moral economy" of peasantries, see Scott, *Moral Economy of Peasant*; applied to the covenantal law tradition in ancient Israel in Horsley, *Covenant Economics*, esp. chs. 2–3.

assemblies (*synagogai*) of Judeans in other cities, the practice of sharing resources—especially to aid the needy—was extended to relations between communities of Jesus loyalists. In a time of severe famine under Claudius, the disciples in the community in Antioch "determined [that] according to their ability, each would send relief [*diakonia*] to the brothers and sisters living in Judea" (Acts 11:27–30). That this was delivered by Barnabas and Saul, according to the narrative, prefigures the Jerusalem apostles' charge to "remember the poor" (in Jerusalem) when they agreed to allow Barnabas and Paul to further expand the movement in a mission among "the uncircumcised" (Gal 2), as noted above.

Epistle of James

It is well known that Martin Luther saw the Epistle of James as an "epistle of straw." He took its focus on "works" as the virtual opposite of Paul's emphasis on faith. James bases social-economic relations on Israelite covenantal law. Indeed, as may be suggested by its being addressed ostensibly to "the twelve tribes in dispersion" (Jas 1:1), the exhortation throughout the epistle stands in continuity with Israelite covenantal and prophetic tradition.

James begins with trials that its community is undergoing (1:1–16). The scenario of favoritism shown to a wealthy person "with gold rings and fine clothes" who visits their assembly, in contrast to the treatment of a poor person with dirty clothes, is evidently hypothetical (2:1–4). It may be addressed to some in the community who have pretensions. But the scenario sets up the rhetorical questions that point to the concrete situation of the assembly. "Has not God chosen the poor in the world to be rich in faith and to be heirs of the kingdom . . . ? Is it not the rich who oppress you? Is it not they who drag you into court?" (2:5–7). With reference to the situation of the community under attack by the wealthy (also local rulers?), the concern of James is to exhort the people to aid the needy, including but not limited to "care for orphans and widows in their distress" (1:26–27, 4:13–17).

James insists that members of the assembly not be drawn into the ways of "the world," presumably the Roman imperial order (in whatever area they were located). In terms reminiscent of the declaration of Jesus that "one cannot serve (both) God and mammon" (Matt 6:24) comes the stark statement that "friendship with the world is enmity with God; therefore, whoever wishes to be a friend of the world becomes an enemy of God" (Jas 4:4). It is utterly unacceptable to imagine becoming engaged in business and seeking gain (4:13). The epistle knows exactly how the urban elite are gaining their wealth. James charges the wealthy with words that echo the indictments by several Israelite prophets: "Listen! The wages of the laborers who mowed your fields, which you kept back by fraud, cry out; and the cries of the harvesters have reached the ears of the Lord of hosts" (Jas 5:40). With such exploitation of their tenants and laborers by the wealthy elite as the foil, James insists that the assembly maintain nonexploitative and non-conflictual relations among their members in following the principles of the covenantal commandments and Mosaic covenantal torah at the center of Israelite tradition.

The Alternative Political-Economic Practices of Communities of Christ Loyalists

These texts later included in the New Testament and other "early Christian" texts provide abundant indications of the political-economic situations and social-economic practices of the communities they address. This enables us to move beyond the artificial and anachronistic separation of the political-economic and religious aspects of the texts and those communities. And this enables us to move well beyond a reductionist reading of these texts as expressions of theological ideas and ethical exhortation for individual believers to recognition of their purpose and function. They were about and were addressed to communities of movements of subjected people struggling to maintain themselves and make adjustments in difficult political-economic circumstances and what was often a hostile environment.

The exploration of the political-economic situations and social-economic practices of these texts (and communities) of Christ loyalists in the Roman imperial context suggests that there were likely some links between the practices indicated in the different texts. Two of the cases examined, of course, were different "legacies" of Paul's mission and "Pauline" communities. The deutero-Pauline letters of two or more generations after Paul and his coworkers' mission indicate that some "Pauline" communities became solidly established in cities of the Greek East. They indicate the kinds of compromises one strand of the expanding movement made in the process. That they were incorporated in a Pauline collection of letters and included in the New Testament in late antiquity meant that they tended to determine the way "the canonical Paul" was read and used to legitimate and reinforce the kyriarchal family in a hierarchical political-economic order ordained of God, including the subordination of women and the institutionalization and later reinstitutionalization of slavery. However, that a different, more liberation-oriented line of Pauline communities, including their communal practices and authority figures persisted into late antiquity suggests that the "authentic" letters of Paul should not necessarily be read as scriptural support for the subordination of women and the legitimation of slavery and other forms of political-economic subjugation.

The apparent communal sharing of goods in the communities addressed by the Didache is closely related to the sustained exhortation of Mosaic covenant renewal that has also taken for a form of the "two ways" in Israelite tradition. This has significant parallels in the major covenant renewal speeches in the Gospels of Matthew and Luke and in the dialogues of Jesus and his sharp condemnation of the scribes and Pharisees in the Gospel of Mark (as discussed in ch. 3 of this volume). This suggests that the communal sharing of goods in the Didache—and perhaps in the speeches early in the Acts narrative as well—may have roots in the mission of Jesus that centered on the renewal of Mosaic covenantal community. And customs and mechanisms of aid to the needy in the covenantal village communities, the fundamental social-economic form of Israelite society had deep roots in Israelite tradition that can be seen operative in the legal collections in the books of the Torah. In much of Israelite (now "biblical") tradition and continuing into the gospels and other texts of early Jesus movements, the twin guiding principles that people have economic rights to a subsistence livelihood and that the community or people as a whole have a communal responsibility to honor and guarantee those rights were central to the life of the people and the practice of communities.

Bibliography

Adams, Edward. "First-Century Models for Paul's Churches: Selected Scholarly Developments since Meeks." In *After the First Urban Christians: The Social Scientific Study of Pauline Christianity Twenty-Five Years Later*, edited by Todd D. Still and David G. Horrell, 60–78. New York: T&T Clark, 2007.

Alcock, Susan E. *Graecia Capta: The Landscapes of Roman Greece*. Cambridge: Cambridge University Press, 1993.

Anderson, Benedict. *Imagined Communities*. New York: Verso, 1983.

Ascough, Richard A., et al. *Associations in the Greco-Roman World: A Sourcebook*. Waco: Baylor University Press, 2012.

Bartchy, S. Scott. "Community of Goods in Acts: Idealization or Social Reality?" In *The Future of Early Christianity: Essays in Honor of Helmut Koester*, edited by Birger Pearson et al., 309–18. Minneapolis: Fortress, 1991.

Blanton, Thomas R., IV, and Raymond Pickett, eds. *Paul and Economics: A Handbook*. Minneapolis: Fortress, 2017.

Boer, Roland, and Christina Petterson. *Idols of Nations: Biblical Myth at the Origins of Capitalism*. Minneapolis: Fortress, 2014.

———. *Time of Troubles: A New Economic Framework for Early Christianity*. Minneapolis: Fortress, 2017.

Butler, Judith. *Excitable Speech: A Politics of the Performative*. New York: Routledge, 1997.

Callahan, Allen Dwight. *Embassy of Onesimus*. Valley Forge, PA: Trinity International, 1997.
———. "Paul's Epistle to Philemon: Toward an Alternative *Argumentum*." *HTR* 86 (1993) 357–76.
Callahan, Allen Dwight, and Richard A. Horsley. "Slave Resistance in Classical Antiquity." *Semeia* 83/84 (1998) 133–51.
Callender, Dexter E., Jr. "Servants of God(s) and Servants of Kings in Israel and the Ancient Near East." *Semeia* 83/84 (1998) 67–81.
Conzelmann, Hans. *First Corinthians: A Commentary on the First Epistle to the Corinthians*. Hermeneia. Minneapolis: Fortress, 1975.
Donfried, Karl. "The Imperial Cults of Thessalonica and Paul's Conflict in 1 Thessalonians." In *Paul and Empire: Religion and Power in Roman Imperial Society*, edited by Richard A. Horsley, 215–23. Harrisburg, PA: Trinity International, 1997.
Downs, David J. *The Offering of the Gentiles: Paul's Collection for Jerusalem in Its Chronological, Cultural, and Cultic Contexts*. WUNT 2/248. Tübingen: Mohr Siebeck, 2008.
Draper, Jonathan A. "The Social Milieu and Motivation of the Community of Goods in the Jerusalem Church of Acts." In *Church in Context: Early Christianity in Social Context*, edited by Cilliers Breitenbach, 77–88. Pretoria: Kerk, 1988.
Elliott, John H. "Social-Scientific Criticism of the New Testament and its Social World." *Semeia* 35 (1986) 1–33.
Elliott, Neil. *The Arrogance of Nations: Reading Romans in the Shadow of Empire*. Minneapolis: Fortress, 2008.
———. "Diagnosing an Allergic Reaction: The Avoidance of Marx in Pauline Scholarship." *Bible and Critical Theory* 8 (2012) 1–12.
———. "Ideological Closure in the Christ-Event: A Marxist Response to Alain Badiou's Paul." In *Paul, Philosophy, and the Theopolitical Vision: Critical Engagements with Agamben, Badiou, Žižek, and Others*, edited by Douglas Harink, 135–54. Theopolitical Visions. Eugene, OR: Cascade Books, 2010.
———. "When Bridges Fail Us: Studying Economic Realities in the New Testament World." In *Bridges in New Testament Interpretation: Interdisciplinary Advances*, edited by Werner H. Kelber and Neil Elliott, 203–32. Lanham, MD: Fortress Academic, 2018.
Finley, Moses. *The Ancient Economy*. Rev. ed. Berkeley: University of California Press, 1999.
Friesen, Steven J. "Poverty in Pauline Studies: Beyond the So-Called New Consensus." *JSNT* 26 (2004) 323–61.
Garnsey, Peter, and Richard Saller. *The Roman Empire: Economy, Society, and Culture*. Berkeley: University of California Press, 1987.
———. *The Roman Empire: Economy, Society, and Culture*. 2nd ed. Berkeley: University of California Press, 2015.
Gouldner, Alvin. *The Coming Crisis of Western Sociology*. New York: Basic, 1970.
Harrill, J. Albert. *The Manumission of Slaves in Early Christianity*. HUT 32. Tübingen: Mohr Siebeck, 1998.
Hopkins, Keith. *Conquerors and Slaves*. Sociological Studies in Roman History 1. Cambridge: Cambridge University Press, 1978.
Horsley, Richard A. *1 Corinthians*. Abingdon NT Commentaries. Nashville: Abingdon, 1997.
———. *Covenant Economics: A Biblical Vision of Justice for All*. Louisville: Westminster John Knox, 2009.

———. *Jesus and the Politics of Roman Palestine*. Columbia: University of South Carolina Press, 2014.

———, ed. *Paul and Empire: Religion and Power in Roman Imperial Society*. Harrisburg, PA: Trinity International, 1997.

———. "Paul and Slavery: A Critical Alternative to Recent Readings." *Semeia* 83/84 (1998) 153–200.

———. "Paul's Assembly in Corinth: An Alternative Society." In *Urban Religion in Corinth: Interdisciplinary Approaches*, edited by Daniel Schowalter and Steven Friesen, 371–95. Cambridge: Harvard University Press, 2005.

———. "Paul's Shift in Economic 'Location' in the Locations of the Roman Imperial Economy." In *Paul and Economics: A Handbook*, edited by Thomas R. Blanton IV and Raymond Pickett, 89–123. Minneapolis: Fortress, 2017.

———. *Revolt of the Scribes: Resistance and Apocalyptic Origins*. Minneapolis: Fortress, 2010.

———. "The Slave Systems of Classical Antiquity and their Reluctant Recognition by Modern Scholars." *Semeia* 83/84 (1998) 18–65.

———. *Sociology and the Jesus Movement*. New York: Crossroad, 1988.

———. *Wisdom and Spiritual Transcendence in Corinth: Studies in First Corinthians*. Eugene, OR: Cascade Books, 2008.

Jameson, Fredric. *The Political Unconscious*. London: Methuen, 1981.

Joubert, Stephen. *Paul and Benefactor: Reciprocity, Strategy, and Theological Reflection in Paul's Collection*. WUNT 2/124. Tübingen: Mohr Siebeck, 2000.

Kloppenborg, John S. "Paul's Collection for Jerusalem and the Financial Practices in Greek Cities." In *Paul and Economics: A Handbook*, edited by Thomas R. Blanton IV and Raymond Pickett, 307–32. Minneapolis: Fortress, 2017.

Knight, Douglas A. *Law, Power, and Justice in Ancient Israel*. Louisville: Westminster John Knox, 2011.

Liu, Jinju. "Urban Poverty in the Roman Empire: Material Conditions." In *Paul and Economics: A Handbook*, edited by Thomas R. Blanton IV and Raymond Pickett, 23–56. Minneapolis: Fortress, 2017.

Longenecker, Bruce W. "Exposing the Economic Middle: A Revised Economy Scale for the Study of Early Christianity." *JSNT* 31 (2009) 243–78.

———. *Remember the Poor: Paul, Poverty, and the Greco-Roman World*. Grand Rapids, 2010.

Luther, Martin. *Luther's Works*. Edited by Jaroslav Pelikan and Helmut T. Lehmann. 55 vols. Minneapolis: Fortress and Concordia, 1957.

Marchal, Joseph A. "The Usefulness of an Onesimus: The Sexual Use of Slaves and Paul's Letter to Philemon." *JBL* 130 (2011) 749–70.

Mayer, Emanuel. *The Ancient Middle Classes: Urban Life and Aesthetics in the Roman Empire, 100 BCE–250 CE*. Cambridge: Harvard University Press, 2012.

Meeks, Wayne. *The First Urban Christians*. New Haven, CT: Yale University Press, 1983.

Morley, Neville. "Economy and Economic Theory, Roman." In *The Oxford Encyclopedia of Ancient Greece and Rome*, edited by Michael Gagarin and Elaine Fantham, 8–13. Oxford: Oxford University Press, 2010.

Murphy, Catherine M. *Wealth in the Dead Sea Scrolls and in the Qumran Community*. STDJ. Leiden: Brill, 2002.

Nasrallah, Laura. "You Were Bought with a Price: Freedpersons and Things in 1 Corinthians." In *Corinth in Contrast: Studies in Inequality*, edited by Steven J. Friesen et al., 54–73. NovTSup 155. Leiden: Brill, 2014.

Oakes, Peter S. *Empire, Economics, and the New Testament*. Grand Rapids: Eerdmans, 2020.

Osiek, Carolyn. *The Shepherd of Hermas: A Commentary*. Hermeneia. Minneapolis: Fortress, 1999.

Osiek, Carolyn, et al. *A Woman's Place: House Churches in Earliest Christianity*. Minneapolis: Fortress, 2006.

Petersen, Norman R. *Rediscovering Paul: Philemon and the Sociology of Paul's Narrative World*. 1985. Reprint, Eugene, OR: Wipf & Stock, 2008.

Price, S. R. F. *Rituals and Power: The Roman Imperial Cult in Asia Minor*. Cambridge: Cambridge University Press, 1984.

Saller, Richard. *Personal Patronage under the Early Empire*. Cambridge: Cambridge University Press, 1982.

Scheidel, Walter, ed. *The Cambridge Companion to the Roman Economy*. Cambridge Companions to the Ancient World. Cambridge: Cambridge University Press, 2012.

———. "Real Wages in Early Economies: Evidence for Living Standards from 1800 BCE to 1300 CE." *JESHO* 53 (2010) 425–62.

Scheidel, Walter, and Steven Friesen. "The Size of the Economy and the Distribution of Income in the Roman Empire." *JRS* 99 (2009) 61–91.

Scott, James C. *The Moral Economy of the Peasant*. New Haven, CT: Yale University Press, 1976.

Ste. Croix, G. E. M. de. *Class Struggle in the Ancient Greek World: From the Archaic Age to the Arab Conquests*. London: Duckworth, 1981.

Still, Todd D. "Did Paul Loathe Manual Labor?" *JBL* 125 (2006) 781–95.

Temin, Peter. *The Roman Market Economy*. Princeton Economic History of the Western World 71. Princeton, NJ: Princeton University Press, 2012.

Theissen, Gerd. "The Social Stratification in the Corinthian Community." In *The Social Setting of Pauline Christianity: Essays on Corinth*, edited and translated by John H. Schütz, 69–119. Philadelphia: Fortress, 1982.

Welborn, L. L. "The Polis and the Poor: Reconstructing Social Relations from Different Genres of Evidence." In *Methodological Foundations*, edited by James Harrison and L. L. Welborn, 189–244. First Urban Churches 1. Atlanta: SBL, 2015.

Winter, Sara C. "Paul's Letter to Philemon." *NTS* 33 (1987) 1–15.

Wright, Benjamin G., III. "'*Ebd/Doulos*: Terms and Social Status in the Meeting of Hebrew Biblical and Hellenistic Roman Culture." *Semeia* 83/84 (1998) 83–111.

Zanker, Paul. *The Power of Images in the Age of Augustus*. Ann Arbor: University of Michigan Press, 1988.

8. Apocalypse in Response to Roman Economic Ideology

Kelly J. Murphy

Introduction

Footage from the documentary *Apocalypse Later: Harold Camping vs. the End of the World* includes a scene where Harold Camping, famous for his (incorrect) prediction that the world would end on May 21, 2011, describes how his church subsequently spent "millions of dollars" advertising his new, recalculated prediction for the end: October 21, 2011. In the next scene, a congregant approaches Camping and quietly says, "I have a question about donations. I've been donating as much as I can ... I don't want anything to be left in my bank account." Camping replies, "Talk to the Lord about it, that's between you and the Lord," but makes no move to discourage the man from giving all his savings to Camping's Family Radio before October 21.[1] Camping frequently turned to the book of Revelation as proof of his end times prediction.[2] Famously, the final chapter of the book of Revelation warns readers not to "seal up the words of the prophecy of this book, for the time is near" (Rev 22:10).

Today, it seems safe to assume that John of Patmos—who lived in Asia Minor and is credited with the book of Revelation's authorship—would be surprised to learn that a man would invoke the work two thousand years later as proof of the world's imminent end. After all, the author likely composed Revelation around 95 CE and wrote with the conviction of someone who

1. Piestrup, *Apocalypse Later*, 57:43–58:42.
2. Amira, "Conversation with Harold Camping."

believed the end would come "soon" (Rev 22:20).

But what may *not* surprise John of Patmos is that these recent discourses about the end of time—where the book of Revelation, an ancient text, is invoked and actualized for the present as a way to anticipate the future—implicate money. As scholars have long noted, the book of Revelation is concerned with wealth, poverty, participation in mundane economies, and a coming future economy. From early Christian commentators forward, interpreters have explained that when John cries out "Fallen, fallen is Babylon the great!" (Rev 18:2) he is not only looking backward at the Babylonian Empire's fall, but also looking forward to the fall of Rome with the return of Jesus as Christ to earth (Rev 21–22). This chapter explores Roman urban economics in Asia Minor and how the book of Revelation is a response to this environment, seeing in John's visions of the future glimpses of his own present, especially in how its author believed followers of Jesus should interact with the Roman imperial economy and how intricately his ideology intersected with the empire that surrounded him.

Setting the Scene

The book of Revelation, also sometimes called the Apocalypse of John, is the twenty-seventh and final book of the Christian New Testament. Revelation 1:1 opens,

> The revelation [*apokalypsis*] of Jesus Christ, which God gave him to show his servants what must soon take place; he made it known by sending his angel to his servant John, who testified to the word of God and to the testimony of Jesus Christ, even to all that he saw.

In the following verses, the author sends a message to seven churches in Asia Minor, writing,

> Grace to you and peace from him who is and who was and who is to come, and from the seven spirits who are before his throne, and from Jesus Christ, the faithful witness, the firstborn of the dead, and the ruler of the kings of the earth. (Rev 1:4–5)

As the book continues, its author—identifying himself as John—explains:

> I, John, your brother who share with you in Jesus the persecution and the kingdom [*basileia*] and the patient endurance, was on the island called Patmos because of the word of God and the testimony of Jesus. (Rev 1:9)

> From the outset, readers are informed of three things. First, whoever this

John is, the book presents him as living on Patmos, a small island located in the Aegean Sea. Second, the author explains he came to be on Patmos "because of the word of God and the testimony of Jesus"; in other words, because of his belief in Jesus Christ, making John what Ellen Davis calls "a displaced person, if not necessarily a prisoner."[3] For John's original audience, his introduction was not simply a statement of belief about who Jesus was, but also "political counterpropaganda."[4] John's proclamation that his God "is, was, is to come," in John's Greco-Roman world, was "a commonplace way of celebrating a deity's eternity and immutability," used for, among others, the Greek gods Zeus and Athena.[5] Moreover, John calls Jesus "ruler of the kings of the earth" in a world that saw only the Roman emperor as king. Thus, Brian K. Blount notes, "in a cultural context where Rome already lays claim to ultimate kinship," this declaration "necessarily *resists* any established rule making the same claim."[6] And so as John begins, it is clear that the author has set Jesus against the Roman emperor and is calling on the audience to do the same. Third, the author explains that he is a recipient of a "revelation" concerning "what must soon take place." What follows in the ensuing twenty-two chapters is a dizzying array of material, including (but by no means limited to) exhortations to established communities of Jesus followers across Asia Minor; descriptions of the heavens; visions of angels, dragons, and beasts; and a portrayal of the coming new Jerusalem. As Timothy K. Beal summarizes, "The literary text of Revelation is an intertextuality, an amalgamation of hundreds and hundreds of bits, pieces, and larger chunks from Jewish Scriptures and other ancient Near Eastern and Greco-Roman mythologies, all stitched together, brought to life, and adopted by an otherwise unknown, unhomed visionary."[7] Yet for as much as John's text looks backward and forward, his revelation is also deeply concerned with his present.

Apokalypsis *in Ancient Context*

In its opening words the book declares it contains an *apokalypsis*, or revelation, while simultaneously situating itself both within the world created by the Hebrew Bible and also in the context of Asia Minor. Although the English word *apocalypse* is now often shorthand for "end of the world" or "disaster," the

3. Davis, Biblical Prophecy, 114.
4. Blount, Revelation, 34.
5. Blount, Revelation, 34.
6. Blount, Revelation, 36; emphasis original.
7. Beal, Book of Revelation, 48.

Greek word from which it derives—*apokalyptein*—means "to uncover, disclose, or reveal." In the ancient world:

> One of the most common uses of this word in everyday Greek was to describe the process by which a husband lifted the veil covering the bride's face at a wedding ceremony. A common ritual—which, of course, still occurs in many cultures to this day—had the effect of *revealing* the bride to the husband. The process of unveiling the bride's face, which was initially either entirely or partially covered by the veil, allowed the bride's face to be seen clearly and in plain view of everyone present. The act of *uncovering* constitutes the essence of an *apocalypse*, and it provides a starting point for considering a body of ancient literature by the same name.[8]

The Greek noun *apokalypsis* came to define a certain set of Jewish and early Christian literature, including Dan 7–12 in the Hebrew Bible and the book of Revelation in the New Testament, as well as extrabiblical texts like 2 Baruch, 4 Ezra, Apocalypse of Zephaniah, the Apocalypse of Abraham, the Testament of Abraham, the Apocalypse of Paul, and the Apocalypse of Peter (among others). In a now-famous definition in the field of biblical scholarship, John J. Collins explains that an *apocalypse* is "a genre of revelatory literature with a narrative framework in which a revelation is mediated by an otherworldly being to a human recipient, disclosing a transcendent reality which is both temporal, insofar as it envisages eschatological salvation, and spatial, insofar as it involves another, supernatural world."[9] Biblical scholars trace the beginnings of the genre of apocalypse to the ancient Near East, but "the very first apocalypses *per se* appear to have been written by Jewish authors, beginning sometime in the third century BCE."[10] And while the origins of apocalypse as a genre is debated, the texts we now call apocalypses often arose out of occupation and colonization.[11] In this vein, these books sought to reveal to their audiences how the world ought to be. In so doing, they often focused on economic issues, including social inequality and interaction with empire. The book of Revelation, which

---

8. Murphy and Jeffcoat Schedtler, "Introduction," 6; emphasis original.

9. J. Collins, *Apocalyptic Imagination*, 5.

10. Murphy and Jeffcoat Schedtler, "Introduction," 6. On ancient Near Eastern precedents, see Hays, "'Proto-Apocalyptic' Constellations."

11. For a nuanced discussion of reading Revelation as an apocalypse, see Linton, "Reading the Apocalypse"; as well as J. Collins, *Apocalypse*, 1–20. While the entire debate about how and where the genre originated is outside the scope of this chapter, readers are pointed to A. Y. Collins, *Crisis and Catharsis*, J. Collins, *Apocalyptic Imagination*; Cook, *Prophecy and Apocalypticism*; P. Hanson, *Dawn of Apocalyptic*; Horsley, *Revolt of the Scribes*; Rowland, *Open Heaven*; Schüssler Fiorenza, *Book of Revelation*.

weaves together apocalypse, epistle, and prophecy,[12] is one such "uncovering": John of Patmos seeks to show his audience that Jesus—the risen Christ—and not Caesar, is king. The book uses visions and symbols to convey this message, addressing issues of the imperial rule of Rome throughout.[13] In fact, according to Greg Carey, "the very apocalyptic form of Revelation leads us to read for its imperial political concerns."[14]

Debate on the Book's Authorship

Though some early Christian writers (and others throughout the book's interpretive history) suggest that the author of the book of Revelation was the apostle of the same name and, accordingly, also the author of the Gospel of John, scholars find several clues in the text that suggest otherwise. As is regularly noted, Dionysius, a Christian bishop in Egypt, observed significant literary dissimilarities between the Gospel of John and the book of Revelation in the third century CE, which are now recounted in the early historian Eusebius's history of the church:

> However, I could not readily agree that this person is the Apostle, the son of Zebedee, the brother of James, to whom belong[s] the Gospel entitled "According to John." ... I base my judgment on the character of each [book] and the forms of expression and the so-called argument of the book that the author is not the same. (*Hist. eccl.* 7.25.7–8)

While the Gospel of John is written in a more literary Hellenistic Greek, the book of Revelation is written in "a kind of Semiticized Greek that suggests someone whose native language was not Greek but the Aramaic spoken by Palestinian Jews."[15] Based on this and other literary observations, scholars

---

12. On Revelation's complex genre, see Linton, "Reading the Apocalypse."

13. As Carey writes, when Revelation addresses imperial rule, it "stands in the sustained Judean tradition of revelatory visions that enabled Judean scribes to resist imperial rule" ("Book of Revelation," 158–59). For a longer discussion of different approaches to Revelation vis-à-vis empire, see Diehl, "Babylon."

14. Carey, "Book of Revelation," 159.

15. Blount, *Revelation*, 8. Carey explains that, "Like others living under imperial rule, John employs a hybrid language. Resistance literatures often appropriate the language of empire but violate its syntactic rules. Moreover, John builds his Apocalypse upon the foundation of Jewish Scriptures. Revelation never quotes Scripture directly, but it has scores, even hundreds of allusions to Scripture—more than any other book of the New Testament. Thus, Revelation expresses its counter-imperial agenda through its foundation in subaltern Jewish tradition" ("Book of Revelation," 159–60).

have long argued that the two books stem from different authorial hands.[16] Additionally, the author of the book appears familiar with "the topography of Jerusalem, the design and cultic practice of the Jerusalem temple, even prior to its destruction in 70 CE, and the broader landscape of Palestine itself."[17] For example, Rev 11:1–13, which describes a series of forty-two months when nations will trample on Jerusalem, "likely reflects the Romans' devastation of Jerusalem."[18] The book also demonstrates a "massive assumption of continuity" with the story of ancient Israel;[19] over half of the book's verses allude to various texts from the Hebrew Bible.[20] As one example, the beasts from Dan 7 reappear, slightly reconfigured, in Rev 13. Similarly, the author of the book of Revelation clearly sees himself as engaged in prophecy in a way similar to the prophets of the Hebrew Bible (e.g., Rev 1:3; see also 22:7, 10, 18, 19). These various clues have led many scholars to suggest that the author was originally a Palestinian Jew.[21]

Dating the Book of Revelation

Yet while John might have originally hailed from Palestine, he now seems to write as an exile on a small island in Asia Minor. He clearly identifies as a follower of Christ: he is a slave (*doulous*) of God (Rev 1:1) who "testified to the word of God and to the testimony of Jesus Christ" (1:2).[22] John's audience appears to be primarily Jewish followers of Jesus;[23] the book never calls the communities that John addresses Christians.[24] In addition to knowledge of the texts of the Hebrew Bible, the author of the book is familiar with Greco-Roman texts, traditions, and imagery. For example, as is often noted, coins issued by Domitian that proclaimed the divine status of his deceased son included seven stars, which some suggest may now be reflected in John's use of seven stars when describing Jesus (1:16). Interpreters have also found numerous

16. For an older article that outlines many of the "Hebraisms" in the apocalypse, see Ozanne, "Language of the Apocalypse." Note that Ozanne's conclusion about the identity of the author of the book of Revelation—John the apostle—is not widely accepted.

17. Blount, *Revelation*, 8.

18. Carey, "Book of Revelation," 160.

19. A. Y. Collins, *Crisis and Catharsis*, 46.

20. For example, see Allen, "Scriptural Allusions."

21. A. Y. Collins, *Crisis and Catharsis*, 46–47.

22. See Koester, "Roman Slave Trade."

23. Carey argues, "Revelation reflects no awareness of a 'Gentile'-dominated 'Christianity' that has abandoned the primary symbols of Jewish identity" ("Book of Revelation," 159).

24. See Friesen, *Imperial Cults*, 183.

similarities between the description of the throne room in Rev 4–5 and Roman imperial language, including that "the acclamation, 'Worthy art thou', addressed to God or the Lamb by those assembled around the heavenly throne (4:11, 5:9; see 5:12), was also employed in Roman imperial court ceremonial to greet the emperor."[25]

However, despite the author's familiarity with Greco-Roman culture and his use of associated ideas and images, his attitude toward the Roman imperial apparatus is far from positive. The author claims to share with his audience "the persecution [*tē thlipsei*] and the kingdom and the patient endurance [*hypomonē*] . . . because of the word of God and the testimony of Jesus [*dia ton logon tou theou kai tēn martyrian Iēsou*]" (Rev 1:9). The scholarly consensus places the date of the book's composition sometime near the end of the first century CE, after the fall of the temple in 70 CE. Most scholars date the book during the reign of Domitian (81–96 CE), often based on a letter from Irenaeus now quoted by Eusebius, who claimed that John's vision "was not even seen a long time ago, but almost in our own generation at the end of the reign of Domitian" (*Hist. eccl.* 3.18.1–3).[26] Yet such a dating places the composition of the book long before widespread persecution of Christians began. A letter from the Emperor Trajan—who reigned immediately after Domitian—to Pliny the Younger is regularly cited extra-biblical evidence about the then-current Roman attitude toward Christians: "Christians are not to be sought out. If brought before you and found guilty, they must be punished, but in such a way that a person who denies that he is a Christian and demonstrates this by his action, that is, by worshipping our gods, may obtain pardon for repentance" (*Ep.* 10:96–97). In short, despite John's claim of persecution, there is no evidence of intense, widespread, and organized persecution of Christians by the Romans during the reign of Domitian.

So how do we account for his claim? Various scholars have offered different theories. Perhaps John felt persecuted, expected to be persecuted for his refusal to assimilate to life under the Roman imperial system, or was even attempting to create a crisis himself.[27] Another possibility is that in John's call for patient endurance (*hypomonē*), the author was "championing an active response

---

25. Moore, "Revelation to John," 442; longer list of similarities, 442–43. For different readings that examine the use of imperial language and imagery in Rev 4–5, see, e.g., Aune, "Influence"; Jeffcoat Schedtler, "Praising Christ the King."

26. For a review of the arguments on dating John's apocalypse, see Blount, *Revelation*, 8.

27. For different arguments on John's proclamation, see A. Y. Collins, *Crisis and Catharsis*; Schüssler Fiorenza, *Book of Revelation*; Thompson, *Book of Revelation*. For a short summary, see Blount, *Revelation*, 41–42.

of faith that resists both the belief in the lordship of Rome and the hostile practices Rome wields to propagandize that belief."[28] In this case, such resistance could surely lead to (localized) persecution in some form. Nevertheless, whatever "crisis" might have produced the book of Revelation, it does not appear to have been a widespread movement that oppressed early Christians.

Yet even if there is no widespread, organized persecution of Christians around the time that the book of Revelation was composed, John of Patmos lived in a present where memories of previous crises—religious, political, and economic—prevailed. While they are not all directly invoked in the book of Revelation, they nevertheless haunt its pages, beginning with the fall of the kingdom of Judah to the Babylonian Empire, the resulting destruction of the First Temple in Jerusalem in 586 BCE, and the ensuing Babylonian exile. From that point forward in Jewish history, the land of Palestine remained under the rule of one foreign empire after another: after the fall of Babylon at the hands of the Persians, some of the exiled people returned to rebuild the temple around 515 BCE, but even while the biblical texts generally depict Persian rule positively, these people still lived under a foreign empire. In 333 BCE, Alexander the Great's conquest of the Persian Empire brought the region under the rule of the Greeks. After Alexander the Great's death in 323 BCE a long period of conflict followed, including a series of ensuing battles between the Ptolemies and the Seleucids over the region. With the eventual success of Antiochus III, a Seleucid, in gaining control over Jerusalem in 198 BCE, more regional unrest followed. This was especially the case under the rule of Antiochus IV, who outlawed certain Jewish practices and desecrated the Jerusalem temple (see 1 and 2 Maccabees), leading to the eventual Maccabean revolt and the establishment of the Hasmonean rule.[29] In this continued story of rising and falling empires, Pompey—a Roman general—invaded Palestine and took control over Jerusalem, establishing Roman rule and imposing taxes on its inhabitants in 63 BCE. From an economic perspective, as Richard Horsley explains, "The Romans impacted economic relations in Judah and Galilee in three main areas: the devastating effects of their repeated wars of (re-)conquest, their extraction of tribute, and the complications they introduced in their shifting arrangement of client rulers."[30] In 66 CE an unsuccessful Jewish revolt against the Romans

28. Blount, *Revelation*, 42.

29. For a history of early Judaism during these periods, see VanderKam, *Introduction to Early Judaism*.

30. Horsley, *Covenant Economics*, 82. For a different discussion of the economic realities of life in ancient Israel and Judah, readers are pointed to Boer, *Sacred Economy*; and Knight, *Law, Power, and Justice*.

ended with the Roman destruction of the temple in Jerusalem in 70 CE.

As J. Nelson Kraybill observes, "By the time John wrote Revelation, the Jewish nation in Palestine had experienced nearly the full spectrum of possible political relationships with the great power from Italy," including friend/ally, vassal state, rebellion/defeat.[31] Even though John is writing from Patmos, the realities of life in Judah—and Roman rule there—run throughout the book of Revelation. While the destruction of the temple at the hands of the Romans is never mentioned in Revelation, Carey explains that "the fear of persecution would have been intensified by the hostility against Jews in the aftermath of the Jewish Revolt of 66–70 CE."[32] Even in exile, numismatic evidence suggests that John's present was rife with reminders of the loss of the temple. For example, Kraybill notes that during the period in which John likely wrote:

> More than two dozen coin designs from the reigns of Vespasian through Domitian carried the words IVDAEA DEVICTA ("Judaea defeated") or IVDAEA CAPTA ("Judaea captive"). Most coins of the series portray Judea as a woman, seated and weeping under a palm tree—with a triumphant Roman soldier (sometimes Emperor) standing nearby. A few coins also depict a Jewish man with hands bound behind his back. In addition to bearing blasphemous imagery of the Emperor as divine, these coins were a constant reminder to Jews of their ill treatment at the hands of Rome.[33]

Such coinage illustrates the *imperium populi Romani*—the power that the Roman Empire exercised over the peoples and places it ruled.

Turning from Palestine to the island of Patmos, located in Asia Minor, a slightly different portrait of the Roman Empire emerges. Kraybill writes that following years of turmoil in the region under Alexander the Great, the arrival of Roman rule under Augustus in 31 BCE "brought physical and economic security to many people in Asia Minor."[34] While "when the Jews revolted in 66–70 CE, Rome brought Jerusalem to its knees with a ruthless siege and gruesome slaughter," many others were eager to welcome Rome. In fact, "most provincials did not resist Roman rule, and many were pleased to be part of the empire. Every province had native groups eager to show loyalty to the Emperor,

---

31. Kraybill, *Imperial Cult*, 168; full discussion, 166–70.
32. Carey, "Book of Revelation," 160.
33. Kraybill, *Imperial Cult*, 203–4.
34. Kraybill, *Imperial Cult*, 59.

since Rome provided security and prosperity to its friends."[35] And so, according to Stephen D. Moore, Rome's colonization of Asia Minor better reflects "colonies of occupation," where "the indigenous population remains in the majority numerically, but is administered by foreign power," rather than "settler colonies," where the colonizers become the majority population.[36] Augustus's rule ushered in the (in)famous Pax Romana; namely, a period of (relative) peace and (relative) economic prosperity throughout the Roman Empire that would last until 180 CE.

Yet it is also important to remember that "Rome ruled an estimated sixty to sixty-five million people of diverse ethnicities and cultures."[37] As Warren Carter writes, "The empire was very hierarchical, with vast disparities of power and wealth. For the small ruling elite, life was quite comfortable. For the majority non-elite, it was at best livable and at worst very miserable."[38] The hierarchical structure of Roman society appears in the pages of John's apocalypse when John lists the events that unfold following the opening of the sixth seal: "Then the kings of the earth and the magnates and the generals and the rich and the powerful, and everyone, slave and free, hid in the caves and among the rocks of the mountains" (Rev 6:15). Here, as is often observed, every layer of Roman society is present: from the rich and the powerful to the enslaved and the freed.[39]

For the agrarian empire of Rome, Asia Minor provided a wealth of resources, ranging from textiles, pottery, leather goods, perfumes, and various food supplies such as olive oil, grains, and wines.[40] As a result, "it is not surprising Rome placed loyal subordinates in Asia Minor, since the province had natural and human resources that would be the envy of any Empire." In addition to providing materials for export (see Rev 18), Asia Minor also "played a vital role in collecting trade taxes for Rome." Famously, however, Rome took more than it gave. Yet even in doing so, there is evidence that Rome provided opportunity for "upward mobility" for some in Asia Minor, especially those who could create and export the goods Rome needed.[41]

35. Kraybill, *Imperial Cult*, 57.
36. Moore, "Revelation to John," 438.
37. Carter, *Roman Empire*, 3.
38. Carter, *Roman Empire*, 3.
39. See Kraybill, *Imperial Cult*, 74–75. Blount observes that "the lengthy enumeration of the fleeing powerful people and the servants and free ones connected with them reads like a laundry list of persons who would either run the political and economic infrastructure of the Greco-Roman world or accommodate themselves to it" (*Revelation*, 139).
40. See, for example, the discussion in Kraybill, *Imperial Cult*, 65–68.
41. Kraybill, *Imperial Cult*, 65; larger discussion, 65–68, 70–72, 80–100.

Perhaps most significantly for a reading of Revelation as a response to Roman imperial economics, the imperial cult took root and grew in Asia Minor.[42] When the Roman Senate recognized Julius Caesar as *divus*—bestowing divine status upon him—in 42 BCE, the imperial cult—in other words, the worship of the emperor as divine—appeared throughout Asia Minor.[43] Roman rule over Asia Minor was bolstered by the presence of the imperial cult, which created rivalry between the urban centers of the region as they sought to gain imperial support.[44] As Moore explains:

> The mainspring of the complex hegemonic mechanism that enabled Roman governance of Asia, however—economically a jewel in the imperial crown, rich in natural resources, agriculture and industry—was the competition for imperial favour and recognition in which the principal Asian cities were perpetually locked (Ephesus, Pergamum and Smyrna in particular, although the rivalry extended to many lesser cities as well). An important expression of this competition was the city's public demonstration of the measure of its loyalty to the emperor, the ultimate patron or benefactor in relation to whom the city was a client or dependent, and as such in rivalry with the other client cities of the province for a limited quantity of goods and privileges. The principal mechanism in turn for formal demonstrations of such loyalty was the imperial cult, the rendering of divine honours to Roman emperors, living or dead.[45]

By the time John composed the book of Revelation, some thirty-five cities in Asia Minor had the title *neōkoros* (temple warden), often competing for the honor,[46] and each of the cities that John addresses had temples or altars dedicated to the imperial cult.[47] This set up a system of exchange with the Roman

---

42. For fuller discussions of the imperial cult, readers are pointed to the work of Price, *Rituals and Power*; and, in his footsteps, Kraybill, *Imperial Cult*; and Friesen, *Imperial Cults*.

43. On how Domitian may have promoted himself and his family to divine status while he was alive, see Kraybill, *Imperial Cult*, 60.

44. For a thorough discussion of competition, see Friesen, *Imperial Cults*.

45. Moore, "Revelation to John," 439.

46. See, for example, Kraybill, *Imperial Cult*, 65. Here people "made sacrifices to the gods on the Emperor's behalf, not to the Emperor himself" (61). On cults in Asia Minor, see Price, *Rituals and Power*, 66–67.

47. Moore continues, "In due course, therefore, each of Revelation's seven cities, along with others in the province, erected temples or altars to Roman potentates living or dead: Julius Caesar (coupled with *Dea Roma*), Augustus (also with *Dea Roma*), Tiberius (with the Roman senate), Vespasian, Domitian and Hadrian. The leading cities competed for the coveted title of *neokoros*, 'temple warden/care-taker,' awarded at the discretion of the senate and the emperor to cities containing an imperial temple with pan-provincial status. Elaborate

emperors as benefactors of the cities.[48] Accordingly, behind many of the texts found in the book of Revelation, interpreters see a tension between participation in the imperial cult with its focus on the Roman emperor and John's assertion that Jesus, as the risen Christ, is the true king.

It's Not the End of the World: Ways of Reading Revelation

The book of Revelation has been read over the centuries in a myriad of ways, including with a focus on the history behind the text and attempts to (unsuccessfully) use the text to predict the future. However, as Walter Brueggemann notes, "While the rhetoric of the 'end of the world' and the coming 'new world' has provided ample ground for much misinformed religious speculation, the world that is to end is not the planet Earth ... but the ordered cosmos administered by the Roman Empire." In other words, in the book of Revelation "the end of the world equals termination of the empire of Rome."[49] While scholars debate the origins of the genre of apocalypse—and while there are certainly many different examples of apocalypse-as-genre—one common thread running throughout these texts is empire. A few regularly cited examples include: apocalyptic texts in the books of Isaiah and Ezekiel are reactions to the devastating effects of the Babylonian Empire on Judah; during the Hellenistic period, texts like Dan 7–12 reflect the crushing results of the Seleucid Empire's presence in Jerusalem; and in the book of Revelation, the apocalypse of John, we find a response to the Roman Empire's presence and influence on early Christianity in Asia Minor. Across all three, the textual answer to each successive empire is, by and large, the same: it may seem like Babylon (or Antiochus IV or Caesar) is in charge, but in reality God is sovereign over creation. Each text seeks to "uncover" that truth and to show its readers how, despite appearances, reality is quite different from the veiled world of their present.

Yet while early apocalyptic texts like the book of Isaiah were addressing Babylon specifically (e.g., Isa 47), later apocalypses took up the name "Babylon" as a cipher for the empire they currently addressed. So, for example, the book of Daniel is set, literarily, in the period of "the first year of King Belshazzar of Babylon," when "Daniel had a dream and visions of his head as he lay in bed"

---

imperial festivals became a prominent feature of the religious life of the province, enmeshing the populace in a communal symbolic articulation of the omnipresence and immanence of absolute power in the absent person of the Roman emperor, whose arms encircled the civilized world by virtue of the imperium Romanum" ("Revelation to John," 441).

48. See Price, *Rituals and Power*, 78–101.

49. Brueggemann, *Money and Possessions*, 265.

(Dan 7:1). However, scholars agree that the vision Daniel reacts to life under Seleucid rule; specifically, the rule of Antiochus IV, the "little horn" of Dan 7:9 who speaks arrogantly. In Revelation, Rome is never named; throughout, the text bemoans the horrors and evils of Babylon, which serves yet again as a cipher. Such an identification, as is often noted, makes sense as Babylon and Rome are linked through their mutual destructions of Jerusalem and the temple.[50] When John invokes Babylon, we see one example of the "massive assumption of continuity" that connects the narrative world of Revelation with Israel's past, especially economic imagery.[51] From where John stands, the exploitive Roman imperial economy begins not in western Asia Minor but already in Judah, with the destruction of Jerusalem and the temple. By using Babylon as a cipher for Rome, John borrows from Israel's economic past in order to address the present and look to the future.

To read Revelation as a response to Roman urban economics in Asia Minor, it helps to keep four things in mind. First, with Walter Scheidel, we must remember that when we try to understand Roman economic history our "explanations must be grounded in the empirical record but do not directly emerge from it: the evidence never speaks for itself."[52] We should look to Revelation, but we should also read the biblical text alongside ancient inscriptions, other texts, coins, and archaeological evidence in order to put together as complete a picture of the period as possible. Second, we must remember that the economy of ancient Rome was an "extractive" economy, one where all roads and goods led to Rome and the emperor.[53] Third, we must keep the category of empire in mind, from John's depiction of the Roman Empire as Satanic to how John also continues to employ language of Rome and empire to imagine a future without Rome.[54] Fourth, we must also listen for the voices of other early Jesus followers that are hidden behind John's rhetoric, which provide us with insights into competing responses to Roman urban economics in Asia Minor.

Case Studies: Ideological Division, Imperial Cult,

50. Carey, "Book of Revelation," 160.
51. A. Y. Collins, *Crisis and Catharsis*, 47.
52. Scheidel, "Approaching the Roman Economy," 2.
53. K. C. Hanson and Oakman, *Palestine*, 105, 181–82.
54. For helpful studies of empire in the book of Revelation and/or apocalyptic literature more broadly see, for example, Moore, *Empire and Apocalypse*, 97–121; Friesen, "Apocalypse and Empire"; Frilingos, *Spectacles of Empire*; Howard-Brook and Gwyther, *Unveiling Empire*; Lopez, "Victory and Visibility."

and Imperial Commerce

John composes Revelation in response to both Roman imperial rule in Judah and Galilee—especially the devastating loss of the temple—and, more immediately, to the practices of Roman urban economics, the realities of the Roman's social hierarchies, and the development of the imperial cult.[55] What, then, does John's apocalypse seek to "unveil" or "uncover" about the Roman economy, the ramifications of Roman urban economics, and how the Roman imperial economy intersected with the ideologies of Jewish and early Christian communities? The most frequent answer has been—from early Christian interpreters to contemporary readers—that Rome and its imperial practices are evil and aligned with Satan, and so the opposite of the imminent apocalyptic future where God's true rule will be revealed.

While it is not possible to do a thorough reading of all the ways that Revelation is a response to Roman economics, four case studies illuminate, briefly, the complex intersections of Roman imperial economics and the ideologies of different Jewish and early Christian communities of which we may catch glimpses in John's apocalypse:

1. An investigation into John's letters to the churches in Rev 2–3 reveals internal ideological divisions regarding participation in the Roman economy among the early communities of Jesus followers in Asia Minor, as well as their differing economic positions in Rome's urban world.

2. An exploration of the two beasts in Rev 13 demonstrates John's anti-assimilationist attitude toward the imperial cult.

3. A survey of the "whore of Babylon" and prophecies of the fall of Rome in Rev 17–18 uncovers John's ideological response to not just the imperial cult but the entire Roman imperial apparatus—as well as the place of some Jews and early Jesus followers within the economy.

4. A review of the "new Jerusalem" described in Rev 21–22 manifests one way in which the apocalypse of John not only repudiates engagement with Rome but also reinscribes elements of empire into its visions of the future.

Together, these illustrate how John's apocalypse presents us with a literary portrait of divided attitudes toward early Jesus followers' participation in the interlocking political, economic, societal, and religious systems that comprised

---

55. According to some readings of the book, John's apocalypse is a response to the imperial cult. For a detailed examination of this, see Friesen, *Imperial Cults*.

the Roman Empire and John's clarion call for followers of Christ to separate themselves from that empire, while also revealing how the book—a product of the culture in which it was produced—sometimes reinscribes the very values it rejects.

The Seven Churches

We find our first case study in the messages to the seven churches now in Rev 2–3, which reveal internal ideological divisions regarding participation in the Roman economy among the early communities of Jesus followers in Asia Minor. In Rev 1:10–11, John writes: "I was in the spirit on the LORD's day, and I heard behind me a loud voice like a trumpet saying, 'Write in a book what you see and send it to the seven churches, to Ephesus, to Smyrna, to Pergamum, to Thyatira, to Sardis, to Philadelphia, and to Laodicea.'" Paul B. Duff notes that while "virtually all of our first-century evidence about Christianity in Western Asia Minor is sketchy and indirect," what is clear is that it was an "urban phenomenon."[56] To varying degrees, each of the cities that John addresses in the book of Revelation played a significant role in production and trade in Asia Minor (and, accordingly, in the overall Roman imperial economy as most goods found their way to Rome). In particular, the region produced textiles, along with pottery, leather, parchment, perfumes, gold and silver metalworks, and various crops.[57] Accordingly, John's apocalypse can be mined for clues about the "urban phenomenon" of early Christianity and the different ideologies about the right relationship between life as a follower of Jesus and engagement in Roman imperial economics, as well as the right relationship between life as a follower of Jesus and poverty and wealth more broadly.

The material in Rev 2–3 consists of seven short messages addressed to an early community of Jesus followers in each of these seven cities, providing a window into the communities in Asia Minor that John addressed. As Beal observes, "Reading them now feels a little like listening in on one end of a phone

56. Duff, *Who Rides the Beast*, 17, 18.

57. As Kraybill describes, "The most important source of wealth for the seven cities mentioned in Revelation was the manufacture of textiles. At Ephesus there were prosperous guilds of wool-workers and cloak dealers. Smyrna was famous for its purple garments, and Sardis was a leader in the manufacture of carpets and dyes. Philadelphia, Thyatira, and Laodicea each produced tapestries, garments and textile luxuries that went to cities throughout the Roman world. In addition to textiles, Asia produced and exported pottery on a large scale. A leather industry thrived, and Pergamum manufactured world-famous parchment. Ephesus, Sardis and Smyrna all made perfumes for the world market, and several cities of the region were noted for their metal-working in gold or silver (cf. Acts 19:23–27)" (*Imperial Cult*, 65).

call. Sometimes the issue is fairly clear, as when [John] criticizes a church for assimilating to mainstream Roman civil religion. Other times he focuses on now unknown persons or movements."[58] Yet even if sometimes murky, these passages provide clues about the kinds of people who constituted these various communities, differing ideologies within those communities, especially vis-à-vis economics, as well as the external pressures of the Roman imperial apparatus on them. A comparison between John's message to the community in the city of Smyrna and John's message to the community of the city in Thyatira illustrates these issues.

The city of Smyrna was "well known for its dedication to Rome and Greco-Roman cultic religion."[59] Situated in a geographically important pocket of the Aegean coast of Asia Minor, Smyrna had long preexisting ties to the Roman Empire by the time John wrote Revelation. A few examples help show this: following its separation from the rule of Pergamum, Smyrna turned to Rome for aid, and the city subsequently constructed a temple to the goddess Roma in 195 BCE. Later, under the rule of the emperor Tiberius (42 BCE to 37 CE), the city dedicated a temple to Augustus. The city was also declared a *neōkoros* by Tiberius and the Roman Senate in 26 CE. As a wealthy port city, Smyrna provided numerous exports, including textiles, and was also home to silversmiths and goldsmiths.[60] Smyrna thus serves as an illustration of the ways that the religious, economic, and political intersected in urban Asia Minor.

John's message to Smyrna is entirely positive,[61] beginning, "And to the angel of the church in Smyrna write: These are the words [*tade legei*] of the first and the last, who was dead and came to life" (Rev 2:8). Though the NRSV translates the first part of the message as "these are the words," the phrase is

---

58. Beal, *Revelation*, 13–14. Duff separates the letters into two types. The first type consists of the letters to Ephesus, Pergamum, and Thyatira, which exhibit "no definitive evidence of either persecution or harassment of the members of the churches by anyone outside the Christian communities at the time of John's writing," but do suggest that John sees rival leaders in these churches and that the letters attest to internal struggles within the Christian movement in Asia Minor (*Who Rides the Beast*, 40). Additionally, the letters to Sardis and Laodicea appear to be communities where John has "the least influence" (43). The second type includes the letters to Smyrna and Philadelphia, where Duff sees no evidence of factionalism or criticism (46; larger discussion, 43–46). However, he suggests based on John's description of Smyrna as poor and Philadelphia as powerless that perhaps "John's type of Christianity finds its strongest support among the economically and socially disenfranchised" (46).

59. Blount, *Revelation*, 53.

60. Thompson, *Book of Revelation*, 152–53.

61. The only other message to a community that is entirely positive is addressed to Philadelphia in Rev 3:7–13. See Blount, *Revelation*, 48.

better translated "thus says" as it originates from the prophetic utterances of the Hebrew Bible (e.g., "Thus says the LORD, your Redeemer, the Holy One of Israel: I am the LORD your God, who teaches you for your own good, who leads you in the way you should go" [Isa 48:17]). Yet while John frames the following message in line with the prophets, he is simultaneously drawing on the language of imperial Rome: "The 'thus says . . .' formula was just as typical of imperial decrees of the period."[62] According to Blount, "The feel John inspires by establishing a link between the imperial edict and his own letters is consistent with the combative political tone he strikes throughout."[63] The addition of the phrase "who was dead and came to life" ensures that readers know the following message is from Christ, the true king.

The message continues in Rev 2:9–11, offering insight into socioeconomic status in the community, internal divisions on economic engagement, and that there existed a (perceived) external threat to the people there. First, John appears to address the socioeconomic status of (at least some of) the members of the Smyrna community: "I know your affliction and your poverty [*thlipsin kai tēn ptōcheian*], even though you are rich [*plousios*]" (2:9a). As Duff notes, "It is tempting to associate [affliction] with external persecution or harassment, for, of course, the word can have this meaning." However, *thlipsis* can also "simply indicate unspecified suffering."[64] The word for poverty, from the Greek *ptōcheia*, literally means "destitution." Given that it is followed by "But you are rich!," Duff argues that "we should understand that here the author comforts the community for its actual poverty by reminding them that they are rich in other ways." Accordingly, despite the wealth of Smyrna, it seems that members of the community there "came from the lower socioeconomic strata of society."[65]

Second, John writes "I know the slander [*blasphēmian*] on the part of those who say that they are Jews and are not, but are a synagogue of Satan [*legontōn Ioudaious einai heautous kai ouk eisin, alla synagōgē tou Satana*]" (Rev 2:9b). Scholars are divided on how to understand the *blasphēmia* of which John speaks, along with his claim that this comes from "those who say that they are Jews and are not, but are a synagogue of Satan." For example, Adela Yarbro

---

62. Blount, *Revelation*, 47.

63. Blount, *Revelation*, 47–48. Blount also cites Aune, who writes, "The author's use of the royal/imperial edict form is part of strategy to polarize God/Jesus and the Roman emperor . . . In his role as the eternal sovereign and king of kings, Jesus is presented as issuing solemn and authoritative edicts befitting his status" (Aune, *Revelation 1–5*, 129).

64. Duff, *Who Rides the Beast*, 43. As Duff notes, the word will also appear in Rev 2:22 in the letter to Thyatira.

65. Duff, *Who Rides the Beast*, 44.

Collins suggests that "the name 'Jews' is denied [to the Jewish community in Smyrna] because the followers of Jesus are held to be the true Jews." Thus, "the juxtaposition of the attack on the Jews with the exhortation about persecution suggests that the Roman authorities were being pressed by certain representatives of the local Jewish community to take action against Christians in Smyrna."[66] As a result, "Christians in Smyrna thus no longer enjoyed the social, economic, and political security afforded by association with and attachment to the local Jewish community."[67] Blount makes a similar argument: "Knowing that the Christ-believers, many of whom were themselves probably Jews, would not acknowledge Caesar's lordship, synagogue members pointed them out and thereby offered them up to persecution." For this reason, Blount argues, the phrase "synagogue of Satan" "is not so much an anti-Jewish denunciation as it is a reference to an intra-Jewish conflict that leads to betrayal," adding, "the witness to the lordship of Christ rankled Smyrna's synagogue community as much as it did the Romans, if for quite different reasons."[68] Duff is more cautious: "The text could just as easily suggest two rival groups taking 'pot shots' at each other."[69]

Although it is impossible to know for sure which is the case, John's message does illustrate the difficulty of separating "Jews" from "Christians" in these communities in Asia Minor, and that the community at Smyrna was undergoing a turbulent period as groups worked out their differences. Third, John offers advice on suffering that has not yet happened: "Do not fear what you are about to suffer [*paschein*]. Beware, the devil is about to throw some of you into prison so that you may be tested, and for ten days you will have affliction. Be faithful until death, and I will give you the crown of life" (Rev 2:10). Duff sees this outside threat as coming from either "civic or imperial forces" because of the reference to imprisonment, but stresses "that this is a future threat, and, as such, does not necessarily indicate any previous or current harassment or persecution by governmental forces."[70] Still, if faithful, the community at Smyrna will be "much richer" in the end, earning "the crown of life."[71] John's message to the community at Smyrna provides us with insight—however murky—into one

---

66. A. Y. Collins, *Crisis and Catharsis*, 85.

67. A. Y. Collins, *Crisis and Catharsis*, 85–86.

68. Blount, *Revelation*, 54. See Blount's nuanced and helpful discussion on the dangers of preaching this text (54–55).

69. Duff, *Who Rides the Beast*, 4.

70. Duff, *Who Rides the Beast*, 43. On the topic of imprisonment, see 147n38.

71. Blount, *Revelation*, 55.

community's embeddedness in Roman imperial politics and economics, while deploying discourses of wealth and imperial power to construct their identity and ideology.

In comparison, John's charge against the followers of "Jezebel" in his message to Thyatira provides us with a different window into how the book of Revelation is a response to the intersection of Roman urban economics and the competing ideologies of Jewish and early Christian communities of John's present. Unlike Smyrna, Thyatira was inland, roughly thirty miles from the Aegean. The city was famous for its purple garment production. So, for example, in the New Testament book of Acts, a woman named Lydia from Thyatira is introduced as "a dealer in purple cloth" (Acts 16:15). In addition, numerous inscriptions at Thyatira confirm the city as a place famous for wool production as well as the establishment of guilds for wool. Moreover, the city also included leatherworks, coppersmiths, and tanners.[72] Altogether, the evidence suggests that Thyatira's population included a "prosperous merchant class."[73] Like Smyrna, Thyatira was home to the imperial cult and so also serves as an example of the ways that the religious, economic, and political intersected in urban Asia Minor. Accordingly, "this religious-political alliance heightened the risk for persons who tried to opt out of the Greco-Roman cultic infrastructure," and the presence of trade guilds—like that for wool—"[complicated] matters even further."[74]

John's message to the community in Thyatira begins positively: "I know your works—your love, faith, service, and patient endurance. I know that your last works are greater than the first" (Rev 2:19). However, the tone abruptly changes in what follows: "But I have this against you: you tolerate that woman Jezebel, who calls herself a prophet and is teaching and beguiling my servants to practice fornication and to eat food sacrificed to idols [*porneusai kai phagein eidōlothyta*]" (2:20). The gravity of John's charge against "Jezebel," who appears to be his rival, is clear in the way that John links "fornication," probably best understood as "idolatry," with eating the sacrificed food.[75] Most scholars conclude that whoever "Jezebel" was, like Paul before her, she either advocated for or at least tolerated her community's engagement with Roman society, including

---

72. Thompson, *Book of Revelation*, 152–53; Duff, *Who Rides the Beast*, 20.
73. Duff, *Who Rides the Beast*, 26.
74. Blount, *Revelation*, 62.
75. E.g., A. Y. Collins, *Crisis and Catharsis*, 87; Duff, *Who Rides the Beast*, 40; Thompson, *Book of Revelation*, 122–24.

economic exchanges that might have involved eating *eidōlothyta*.[76]

What was at stake in this decision? In Roman society, the practice of eating food sacrificed to idols was a religious act, but it was also political, social, and intricately connected to economics. Blount explains, "Artisan, trade, and other business associations aligned their groups with patron deities," and "participation in such groups, which allowed for upward social and economic mobility, often included the obligatory participation in such a group's cultic activities."[77] Beyond the merchant class, food sacrificed to idols could appear in public festivals, the market place, and private dinners, and so "could have been encountered by the average person in a variety of contexts."[78] Accordingly, "refusal to share a meal could severely hinder such a person's livelihood."[79] Consequently, the ability to succeed economically could depend precisely on the decision a person made regarding this issue.

Scholars have long concluded that the name "Jezebel" was unlikely the real name of the prophet in Thyatira. Rather, "it is demagoguery by association."[80] To early Jewish followers of Jesus, the name would have been associated with King Ahab's foreign wife from the book of Kings, who encouraged worship of Ba'al rather than Yhwh. The connection John is making between the two is clear: Jezebel of the book of Kings attempted to lead God's people into idolatry just as the "Jezebel" of Thyatira is luring God's people into idolatry through association with the Roman imperial economic system. However, John's message to the community in Thyatira suggests that John had not yet given up on the people there, whose own ideology vis-à-vis participating in the world of Rome differed so much from his own. Jezebel was given "time to repent" (Rev 2:21), and though she refused, those "who commit adultery with her" are also given a chance to repent (2:22). The message also implies John has a following in Thyatira: "But to the rest of you in Thyatira, who do not hold this teaching, who have not learned what some call 'the deep things of Satan,' to you I say, I do not lay on you any other burden; only hold fast to what you have until I

76. Duff, *Who Rides the Beast*, 61. That this issue, and other ideological differences, were likely a widespread ideological divide among early Christian communities in Asia Minor is suggested by John's messages to two other churches: first, he praises the people of Ephesus for hating the "works of the Nicolaitans" (Rev 2:6); second, he accuses the community at Pergamum of following someone named Balaam, who encourages eating food sacrificed to idols, as well as listening to the Nicolaitans (2:14–15).

77. Blount, *Revelation*, 59.

78. Duff, *Who Rides the Beast*, 52; larger discussion, 51–55.

79. Duff, *Who Rides the Beast*, 55.

80. Blount, *Revelation*, 63.

come" (2:23–24). Thus, John's words to Thyatira suggest that while there were internal differences among early Jesus followers as to how they should approach the question of eating food sacrificed to idols, the differences were not yet so entrenched that the author of Revelation thought they could not be resolved.

The messages for Smyrna and Thyatira exemplify two major economic concerns and the developing ideologies in response to these issues that scholars see in the book of Revelation: right economic practices *within* these early communities of Jesus followers and right economic practices as these communities engaged with the world of Roman commerce and cult in which they were embedded. First, the evidence suggests that the communities John addresses were made up of many people who participated in this imperial economy, from the wealthier merchants to the poor.[81] For example, John complains of Laodicea, "I know your works; you are neither cold nor hot. I wish that you were either cold or hot" (Rev 3:15), continuing, "For you say, 'I am rich, I have prospered, and I need nothing.' You do not realize that you are wretched, pitiable, poor, blind, and naked" (3:16).[82] In contrast, he writes to the church at Smyrna, "I know your affliction and your poverty, even though you are rich" (2:9). John's charge that Laodicea is rich but actually poor, while Smyrna is poor but actually rich, insinuates that John had particular opinions about what it meant to be a Christ follower who lived in an epicenter of Roman urban economics. Second, John's apocalypse also responds to the question of whether a Christ follower can participate in Roman social/political/religious practices, ultimately arguing against it.[83] At the same time, John's letter to the churches lets us hear other voices on the matter, suggesting that there was significant intra-communal disagreement on appropriate levels of engagement in Roman economy. In other words, multiple ideologies emerged in light of Roman economics. On the one hand, this was internal: different churches/leaders made different choices vis-à-vis the Roman economy. On the other hand, this also represented an external threat: the need to participate in the Roman imperial cult in order to be

---

81. Duff, *Who Rides the Beast*, 29.

82. Duff suggests it is physical, not metaphorical, wealth (*Who Rides the Beast*, 42–43).

83. On opposing factions in Pergamum, Thyatira, and (maybe) Ephesus, Duff sees a split between those on John's side and those who participate in the imperial cult (*Who Rides the Beast*, 46–47) and issues of wealth and poverty in Smyrna and Laodicea (47). Koester reminds readers: "Instead, we find readers facing a spectrum of challenges. Some encountered local hostility against the church. For others, the principal threat was assimilation into the dominant Greco-Roman culture. For still others, the issue was the complacency that grows out of economic prosperity" ("Revelation's Visionary Challenge," 7; larger discussion, 7–9).

economically secure.[84]

When we now read Revelation, Craig R. Koester argues that "the contrast between God and God's opponents is clear in the visionary world of Revelation." However, he continues by explaining that "it almost certainly would not have been so clear in the social world of its early readers." He notes that the book addresses Jesus followers in a geographic area "where many Christians lived relatively comfortable lives. Some were poor but others were well off; some found themselves in conflicted situations while others blended more easily into society." Accordingly, "for many, John's critique of the empire would have seemed strange and excessive. It would not have been obvious to them that the empire posed a threat to the faithful."[85] But for John, the threat is clear: participation—even if only through the extension of eating foods sacrificed to them—in the worship of Roman deities is tantamount to idolatry and is thus a failure to recognize that Christ, not Caesar, is king.

The Two Beasts

Our second case study turns to an exploration of the two beasts in Rev 13. Here John introduces two beasts, both of which scholars connect to Rome and its imperial economic practices.[86] The first beast rises

> out of the sea, having ten horns and seven heads; and on its horns were ten diadems, and on its heads were blasphemous names. And the beast that I saw was like a leopard, its feet were like a bear's, and its mouth was like a lion's mouth. And the dragon gave it his power and his throne and great authority. One of its heads seemed to have received a death-blow, but its mortal wound had been healed. In amazement the whole earth followed the beast. They worshiped the dragon, for he had given his authority to the

---

84. On internal challenges, see Thompson, *Book of Revelation*. For arguments on how external pressures are more prominent in the letters of Rev 2–3, see Friesen, *Imperial Cults*.

85. Koester, "Revelation's Visionary Challenge," 5.

86. Carey writes of the beast in Rev 13: "This Beast, symbol of Rome's pretension of imperial rule, dominates the inhabitants of the earth: 'Who is like this beast, and who can make war against it?' (13:4). Another Beast emerges from the earth and leads the inhabitants to worship the Beast from the Sea (13:12). This other Beast depicts how the city elites in the province of Asia promoted festivals, shrines, temples, and elaborate ceremonies lavishing divine honors on the Roman emperors. All of these activities enacted submission and loyalty to Rome. The Greek verb *proskyneo*, rendered 'to worship' in modern translations, literally meant to bend the knee, to demonstrate submission in the face of a great power" ("Book of Revelation," 158). For more extended arguments on the connection between the book of Revelation and imperial cults, esp. Rev 13, see Friesen, "Myth and Symbolic Resistance"; Thompson, *Book of Revelation*, 160–64.

beast, and they worshiped the beast, saying, "Who is like the beast, and who can fight against it?" (Rev 13:1–4)

Scholars commonly suggest that the beast from the sea that appears in Rev 13 symbolizes Roman imperial power. In particular, this argument is made based on the fact that John's beast is modeled after the beasts in Dan 7:3–7:

> And four great beasts came up out of the sea, different from one another. The first was like a lion and had eagles' wings. Then, as I watched, its wings were plucked off, and it was lifted up from the ground and made to stand on two feet like a human being; and a human mind was given to it. Another beast appeared, a second one, that looked like a bear. It was raised up on one side, had three tusks in its mouth among its teeth and was told, "Arise, devour many bodies!" After this, as I watched, another appeared, like a leopard. The beast had four wings of a bird on its back and four heads; and dominion was given to it. After this I saw in the visions by night a fourth beast, terrifying and dreadful and exceedingly strong. It had great iron teeth and was devouring, breaking in pieces, and stamping what was left with its feet. It was different from all the beasts that preceded it, and it had ten horns.

As the angel tells Daniel, each of the beasts in Daniel's vision represents an empire, each destined to fall to God (Dan 7:17), resulting in a divine and "everlasting kingdom" (7:27). The beasts from the book of Daniel provide the background for interpreting this new terrible beast that John sees, who is "more fearsome than Daniel's beasts, embodying aspects of all of the great empires of history."[87] Yet while this beast may describe empire broadly, at the same time the text provides clues that John was also using this beast as a metaphor specifically for the Roman Empire: the seven heads represent the seven hills and emperors of Rome (Rev 17:9); the diadems—jeweled crowns associated with sovereigns—represent Rome's claim to power, a grotesque inversion of the claim that Christ is king (19:16); the "mortal wound" healed a reference to the

---

87. Carey, "Book of Revelation," 165. Similarly, Koester writes, "The beast is an image for the Roman Empire—and yet is more than that. John's imagery lumps Rome together with other great empires that have risen and fallen. The monster that John sees rising from the deep looks very much like the four great beasts that Daniel saw coming from the sea. In Dan 7:1–7 there are four separate beasts: a lion, a leopard, a bear, and a ten-horned monster. And the four beasts represent successive empires: the Babylonians, the Medes, the Persians, and the Hellenistic kingdoms of Alexander. Yet Revelation blends the traits of all of the beasts together in its vision of the sea beast. The implication is that the many empires that rise and fall over time belong to the same phenomenon: that of empire itself" ("Revelation's Visionary Challenge," 14).

legend of *Nero redivivus* that circulated around the time of the composition of Revelation—namely, the popular idea that the emperor Nero, who died in 68 CE, would one day return alive to Rome.[88]

John's vision then includes a second beast: one that "rose out of the earth" (Rev 13:11). The book describes the beast from the earth, like the beast from the sea, with monstrous language: "It had two horns like a lamb and it spoke like a dragon" (13:11). That it is connected to Rome is made clear in John's description, for the beast from the earth "exercises all the authority of the first beast on its behalf, and it makes the earth and its inhabitants worship the first beast, whose mortal wound had been healed" (13:12). Yet, as many scholars have argued, the earthly beast can be read as referring specifically to John's negative stance toward the participation of Jesus followers in the Roman imperial cult. For example, Justin Jeffcoat Schedtler identifies three aspects of the passage that allude to practices associated with the imperial cult.[89] First, the passage describes making an "image for the beast," likely a reference to the cult statues of the emperor that would have been found in many cities in Asia Minor (13:12).[90] Second, the passage appears to allude to the ways that the imperial priests maintained the imperial cult, especially "the well-known ancient phenomena of the animation of cult statues" (13:13–15, esp. v. 15). Third, the passage describes the threat that many early followers of Jesus might have felt regarding nonparticipation in the imperial cult: "The image of the beast could even speak and cause those who would not worship the image of the beast to be killed" (13:15).[91] As Jeffcoat Schedtler notes, "By refusing to participate in the imperial cultic sacrifices, many Christians were likely ostracized, and may have been persecuted outright."[92] Furthermore, some form of ostracization or localized persecution of Jesus followers for refusing to participate in the imperial cult might have been considered along similar lines as refusing to participate in cults of Roman deities.[93]

John's position on involvement in the imperial cult is made clear in Rev 13 (and the ensuing chapters of the book): the dragon (Satan) introduced in Rev 12 gives the first beast (Rome) authority, while the second beast (the imperial

88. For more on this legend—and its various strands—see Blount, *Revelation*, 248–49; Frilingos, *Spectacles of Empire*, 56; Jeffcoat Schedtler, "Beast or the Lamb," 155; Klauck, "Do They Never."
89. Jeffcoat Schedtler, "Beast or the Lamb," 152–57.
90. Jeffcoat Schedtler, "Beast or the Lamb," 156.
91. Jeffcoat Schedtler, "Beast or the Lamb," 157.
92. Jeffcoat Schedtler, "Beast or the Lamb," 157.
93. Price, *Rituals and Power*, 220–22.

cult) causes "both small and great, both rich and poor, both free and slave, to be marked on the right hand or the forehead, so that no one can buy or sell who does not have the mark, that is, the name of the beast or the number of its name" (13:16–17; see Rev 12–13). This mark is at odds with those marked by the seal of God on their foreheads in 7:1–8 and 22:4. According to many interpretations, when John refers to the "mark of the beast," he is likely describing the use of Roman coins marked by the emperor's image.[94] Without these coins, early followers of Jesus could not participate in commerce. Yet as Blount notes, the symbolism of the mark is "much broader than imperial coinage." John is worried about "all the enticements that draw his people toward accommodation to imperial cultic practice," including "eating meat sacrificed to idols" in order to maintain their status in trade guilds.[95] The logical procession is clear: "Participation in the imperial cult means not just worship of the emperor but worship of the devil."[96] For John, participation in the commercial life of the empire was dangerously adjacent, perhaps even identical, to participation in the imperial cult.

Revelation 13:18 concludes, "This calls for wisdom: let anyone with understanding calculate the number of the beast, for it is the number of a person. Its number is six hundred sixty-six." The "number of the beast," which is really "the number of a person," connects the second beast back to the first, where one of the beasts from the sea's seven heads "seemed to have received a death-blow, but its mortal wound had been healed" (13:3). Here many scholars again see a reference to the legend of *Nero redivivus*. "In amazement," the book says, "the whole earth followed the beast" (13:3), and "they worshiped the dragon, for he had given his authority to the beast, and they worshiped the beast, saying, 'Who is like the beast, and who can fight against it?'" (13:4). And while the world may think the answer to that question is Rome, John knows otherwise.

When John returns to Nero in Rev 13:18, he gives him the number 666, and John's audience would likely have made a historical connection that later readers cannot. The Greek *Neron Caesar*, when transliterated into Hebrew, where every letter of the Hebrew alphabet is associated with a number, totals 666. With this, some readers have understood John to be taking a symbolic potshot at the Roman Empire: the number seven represents wholeness, but the beast is a repetitive 666, suggesting "that the beast keeps trying to approach the

---

94. For other suggestions, including how this might refer to participation in trade guilds, see A. Y. Collins, *Crisis and Catharsis*, 88; Kraybill, *Imperial Cult*, 114–17, 135–41.

95. Blount, *Revelation*, 260.

96. Carter, *Roman Empire*, 81.

level of completeness ... but cannot quite make it."[97] In a slightly different vein, Koester explains, "The idea is not that the beast actually is Nero. Rather, it is that in the savagery of Nero, the empire shows its true face. If the slaughtered and living Lamb 'conquers' by faithfully enduring suffering, the Nero-like beast conquers by brutally inflicting suffering on the faithful (Rev 5:5–6; 13:7)."[98]

The emerging ideology in the book of Revelation tells its audience that participation in the exploitive economics of Rome should be abhorrent to followers of Christ. According to Christopher Frilingos, the beasts remind Revelation's audience that "the 'great and amazing' deeds of God ought to remain the focus of attention, because the spectacles of the beast lead to destruction."[99] In reality, however, early Jews and Christians lived in Asia Minor under the Roman Empire, a feat that was nearly impossible to do without participating in that economy—and, accordingly, the political/religious life of Rome. So, as Carey observes, "The joint images of the Beast from the Sea and the Beast from Earth point to one of the great dilemmas caused by imperialism. Imperialism cannot survive simply by imposition from 'across the sea': instead, it requires indigenous collaboration. Such is John's view of the Asian imperial cults."[100] In John's derogatory view of participation in the imperial cults, we can witness—if we stop to listen to their (admittedly muffled) voices as they are preserved in John's rhetoric against them—how some early followers of Jesus seem to have been comfortable with such collaboration.

The Whore of Babylon

Our third case study turns to a survey of the "whore of Babylon" and prophecies of the fall of Rome found in Rev 17–18, which uncover John's ideological response to the economic effects of the larger Roman imperial apparatus beyond the question of eating food sacrificed to Roman gods or participation in the imperial cult. These chapters further continue John's argument for what Davis calls "commerce as fornication."[101] While shrouded in symbolism and prophesy, Rev 17–18 includes some of John's clearest attacks on Rome, and, specifically, John's understanding of the realities of Roman economic practices. Yet even while John critiques Rome's economic practices—and, so, the empire of Rome—he also employs problematic gendered imagery that, as Lynn R. Huber

97. Blount, *Revelation*, 262.
98. Koester, "Revelation's Visionary Challenge," 15.
99. Frilingos, *Spectacles of Empire*, 57.
100. Carey, "Book of Revelation," 166.
101. Davis, *Biblical Prophecy*, 115–19.

explains, "mimics how Roman discourses think about women."[102]

Revelation 17 begins with one of the most famous images from the book: an angel beckons John, saying, "Come, I will show you the judgment of the great whore [*pornēs*] who is seated on many waters, with whom the kings of the earth have committed fornication [*eporneusan*], and with the wine of whose fornication [*porneias*] the inhabitants of the earth have become drunk" (Rev 1:1–2).[103] John then describes his vision: "A woman sitting on a scarlet beast that was full of blasphemous [*blasphēmias*] names," with "seven heads and ten horns" (17:3). For John's audience, the meaning behind the scene—and its economic implications—would be clear: the woman "seated on many waters" is a not-so-subtle depiction of the widespread Roman Empire; the "kings of the earth" and the "inhabitants" of the earth refer to how both those with more power and those with less power in Asia Minor often welcomed Rome and their place in its imperial infrastructure; and seven is the number of hills associated with Rome and, perhaps, the number of its emperors (see 12:3, 13:1, 17:9–14). As in previous chapters, John's use of the Greek *porneúō*, while often translated as "fornication," is best understood as read alongside the long use of using "sexual fidelity/infidelity as a metaphor for faithfulness to the ways of Yhwh versus faithfulness to the competing imperial structures of the day" already found in the prophetic books of the Hebrew Bible.[104] As Wes Howard-Brook and Anthony Gwyther note, John's use of such language connects infidelity to the powers of seduction.[105]

The woman is "clothed in purple and scarlet, and adorned with gold and jewels and pearls, holding in her hand a golden cup" (Rev 17:4). This depiction has led scholars to various conclusions: for example, the woman represents the goddess Roma herself[106] or the goddess Cybele.[107] Alternatively, "the woman

---

102. Huber, *Thinking and Seeing*, 55.

103. On the use of "whore" over prostitute, see Howard-Brook and Gwyther, *Unveiling Empire*, 159n6.

104. Howard-Brook and Gwyther, *Unveiling Empire*, 168.

105. Howard-Brook and Gwyther, *Unveiling Empire*, 168, 176.

106. For example, Bauckham writes, "Chapter 17 brings the two images together: the harlot is enthroned on the seven heads of the beast (17:3, 9–10). In other words, Roman civilization, as a corrupting influence, rides on the back of Roman military power" (*Climax of Prophecy*, 343), continuing, "it may be that in the woman in Revelation 17 John's readers would have recognized the goddess Roma, revealed by the vision in her true character: a Roman prostitute, wearing her name on a headband on her forehead (17:5) as prostitutes did in the streets of Rome" (*Climax of Prophecy*, 344). Who do people say this woman is?

107. Jeffcoat Schedtler, "Mother of Gods."

and the beast both seem to represent the same entity, the city of Rome."[108] First seated on many waters, then on a beast—red like the dragon of 12:3 and the city of Rome in 18:16—and then on "peoples and multitudes and nations and languages" in 17:15, "the woman, as 17:18 confirms, is the great city of Rome, enthroned upon the bestial empire whose commerce she uses to seduce the world into her idolatrous, prostituting behavior."[109] John's vision briefly illustrates how the book of Revelation sometimes admits the allure of empire, especially Rome's economic prosperity: clothed in purple, the color of royalty, with gold, jewels, and pearls, and holding a golden cup, the woman depicts the material spoils of an imperial economic policy. But the apocalypse quickly turns the seductive image on its head to reveal what John sees as the revolting realities of empire and imperialism: the cup is "full of abomination and the impurities of her fornication" (17:4). The reality of Roman imperialism is that its success rested on the extraction of goods and the labors of the colonized, and, whether they were willing participants or not, few of them saw the rewards that Rome, their "benefactor," did.

John then describes how "on her forehead was written a name: 'Babylon the great, mother of whores and of earth's abominations'" (Rev 17:5). John also sees "that the woman was drunk with the blood of the saints and the blood of the witnesses to Jesus" (17:6a). Yet as Jennifer Glancy and Stephen D. Moore have shown, while the woman is dressed as one may expect a wealthy Roman woman to be dressed, this is but a deception: the tattoo on her forehead identifies her as a regular prostitute, not a courtesan.[110] As Huber observes, the image of a whore drunk on the blood of Jesus followers should disgust John, but instead "of all the things that John witnesses on his visionary tour, the Whore is the only thing at which he *shows* amazement, although he does fall at the feet of the risen Christ when he sees him."[111] In short, the book of Revelation's presentation of Rome as whore reveals deep horror and disgust while simultaneously acknowledging the intoxicating allure of wealth. The chapter also draws on a long-standing tradition of depicting a city as unfaithful female, known not only from religious literature but from actual Roman "Judaea Capta" coins minted after the revolt of 70 CE, which depict Judea as a captive woman sitting on the ground following her defeat at the hands of the Romans. Yet in the book of Revelation we find the opposite: Rome—not Judea—is described as a woman

108. Blount, *Revelation*, 314.
109. Blount, *Revelation*, 314.
110. See Glancy and Moore, "How Typical."
111. Huber, "Gazing at the Whore," 306; emphasis original.

and, ultimately, as a woman who is physically and sexually violated. And so, "by depicting Rome as a woman, specifically as a Whore, in terms of violation and destruction, John takes what some may have found comforting (i.e. Roman peace and power) and tries to unsettle his audience—the city as Whore is not a safe space."[112]

The image of the woman on the beast also builds on John's previous use of a woman to make a rhetorical point related to Roman economic practices. Returning to our earlier discussion of Jezebel, we remember that John portrays her as representing a threat from inside the community of Jesus followers at Thyatira; at the same time, her position on eating food sacrificed to idols means to John that "the threat from outside is not *purely* external: the outside has infiltrated the inside." The whore, to borrow from Moore, "represents the threat to Christianity from without."[113] Reading with an eye toward John's ideological criticism of engagement with the Roman imperial economy, John's depictions of Jezebel and the whore "represent but two sides of the same (counterfeit) coin in Revelation: on the one hand, an inside that has somehow strayed outside; on the other hand, an outside that has somehow stolen inside."[114] Both Jezebel and the whore are alluring, seductive, and attractive, but in John's literary imagination both meet a violent death, thus severing the community of Jesus followers from Roman economy, within and without. And so Rev 17 closes by imagining Rome's violent end: the "great city that rules over the kings of the earth" (17:18) will be made "desolate and naked," devoured, and burned (17:16). The chapter continues the book's employment of negative images of women, sexuality, and violence to unveil John's ideology concerning the realities of Roman Empire and the proper place of Jesus followers within the Roman Empire—an issue inextricably linked with ideologies of prosperity.

Finally, John's use of a whore to symbolize Rome and its economic practices draws our attention to the complex afterlives of the symbol of the whore for later readers, who sometimes identify with her, find catharsis in her defeat and the defeat of the beast, or who are horrified at the abuse the woman, a marginal figure much as John imagines his own community to be marginalized, suffers.[115] While some scholars argue that the gendered metaphor should not

---

112. Huber, *Thinking and Seeing*, 88.
113. Moore, "Revelation to John," 450; emphasis original.
114. Moore, "Revelation to John," 450–51.
115. For different ways of understanding this figure, see, as just a few examples, Huber, "Gazing at the Whore" and *Thinking and Seeing*; Keller, *Apocalypse Now and Then*; Kim, "'Uncovering Her Wickedness'"; Pippin, *Apocalyptic Bodies*; Schüssler Fiorenza, *Power of the Word*; Smith, *Woman Babylon*; Vander Stichele, "Re-Membering."

be overanalyzed, others connect its use with real life economics. For example, Tina Pippin writes, "Sex workers in the United States identify with the Whore of Babylon. In their reading, she is a prostitute like them and a victim of male violence." Of course, "the violence done to the Whore is extreme; why does the demise of empire have to be symbolized by a sexually abused and devoured woman?"[116] For many readers, as Caroline Vander Stichele writes, the whore is more than simply a metaphor for Rome; she is also "a woman both within the text of Revelation (as Jezebel) and without it in terms of the correspondence with female identity in the larger sociocultural world of the text's readers and in the biblical landscape of female imagery upon which the text draws."[117] In Rev 17, critique and religious ideology are mutually constituting in the text and its reception.

In what follows in Rev 18, the woman is imagined as a city, and the text turns to a prophesy of Rome's fall, beginning in vv. 2–3:

> Fallen, fallen is Babylon the great!
>   It has become a dwelling place of demons,
> a haunt of every foul spirit,
>   a haunt of every foul bird,
>   a haunt of every foul and hateful beast.
> For all the nations have drunk
>   of the wine of the wrath of her fornication,
> and the kings of the earth have committed fornication with her,
>   and the merchants of the earth have grown rich from the power of her luxury.

That "the kings of the earth have committed fornication [*eporneusan*] with her" suggests the intricate ties between politics, religion, and economics in the Roman Empire, especially if the verb *porneuō* is read metaphorically for the allures of economic gain found by those who participate in the imperial cult and the overall Roman economy (Rev 18:3). Furthermore, "the merchants of the earth have grown rich from the power of her luxury" suggests the vast Roman trading system found throughout Asia Minor—including in the communities of early Jesus followers that John addresses—that provided an avenue for economic advancement for some individuals but not all (18:3). As in Rev 17, that both the kings and the merchants are implicated by John reminds the audience of how many people across the hierarchy of Roman society welcomed Rome willingly. As the chapter unfolds, the city declares: "I rule as a queen; I am no

---

116. Pippin, "Revelation/Apocalypse," 630.
117. Vander Stichele, "Re-Membering," 114.

widow; and I will never see grief" (18:7), referencing Rome's belief in its own never-ending power and immortality. Yet for this "her plagues will come in a single day pestilence and mourning and famine—and she will be burned with fire; for mighty is the Lord God who judges her" (18:8).

Revelation 18 continues the use of Babylon as a cipher to condemn Rome's luxurious lifestyle, with John invoking imagery from the Hebrew Bible to make his case. For example, a voice from heaven says, "Come out of her, my people" (18:4), recalling the same command from Isa 48:20–22 and Jer 50:8–10, 51:6–10. Revelation 8:9–20 invokes the weeping, wailing, and mourning kings, merchants, shipmasters, seafarers, and sailors who appear originally in the book of Ezekiel's condemnation of Tyre (Ezek 27). A famous trade center, Tyre often incurred the wrath of the prophets of the Hebrew Bible. Thus, Isaiah also denounces Tyre, "the merchant of the nations" (Isa 23:3), who the prophet implies "store[s] and hoard[s]" its merchandise at the expense of others (though there is a time in the future when "her merchandise will supply abundant food and fine clothing for those who live in the presence of the Lord" [Isa 23:18]). What those prophets of old once said to their audiences, John repeatedly raises to explain the present economic realities of the world around him and to decry participation in the imperial economy. John's apocalypse borrows from "an implicit critique of an exploitive imperial economy" found in the texts of the Hebrew Bible; Israel's past experiences with exploitive economies continue into the present.[118]

In the wake of Rome's destruction, Rev 18:11 explains how "the merchants of the earth weep and mourn for [Babylon/Rome], since no one buys their cargo anymore." As Kraybill and others have outlined, working in commerce—and particularly on the sea—was one avenue providing an opportunity for upward mobility for both Jews and early Jesus followers in Asia Minor.[119] For example, Davis argues that "maritime trade may have been the life of some loyal Christians in the mid-first century ... a few decades later, John repudiated it entirely as an option for Christians."[120] And so Rev 18 seems to provide a window into competing ideologies among early Jews and Jesus followers in Asia Minor, particularly around engaging in trade that was headed to Rome. The famous list of cargo items in Rev 18:12–13 ties back to the kinds of exports the seven cities of Rev 2–3 are known to have produced:

---

118. Howard-Brook and Gwyther, *Unveiling Empire*, 173.

119. Kraybill, *Imperial Cult*, 99–101.

120. Davis, *Biblical Prophecy*, 117. For relevant passages, see Rev 13:16–17, 20:4.

gold, silver, jewels and pearls, fine linen, purple, silk and scarlet, all kinds of scented wood, all articles of ivory, all articles of costly wood, bronze, iron, and marble, cinnamon, spice, incense, myrrh, frankincense, wine, olive oil, choice flour and wheat, cattle and sheep, horses and chariots, slaves—and human lives [sōmatōn kai psuchas anthrōpōn]

Scholars have long observed that the list appears to be modeled after a similar list found in Ezekiel (see Ezek 16:9–13; 27). Of the list in Revelation, Richard Bauckham writes, "Most of these items were among the most expensive of Rome's imports."[121] Yet as Howard-Brook and Gwyther observe, it is also the case that some of the items "are simply the staples of life." In this way, "rather than portraying a city that extracted simply *luxury goods* from the entire earth, the list depicts Babylon as appropriating *everything* from the entire earth."[122]

This "everything" includes something not found in Ezekiel's list: humans. In Rev 18:13, the final cargo item is not an object but enslaved people: *sōmatōn kai psuchas anthrōpōn*. Famously, the Roman economy was built on the backs of enslaved people,[123] and some of the cities in Asia Minor provided these slaves, including Ephesus, Thyatira, and Sardis.[124] Thus, while "John does not take up slavery as a topic in its own right . . . the way he tells of merchants selling human 'souls'—and not just human 'bodies'—along with gold, grain, cattle, and horses underscores the problems inherent in a society that turns everything into commodities that can be sold to meet the insatiable demand of the ruling power."[125] Even as John uses the past world of the prophets to explain the present, he also modifies that world to underscore what he sees as the horrific economic realities of his present world.

Revelation 18, like the preceding chapter, ends by imagining the devastation of those who participated in the imperial economy while relishing Rome's forthcoming violent demise. So, John writes, "The merchants of these wares, who gained wealth from her, will stand far off, in fear of her torment, weeping and mourning aloud" (Rev 18:15), lamenting the fall of the city, and so too will "all shipmasters and seafarers, sailors and all whose trade is on the sea" (17:18), crying out from afar as they see the city burn (18:18). Then, finally, in Rev 18:21, "a mighty angel took up a stone like a great millstone and threw it into

121. Bauckham, *Climax of Prophecy*, 366.
122. Howard-Brook and Gwyther, *Unveiling Empire*, 173; emphasis original.
123. For an extensive look at the role of slavery in early Christianity, see Glancy, *Slavery in Early Christianity*; as well as Boer and Petterson, *Time of Troubles*, esp. 103–90.
124. Koester, "Roman Slave Trade," 777.
125. Koester, "Roman Slave Trade," 785–86.

the sea," saying:

> With such violence Babylon the great city
>   will be thrown down,
>   and will be found no more;
> and the sound of harpists and minstrels and of flutists and trumpeters
>   will be heard in you no more;
> and an artisan of any trade
>   will be found in you no more;
> and the sound of the millstone
>   will be heard in you no more;
> and the light of a lamp
>   will shine in you no more;
> and the voice of bridegroom and bride
>   will be heard in you no more;
> for your merchants were the magnates of the earth,
>   and all nations were deceived by your sorcery.
> And in you was found the blood of prophets and of saints,
>   and of all who have been slaughtered on earth. (Rev 18:21–24)

In miniature, Rev 7–18 demonstrates how John's apocalypse responds to Roman imperial economy, with attraction, disgust, and, ultimately, violence. Readers are left to wrestle with this violence: "Is this vision the ultimate dream of humiliating the conqueror?"[126] Only subtly veiled in metaphors, visions, and prophecies, John uses the book of Revelation to offer up a scathing indictment of Rome and, in particular, Roman economics. Yet while John's ideological stance can be understood as anti-imperial and anti-assimilationist—unlike, according to him, the attitudes of some of his fellow Christ followers—it is also the case that he reinscribes aspects of the Roman Empire into the gendered depiction of Rome.

By using Babylon as a cipher for Rome, John borrows from Israel's economic past in order to address the present and look to the future. Paradoxically, in the story of Israel's past economic devastation at the hands of the Babylonians in 587 BCE, John also finds hope for a future—the kingdom of Jesus. Though the fall of the First Temple was an event preceded and followed by economic ruin, eventually even mighty Babylon fell. So too, says John of Patmos, will Rome.[127] Revelation 18, invoking the past, called for early Jesus followers "to sever all economic and political ties with an Empire that had sold out to

---

126. Pippin, "Revelation," 630.
127. See Kraybill, *Imperial Cult*, 16. Also see A. Y. Collins, *Crisis and Catharsis*, 106–7.

injustice, idolatry, and greed."[128] In the final chapters of the book, John envisions a future where (almost) everyone—including the kings of the earth—has the opportunity to "come out, come!" of the empire (Rev 18:4).[129] Even as the call "come out, come!" refers to the past and a promise of return from Babylon, John also looks forward by using this call as an invitation to participate in a new, quickly approaching, economic reality on earth: "The audience of Revelation is called to undertake an exodus 'out' from Babylon as a preparation for entry 'into' God's new Jerusalem... [setting] in motion the 'either-or' choice that the audience must make."[130] Yet despite John's rising crescendo against the Roman Empire and its economic practices, the reality he envisions—a new city that contrasts with the city of Rome—in some ways resembles the very one he decries throughout the book.[131]

The New Jerusalem

Our fourth and final case study illustrating how Revelation responds to Roman imperial economics is found in the closing chapters: Rev 21–22. Here John unveils how he imagines the imminent future will look. This future is one with a new heaven, a new earth, and a new Jerusalem, which John sees "coming down out of heaven from God, prepared as a bride adorned for her husband" (Rev 21:2). The two cities are presented as opposites: one a whore, the other a virginal bride.[132] Yet even as Rev 21–22 depicts a city with a new economic order personified as a woman—one that rights the wrongs of Rome's imperial economy—it also, in some ways, rebuilds the empire that the apocalypse has spent chapters tearing down.

In this imagined future, concerns about wealth and poverty continue even as historical time ends. At first glance, the alternative provided by the new Jerusalem appears idyllic, peaceful, welcoming—nothing like the "'evil woman'

---

128. Kraybill, *Imperial Cult*, 16.

129. Scholars have suggested different ways of understanding what the author of Revelation means here: perhaps listeners are to stop participating in the imperial cult (Kraybill, *Imperial Cult*); perhaps this is a call "for social exclusivism" (A. Y. Collins, *Crisis and Catharsis*, 157); or perhaps the call "is not only an entreaty to exit; it is also an order to engage" with God by "witnessing actively to the lordship of God and Christ as the only measure of present and eschatological security" (Blount, *Revelation*, 328).

130. Rossing, "City Visions," 194.

131. For more on the "'two-women' ethical *topos*" found in Revelation and other early Jewish and Christian texts, see Rossing, "City Visions."

132. See Huber, *Thinking and Seeing*; Rossing, "City Visions."

Babylon," with her "unjust political economy and military empire."[133] As the book closes, a voice from the divine throne exhorts John:

> See, the home of God is among mortals.
> He will dwell with them;
> they will be his peoples,
> and God himself will be with them;
> he will wipe every tear from their eyes.
> Death will be no more;
> mourning and crying and pain will be no more,
> for the first things have passed away. (Rev 21:2–4)

In many ways, these verses reflect John's own economic concerns: they imagine a reversal of the situation described in Rev 18.[134] In the new Jerusalem, "death will be no more; mourning and crying and pain will be no more, for the first things have passed away" (Rev 21:4), a clear contrast with the mourning, crying kings, merchants, and shipmasters of Rev 8. It seems as if everyone is welcome here: the text describes how the "nations will walk" and "the kings of the earth will bring their glory" to the new Jerusalem (21:24), in sharp contrast with a cargo list of items that ends with humans as objects to meet the demands of nations and kings under the sway of the beast in Rev 18. The economic ideology of these final chapters appears to be a call for coexistence between peoples and former empires, all under God's new rule on earth. In addition to the serene description of what life will be like in the new Jerusalem, the city itself is described: this is an earthly, material city, which is adorned with luxurious, splendid, radiant things. The extravagance of the new Jerusalem serves as a reminder that John's ideological response to wealth is not always negative. Rather, John's diatribe can be read as "against wealth that is situated in the autonomy, self-sufficiency, and arrogance of Rome."[135] In contrast, "the wealth situated in obedience to God is acceptable" and measured by "adherence to the God of the gospel rather than to the norms and passions of Rome."[136]

Yet a closer examination of his vision for the future illustrates how, though John has spent several chapters tearing down the empire, in some ways he ironically ends up using pieces of that empire to build the new Jerusalem. As Davina C. Lopez writes, "Insofar as Revelation imagines something 'new,' it

---

133. Rossing, "City Visions," 196.

134. For example, see Rossing, "City Visions," 190–96.

135. Brueggemann, *Money and Possessions*, 278. As Brueggemann notes, it is not that Revelation is anti-wealth, pointing readers to Rev 1:12, 4:4, 5:8, 8:3, as well as the message to the church in Laodicea (Rev 3:17–18). See A. Y. Collins, *Crisis and Catharsis*, 134–35.

136. Brueggemann, *Money and Possessions*, 279.

does so at least in part by interacting with the available discourses that were thought to be persuasive or at least those with which an audience would be familiar."[137] In other words, throughout the final chapters of the book, scholars see images, ideas, and rhetoric that reflect Roman imperial ideology.

Five regularly cited examples help illustrate, in miniature, some of the ways in which scholars see Roman imperial ideology at work in Revelation's description of the new Jerusalem: the city is depicted as urban, hierarchal, full of riches that go to those who conqueror, and ruled by an enthroned emperor. First, John imagines the divinely perfect future as urban. This is a city with walls, gates, and foundations, where "eschatological living is envisioned . . . as a complex, other-connected and no doubt other-oriented relationship that brings with it all of the social and political ramifications that life in any city engenders."[138] As John urbanizes the apocalyptic future, he reproduces the urbanization process that Asia Minor experienced under the Romans.

The second example, as Lopez notes, pertains to how the world within (and without) the new Jerusalem's walls remains hierarchal.[139] Not everyone is allowed into this new city: "But as for the cowardly, the faithless, the polluted, the murderers, the fornicators, the sorcerers, the idolaters, and all liars, their place will be in the lake that burns with fire and sulfur, which is the second death" (Rev 21:8); "nothing unclean will enter it, nor anyone who practices abomination or falsehood, but only those who are written in the Lamb's book of life" (22:27). Moreover, Rev 22:4 tells us that those allowed into the city are those who have "his name . . . on their foreheads," whom the text describes as "slaves [*douloi*] of God" (22:3). Just as Rome's slaves were marked on their forehead, so too will the new Jerusalem's inhabitants be marked.[140] In this way, the new Jerusalem "appears like a reincarnation of the imperial landscape," with "imagery associated with slavery therein."[141]

The third example is found in how the description of the new Jerusalem

137. Lopez, "Victory and Visibility," 293. Similarly, Frilingos writes, "Despite the assurance that 'the first things have passed away,' the 'new heaven and new earth' that the audience glimpses in the Apocalypse reconstitutes the viewing relations of the old world. The New Jerusalem invites the audience into the imperial arena: the crowds gather, the editor sits in attendance, and the throng, composed of worshipful servants, venerates the divine emperor" (*Spectacles of Empire*, 115). Moore writes that "in the construction of the New Jerusalem," Rome is both "absent (because already annihilated)" and yet also "present" ("Revelation to John," 444).

138. Blount, *Revelation*, 378.
139. Lopez, "Victory and Visibility," 289–90.
140. Lopez, "Victory and Visibility," 289.
141. Lopez, "Victory and Visibility," 290.

in Rev 21:18–21 is, as Duff writes, "quite similar" to how Rome's wealth is described.[142] This is a city made of pure gold, every jewel, and pearls—the very things that adorned Babylon the woman (see 17:4). Fourth, Rev 21:7 declares that it is "those who conquer [*nikōn*]" who will inherit all of the good things of the new Jerusalem.[143] From the Greek verb *nikaò* (to conquer), the verb carries with it the connotation of battle. This is the same verb used when John describes how "the beast that comes up from the bottomless pit" will make war on the olive trees and lampstands that stand before God, "and conquer [*nikēsei*] them and kill them" (11:7; see 11:4–6). In order to gain the spoils of new Jerusalem, people must take on the actions of empire.

Fifth, and finally, as the book of Revelation closes with God enthroned (Rev 22:3), we are reminded that Revelation even adopts imperial ideologies for God. As Moore writes:

> More than any other early Christian text (prior to Tertullian, at any rate), Revelation epitomizes the theo-imperialist orientation that enabled the Roman state effortlessly to absorb Christianity into itself, to turn Christianity into a version of itself, to turn itself into a version of Christianity—notwithstanding the fact that Revelation is also ostensibly more hostile to Rome than any other early Christian text. The flaw inheres in three mutually reinforcing—and inescapably obvious?— features of Revelation (although the obvious is always hedged about with obliviousness, and hence never as inescapable as one would like). First of all, the throne is the paramount metonym for God in this book. Second, the principal attributes of "the one seated on the throne" are stereotypically imperial attributes: incomparable glory and authority, overwhelming power and punitive wrath. Third, the principal activities of the one seated on the throne and those of his elite agents are quintessentially imperial activities: the conduct of war and the enlargement of empire.[144]

And so even as John imagines a new future, free of Rome, he fills it with images and ideas from Rome—a hierarchical urban city where the conquerors take the spoils, while a ruler sits enshrined on a throne. Lest we be surprised by this, though, Jacqueline M. Hidalgo reminds us that "a community purified of Roman-ness would not have been possible"; indeed, "we must recognize that Revelation is an alter-imperial text written with the possibilities of the Roman

---

142. Duff, *Who Rides the Beast*, 63.
143. See Blount, *Revelation*, 382.
144. Moore, "Revelation to John," 451.

Empire and not always strictly opposed to them."[145]

Conclusion

Reading Revelation with an eye toward economic issues—and, especially, toward the ways that the book responds to Roman imperialism and the realities of life in urban Asia Minor—shows us that John's apocalypse is a literary portrait of divided attitudes on how early followers of Jesus should participate in the interlocking political, economic, societal, and religious systems that comprised Rome. John calls for his listeners—and all followers of Jesus—to divest themselves from the empire. Accordingly, scholars have often seen the book of Revelation as a call to "social radicalism."[146] After all, John asks his listeners to refuse to engage in Roman economics, which he sees as fundamentally corrupt, and to "come out, come!" (Rev 18:4) from Rome. In place of this corrupt system, scholars see John envisioning "God's alternative to Rome's empire."[147] Yet a closer look at John's world shows that there is an alternative way to read the emerging discourse about Roman imperial economics in the book: one that takes seriously how present Rome remains in John's apocalyptic future, long after the Rome of John's present is gone.

Here we return, briefly, to Harold Camping. The story of Camping's (many) failed predictions of the end of the world shows how Revelation's concern with economics plays out far into a future beyond John of Patmos's imagination. Camping's story is one that highlights how Revelation may be twisted to create economic distress (even if those who do the twisting genuinely believe they do so in hopes that a new utopian present will come *soon*). But there are many other examples of the *actual* future of Revelation that we could likewise mention, including those who continue, along with John of Patmos, to critique injustice, exploitation, and the overreach of empire. As just one frequently cited example, we could turn to Martin Luther King Jr., in whom many see the influence of the theology of the book of Revelation: "Let us be dissatisfied until the empty stomachs of Mississippi are filled and the idle industries of Appalachia are revitalized . . . Let us be dissatisfied until our brothers and sisters of the Third World—Asia, Africa, and Latin America—will no longer be victim of imperialist exploitation, but will be lifted from the long night of poverty,

---

145. Hidalgo, *Revelation in Aztlán*, 84; see also Frilingos, *Spectacles of Empire*; and Lopez, "Victory and Visibility," 294–95.

146. A. Y. Collins, *Crisis and Catharsis*, 137.

147. Carter, *Roman Empire*, 63.

illiteracy, and disease."[148] Or we could turn to the significant work that has been done on the women of the book of Revelation. After all, it can hardly escape our notice that John's economic discourses are also deeply entwined with John's often severely problematic depiction of women: Babylon the whore (past), Jezebel the fornicator (present), and a (presumably virgin) bride (future). Each of these female figures constitutes part of Revelation's response to Roman imperialism and economics and represents a way that Revelation's concern with economics (and gender) plays out in the *actual* future. So Glancy and Moore remind us how "the story of Babylon's demise is the story of a great many sex workers in every age, including our own."[149] Beyond these examples, a host of other readings of Revelation help us to see how we can approach the text, with its focus on wealth, poverty, and participation in mundane economies—as well as its tendency toward replicating empire—to (re)examine our own roles in the economic systems in which we live.[150]

While the economic discourses found in Revelation are woven together in the book's concept of temporality—from the past, John's own present, to the apocalyptic future the work seeks to unveil—its concern with economics also weaves into the actual future, for better or for worse, over the course of the text's reception history, and calls us to take seriously what the book says and the many ways the book is used when it comes to all things economic.

Bibliography

Allen, Garrick. "Scriptural Allusions in the Book of Revelation and the Contours of Textual Research 1900–2014: Retrospect and Prospects." *CurBR* 14 (2016) 319–39.

Amira, Dan. "A Conversation with Harold Camping, Prophesier of Judgment Day." *Intelligencer*, May 11, 2011. https://nymag.com/intelligencer/2011/05/a_conversation_with_harold_cam.html.

Aune, David. "The Influence of Roman Imperial Court Ceremonial on the Apocalypse of John." *Papers of the Chicago Society of Biblical Research* 28 (1983) 5–29.

Aune, David. *Revelation 1–5.* WBC 52A. Dallas: Word, 1997.

———. *Revelation 6–16.* WBC 52B. Nashville: Thomas Nelson, 1998.

———. *Revelation 7–22.* WBC 52C. Nashville: Thomas Nelson, 1998.

Bauckham, Richard. *The Climax of Prophecy: Studies on the Book of Revelation.* Edinburgh: T&T Clark, 1993.

Beal, Timothy K. *The Book of Revelation: A Biography.* Princeton, NJ: Princeton University Press, 2018.

---

148. King, "Honoring Dr. Du Bois," 110–11.

149. Glancy and Moore, "How Typical," 568.

150. As just a few examples: Blount, *Can I Get Witness*; Darden, *Scripturalizing Revelation*; Hidalgo, *Revelation in Aztlán*; Huber, "Gazing at the Whore"; Smith, *Woman Babylon*.

Blount, Brian K. *Can I Get a Witness? Reading Revelation through African American Culture.* Louisville: Westminster John Knox, 2005.

———. *Revelation: A Commentary.* Louisville: Westminster John Knox, 2009.

Boer, Roland. *The Sacred Economy of Ancient Israel.* LAI. Louisville: Westminster John Knox, 2015.

Boer, Roland, and Christina Petterson. *Time of Troubles: A New Economic Framework for Early Christianity.* Minneapolis: Fortress, 2017.

Boesak, Allan A. *Comfort and Protest: The Apocalypse from a South African Perspective.* Philadelphia: Westminster, 1997.

Brueggemann, Walter. *Money and Possessions.* Louisville: Westminster John Knox, 2016.

Carey, Greg. "The Book of Revelation as Counter-Imperial Script." In *In the Shadow of Empire: Reclaiming the Bible as a History of Faithful Resistance*, edited by Richard A. Horsley, 157–76. Louisville: Westminster John Knox, 2008.

Carter, Warren. *The Roman Empire and the New Testament: An Essential Guide.* Nashville: Abingdon, 2006.

Collins, Adela Yarbro. *Crisis and Catharsis: The Power of the Apocalypse.* Philadelphia: Westminster, 1984.

Collins, John J. *Apocalypse, Prophecy, and Pseudepigraphy: On Jewish Apocalyptic Literature.* Grand Rapids: Eerdmans, 2015.

———. *The Apocalyptic Imagination: An Introduction to Jewish Apocalyptic Literature.* 2nd ed. Grand Rapids: Eerdmans, 1998.

Cook, Stephen L. *Prophecy and Apocalypticism: The Postexilic Social Setting.* Minneapolis: Fortress, 1995.

Darden, Lynne St. Clair. *Scripturalizing Revelation: An African American Postcolonial Reading of Empire.* Atlanta: SBL, 2015.

Davis, Ellen. *Biblical Prophecy: Perspectives for Christian Theology, Discipleship, and Ministry.* Louisville: Westminster John Knox, 2014.

Decock, Paul B. "Hostility against the Wealth of Babylon: 7:1—19:10." In *Animosity, the Bible, and Us: Some European, North American, and South African Perspectives*, 263–86. Atlanta: SBL, 2009.

DeSilva, David A. "The Strategic Arousal of Emotion in John's Visions of Roman Imperialism: A Rhetorical-Critical Investigation of Revelation 4–22." *Neot* 42 (2008) 1–34.

Diehl, Judy. "'Babylon': Then, Now and 'Not Yet': Anti-Roman Rhetoric in the Book of Revelation." *CurBR* 11 (2013) 168–95.

Duff, Paul B. *Who Rides the Beast? Prophetic Rivalry and the Rhetoric of Crisis in the Churches of the Apocalypse.* Oxford: Oxford University Press, 2001.

Eusebius. *Ecclesiastical History: Books 1–5.* Translated by Roy J. Deferrari. FC. Washington, DC: Catholic University of America Press, 2005.

———. *Ecclesiastical History: Books 6–10.* Translated by Roy J. Deferrari. FC. Washington, DC: Catholic University of America Press, 2005.

Friesen, Steven J. "Apocalypse and Empire." In *The Oxford Handbook of Apocalyptic Literature*, edited by John J. Collins, 163–79. Oxford Handbooks. Oxford: Oxford University Press, 2014.

———. *Imperial Cults and the Apocalypse of John: Reading Revelation in the Ruins.* Oxford: Oxford University Press, 2001.

———. "Myth and Symbolic Resistance in 3." *JBL* 123 (2004) 281–313.

———. "Satan's Throne, Imperial Cults and the Social Settings of Revelation." *JSNT* 27 (2005) 351–73.
Frilingos, Christopher A. *Spectacles of Empire: Monsters, Martyrs, and the Book of Revelation*. Divinations: Rereading Late Ancient Religion. Philadelphia: University of Pennsylvania Press, 2004.
Glancy, Jennifer A. *Slavery in Early Christianity*. New York: Oxford University Press, 2002.
Glancy, Jennifer A., and Stephen D. Moore. "How Typical a Roman Prostitute Is Revelation's 'Great Whore'?" *JBL* 130 (2011) 551–69.
Hanson, K. C., and Douglas E. Oakman. *Palestine in the Time of Jesus: Social Structures and Social Conflicts*. 2nd ed. Minneapolis: Fortress, 2008.
Hanson, Paul D. *The Dawn of Apocalyptic*. Philadelphia: Fortress, 1975.
Hays, Christopher B. "'Proto-Apocalyptic' Constellations in the Bible and the Ancient Near East: Revelation, Interpretation, Combat, and Judgment." In *Apocalypses in Context: Apocalyptic Currents through History*, edited by Kelly J. Murphy and Justin Jeffcoat Schedtler, 37–60. Minneapolis: Fortress, 2016.
Hidalgo, Jacqueline M. *Revelation in Aztlán: Scriptures, Utopias, and the Chicano Movement*. The Bible and Cultural Studies. New York: Palgrave MacMillan, 2016.
Horsley, Richard A. *Covenant Economics: A Biblical Vision of Justice for All*. Louisville: Westminster John Knox, 2009.
———. *Revolt of the Scribes: Resistance and Apocalyptic Origins*. Minneapolis: Fortress, 2010.
Howard-Brook, Wes, and Anthony Gwyther. *Unveiling Empire: Reading Revelation Then and Now*. Bible and Liberation. Maryknoll, NY: Orbis, 1999.
Huber, Lynn R. "Gazing at the Whore: Reading Revelation Queerly." In *Bible Trouble: Queer Reading at the Boundaries of Biblical Scholarship*, edited by Teresa J. Hornsby and Ken Stone, 301–20. Atlanta: SBL, 2011.
———. *Thinking and Seeing with Women in Revelation*. LNTS 475. London: Bloomsbury T&T Clark, 2013.
Hylen, Susan. "The Power and Problem of 8: The Rhetorical Function of Gender." In *Pregnant Passion: Gender, Sex, and Violence in the Bible*, edited by Cheryl A. Kirk-Duggan, 205–19. Atlanta: SBL, 2003.
Jeffcoat Schedtler, Justin. "The Beast or the Lamb in the Apocalypse to John." In *Apocalypses in Context: Apocalyptic Current through History*, edited by Kelly J. Murphy and Justin Jeffcoat Schedtler, 143–62. Minneapolis: Fortress, 2016.
———. "Mother of Gods, Mother of Harlots: The Image of the Mother Goddess behind the Depiction of the 'Whore of Babylon' in 7." *NovT* 59 (2017) 52–70.
———. "Praising Christ the King: Royal Discourse and Ideology in Revelation 5." *NovT* 60 (2018) 162–82.
Keller, Catherine. *Apocalypse Now and Then: A Feminist Guide to the End of the World*. Boston: Beacon, 1996.
Kim, Jean K. "'Uncovering Her Wickedness': An Inter(con)textual Reading of 7 from a Postcolonial Feminist Perspective." *JSOT* 73 (1999) 61–81.
King, Martin Luther, Jr. "Honoring Dr. Du Bois." *Freedomways* 8 (1968) 104–11.
Klauck, Hans-Josef. "Do They Never Come Back? 'Nero Redivivus' and the Apocalypse of John." *CBQ* 63 (2001) 683–98.
Knight, Douglas A. *Law, Power, and Justice in Ancient Israel*. Louisville: Westminster John Knox, 2011.
Koester, Craig R. "Revelation's Visionary Challenge to Ordinary Empire." *Int* 63 (2009) 5–18.

———. "Roman Slave Trade and the Critique of Babylon in 8." *CBQ* 70 (2008) 766–86.
Kraybill, J. Nelson. *Imperial Cult and Commerce in John's Apocalypse*. JSNTSup 132. Sheffield: Sheffield Academic, 1996.
Linton, Gregory L. "Reading the Apocalypse as Apocalypse: The Limits of Genre." In *The Reality of Apocalypse: Rhetoric and Politics in the Book of Revelation*, edited by David L. Barr, 9–41. SymS 39. Atlanta: SBL, 2006.
Lopez, Davina. "Victory and Visibility: Revelation's Imperial Textures and Monumental Logics." In *An Introduction to Empire in the New Testament*, edited by Adam Winn, 273–96. Atlanta: SBL, 2016.
Macaskill, Grant. "Critiquing Rome's Economy: Revelation and Its Reception in the Apostolic Fathers." In *Engaging Economics: New Testament Scenarios and Early Christian Reception*, edited by Bruce W. Longenecker and Kelly D. Liebengood, 243–59. Grand Rapids: Eerdmans, 2009.
Moore, Stephen D. *Empire and Apocalypse: Postcolonialism and the New Testament*. The Bible in the Modern World 12. Sheffield: Sheffield Phoenix, 2006.
———. "The Revelation to John." In *Postcolonial Commentary on the New Testament Writings*, edited by Fernando Segovia and R. S. Sugirtharajah, 436–54. Bible and Postcolonialism. New York: T&T Clark International, 2007.
Murphy, Kelly J., and Justin Jeffcoat Schedtler. "Introduction—From before the Bible to beyond the Bible." In *Apocalypses in Context: Apocalyptic Current through History*, edited by Kelly J. Murphy and Justin Jeffcoat Schedtler, 3–18. Minneapolis: Fortress, 2016.
Ozanne, C. G. "The Language of the Apocalypse." *TynBul* 16 (1965) 3–9.
Park, Rohun. "Revelation for Sale: An Intercultural Reading of 8 from an East Asian Perspective." *The Bible & Critical Theory* 4 (2008) 25.1–12.
Piestrup, Zeke, dir. *Apocalypse Later: Harold Camping vs the End of the World*. El Segundo, CA: Gravitas Ventures, 2014.
Pippin, Tina. *Apocalyptic Bodies: The Biblical End of the World in Text and Image*. London: Routledge, 1999.
———. "Revelation/Apocalypse of John." In *Women's Bible Commentary*, edited by Carol A. Newsom et al., 627–32. 3rd ed. Louisville: Westminster John Knox, 2012.
Pixley, Jorge V. "Revelation 21:1—22:5: A Latin American Perspective." In *Return to Babel: Global Perspectives on the Bible*, edited by Priscilla Pope-Levison and John R. Levison, 201–5. Louisville: Westminster John Knox, 1999.
Pliny the Younger. *The Complete Letters*. Translated by P. G. Walsh. New York: Oxford University Press, 2009.
Price, S. R. F. *Rituals and Power: The Roman Imperial Cult in Asia Minor*. Cambridge: Cambridge University Press, 1984.
Rossing, Barbara R. "City Visions, Feminine Figures and Economic Critique: A Sapiential Topos in the Apocalypse." In *Conflicted Boundaries in Wisdom and Apocalypticism*, edited by Benjamin G. Wright III and Lawrence M. Wills, 181–96. Atlanta: SBL, 2005.
Rowland, Christopher. *The Open Heaven: A Study of Apocalyptic in Judaism and Early Christianity*. 1982. Reprint, Eugene, OR: Wipf & Stock, 2002.
Scheidel, Walter. "Approaching the Roman Economy." In *The Cambridge Companion to Roman Economy*, edited by Walter Scheidel, 1–22. Cambridge Companions to the Ancient World. Cambridge: Cambridge University Press, 2012.
Schüssler Fiorenza, Elisabeth. *The Book of Revelation: Justice and Judgment*. Philadelphia: Fortress, 1985.

———. *The Power of the Word: Scripture and the Rhetoric of Empire*. Minneapolis: Fortress, 2007.

Smith, Shanell T. *The Woman Babylon and the Marks of Empire: Reading Revelation with a Postcolonial Womanist Hermeneutics of Ambiveilence*. Emerging Scholars. Minneapolis: Fortress, 2014.

Song, Choan-Seng. "Revelation 21:1–22:5: an Asian Perspective." In *Return to Babel: Global Perspectives on the Bible*, edited by Priscilla Pope-Levison and John R. Levison, 213–19. Louisville: Westminster John Knox, 1999.

Thompson, Leonard L. *The Book of Revelation: Apocalypse and Empire*. Oxford: Oxford University Press, 1990.

VanderKam, James C. *An Introduction to Early Judaism*. Grand Rapids: Eerdmans, 2001.

Vander Stichele, Caroline. "Re-Membering the Whore: The Fate of Babylon According to 7.6." In *A Feminist Companion to the Apocalypse of John*, edited by Amy-Jill Levine with Maria Mayo Robbins, 106–20. Feminist Companion to the New Testament and Early Christian Writings. New York: T&T Clark, 2010.

Ancient Document Index

Ancient West Asian Documents

Code of Ur-Nammu

    7

Hebrew Bible

Genesis

	16, 25
1:27	210
2–3	14
23	22, 25
23:4	23
23:9	23
23:20	23
33:19–29	25
33:19–20	22, 24, 25
34:10	23
41—Exod 15	14
41–50	15
41	14
41:1–8	14
41:33–45	14–15
41:46–49	15
41:53–57	15
42:6	15
42:18–25	15
43:8–10	15
43:18	15
44:16–17	15–16
44:10–13	15
44:16–17	15–16
44:18–34	15
45:4–14	15–16
45:26	17
46:1–4	15–16
46:8–27	15
47:1–6	16
47:11	16
47:13–26	15

Exodus

1–15	16
1:8–22	16
1:8	14
1:11	16
2:11–15	16
2:23–25	16
5:1—12:36	15
5:10–21	16
13:17—15:21	16
21–23	222
21:2	8
21:7	8
22:24	57
22:25–27	75, 76
23:4	23
23:9	23
23:10–11	65
23:20	23
24	82

Leviticus

	74, 222
19:2	76
19:17–18	77
19:36	22
25	7, 22, 25
25:2–7	57
25:23	25
25:25–55	26
25:35–37	75
25:36	57
27	22, 25

Numbers

16	30
27	26

Deuteronomy

3:4	24
3:13–14	24
6:11	25
15:1–6	65
15:1–2	57, 75
15:4	223
15:7–11	57, 76
15:7–8	75
15:12–15	57, 75
15:12	8
17:14–20	22
19:14	24
23:19	57
24:1–4	78
24:10–13	76
24:21	57
25:13	22
27:17	24
32:9	24
32:11	91

Joshua

	25
14:2	24
18:2–10	24
24:13	25

Judges

	66
6:24	15
8:32	15

Ruth

3:2	26
4	22, 25, 26, 27
4:1–12	27
4:3	24, 27
4:5	27
4:10	27

1 Samuel

	66
12	57
28:24	14

2 Samuel

	66
2:1–4	66
5:1–4	66
8:2	26
14:7	15
14:30–31	24
24:18–25	22, 25

1 Kings

	66
1:9	14
1:19	14, 27
1:25	14
4:10–26 [MT 4:20—5:6]	19
5:11	21
9:11–13	21
10	17
10:11–12	19
10:15	19
10:20	18
10:22	17, 18
10:28–29	19–20

ANCIENT DOCUMENT INDEX 275

15:17	14
18	3, 7
21	22
21:3	27
21:4	27
21:19	27

2 Kings

9:21	24, 27
9:25	24
18:22	4

1 Chronicles

21:1—22:1	22
21:18–22	25

2 Chronicles

9:13–29	6
32:12	4

Ezra

	233
1:2–4	56

Nehemiah

	58
5:1–13	55, 58
5:4	56
9:35–37	56
10:32–39	56
12:44	56
13:10–13	56
13:20	22

Job

24:2	24

Psalms

	23, 26
16:6	24, 26
68	3
78:55	24, 26
105:11	24
118	90

Proverbs

16:11	22
20:10	22
20:23	22
22:28	7, 24
23:10	24
31	119

Song of Songs/Solomon

	14

Isaiah

	22, 58, 85, 87, 93, 109, 241
5:1–10	89
5:6	89
5:8	55
6:8	7, 89
23:2–3	22
23:3	22
23:8	22
23:17	22
23:18	260
47	241
48:17	246
48:20–22	260
51:17–18	91
56	89
56:7	88
56:8	89
60	177

Jeremiah

	58, 93
3:14	15
7:1–15	88–89
7:11	88, 89
12:10	24
26	89
27–28	89
31:27–34	77

(*Jeremiah continued*)

32:6–15	22–23
32:7	26
32:8	26
32:15	26
34:9	8
37:12	24, 27
46:21	14
50:8–10	260
51:6–10	260

Ezekiel

	241
16:9–13	261
16:27	
17:3–4	22
27–28	17
27	260
27:12–25	21
28:5	22
38:13	22

Daniel

	241, 242, 252
7–12	233, 241
7	52, 203, 235
7:1–7	252
7:1	242
7:3–7	252
7:9	242
7:17	252
7:27	252
8	52
10–12	52
11–12	203
11:32–35	204
12:3	204

Hosea

5:10	24
12:7–8 [MT 8–9]	22
12:8	22

Amos

	85, 87
4:7	24
5:11	25
5:22	14
7:17	24, 26

Micah

	6, 87
2:5	24, 26

Nahum

3:16	22

Zephaniah

1:11	22
1:13	25
2:6–7	24

Haggai

	56

Zechariah

2:1 [MT 2:5]	24, 26
10:1	3
14:21	22

Apocrypha & Pseudepigrapha

Ben Sira/Sirach

13:19	59
38:24–34	109

1 Enoch

85–90	52, 91
90:6–19	20
98:2	108
102:9–11	108
104:2–6	203

ANCIENT DOCUMENT INDEX

2 Esdras/4 Ezra
   233

1 Maccabees
   237

2 Maccabees
   237
4–5   60
7–15   60

Wisdom of Solomon
   205

New Testament

Matthew
   29, 37, 70, 73, 74, 75, 78, 81, 83, 85, 108, 226
2   47
5–7   78
5:3–12   108
5:17–20   73, 83
5:20–48   77, 79
5:21–48   73
5:25   108
5:38–48   75
5:40–42   108
6:12   108
6:24   224
6:25–34   108
6:27–36   76
7:24–27   36
8:22   110
9:1–8   84
10:17–20   94
10:29–33   94
10:34–36   110
10:37   110
11:8   108
11:25   82
12:28   113
13:1–23   36
13:36–43   36
13:55   108
18:23–36   29
18:23–35   108
18:25   126
19:23–24   38
20:1–16   29
21:20–22   89
21:33–46   28
22:1–14   108
22:1–13   29
23   108
23:9   110–11
23:37–38   91
24:45–51   38
25:14–30   4, 38
25:21–48   73
25:31–46   108
26:69–71   126
27:55–56   137
27:55   123

Mark
1:21   70
1:23–27   113
2:1–12   74, 84
2:1   70
2:10   113
3:6   85
3:20–22   110, 111
3:22–30   113
3:31–35   72, 79, 110, 111
4:2–20   36
4:11–12   36
6   79
6:1–6   110, 111, 113
6:3   108
6:6   70
6:7–13   71
6:16–29   68
6:17   78
7:1–13   85–86
8:34–38   44, 94

(Mark continued)		6:27–42	75
10:2–45	72, 78	6:29	76
10:3–4	78	6:30–36	76
10:13–16	79	6:35	108
10:17–31	108	6:37–42	77
10:17–22	79	6:43–49	77
10:23–25	79	6:43–45	77
10:26–31	79	6:46–49	77
10:28–30	81	7:25	108
10:29–30	110	8:2–3	137
10:35–37	79	8:2	137
11:11	88	8:3	123
11:12–14	89	8:4–15	36
11:17	89	9:60	110
11:18–19	88	10:1–16	71
11:20–24	89	10:7	208
11:27–33	91, 113	10:21	82
12:1–12	28, 89	10:30	106
12:1	35, 89	11–12	208
12:38—13:2	86	11:2–4	44
13:3	88	11:20	113
13:9–11	94	11:27–42	75
13:9	44	11:37–52	85
14:1–3	88	12:2–12	44, 94
14:12–17	88	12:13–21	38, 108
14:26	88	12:22–31	108
14:43–49	88	12:35–38	29
14:58	90	12:41–48	38
15:16	107	12:51–53	110
15:27	107	12:57–59	108
15:29	90	13:34	91
15:40–41	137	14:12–24	108
15:41	123	15:1–7	38
16:1–8	47	15:7–11	76
		15:8–10	38
Luke		15:11–32	38
	37, 70, 73, 74, 75, 77, 78, 79, 83, 226	16:1–8	108
		16:13–18	83
2	47	16:13	37, 83, 108
4:16–30	108, 109	16:19–31	4, 108
6:20–49	73, 78	17:3–10	29
6:20–26	108	17:7–10	38
6:20–21	108	18:18	80
6:24–25	108	18:24–25	38

19:11–27	29
20:9–19	28
20:45—21:6	86
24	63

John

	234
2:13–22	86
3:16	2
19:25	123

Acts

	196, 198, 202, 248
2	94
2:14	119
2:32–37	215
2:44–47	220
2:44–45	215, 220
2:44	220
2:46	220, 221
4	94
4:32–37	215, 220
4:32–35	221
4:34	223
4:36–37	222
5:1–11	222
5:35	119
5:36	107
6	138
6:1–6	221
6:2	138
6:4	138
7:2	119
8:1–5	33
8:28	35
11:27–30	224
11:27–29	215
12:13–15	126
13:16	119
16	123, 133
16:12	149
16:14–15	125
16:15	248
16:16–18	126
16:40	125
17:1–9	202
17:4	120, 137
17:22	120
17:34	120
18:1–3	124
19:23–27	244
21:38	107
22:1	120
22:27–28	131
22:44–45	215, 220
23–25	131

Romans

	171, 172, 200
8	209
10:1–13	207
10:14–22	207
11:17–24	200
12	172, 177
12:5	178
12:10	178
12:16	
13:8	178
15	
15:5	178
15:7	178
15:14	178
15:25–27	176
16	123
16:1–2	137, 170
16:2–3	123, 170
16:22	34
16:23	170

1 Corinthians

	137, 166, 167–68, 204, 205, 211, 213, 215
1:10—4:21	205
1:10—4:13	204, 205
1:11	32, 33, 35, 137, 170, 205, 211
1:16	211
1:26–31	205

(1 Corinthians continued)

1:26–28	166, 167, 174, 175
1:26–27	165, 168
1:26	204
2:6–8	188, 201
4:8–13	205
4:8	205
5–6	205
6:12	206
6:13–20	129
7	212
7:1–7	129
7:1	212
7:2–16	212
7:5a	212
7:9	212
7:11a	212
7:15	212
7:18–20	212
7:21–24	211
7:21–23	211, 212
7:21	209, 212, 213, 214
7:24	212
7:29–31	206
7:29	212
8–9	176
8	215
8:1—11:1	205, 206
8:1–4	215
8:5b	207
8:9–14	216
9	208, 216
9:15–23	208
10:1–13	207
10:14–22	207
10:23—11:1	207
10:23	206, 207
11:17–22	178
12–14	205
12	177, 207
12:25	178
13	216
15	205
15:1–28	188, 201
15:12–28	201
15:8–10	208
15:20–28	176
16:1–4	176
16:1–2	215
16:3–4	215
16:15–17	211
16:21	34

2 Corinthians

8–9	176
8:1–4	215
8:1–2	208
8:2	166
8:9–14	216
9	216

Galatians

	200, 201, 209, 210
1:15–20	199
2	224
2:9–10	215
2:10	176
3–5	209
3–4	200
3:28	211
5:13	37, 178
6:11	34

Ephesians

	200, 209, 217
4:2	178
4:25	178
4:32	178
5:21—6:9	119, 217
5:21	178
6:5–8	126, 129, 217

Philippians

	200, 202, 204
1–2	202
1:1	138
1:19–23	203
1:27–29	204
1:29	204

2:5–11	201
2:15–17	204
3:18–21	188
3:19–21	201
3:20—4:1	204
4:15–19	204
4:15–16	208

Colossians

	200, 209, 217
3:9	178
3:13	178
3:18—4:1	119
3:18–25	217
3:22–25	126, 129
4:15	123
4:18	34

1 Thessalonians

	200, 202
1–2	208
1:2–10	202
1:2–3	202
2:2	202
3:1–5	202
3:6–10	202
3:12	178, 203
4:3–7	129
4:9	178
4:18	178
5:1–11	202
5:11	178
5:13	178

2 Thessalonians

	200
1:3	178
3:17	34

1 Timothy

	200
5:14	122
6:1–2	129, 217
6:17–18	217

2 Timothy

	200

Titus

	200
2:3–5	119
2:4–5	122
2:9–10	129, 217

Philemon

	31–32, 200, 209, 213, 214
10	213
11	213
13	213
14	214
16	214
17–19	34
17	214
22	170

James

	224–25
1:1–16	224
1:1	224
1:26–27	224
2:1–4	224
2:5–7	224
4:4	224
4:13–17	224
4:13	224
5:40	225

1 Peter

2:18—3:7	119
2:18–25	126, 129, 217

Revelation

	164, 230, 231, 233–34, 235, 237, 238, 240, 241, 244, 248, 250, 255, 257, 262, 266, 267, 268
1:1–2	256
1:1	231, 235
1:2	235

(Revelation continued)		13:4	251, 254
1:3	235	13:7	255
1:4–5	231	13:11	253
1:9	231, 236	13:12	251, 253
1:10–11	244	13:13–15	253
1:12	264	13:16–17	254, 260
2–3	243, 244, 260	13:18	254
2:6	249	17–18	243, 255
2:8	245	17	256, 258, 259
2:9–11	246	17:3	256
2:9	250	17:4	256, 257, 266
2:9a	246	17:5	256, 267
2:9b	246	17:6a	257
2:10	247	17:9–14	256
2:14–15	249	17:9	252, 256
2:19	248	17:15	257
2:20	248	17:16	258
2:21	249	17:18	257, 258, 261
2:22	246, 249	18	159, 239, 259, 260, 264
2:23–24	249–50	18:2–3	259
3:7–13	245	18:2	231
3:15	250	18:3	259
3:16	250	18:4	260, 263, 267
3:17–18	264	18:7	260
4–5	236	18:8	260
4:4	264	18:11–14	191
5:5–6	255	18:11–13	158
5:8	264	18:11	159, 260
6:15	239	18:12–13	260
7–18	262	18:13	261
7:1–8	254	18:14b	159
8	264	18:15	261
8:3	264	18:16	257
8:9–20	260	18:18	261
11:1–13	235	18:19	159
11:4–6	266	18:21–24	261–62
11:7	266	18:21	261
12–13	254	19:16	252
12	253	20:4	260
12:3	256, 257	21–22	231, 243, 263
13	235, 243, 251, 252	21:2–4	264
13:1–4	252	21:2	263
13:1	256	21:4	264
13:3	254	21:7	266

21:8	265
21:18–21	266
21:24	264
22:3	265, 266
22:4	254, 265
22:7	235
22:10	230, 235
22:18	235
22:19	235
22:20	231
22:27	265

Dead Sea Scrolls

1QS	59
1QS 5:1–3	222
1QS 5:5–7	91
1QS 6:18–24	222
1QS 8:4–10	91
1QS 9:3–6	91
4QFlor 1:1–13	91

Rabbinic Writings

b. Pesahim

57a	64

m. Shebi'it

10:3–7	65

Roman-Era Writings

Athenaeus
Deipnosophistai

6.265d–266e	197

2 Baruch

	233

1 Clement

55:2	218

Augustus, Gaius Julius Caesar
Res Gestae

15	191
25	197

Apocalypse of Zephaniah

	233

Apocalypse of Abraham

	233

Apocalypse of Peter

	233

Apocalypse of Paul

	233

Corpus Inscriptionum Latinarum (CIL)

10.874	154
10.875	154, 159

Dio, Cassius

49.12.5	197

Dionysius of Halicarnassus
Roman Antiquities

4:13	160

Epistle of James

	224–25

Eusebius of Caesarea
Historia ecclesiastica

3.18.1–3	236
7.25.7–8	234

Josephus

Antiquities of the Jews

3.280–284	65
8.261–288	68
12.375–378	65
13.296–298	85
13.318–319	60
14	62
14.202–210	65
14.202–210	65
14.202–203	62
14.450	61
14.475	65
15.5–7	65
15.299–312	62
16.271–272	106
17.270–284	106
17.271–284	66
17.286–295	62
18.23	67
18.27	110
18.36–38	112
18.85–87	68
18.106–118	79
18.116–119	68, 107
18.269–275	106
20.97–98	68, 107
20.105–109	88
20.113–117	106
20.118–119	106
20.121	106
20.160–161	106
20.168	68
20.169–171	68, 107
20.180–181	63
20.206–207	63
20.232–235	106
20.255–257	106

The Jewish War

1.204–259	62
1.303	61
1.326	61
2.56–65	66
2.60–65	106
2.66–75	62
2.125	106
2.175–177	84
2.185–203	68
2.223–226	88
2.228–231	106
2.232–235	106
2.253	106
2:254–265	107
2.259	68
2.259–263	107
2.259	68
2.261–263	68
2.272–276	106
2.427–448	106
2.511	110
2.595	69
4.159–160	62
4.271–274	62
4.507–510	67
5.58–85	106
6.300–309	91

The Life of Flavius Josephus

26	24
30	110
39	110
65–66	69
66	106
66–68	110
70–73	69
99	110
119–120	69
126–131	69
175	106
246	61
346	110
372	106
374–384	110

Justin Martyr
1 Apology

67.6	218

Ignatius of Antioch
Letter to Polycarp

4.3	133, 218

Letter to the Smyrnaeans

6.2	218
13.2	123, 137

Letter to the Ephesians

	200, 209, 217

Oxyrhynchus Papyri

1205	219

Petronius
Satyricon

	131
76:3–9	159

Philo
Legatio ad Gaium

	68

De specialibus legibus

3.169–70	119

Pliny the Younger
Epistulae (Letters)

7.24.5	123
10:96–97	236

Plutarch
Cato the Elder

21:5–6	156, 159

Advice about Keeping Wel

	122

Pseudo-Aristotle
Oeconomica

	122

Shepherd of Hermas
Mandata(s)

8:10	218

Similtude(s)

1:8	218

Vision(s)

1:1	130

Suetonius
Claudius

18–19	191

Testament of Abraham

	233

Xenophon
Oeconomicus

	122

Author Index

Adams, Edward, 123, 139, 196, 226
Alcock, Susan, 96, 193, 195, 226
Aldrete, Greg, 155, 156, 180
Alikin, Valeriy A., 123, 135, 138, 139
Allen, Garrick, 235, 268
Allison, Dale C., 45, 96, 107, 115
Alt, Albrecht, 24, 39
Althusser, Louis, 35, 39
Anderson, Benedict, 199, 226
Anderson, Lisa, 5, 11
Andreau, Jean, 161, 162, 180
Arnal, William, 105, 115
Arzt-Grabner, Peter, 33, 39
Ascough, Richard A., 196, 226
Aubert, Jean-Jacques, 160, 180
Aune, David, 236, 246, 268
Avigad, Nahman, 63, 96

Bagnall, Roger S., 121, 127, 139
Bailey, Kenneth E., 29, 39
Bain, Katherine, 125, 127, 133, 135–39
Bakirtzzis, Charalambos, 149, 180
Balzer, Klaus, 59, 96
Bammel, Ernst, 102, 115
Bartchy, S. Scott, 220, 221, 226
Barclay, John, 32, 33, 35, 39, 170–71, 180
Bartchy, S. Scott, 220, 221, 226
Barton, John, 11
Bauckham, Richard, 158–59, 180, 256, 261, 268
Bayly, C. A., 5, 11
Beal, Timothy K., 232, 244–45, 268

Becker, Michael, 116
Bendor, Shunya, 24, 39
Berlin, Andrea, 98, 111, 115
Bermejo-Rubio, Fernando, 102, 115
Blanton, Thomas, 42, 194, 226, 228
Bloch, Ernst, 31
Blount, Brian K., 232, 234, 235, 236–37, 239, 245–46, 247, 248, 249, 253, 254, 255, 257, 263, 265, 266, 268, 269
Boer, Roland, ix, 9, 11, 12, 13, 14, 20, 23, 30, 36, 39, 40, 48, 49, 54, 96, 105, 115, 190, 191, 193, 226, 237, 261, 269
Boesak, Allan A., 269
Bond, Helen, 111, 115
Borg, Marcus, 102–3, 115,
Bornkamm, Günther, 101–2, 115
Borowski, Oded, 24, 40
Boyer, Robert, 13, 40
Brandon, S. G. F., 102, 115
Brewer, Douglas, 14, 40
Briant, Pierre, 18, 19, 40
Bright, John, 20, 23, 40
Brinkman, Carl, 23, 40
Brodie, Thomas, 16, 40
Broshi, Magen, 63, 96
Bruce, F. F., 33, 40
Brueggemann, Walter, 241, 264, 269
Butler, Judith, 201, 226

Callahan, Allen Dwight, 197, 213–14, 218, 227
Callender, Dexter E., Jr., 221, 227
Cantor, Norman F., 9, 11
Carey, Greg, 234, 235, 238, 251, 252, 255, 269
Carr, David M., 50, 71, 96
Carroll, Robert P., 26, 40
Carter, Warren, ix, 110, 115, 141, 190, 239, 254, 267, 269
Casey, Maurice, 107, 115
Chakrabarty, Dipesh, 96
Chandler, Tertius, 142, 143, 180
Chaney, Marvin L., 24, 40, 57–58, 80, 96
Chase-Dunn, Christopher, 18, 40
Ciarallo, Annamaria, 155, 180
Clines, David. J. A., 23, 40
Collins, Adela Yarbo, 233, 235, 236, 242, 246–47, 254, 262, 263, 264, 267, 269
Collins, Billie Jean, 40
Collins, John J., 233, 269
Conzelmann, Hans, 206, 227
Cook, Stephen L., 233, 269
Cooley, Alison, 155, 180
Coomber, Matthew J. M., ix, 1, 4, 11, 39, 96, 99,
Cooper, Kate, 120, 124, 139
Coote, Robert B., 5, 11, 87, 96
Corbier, Mireille, 144, 180
Cremin, Ciara, 102, 115
Cronauer, Patrick T., 27, 40
Crossan, John Dominic, 45, 96, 102, 103, 110, 115
Crossley, James G., x, 96, 101, 102, 105, 110, 111, 112, 116,

Dalby, Andrew, 156, 180
Darden, Lynne St. Clair, 268, 269
Davies, Philip R., 6, 11, 42
Davis, Ellen, 232, 255, 260, 269
Decock, Paul B., 269
de Geus, Cornelis. H. J., 23, 40
Deissmann, Adolf, 164, 165–66, 167, 169, 180

Deist, Ferdinand E., 23, 24, 40
DeLaine, Janet, 161, 180
deSilva, David A., 169
Dever, William G., 23, 40
DeVries, Simon J., 27, 40
Diehl, Judy, 234, 269
Donfried, Karl, 202, 227
Dodd, C. H., 28, 36–37, 40
Downs, David J., 176, 180, 215, 227
Draper, Jonathan A., 73, 85, 98, 221, 227
Duff, Paul B., 244, 245, 246, 247, 248–50, 266, 269
Duncan-Jones, Richard, 142, 143, 178, 180

Ehrman, Bart D., 45, 96
Elliger, Karl, 24
Elliot, John H., 194, 227
Elliot, Neal, xi, 102, 116, 189, 194, 201, 227
Engels, Donald, 143, 144, 150–53, 180
Engels, Friedrich, 164, 165, 166, 181
Erdkamp, Paul, 143, 145, 155, 156, 157, 181, 182, 183, 185, 186

Fiensy, David A., 110, 116
Finkelstein, Israel, 19, 40
Finley, Moses, 141, 143, 144, 146, 147, 148, 149, 150, 152, 153, 155, 156, 168, 173, 175, 179, 181, 183, 189, 227
Fisher, Mark, 102, 103, 116
Fox, Gerald, 142, 143, 180
Fredriksen, Paula, 107, 116
Frey, Jörg, 107, 116
Freyne, Sean, 60, 96, 110, 116
Frier, Bruce W., 121, 127, 139
Friesen, Steven J., 42, 102, 116, 155, 163, 169–71, 172–73, 175, 17677, 179, 180, 181, 183, 184, 193, 194, 227, 228, 229, 235, 240, 243, 251, 269,
Frilingos, Christopher A., 33, 40, 242, 253, 255, 265, 267, 270
Fulford, Michael, 145, 181

AUTHOR INDEX

Gager, John G., 52, 96
Galbraith, Deane, 205, 116
Garnsey, Peter, 142, 146, 156, 156, 157–58, 181, 184, 191, 227
Giardina, Andrea, 162, 180, 181, 182, 183, 185
Glancy, Jennifer, 32, 33, 36, 37, 41, 257, 261, 268, 270
Godelier, Maurice, 23, 41
Goodman, Martin, 51, 63, 65, 96
Gouldner, Alvin, 227
Graham, Shawn, 157, 160, 181
Greene, Kevin, 144, 181
Guha, Ranajit, 96
Guijarro, Santiago, 28, 41
Guillaume, Philippe, 23, 25, 27, 41
Gwyther, Anthony, 242, 256, 260, 261, 270

Hanson, John S., 51, 54, 58, 66, 76, 97, 98, 105–6
Hanson, K. C., xi, 65, 97, 110, 116, 242, 270
Hanson, Paul D., 233, 270
Harland, Philip A., 123, 125, 139
Harnack, Adolf von, 45, 97
Harrill, J. Albert, 32, 41, 213, 219, 227
Harris, William V., 50, 97
Harrison, James, 176, 181, 229
Hawkins, Cameron, 144, 182
Hidalgo, Jacqueline M., 266–67, 268, 270
Hill, Christopher, 105, 114, 116
Hilton, Rodney, 105, 113, 116
Hirth, Kenneth, xii, 3, 11, 118
Herzog, William R., II, 29–30, 41, 54, 88–89, 97, 110, 116
Hezser, Catherine, 50, 97
Hitchner, R. Bruce, 142, 182
Hobsbawm, Eric J., 52, 97, 104–105, 116
Holladay, William L., 26, 41
Holleran, Claire, 157, 160, 182
Holmberg, Bengt, 163, 182
Hopkins, A. G., 11

Hopkins, Keith, 142, 143, 151, 163, 182, 190, 227
Horden, Peregrine, 145, 146, 155, 159, 182
Hornsby, Teresa J., 270
Horsley, Richard A., x, xii, 46, 50, 51, 52, 54, 56, 58, 59, 60, 61, 63, 66, 67, 68, 69, 71, 72, 73, 78, 85–86, 87, 88, 89, 91, 93, 97, 98, 100, 102, 105–6, 110, 117, 185, 187, 192, 194, 195, 196, 197, 204, 205, 211, 223, 227, 233, 237, 269, 270
Houston, Walter, 23, 41
Howard-Brook, Wes, 242, 256, 260, 261, 270
Huber, Lynn R., xii, 255–56, 257–58, 263, 268, 270
Hylen, Susan, 270

Jameson, Fredric, 35, 41, 201, 228
Jankowska, Ninel B., 15, 41
Jashemski, Wilhelmina, 155, 182
Jeffcoat Schedtler, Justin, 233, 236, 253, 256, 270, 271
Jensen, Morten H., 111, 117
Jessop, Bob, 13, 41
Jongman, Willem, 153, 182
Joseph, Simon J., 98
Joubert, Stephan, 176, 182, 215, 228

Kazen, Thomas, 98
Kaufman, Stephen A., 24, 41
Kautsky, John H., 110, 117
Kautsky, Karl, 164–65, 166, 182
Kearsley, R. A., 135, 136, 139
Kehoe, Dennis, 162, 182
Keith, Chris, 108, 117
Keller, Catherine, 258, 270
Kim, Hyuan Chul Paul, 16, 41
Kim, Jean K., 258, 270
King, Martin Luther, Jr., 213, 267, 270
King, Rebekka, 102, 117
Kirk, Alan, 99
Kirk-Duggan, Cheryl A., 270

Kitz, Anne M., 24, 41
Klauck, Hans-Josef, 253, 270
Kloppenborg, John S., 215, 228
Knapp, Bernard A., 4, 11
Knight, Douglas A., 54, 57, 99, 222, 228, 237, 270
Koehler, Ludwig, 23, 41
Koester, Craig R., 235, 250, 251, 252, 255, 261, 270
Koester, Helmut, 149, 180
Kohler, Josef, 24, 41
Kolendo, Jerzy, 162, 182
Kron, Geoffrey, 144, 182
Kraybill, J. Nelson, 238–39, 240, 244, 254, 260, 262–63, 271

Last, Richard, 123, 125, 139
Launderville, Dale F., 22, 41
Laurence, Ray, 153, 154, 155, 156–57, 182
Lemche, Niels Peter, 24, 41
Lenski, Gerhard E., 113, 117
Levine, Amy-Jill,, 272
Levine, Baruch A., 7, 8, 11, 23, 42, 43
Linton, Gregory L., 233–34, 271
Lipietz, Alain, 13, 42
Liu, Jinju, 197, 228
Loader, William, 111, 117
Long, Burke, 18, 42
Longenecker, Bruce W., 139, 163, 172–74, 175, 179, 182, 193, 194, 228, 271
Lopez, Davina, xii, 242, 264–65, 267, 271
Lovén, Lena Larsson, 124, 139
Luckhardt, Courtney, 9, 11
Luther, Martin, 213, 224, 228

Macaskill, Grant, 271
MacDonald, Margaret, x
MacDonald, Nathan, 43
Malherbe, Abraham, 167, 169, 182
Mann, Michael, 141, 182
Manning, J. G., 48, 99, 141, 182, 183
Marchal, Joseph, 32, 42, 183, 213, 228

Marshall, I. Howard, 33, 42
Martin, Dale, 30, 42
Marx, Karl, 181
Mason, Steve, 99
Mattern, Susan P., 63, 99
Matthews, Victor H., 23, 24, 42
Mattingly, David J., 144, 145–46, 146–47, 149, 155, 156, 163, 180, 183, 186
Mayer, Emanuel, 48, 99, 160–61, 174, 183, 189, 228
Meeks, Wayne A., 37, 42, 167, 169, 183, 194, 226, 228
Meggitt, Justin, 34–35, 42, 167–69, 173, 175, 176, 183
Meijer, Fik, 159, 183
Mein, Andrew, 116
Mitchell, Stephen, 156, 183
Moeller, Walter, 153, 183
Moore, Stephen D., 236, 239, 240, 242, 257, 258, 265, 266, 268, 270, 271
Moran, William L., 18, 42
Morel, Jean-Paul, 162, 183
Morley, Neville, 143, 144, 159–60, 161, 162, 183, 191, 228
Morris, Ian, 48, 99, 142, 182, 183
Moule, C. F. D., 102, 115
Moxnes, Halvor, 28, 41, 42, 110, 111, 117
Murphy, Catherine, 59, 99, 228
Murphy, Kelly J., x, xii, 230, 233, 270, 271
Myers, Ched, ii, xii, 46, 99
Myles, Robert J., 102, 110, 116, 117

Nam, Roger, xii, 21, 42
Nasrallah, Laura Salah, 33, 42, 201, 229
Neusner, Jacob, 65, 83, 99
Nijf, Onno van, 159, 183

Oakman, Douglas E., 65, 97, 110, 116, 242, 270
Oakes, Peter, 123, 139, 143, 149, 163, 171–72, 179, 183, 229, 229
Odell, Margaret S., 21, 42

AUTHOR INDEX

Öhler, Marcus, 116
Osiek, Carolyn, x, xii, 32, 33, 42, 118, 120, 122, 125, 126, 127, 136, 138, 139, 140, 217, 218, 229
Overman, Andrew J., 98, 115
Ozanne, C. G., 235, 271

Park, Rohun, 183, 184, 271
Parker, A. J, 145, 184
Pastor, Jack, 23, 42
Paterson, Jeremy, 159, 184
Peacock, David P., 145, 147, 149, 154, 184
Perry, Matthew J., 128, 129, 130, 131, 132, 139
Pervo, Richard I., 42
Petersen, Lauren Hackworth, 184
Petersen, Michelle, 157, 162, 184
Petersen, Norman R., 213, 229
Petterson, Christina, x, 9, 12, 13, 20, 23, 34, 40, 42, 48, 96, 105, 115, 190, 191, 226, 261, 269
Pickett, Raymond, 42, 194, 226, 228
Piestrup, Zeke, 230, 271
Pippin, Tina, 258–59, 262, 271
Pixley, Jorge V., 271
Pleket, H. W., 156, 158, 184
Portier-Young, Anathea, 99
Price, Jennifer, 180, 181
Price, S. R. F., 194, 240–41, 253, 271
Purcell, Nicholas, 145, 146, 155, 159, 160, 174, 182, 184

Reden, Sitts von, 141, 184
Renz, Thomas, 22, 42,
Rollens, Sarah E., 113, 117
Roller, Duane W., 99
Rossing, Barbara, R., 263–64, 271
Rostovtseff, Michael, 48, 99
Roth, Ulrike, 31–32, 32–33, 34–35, 42

Saller, Richard, 118, 122, 127, 128, 129, 140, 142, 146, 181, 191, 195, 227, 229
Salmon, John, 144, 180, 183, 186

Sanders, E. P., 90, 99, 111, 112, 117
Sanders, Guy R., 150, 184
Savunen, Liisa, 120, 124, 125, 134, 135, 140
Scheidel, Walter, 118, 141–42, 143, 158, 163, 173, 178–79, 181, 182, 184, 190, 191, 193, 229, 242, 271
Schloen, J. David, 15, 43
Schottroff, Luise, 28–30, 36–37, 43
Schüssler Fiorenza, Elisabeth, xii, 110, 117, 233, 236, 258, 271
Schwartz, Seth, 51, 99
Schweitzer, Albert, 45, 99
Scobie, Alex, 158, 185
Scott, James C., 58, 97, 99, 223, 229
Seibert, Eric A., 21, 43
Silver, Morris, 27, 43,
Sirks, Booudewijn, 155, 185
Shim, SeungWoo, 179, 185
Skinner, John, 15, 43
Solin, Heikki, 34, 43
Smith, Christopher, 184
Smith, Shanell T., 258, 268, 272
Song, Choan-Seng, 272
Spek, Robartus J. Van der, 25, 43
Stark, Rodney, 174–75, 185
Ste. Croix, G. E. M. de., 19, 43, 105, 115, 117, 191, 193, 229
Stegemann, Ekkehard W., 117
Still, Todd D., 226, 229
Stone, Ken, 270
Stone, Timothy, 16, 43
Stravrakopoulou, Francesca, 11
Sweeney, Marvin A., 24, 27, 43
Temin, Peter, 48, 99, 119, 140, 144, 145, 156, 157, 185, 189, 191, 229
Thatcher, Tom, 46, 87, 98
Theissen, Gerd, 33, 43, 72, 99, 167–68, 174, 185, 194, 204, 229
Temin, Peter, 48, 99, 119, 140, 144, 145, 156, 157, 185, 189, 191, 229
Tompkins, Daniel, 152, 185
Thompson, Leonard L., 23, 236, 245, 248, 251, 272
Thompson, Thomas L., 43

Toner, Jerry, 158, 185
Tuck, Steven, 157, 185
Turner, Geoffrey, 36, 43

Udoh, Fabian E., 62, 100
Ulrich, Eugene, 50, 100

Vanderkam, James C., 237, 272
Vander Stichele, Caroline, 258, 259, 272

Walbank, Mary E. Hoskins, 150, 185
Wallace-Hadrill, Andrew, 145, 154, 180, 185
Wallerstein, Immanuel, 18, 19, 43
Walsh, Jerome T., 27, 43
Walsh, P. G., 271
Webb, Robert L., 67, 79, 100
Welborn, L. L., 229
Whitelam, Keith W., 5, 11

Whittaker, C. R., 141, 142, 152, 157, 158, 179, 185
Williams, D. F., 145, 147, 149, 153, 184
Williams, David J., 176, 185
Wilson, Andrew, 139, 144–45, 148–49, 152, 185
Winter, Sara C., 213, 229
Wiseman, James, 150, 186
Witcher, Robert, 160, 186
Witherington, Ben, III, 33, 43
Wright, Benjamin G., III, 24, 43, 211, 229, 271
Wright, Christopher J. H., 43
Wright, N. T., 102, 103, 117

Yves Saillard, 40

Zanker, Paul, 194, 229

www.ingramcontent.com/pod-product-compliance
Lightning Source LLC
Chambersburg PA
CBHW032051220426
43664CB00008B/952